# Inner Loops

## A Sourcebook for Fast 32-bit Software Development

Rick Boo

**Addison-Wesley Developers Press**

**An imprint of Addison Wesley Longman, Inc.**

Reading, Massachusetts • Harlow, England • Menlo Park, California
Berkeley, California • Don Mills, Ontario • Sydney
Bonn • Amsterdam • Tokyo • Mexico City

Many of the designations used by manufacturers and sellers to distinguish their products are claimed as trademarks. Where those designations appear in this book, and Addison Wesley Longman, Inc. was aware of a trademark claim, the designations have been printed in initial capital letters or all capital letters.

The author and publisher have taken care in preparation of this book, but make no express or implied warranty of any kind and assume no responsibility for errors or omissions. No liability is assumed for incidental or consequential damages in connection with or arising out of the use of the information or programs contained herein.

*Library of Congress Cataloging-in-Publication Data*

Booth, Rick.
    Inner loops : a sourcebook  for fast 32-bit software development / Rick Booth.
            p.   cm.
    Includes index.
    ISBN 0-201-47960-5
        1.  Computer software--Development.    2.  Pentium (Microprocessor)--Programming.
    3.  Intel 80486 (Microprocessor)--Programming.
    I.  Title.
    QA76.76.D47B68    1997
    005.265--dc20                                                            96-36332
                                                                                CIP

Sponsoring Editor: Mary Treseler
Project Manager: Sarah Weaver
Production Coordinator: Erin Sweeney
Cover design: Square One Design
Set in 11-point Times Roman by Octal Publishing, Inc.

1 2 3 4 5 6 7 8 9 -MA- 0099989796
*First printing, December 1996*

Addison Wesley Longman, Inc. books are available for bulk purchases by corporations, institutions, and other organizations. For more information please contact the Corporate, Government, and Special Sales Department at (800) 238-9682.

Find A-W Developers Press on the World Wide Web at:
http://www.aw.com/devpress/

# Contents

*Acknowledgments    ix*
*About the CD-ROM    xi*
*Preface    xiii*

Introduction    1
   Optimized Algorithms for the 32-Bit PC    1
   Who This Book Is For    2
   Overview of the Contents    2
   Playing Devil's Advocate    5
   Inner Loops    6


## Part 1   Theory    9

Chapter 1    The Reference World of the Pentium-100    11
   The Pentium-100 Processor    12
   Memory    13
   The PCI and ISA Buses    15
   Disks    15
   The Modem    18
   The Network Connection    18
   Still Images    19
   Video    19
   Audio    20
   Text    20

Compiled Code   21
Operating Systems   21
Conclusion   22

Chapter 2    32-Bit Assembly Language   23

What to Forget About 16-Bit Assembly Language   24
Basic 32-Bit Assembly Language   26
The Instruction Set   34
Cycle-Counting Conventions   45
Conclusion   46

Chapter 3    Structured Assembly Language   49

Conventional Assembly Language   50
C and Assembly Language Interleaved   52
Calling and Returning   55
Data Structures   57
Structured Assembly Language   58
Debugging   65
Conclusion   65

Chapter 4    Optimizing the 486   67

The CH486.EXE Instruction Timing Program   68
The Instruction Set   69
The Cache   80
The 486 Output Queue   84
Data and Code Alignment   85
Cycle Thieves and Cycle Savers   87
Conclusion   89
References   89

Chapter 5    Optimizing the Pentium   91

The CHPENT.BAT Instruction Timing Program   92
Pentium Features Overview   92
How Instruction Pairing Works   93
The Instruction Set   98
The Cache   109
The Pentium Output Queue   115

Data and Code Alignment    116
Cycle Thieves and Cycle Savers    118
Instruction Stream Timing Oddities    119
Conclusion    121
References    121


Chapter 6    Optimizing the Pentium Pro    123
The CHPPRO.EXE Instruction Timing Program    124
Dynamic Execution    124
Micro-ops    127
New Instructions    129
Instruction Set Timing    130
The Floating-Point Unit    134
The Cache    135
Data Code and Alignment    136
The Partial Register Stall    136
Branch Prediction    137
Optimization Summary    138
Conclusion    139
References    140


Chapter 7    Achieving Speed    141
When and Where to Speed Code Up    142
Rethinking Algorithms    143
The Special Advantages of Assembly Language    146
Data and Stack Alignment    147
Running on Seven Registers    148
Table-Driven Code    150
Unrolling Loops    151
Loop Counter Efficiency    154
Minimizing Pointer Increments    154
Jump Tables    156
Coiled Loops    157
Tandem Loops    158
Prefetching into Cache    160
Setting Flags    161
Fast Multiplication    162
Rethinking in Assembly Language    163
Conclusion    169

Chapter 8    C Performance    171

How C Statements Translate into Assembly Language    172
Compiler Optimization Switch Behaviors    180
Predicting C Performance    182
Conclusion    183

Chapter 9    MMX    185

General Processor Enhancements    186
The MMX Registers    189
The MMX Instructions    190
MMX Instruction Timing and Pairing    195
Software Emulation of MMX    196
Conclusion    202
References    203

# Part 2    Practice    205

Chapter 10    Moving Memory    207

The CHMEM.EXE Program    208
Alignment, the First Rule    208
A Pentium Read-Before-Write Speedup    212
Conclusion    217

Chapter 11    Random Numbers and Primes    219

The Algorithms    220
On the CD-ROM    221
Random Number Theory    222
Random Numbers in Practice    227
Conclusion    250
References    251

Chapter 12    Linked Lists and Trees    253

Nodes in a Nutshell    253
Speed Issues    257

Inner Loops   258
Linked List Searching   259
Binary Tree Searching   261
Traversing a Binary Tree   264
Conclusion   266


Chapter 13   Hashing   267

When to Hash   267
How to Hash   268
Fast Hashing with IL_HashFindSymbol()   268
IL_HashAddSymbol()   278
The Demo Program: CHHASH.EXE   279
Conclusion   279


Chapter 14   Huffman Compression   281

A Huffman Example   281
What Huffman Is Good For   283
Performance   285
Huffman, Step by Step   285
Huffman Compression   286
Huffman Decompression   297
Conclusion   299
References   300


Chapter 15   A Fast Sort   301

Order N Sorting   301
The CHSORT.EXE Program   303
The First Inner Loop of the Distribution Sort   303
The Second Inner Loop of the Distribution Sort   307
Performance   308
The Loop Not Taken   312
Conclusion   313


Chapter 16   Matrix Multiplication   315

Matrix Review   315
Fast Multiplication with a Three-by-Three Matrix   317

The CHMATRX.EXE Demonstration Program    320
Large Matrices    320
Conclusion    322

Chapter 17    JPEG    323
How JPEG Works    324
Taking on the Inverse DCT    329
Conclusion    349
References    349

Epilogue    351

Index    353

# Acknowledgments

This book would not have been written had not David Lubar, a fellow games programmer and ardent writer, suggested it, encouraged it, and placed me in touch with the right editors to make it happen. Thanks, Dave. I must also thank editors Claire Horne and Mary Treseler for their encouragement and help in creating the manuscript. Joe Augenbraun served as the main source of critical feedback, fastidious and unsparing. Tom Lane of the Independent JPEG Group provided technical assistance and advice for the JPEG chapter. And the MMX chapter owes its existence to the consideration of Mark Morris, who thought to send me the critical documentation just in time for inclusion. Thanks to Seth Haberman of Montage Group Ltd. for supplying the Pentium Pro for testing. And thanks to the management of WorldGate Communications for graciously enduring author "brownouts" in the final phases of manuscript preparation.

On the home front, of course, there is a wife who has seen little but the silhouette of her husband against a phosphorescent screen for a year. Thanks, Joyce, for your support, help, patience, love, and attention to life's most important inner loops.

# About the CD-ROM

The CD-ROM accompanying this book contains source and executable example code associated with 11 of the 17 chapters in this book. Each chapter's code is in a separate subdirectory on the CD, and some subdirectories also include test data files and the results of timing tests run on test systems.

All code was compiled in a DOS environment, *for* a DOS environment, using Watcom C/C++ and Microsoft MASM 6.11. All but one of the programs will execute in a "DOS box" under Windows, but the fine-timing mechanisms involved in some programs will work more accurately in a machine booted with DOS. The 486 instruction-timing program requires such a true DOS environment. Many of the programs, though, will not run on a 486, because the Pentium and Pentium Pro fine-timing instruction `rdtsc` is needed to acquire much of the precise timing information used in this book. But the code implementing critical algorithms *will* run, if transplanted to a different context, on anything from a 386 up.

All of the important C algorithm implementations, if exported to another environment, should compile correctly. The C comment delimiter style adopted in the book is, for convenience and readability, the C++-style double slash (//). For compatibility with C compilers that do not support this style, a conversion program that produces files using the "slash-star" convention (/* . . . */) is provided.

All of the assembly language code uses the structured runtime controls of Microsoft's MASM 6. MASM-specific structured assembly language was intentionally chosen for this book, because it represents a powerful advance over conventional assembly language, is worth teaching, and is worth learning (and it's easier to read, once you learn the fundamentals). Chapter 3 explains structured assembly language. This code can be exported to other assemblers with some straightforward manual translation.

All executable programs use the DOS4GW.EXE DOS extender, which must be found either in the connected directory or somewhere in the environment path list. For convenience, a copy of this DOS extender is included in each directory with executable code. If you try to run a program without being connected to such a directory, then the program may fail, giving you an error message citing the absence of the extender file.

Also see the Test Program Alert at the back of the book for further program notes.

# Preface

It started in the twilight of an August night in 1983. My company had just spent $200,000 to install a minicomputer for software development, but I was already concerned about performance.

The major players in the video game industry were uniformly using similar systems to assemble 6502 code for Atari and Commodore machines, but the benchmarks I had just run showed that our upcoming large projects for the Commodore-64—between 10 and 20 thousand lines of code each—would take five to ten minutes to assemble on the stand-alone minicomputer (and 20 or 30 minutes if several users assembled at once). I had visions of interminable coffee breaks, frustrated programmers, and missed deadlines as the projects matured, so . . . I wrote a few lines of code.

I wondered how fast an assembler could run on a PC-XT. The only 6502 assembler for the PC that was on the market at the time had benchmarked fourteen times slower than the minicomputer. Was that really the best a PC could do? I decided to find out.

My reasoning went as follows: An assembler is a fairly simple software tool. It doesn't take very much logic to translate an opcode into a byte of machine language, or an operand into a byte or two of data after the opcode. The single most time-consuming part must be the symbol lookup itself—translating labels and opcodes and operands from text into symbol addresses. So I wrote down these lines:

```
lodsb              ;12 cycles  Fetch a letter.
xlat               ;11 cycles  Encode it.
or      al,al      ; 3 cycles  Check its legality.
je      done       ; 4 cycles  Exit if done.
```

```
xor     dl,al   ; 3 cycles  Randomize a
rol     dx,1    ; 2 cycles  16-bit number.
stosb           ;11 cycles  Record the code.
------------------------
                ;46 CYCLES TOTAL
```

This was the inner loop—to be repeated in-line—for the fastest symbol lookup I could devise for the 8088 processor, the chunk of code that gets executed once for every character in a symbol. (The loop is different but similar for today's 32-bit processors; see Chapter 13, on hashing.) Since the processor clock of the PC-XT was ticking at almost five million cycles a second, the 46 cycles of this loop could be executed about one hundred thousand times in a second. Assuming an average of ten symbol characters per line and a two-pass assembler that looks at every line twice, this inner loop would be executed 20 times per line. So the fastest you could go would be 5,000 lines per second, if that's all there was to do. But since the assembler still had a lot of other work to do, and code always runs a bit slower than the ideal, I suspected that this loop would take up about 20 percent of the CPU time of a fast assembler. That seemed a reasonable guess, since everything else was either disk I/O or very simple logic operations. And it brought the performance expectation down to 1,000 lines per second.

That figure was not only 100 times faster than the commercial PC assembler, it was also nearly ten times faster than the new minicomputer! I stared at the code, checked the figures again and again, and couldn't see a reason in the world why a PC-XT assembler couldn't outrun the $200,000 giant in our computer room by an order of magnitude.

So I built a fast PC-based 6502 assembler in three weeks, every nook and cranny braced for speed. It turned out to be disk-bound and only reached 1,000 lines per second on uncommented code. But it still ran seven times faster than the mini-computer—and 100 times faster than the commercial PC software.

We sold the minicomputer.

Adapted for other 8-bit processors as well, the assembler saw use in the video game industry through 1995. It now runs about 50,000 lines per second on my Pentium-100, still about five times faster than any other PC assembler I've tested. And it wouldn't have been built if seven lines of code—an inner loop—hadn't predicted its astonishing performance.

The embarrassing part of this remarkable software success story is that I was responsible for the purchase of the minicomputer in the first place. After all, everybody else was using one; everybody else used basically the same assemblers, too. And there was *proof* that the minicomputer must be necessary: it outperformed commercial PC software by an order of magnitude. It all looked right until . . . seven lines of code proved it wrong. It hadn't occurred to me that both of the commercial assemblers I was using ran at 1 percent efficiency!

Since then I've discovered that 1 percent efficiency is not uncommon in commercial software. In fact, it's actually encouraged by the conventional wisdoms of well-structured code development: *Nest subroutines. Seek generality. Recurse.* Slow seems safe.

And so it is that this book comes to cover code that often is, in a real sense, a bit risky and at odds with convention. But that's not all bad. Often success comes not from the rules you follow, but from the rules you break.

# Introduction

*When you can measure what you are speaking about, and express it in numbers, you know something about it.*

—Lord Kelvin

You wouldn't write a check you can't cash—at least, not intentionally. And you wouldn't pay a hundred dollars a gallon for gas. That's because you know the rules of money: you can't spend what you don't have, and what you do have should be spent wisely.

But what about the computing power needed to run an application? How do you know how much you have? And how do you spend it wisely?

This book attempts to answer these two questions as they relate to 32-bit code running on IBM PC–compatible computers. It's a book with concrete, performance-related numbers and advice on crafting fast, reliable code—and a selection of practical high-speed algorithms, analyzed and ready to run.

There are two parts to this book. The first, the theoretical part, concerns the design and analysis of fast computer code. It's about optimizing for speed. The second part applies theory to practice on a selection of important algorithms, offering high-performance solutions in both C and assembly language.

## Optimized Algorithms for the 32-Bit PC

This book aims to integrate the principles of code optimization with real-world examples of important algorithms. In fact, this book tries to bridge the gap between optimization and algorithms for 32-bit PC code. Virtually all of the algorithm books

I have seen offer machine-independent C, Pascal, or pseudocode descriptions of algorithms. This presents two difficulties for the high-performance PC programmer: First, there's still guesswork to be done as to how fast things will actually run when implemented. And second, you usually need to translate to assembly language for the last performance doubling.

So now that there are about a hundred million PCs in the world, it seems appropriate to ditch the machine-independent generality and just see what a PC can do. The algorithm chapters contain both C and assembly language implementations, as well as numbers you can use for performance estimates.

Although the 486, Pentium, and Pentium Pro processors are all discussed here, the code examples shown are usually optimized for the Pentium, unless otherwise noted. Likewise, the real-world performance figures discussed in this book are generally stated in terms of the way a Pentium-100 performs. It's easy to scale performance figures up and down from there to estimate how well other PC processors can do.

## Who This Book Is For

This book is designed for programmers who can at least read through PC assembly language listings, if not confidently write them. C is the higher-level language of choice in this book, but programmers not familiar with C should be able to get the gist regardless. The material applies to all PC programming environments that support 32-bit code, including extended DOS, Windows, Windows 95, Windows NT, and OS/2.

There are three important themes developed in these chapters:

1. *Prediction.* Good, bad, or ugly—knowing in advance how well any particular code is likely to run.
2. *Analysis.* Rethinking the "bad" (slow) to make it run "good" (fast).
3. *Speed.* Pulling out all the stops—making good better and better best.

## Overview of the Contents

It's time for a reality check. Grand generalizations are fine, but what's really in this book? Here are some of the high points of the chapters to come.

# Part 1: Theory

This part covers the fine points of processors (486, Pentium, Pentium Pro, and MMX extensions), systems (the capabilities of a Pentium-100 computer), assembly language (32-bit advice and structured coding), C (performance prediction), and the general quest for speed.

***Chapter 1. The Reference World of the Pentium-100.*** Actual performance measurements given throughout this book are based on a "typical" Pentium-100 system (the one used to *write* this book). I describe the reference system as well as various real-world points of reference, such as video frame and pixel rates and audio norms. Also used as a reference is the text of *War and Peace*.

***Chapter 2. 32-Bit Assembly Language.*** The cardinal rules: Shun 16-bit registers. Forget segment registers. And use the core one-cycle instructions. There are handy lists of useful, useless, and useful-but-painful instructions. A good bit of this chapter covers low-level processor mechanics.

***Chapter 3. Structured Assembly Language.*** Between the chaos of ordinary assembly language and the safety of well-coded C lies structured assembly language. Mixing C-like structure with assembly language power, it is an excellent, if little publicized, way to write solid, maintainable assembly language modules without compromising speed. It is implemented in the commercial MASM 6 assembler, and it is used throughout this book. This chapter introduces it.

***Chapter 4. Optimizing the 486.*** Counting cycles was never easier than on the 486. The first truly RISC-like processor in the 80x86 family, the 486 has a distinctly fast subset of instructions—and some distinctly slow legacy instructions. In a few aspects of optimization, the 486 resembles the Pentium Pro even more than it resembles the Pentium.

***Chapter 5. Optimizing the Pentium.*** If you like puzzles, you'll like optimizing the Pentium. You can execute instructions in pairs, but avoiding stalls while keeping the instruction queue full is not a trivial task to be left to compilers. The real scoop on instruction timing and cache performance is found here.

***Chapter 6. Optimizing the Pentium Pro.*** Learn to supplicate before the mysterious, dynamic execution engine at the heart of this high-end processor. Gone is some of the simple predictability of earlier processors, but it's replaced with the opportunity to guess and cajole even greater instruction parallelisms and speed. Find out when a zeroed register might not act like a zeroed register.

***Chapter 7. Achieving Speed.*** There are many techniques for improving speed. Some pertain to C, and others must be done in assembly. Here a simple function undergoes an eight-phase metamorphosis from respectable C to nine-times-faster assembly language. When the optimal Pentium code performs badly on a Pentium Pro, a final fix makes it run right on both.

***Chapter 8. C Performance.*** It's remarkably easy to mentally translate between C and assembly language. This chapter goes over the correlation between C statements and the code they often generate, as well as what optimization switches do. The one-variable, one-cycle rule of thumb makes it easy to make a ballpark estimate of C performance.

***Chapter 9. MMX.*** As of this writing, the new Pentium and Pentium Pro MMX chips aren't out yet—but their specs are. This chapter looks at the kinds of performance boosts multimedia code is going to get. Running two nearly identical loops in parallel looks like the best optimization strategy for many applications.

## Part 2: Practice

This part contains an eclectic mix of algorithms, from memory block transfers to JPEG's inner loop, analyzed, optimized, and ready to run.

***Chapter 10. Moving Memory.*** There is a fine structure to memory: the primary cache (and often a secondary cache), the main memory, cache lines, burst transfers, and write-through and write-back strategies. Simple memory-to-memory block transfer is not a one-size-fits-all proposition. Here are three ways to beat the processor's "bliter." The upshot is that you can transfer large memory blocks on the Pentium about 30 percent faster with a software loop than with the built-in processor block transfer instruction.

***Chapter 11. Random Numbers and Primes.*** There is no one right way to generate random numbers, so here are eight ways to do it at various speeds. There's also a randomness checker, an integration example, and a sieve of Eratosthenes to generate prime numbers. You can generate reasonably good 32-bit random numbers at rates up to about ten million per second.

***Chapter 12. Linked Lists and Trees.*** Few structures are more sensitive to memory layout and access patterns. Sometimes large structures with embedded links are penalized for being an even power of 2 in size. But if you're running in cache, there's a two-cycle-per-link search for a record field match. In good times (cache), link traversal can cost as little as two cycles per node, and binary tree descent as little as six cycles; but in bad times (main memory, dispersed), they can each reach 50 cycles.

***Chapter 13. Hashing.*** What's the fastest way to look up a word in an electronic dictionary or to find a name in an electronic phone book? Usually the answer is "by hashing." Feed a word or a name in, and grind out a little pseudorandom number that helps you locate it *fast*. The result—you can "look up" every word in *War and Peace* in less than a second.

***Chapter 14. Huffman Compression.*** The classic variable-length bit-code compression, Huffman often plays a role within more complex compression schemes (JPEG is part Huffman). The fastest decompression is usually table-driven and tailored to primary cache size. With Huffman compression, you can compress *War and Peace* to about 60 percent of its original ASCII text size in less than a second.

***Chapter 15. A Fast Sort.*** Many sort algorithms degrade in their per-item sorting speed as the number of items to be sorted goes up. The fast sort given in this chapter, though, maintains a fairly constant speed, even when the number of items to be sorted runs into the millions. For very large scale sorting, it performs faster than the more popular alternatives. You can sort as many millions of records as you can stuff into memory (allowing a 9-byte-per-record sorting overhead) on the value of a 32-bit integer field at a rate of just under half a million records per second.

***Chapter 16. Matrix Multiplication.*** Matrix math is often floating-point math; this chapter looks at the best ways to pipeline a series of multiplications and additions through the floating-point unit. The special problems of big matrices are considered, and a common 3x4 rotation-and-displacement matrix problem is solved. Using the techniques discussed here, you can rotate and displace the coordinates of over 50,000 points in three-dimensional space 30 times per second.

***Chapter 17. JPEG.*** One of the biggest and most interesting inner loops around is found in the JPEG image compression and decompression process. This chapter takes a look at the main inner loop of JPEG decompression and shows how the loop can be tuned up in assembly language side by side with the C implementation. Using assembly language, you can squeeze an extra 30 percent performance out of the fast integer inverse discrete cosine transform loop (explained in the chapter) over good compiled C.

# Playing Devil's Advocate

It all sounds great, doesn't it? Faster! Better! Life just got good!

Well . . . maybe not quite *that* good. There are a lot of reasons *not* to optimize code. In fact, a good speed-conscious programmer usually has to hide out from management once in a while. But success breeds respect, and not messing up is the way to get it.

These are the common precautions:

- Changing working code invites bugs. If it ain't broke, don't fix it.
- It usually takes longer to develop fast code than it does to develop slower code.
- Fast code often violates principles of structured program design; that makes it dangerous and difficult to maintain.
- Assembly language code is notoriously unstable in inexperienced hands.
- Often programmers speed up the wrong parts of the code, with little net gain.
- Portability may break.

There is some truth to all of this. Portability to non-PC systems goes out the window with assembly code. Sometimes it is lost when C code is based on machine-specific assumptions, such as integer byte order. But most of the world's computers are PC systems, and portability is not always a problem. Programmers do often target the wrong code for optimization. But experience (and, hopefully, this book) can help on that front. The evils of assembly language truly are legend. But structured assembly language has come to the rescue in the last few years. It's gotten much more civilized down there. And yes, fast code can invite bugs, increase costs, and be difficult to modify. But sometimes the benefits are simply *worth* it.

Therefore, proceed with caution. A speed-demon coder can be his own—and his management's—worst enemy. But, conversely, success breeds success.

# Inner Loops

Inner loops have played a big role in my career. Having worked in the video game and digital video fields for seventeen years, and more recently in cable set-top boxes, I've found that all three fields tend to demand all available performance. In fact, some of the algorithms discussed in this book are ones I've worked on, in one form or another, over the years. And the steps to build them are always the same: Seek out the inner loops that determine top performance. Find the best assembly language loops that do the job. Count the cycles. Extrapolate. Code.

Outer loops can be important, too. I've often had to optimize code one and two levels out from an inner loop just to keep up the pace. And so it is that fast code begets the need for even more fast code. And along a continuum, fast algorithms seek each other out to form systems. Indeed, systems work is the often the ultimate outcome of the quest for speed.

The algorithms presented in this book are crafted in inner loops of C and assembly, both good languages for efficient programming. But assembly language is far superior for efficiency *analysis*. You can't just look at an inner loop of C code, jot down a few numbers, and know within plus or minus 10 percent how fast it will run. You *can* do these things with assembly. In fact, assembly code suggests and predicts C performance. That is why assembly language is the frontline tool for finding the best algorithms and knowing how well they will run. There's nothing contradictory about analyzing in assembly and implementing in C.

The assembly language used in this book is *structured* assembly language. It doesn't look quite the same as most published assembly code. That's because it incorporates constructs usually seen in higher-level languages: `if-else-endif` clauses, `repeat-until` sections, and `while` loops. This code is written for use with Microsoft's MASM 6 assembler. The constructs make for readable code, with fewer opportunities to create bugs. In fact, they make assembly look and feel a lot like C. And there's usually no performance penalty for using them. Chapter 3 explains more about structured assembly language. If you happen to use a different, nonstructured assembler, it's a straightforward process to translate back into ordinary label-intensive code.

To my way of thinking, optimization is a very enjoyable subject. It's where you seek and sometimes touch the limits of silicon, systems, and cycles. I hope you enjoy the book.

# Theory

# The Reference World of the Pentium-100

*You don't know what you've got until it's gone.*
—*Common saying*

It starts as a slight sluggishness, or perhaps an overly pregnant pause. The video may stutter, or clicking sounds may punctuate the unwanted silence on an audio channel. Sometimes the "progress" bar creeps like a gastropod. And once in a while you might as well take lunch while your computer works, without user interaction, on a difficult problem. The common thread is resource exhaustion, and like a car without a gas gauge—you often don't know what you've got till it's gone. And then, of course, you want it back.

A good optimizer *can* often get it back after running out of resources. But a *great* optimizer predicts and avoids resource exhaustion in the first place. This chapter is about knowing what you've got—before it's gone. It's about the ballpark performance figures that are the first stop along the way to efficient code design.

To back up the abstractions with real numbers, this chapter looks at the specific speeds and capabilities of a Pentium-100 system—specifically, the one used to write this book. This test system is a Micron Millenia with a Pentium-100 processor and 32 megabytes of EDO (Extended Data Out) RAM, manufactured in June 1995. The Pentium-100 is, in fact, used for performance reference throughout this book. Its nice round clock speed, 100 megahertz, lends itself well to scaling. For many purposes it is approximately true that a Pentium-75 runs at three-quarters of a Pentium-100's speed, and a Pentium-133 runs about one-third faster.

But this chapter is about more than just hardware, for some of the things that bog down computers most—video, audio, images, modems, and networks—need to be investigated as well. A couple of rules of thumb about compiler and operating system effects round out the chapter's performance eyeballing notes. This is the how-many, how-fast, how-often, and how-much chapter.

# The Pentium-100 Processor

In 1979, when I encountered my first personal computer, the TRS-80 and Apple II were hot. Both were finding their way into business as well as recreational uses, and both had about one one-thousandth the computing power of the Pentium-100. Adding two 32-bit numbers from memory and placing the result back into memory took about 50 microseconds, versus an effective 0.02 microseconds (best case) on the Pentium. Floating-point multiplication? The Pentium-100 is nearly 100,000 times faster. Although the power of today's computers may seem almost unimaginably vast compared to those early machines, the problems addressed by computers have kept pace with their increased power. It's still just about as easy to run out of power as it used to be.

The Pentium chip will be reviewed in more detail in another chapter, but here is a thumbnail sketch of what it can do. The Pentium chip is capable of executing two instructions in a single clock cycle—of which, in the case of a Pentium-100, there are 100 million in a second. It is not always possible to execute two at a time, though. Some instructions take more than one cycle, and some conditions cause further processor delays. The bottom line is that unless the processor is spending most of its time in highly efficient inner loops, you're likely to get 150 million or fewer instructions through, out of the 200 million upper limit.

The fast instructions include data movement, addition, subtraction, most shifts, bitwise logical operators, and most branches—in other words, most of what a computer needs to do. Integer multiplication takes 9 cycles, and division takes usually 41or more cycles. (These are among the most common of the slower instructions.)

There's a floating-point unit on board, which can sometimes operate in parallel with the other instructions, but there's usually not a lot of parallelism there in practice. Within the floating-point unit there is another form of parallelism, such that a multiplication can end up costing as little as one cycle. But in practice, a = b * c tends to often cost 7 cycles or more. Division still costs as much as 39 cycles (unless you intentionally reduce its precision and run in 33 or 19 cycles), and more complex functions like sine and cosine can cost over 100 cycles.

In summary, a Pentium-100 is a powerful computing engine that, when not slowed down by higher math, can deliver well over 100 million simple instructions per second, sometimes achieving nearly 200 million in very tight loops.

# Memory

There are three tiers of memory in a typical Pentium-100 system: the primary cache, the secondary cache, and main memory. Second only to the processor itself, their performance influences the power of the system. From fastest to slowest, here they are.

## The Primary Cache

When the processor accesses memory, much of the time it's reading from, and possibly writing to, the primary cache right onboard its own chip. The Pentium keeps an 8 kilobyte (K) store of recent executable instructions, and almost any time an inner loop is running, it is executing from this rapid access store. And there is another 8 kilobyte store of recently referenced data, organized in chunks of 32 bytes. Many algorithms can execute extensively while hitting the primary cache with data references almost all the time. A data fetch or store from or to the primary cache costs only one cycle, and two such references can usually be executed in the same cycle.

You can copy data from one part of the primary cache to another at a rate of 350 megabytes (MB) per second. But since there's only 0.008 megabytes of primary cache, you can't copy for very long at a stretch. The fastest solution to a problem often revolves around how to fit critical tables into the 8 kilobytes of cache.

For all its memory, Pentium optimization sometimes reduces to an 8K cache game focused on keeping just the right data available at high speeds. Many programs, though, achieve 90 percent hit rates, and better, naturally.

## The Secondary Cache

Most Pentium systems have at least a 256K secondary cache to rapidly feed the 8K primary cache. On the test system, it costs 7 cycles to fetch data from the secondary cache if it's not in the primary cache. But since any data fetched from secondary initiates a 32-byte transfer to the primary cache, subsequent accesses to nearby data are automatically speeded up to one cycle. If I'm sequentially reading bytes not already in the primary cache, the first one I read will take 7 cycles, but the other 31 will usually take just one cycle each, since they were transferred to the primary cache after the first read. An entire 8K can be transferred from secondary cache to primary cache in as little as 2,589 cycles, about 25 microseconds.

## The Main Memory

This is the big-ticket memory, the 8 or 16 or 32 or more megabytes you bought to make Windows 95 or some such environment happy. Despite the 60- or 70- or 90-nanosecond ratings on the RAM, it takes significantly longer than that to transfer data from main memory. On the test system it takes 170 nanoseconds, or 17 cycles, to fetch a piece of data from main memory. Of course, a 32-byte chunk gets transferred as a result, and it can subsequently be accessed from the primary cache. An entire 8K can be transferred from main memory to both the secondary cache and the primary cache in about 5,000 cycles, or about 50 microseconds.

An ordinary RAM-to-RAM copy runs an order of magnitude slower than a cache-to-cache copy, at about 45 megabytes per second, but can be boosted to over 60 megabytes per second on some large transfers using special software described in Chapter 10. Either way, that's still fast enough to make over a dozen copies of *War and Peace* in a second.

## Page Tables

It's possible to access main memory in such a random pattern that you can completely baffle the processor, which is set up to be ready for memory references in the same general vicinity as other recent references. When this happens, the processor has to take time out to reference what are known as page tables in memory, describing how virtual memory maps into physical memory. The upshot is that really random memory references can cost 48 cycles, and in rapid sequence they can cost 60. If you've ever considered solving a problem with a 16 megabyte lookup table for speed, timings like these should make you think twice. (The bigger the lookup table, the more seemingly random the access pattern, from the processor's point of view.) You can perform about 100 primary cache references in the same time it takes to hit one really random spot (that is, one that is not near other recently used data) in main memory!

## Summary

There is a two-order-of-magnitude difference between the fastest and slowest memory access patterns on the Pentium. Fortunately, a lot of software can run mainly on the fastest 8K of the primary data cache and code cache. The secondary cache and main memory, while both much slower than the primary cache for a lone reference, make up for the lone reference speed by rapidly transferring 32-byte chunks to the primary cache so that nearby references won't incur the same penalty. And on the test system, ordinary memory copies, not assisted by a cache, run at 45 megabytes per second.

# The PCI and ISA Buses

After the processor and the memory, one of the most important speed-critical items in a computer is the bus it uses to interface with other devices. For about a decade, from the early 1980s to the early 1990s, the ISA (Industry Standard Architecture) bus ruled the PC world, with IBM's MCA (Microchannel Architecture) bus and the later EISA (Extended ISA) bus challenging it with better speed. You plugged cards, such as video boards, into ISA slots, but bulk data transfer over the ISA bus was arduously slow. As of this writing, most computers still come with an ISA bus and slots, and there are still plenty of ISA boards around, many of which are not significantly impeded in their duties by ISA speed. The test system has an ISA bus as well as the newer and much faster PCI bus.

Although to some extent data transfer rates can be slowed by the peripheral board itself, if you get 3 to 4 megabytes per second out to a video board over an ISA bus, you are doing well. With the PCI bus, that number increases dramatically—to about 21 to 24 megabytes per second (depending on video mode) on the test system, using a Diamond Stealth 64 video card with VRAM. This is the speed of processor-mediated memory-mapped copies over the bus. There are ways to transfer memory over the PCI bus in which the bus essentially performs direct memory access on the data (instead of having the processor feed it the data), and such transfers should be capable of even higher speeds. But for ordinary applications well above the device-driver level, processor copies at 21 to 24 megabytes per second appear to be in the ballpark.

On many 486 and early Pentium systems, there is an alternative to PCI—the VESA local bus, also called the VL bus. The competing, but fading, VL bus design is said to have similar speed characteristics to PCI. In any event, up to 24 megabytes per second is possible on the test system, and that's not a bad working number. (That's seven copies of a certain Russian novel each second.)

An algorithm that picks up data, processes it, and sends it out over the PCI bus can run as fast as about 4 cycles per byte (or 16 cycles per longword) before the bus speed limits it.

# Disks

Next in line in terms of determining system speed are the disks.

## The Hard Disk

I can read from and write to the test system's hard disk, a Conner 1.275-gigabyte disk on an enhanced IDE (EIDE) controller, at about 2.5 megabytes per second. That's a little shy of the size of a long novel each second.

The tests I ran were under the DOS4GW DOS extender, the same environment I used for the rest of the tests in this book. Straight DOS without an extender tends to achieve a slightly higher rate, because the data doesn't have to be copied to or from high extended memory (since most disk controllers can only address low physical memory addresses). And in a multitasking operating system, much of the disk delay can actually be overlapped with the execution of tasks that aren't waiting for the disk operations to complete. So accounting for disk access time is a bit tricky in an environment where the time you wait isn't necessarily the time you lose, all tasks considered.

The processor can execute about 40 instruction cycles in the time it takes to read a streamed byte off the disk. In a multitasking environment, many of those cycles may actually be available, but it does set a processing speed limit for data coming in from disk.

## The Floppy Disk

A standard 1.44-megabyte 3.5-inch floppy can be entirely read or written on the test machine in a little over a minute at a rate of about 23K per second. There aren't many times other than during software installation when that number gets annoying, as the floppy has become a lightly used method of file transfer. But it doesn't hurt to know the numbers.

## The CD-ROM Disk

As of this writing, there are CD-ROM drives available all the way from 1× speed, the normal speed of an audio CD, to 8×, eight times faster. The test system uses a Plextor 4×. Unless something's gone wrong, a CD-ROM disk drive usually delivers data at or near its rated speed. Table 1-1 shows the nominal delivery rates at the various drive speeds. The numbers are theoretically exact.

| Table 1-1 | CD-ROM Data Transfer Rates |
|---|---|
| 1X speed— | 150K/second |
| 2X speed— | 300K/second |
| 3X speed— | 450K/second |
| 4X speed— | 600K/second |
| 6X speed— | 900K/second |
| 8X speed— | 1200K/second |

CD-ROM drivers are notoriously inefficient at reading their disks. They are often set up to read ahead beyond the previous read request, in anticipation of future sequential access to the data stream. In effect, the CD-ROM reading task becomes a background task this way, and DOS or other programs can proceed while the CD-ROM drive fetches ahead. When this happens—sometimes taking up half or more of the processor's power until the transfer is done—you can notice a big performance hit on the processor. As a rule of thumb, assume, until proven otherwise, that you're running at 40 to 60 percent processing power, or even less, when streaming data near full speed off a CD-ROM drive

The capacity of CD-ROMs seemed enormous when they first came out, when I was working with a 30 megabyte drive. But now that I've got a gigabyte, it seems more approachable. At exactly 150K per second of "audio playing time," a 74-minute CD has a raw data capacity of 650 megabytes. And a 4× drive can read one in just under 20 minutes.

The test system processor can execute 160 instruction cycles in the time it takes to read a streamed byte off a 4× CD-ROM drive. But thanks to the high overhead of CD-ROM reads, as few as 60 cycles may be available to an application. This cycle count is a key determinant of what algorithms can be applied to streamed data and what cannot. A data decompression algorithm that runs at 80 cycles per compressed byte probably can't stream at 4×. At 2×, the cycle count per streamed byte is more likely 120, and the former hypothetical algorithm would stand a good chance of keeping up.

# The Modem

In comparison to everything else discussed so far, even a fast telephone modem is slow. The rule of thumb about kilobaud ratings is that you divide the rating number by 10 to get kilobytes per second. The test system has a 28.8-kilobaud modem, which is about as fast as they currently get, so it can only deliver raw data at about 3K per second, about an eighth the speed of a floppy disk. The 14.4-kilobaud modems achieve about half what the 28.8 modems do, and so forth.

When compression and decompression protocols are agreed upon on both ends of the line, the modems sometimes achieve data compression of about a factor of two—so that, for instance, text may seem to come through at a 6K rate, having been squeezed to 3K during transmission. But compressed graphics files like JPGs or GIFs resist compression and take the straight 3K route.

A megabyte takes just over five minutes to send or receive at an uncompressed 28.8 rate. That's about one long Russian novel every 18 minutes, or every 9 if sent through a compressing protocol.

The processing overhead for modem transmissions is fairly small, so for every byte of, say, compressed data arriving or leaving via modem, there are about 30,000 cycles of processing power available. That's about 500 times more processor availability than a byte off a 4× CD-ROM gets, enough to make almost any decompression algorithm happy.

# The Network Connection

If you're attached to a local area network and someone tells you the network runs at 10 megabits per second or better, don't assume you can transfer data at that rate. A few years ago I discovered that even on a nice new 10-megabit ethernet network, individual stations were limited to 2 megabits, or 200 kilobytes, per second. The explanation the manufacturer's representative gave was that the boards plugged into the PCs were rate-limited, but the network as a whole was not.

The moral of the story is that you're better off seeing how long it takes to transfer a large file under an otherwise light network load than taking someone's word about network data rates. Under heavy contention, performance is, of course, predictably worse. But my working rule of thumb about local area networks is that they're about 200K per second—plus or minus 50—until proven otherwise. (That's 16 seconds per novel.)

Before overhead, that's 500 cycles available per byte. And it's only a little faster at streaming than a 1× CD-ROM drive.

# Still Images

How big is a picture? Well, a decent-looking full-screen picture on a PC can range from about 15K to about 3 MB, depending on how perfectly accurate, clean, and precise you want it and how hard you want to work to compress it. Graphics screens range from a resolution of 320×200 with 256 colors to 1024×768 (or higher) with 16 million colors. The range of picture elements, or pixel, counts is from 64,000 to 786,432, and bytes per pixel goes from 1 to 4.

It's easy to see that even highly efficient operations, when performed on each pixel or byte of a large image, can give a Pentium system pause. Decompression of a large JPG image can take several seconds, even if the processor only spends 2 or 3 microseconds on each pixel. And it can take more than a second to read a large uncompressed image file from disk, or many seconds from a CD-ROM. Transferred over even the fastest phone modem, the smallest reasonable full-screen picture file takes 5 seconds, and the largest a quarter of an hour.

Thus images or pictures pose a natural challenge to the Pentium-100's computing power. To put a full-screen 1024×768 picture on the screen in one second, an algorithm has to process pixels in 130 cycles or less, on average. The next level of insult is video.

# Video

As if still images weren't challenging enough, there's video. Until recently, single-speed CD-ROMs were the delivery vehicle of choice for video. It never looked particularly good at full screen, because it was delivering mostly 8K and 9K frames, which just didn't look good blown up to full screen. But double-speed CD-ROM drives deliver 15K to 20K frames at 15 frames per second, a much more respectable-looking basis for full-screen video.

Consider now that even with the smallest number of pixels in full-screen mode (64,000), that's 960,000 pixels per second that need updating. That's roughly 100 cycles per pixel, which tends to be diminished to about 40 after the CD-ROM drive takes its inordinately large cut. Suddenly that's not a lot of time to decompress an input stream and slam pixels out over the PCI bus.

And that doesn't even come close to the quality we're accustomed to from our TV sets. Standard TV runs at nearly 30 frames per second, (actually 30,000/1,001 frames per second) with a very approximate effective pixel density of 640×480. That's twice the frame rate and more than quadruple the pixels mentioned in the paragraph above: about 10 cycles per pixel, not enough time do much of a decompression algorithm at all. Imagine the difficulty of updating the much larger graphics screen modes at comparable rates.

There appear to be hardware video decompression solutions using MPEG (Motion Pictures Expert Group) technology coming down the pike to save the video day, but until they become a standard, Pentiums and their descendants will crank long and hard to create acceptable video.

# Audio

If a Pentium seems to struggle with video, it has the power to do respectable things with audio in real time. An audio recording usually consists of a series of several thousand 8- or 16-bit numbers recorded each second, reflecting the oscillation of sound waves striking the recording microphone. If you graphed the numbers, you would see the wave. Each number is referred to as a sample, and PCs record and play them back at rates from about 4,000 per second (slightly hoarse voice) to 44,100 per second (CD quality). A common middle-of-the-road selection is 11,250 per second, which carries respectable voice as well as music for the less discriminating.

Even at the full CD-quality rate of 44,100 samples per second, that's over 2,000 Pentium-100 cycles from one sample to the next. Audio is inherently an order of magnitude less taxing than video. Some of the easier things to do with audio include combining several streams of audio or changing volume. And you can actually burn up all the available cycles trying to do real-time frequency filters or frequency spectrum analysis.

# Text

*War and Peace* makes up 3.25 megabytes of uncompressed data as a simple ASCII text file. You can slam this much data around RAM at incomprehensibly high speeds, but pulling it off a disk, a network, or a modem takes noticeable to painful amounts of time. Text and database files of similar or larger size are not uncommon, so it's worth considering what you do and do not have to wait for with files of this magnitude.

# Compiled Code

As a rule of thumb, if you're running out of processing power for a CPU-bound algorithm and have also run out of ways to make C go faster, the best hand-assembled code often runs about 50 percent faster still. Badly compiled C code may run at a half or a third the speed of assembly code. I believe most of the currently popular C compilers do rather well with their optimization switches turned on, but I speak mainly from experience with Watcom C, which has a good reputation for efficiency and does achieve a two-thirds efficiency level on average.

When trying to estimate how well C will perform in real time, I often find myself writing an inner loop in assembly language, counting the cycles, and scaling back to two-thirds speed for the C estimate. There is a fair amount of variability, but the relationship seems to hold on average. And it's nice to know, when running out of cycles in C, that there's probably a reserve pool if you recode in assembly.

# Operating Systems

Having considered the primary and secondary cache speeds and sizes, and having assumed that all processor cycles and facilities were dedicated to one's own application, one must finally come to grips with the fact that, increasingly, operating systems and the competing tasks managed by those systems can reduce the size of the resource pie anywhere from a little to a lot.

Aside from taking processor cycles away from a task for its own housekeeping or to give to other tasks, an operating system—or even a simple interrupt service routine, if called often enough—can decrease the total system throughput by causing the cache to be shared, in effect, among the competing tasks. In other words, if you switch tasks often enough and fire enough interrupts, the various tasks can end up spending a lot of time kicking each other's memory out of cache and reloading it with their own.

Using the 50-microsecond figure for how long it takes to reload 8K of primary cache data from main memory, that puts an upper limit of 20,000 complete reloads per second. As a ballpark estimate, a twentieth that number of task switches and interrupt servicings, 1,000 or less, could shave significant percentage points off performance. Sharing the processor in tiny time slices diffuses the effectiveness of the cache, which sees a much more random looking overall access pattern.

There's a price to pay—not so serious as death, but definitely akin to taxes—for being part of a community of concurrent programs, so as a rule of thumb, expect to pay a little tithe from your processor-second when other tasks are running too.

# Conclusion

This chapter has reviewed not only the speeds of operation of a typical Pentium-100 and the devices to which it is normally connected, but also some of the real-world problems that challenge such a system. Resources are not infinite, and it's best to know up front what the capacities and capabilities of the machine are, as well as the magnitude of the problems it will be called upon to address.

Table 1-2 shows the five orders of magnitude of data movement speed typically associated with a Pentium-100, from modem to primary cache. Practical application algorithms are often dominated by one or more of these potential bottlenecks, and good inner loops must be sculpted around them. Sometimes you *can* know what you've got before it's gone. And sometimes you have to.

| Table 1-2 Pentium-100 Environment Data Movement Speeds | |
|---|---|
| Data Transfer Type | Speed (megabytes per second) |
| Primary cache data movement | 400 |
| Main memory data movement | 44 |
| PCI bus data movement | 21 |
| ISA bus data movement | 3 |
| Hard disk read/write | 2.5 |
| CD-ROM read | 0.6 |
| Local area network read/write | 0.2 |
| Floppy disk read | 0.023 |
| Modem | 0.003 |

# 2

# 32-Bit Assembly Language

*O! . . . that I could forget what I have been.*
—*Richard II, Shakespeare*

Once in a long time, the advance of technology makes things simpler. For those who learned 16-bit 80x86 assembly language—juggling segment registers and using special-purpose string and loop instructions—32-bit assembly language is a simplification. And half of learning it is remembering what to forget.

Whether you program in assembly language, C, C++, or any other language, knowledge of assembly language can be very useful. I very often find myself designing algorithms and estimating their performance in assembly language, even if I intend to implement them in another language.

This chapter assumes that the reader is familiar enough with assembly language, whether of the 80x86 family or others, to at least feel comfortable reading through code listings. Assuming that, this chapter presents a quick review of what's new and powerful in 32-bit coding, and it presents a way to group and think about the 80x86 instruction set. Unless otherwise noted, specific timing comments in this chapter refer to the Pentium. Subsequent chapters will cover 486, Pentium, and Pentium Pro specifics in more detail.

The main topics in this chapter are

- What to forget about 16-bit assembly language
- Basic 32-bit assembly language
- The instruction set

# What to Forget About 16-Bit Assembly Language

In the early 1980s, the success of the first IBM PCs was due in large part to the awkward way the 8088 processor stretched beyond the 64K memory-addressing limit of most of its competitors to attain an unthinkably huge 1 megabyte of addressable memory space. The way it did so was basically a "kludge," and until the advent of true 32-bit computing, programmers had to spend extra coding time and cycles dealing with the addressing problem, especially when data structures exceeded, or could exceed, 64K in total size.

Early PCs, though technically able to address an entire megabyte of memory, could only "see" four 64K memory zones at any one time. One of the zones contained the executable code itself, another the processor stack, and another the current working data area. The fourth was a floating spare, so that, for instance, you could copy between the data area and the spare area. Always having to worry about just where your four zones were positioned was a major problem. Copying 70K from one place to another required at least one pit stop to change the "segment registers" so that the processor could see the right parts of memory. And memory pointers came in two sizes, those with and those without a segment register value attached.

The four original, infamous segment registers, called CS, SS, DS, and ES, were augmented by two more, "spare" segment registers, FS and GS, when the 386 came out. So ever since the 386, there have been six 64K windows into memory. From the 286 on, these registers have become windows into an ever-larger physical memory—and even virtual memory—address space.

What happened to simplify things in 32-bit code? In 32-bit applications, the segment registers are all still there, but now they control 4-gigabyte windows into memory instead of the original 64K. (Their addressing range went from 16 bits to 32 bits.) By convention, most applications now operate with the segment registers all looking at the same window of memory in what's known as the "flat" programming model. In the old days, you had to shuffle the segment registers to see objects larger than 64K. Those days are gone.

The first thing to forget about 16-bit assembly language is the need to worry about memory segmentation with segment registers. Almost all the time, you can get away with 32-bit application programming without worrying about them or directly operating on them.

The second thing to forget about 16-bit assembly language is the 16-bit processor registers (other than the segment registers) and most 16-bit operands in general.

A lot of assembly language instructions have a single bit devoted to operand size. The bit used to signal either 8-bit or 16-bit size. In 32-bit assembly language, it signals either 8-bit or 32-bit size. It takes a special instruction prefix byte to signal a 16-bit size in 32-bit code, and that slows things down. Also, mixing 16-bit and 32-bit register instructions can easily lead to bugs. In C, avoid "short" 16-bit variables, unless space conservation requires them.

The third thing to forget about 16-bit coding—or, for that matter, early 32-bit coding on the 386—is use of the special-purpose compound-operation instructions, such as `lods` (load string), `stos` (store string), `loop` (loop test and branch), `xlat` (translate), `jcxz` (jump if `cx` is zero), and most of the `rep` (repeat) instructions, which, with the exception of `rep movs` (repeat move string), are mostly less efficient than the sum of their component parts. For example,

```
lodsb                    ;load a byte and advance the pointer
```

is generally less efficient in terms of speed than the equivalent:

```
mov     al,[esi]         ;load a byte
lea     esi,[esi+1]      ;and advance the pointer
```

More specifics on the more efficient forms are given later in this chapter.

And the fourth and final thing to forget, if you're concerned about Pentium speed and efficiency, is almost any instruction that combines a movement of data, between memory and a register, with a logical or arithmetic operation on that data. Thus

```
add     al,[esi]         ;direct addition to al from memory
```

is usually less efficient, due to potential instruction pairing, than

```
mov     bl,[esi]         ;move memory to a spare register
add     al,bl            ;add from the spare register
```

And

```
inc     byte ptr [esi]   ;increment a memory byte
```

is usually less efficient than

```
mov     bl,[esi]         ;move memory to a spare register
inc     bl               ;increment the byte
mov     [esi],bl         ;move it back to memory
```

If you don't happen to have a spare register available, though, the move-and-operate instructions can still sometimes be useful and efficient in that particular context. In a closely related situation on the Pentium Pro, there are actually cases where move-and-operate instructions lead to greater efficiency. This exception to the general rule is explained in Chapter 6.

In review, the old assembly language habits to break are as follows:

1. Almost all segment register usage, except for use in systems programming
2. Almost all 16-bit register usage
3. Compound instruction usage, like `lods` and `stos` and `loop`
4. Register-memory move-and-operate instructions, like `add al,[esi]`

Following these guidelines leaves you programming with an efficient but "reduced" instruction set. Sound familiar? The 80x86 started life as a CISC (complex instruction set computer) processor, with a lot of redundant instructions. This saved time in the early 1980s but came to bog the processor down a decade later, as its core design became more like a RISC (reduced instruction set computer) processor from the 486 on. (The main feature normally associated with RISC processors but still lacking in the 80x86 is a large number of registers, making efficient use of the handful that *are* available critical.) Today the legacy CISC instructions are still available for backward compatibility, but efficient coding is done mainly with the reduced instruction set, which is what is left after breaking the four old habits just mentioned.

# Basic 32-Bit Assembly Language

If you already know an assembly language, this summary will, hopefully, be enough to get you reading 32-bit 80x86 assembly language. If not, you may want to consult an assembly language text.

## Processor Structure

The processor structure seen and used by 32-bit applications these days is much simpler than it used to be in 16-bit days. Figure 2-1 shows the nesting of the eight 8-bit registers inside four of the eight 16-bit registers, which in turn are inside eight 32-bit registers. Thus, for instance, the AL register contains the low byte of both the 16-bit AX register and the 32-bit EAX register. And AH contains the high byte of

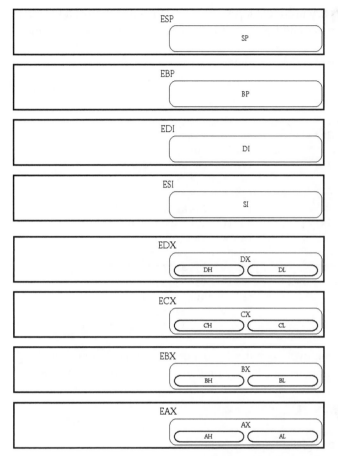

**Figure 2-1   Processor Registers with Nesting Shown**

AX and the next-to-lowest byte of EAX. The AX register is just the low half of EAX, and there is no separate register that addresses the high half.

The registers are fairly interchangeable. You can add or subtract or perform bit-wise logical operations between any two same-sized registers. You can perform shifts, nots, negations, increments, or decrements on any register.

There is also a 32-bit flags register, which will be discussed later in the chapter.

## Addressing Memory

Memory addressing is simple. You can add two 32-bit registers and a 32-bit offset to generate a memory address. One of the registers can be optionally premultiplied by two, four, or eight. And you don't have to use either register or the offset if it's not needed. Whenever registers are used to address memory, they are enclosed in square brackets. Here are seven ways to address memory to fetch a byte using these rules:

```
var1    db    'a1b2c3d4e5'         ;dummy global byte data


        mov   al,[esi]             ;register only
        mov   al,[edx*2]           ;multiplied register only
        mov   al,[esi+edx*2]       ;both registers
        mov   al,var1              ;offset only
        mov   al,var1[esi]         ;register and offset
                                   ;alternate forms:
                                   ;"mov al,[esi+7]"
                                   ;"mov al,var1[esi+7]"
        mov   al,var1[edx*2]       ;multiplied reg and offset
                                   ;alternate forms:
                                   ;"mov al,[edx*2+7]"
                                   ;"mov al,var1[edx*2+7]"
        mov   al,var1[esi+edx*2]   ;all three
                                   ;alternate forms:
                                   ;"mov al,[esi+edx*2+7]"
                                   ;"mov al,var1[esi+edx*2+7]"
```

On the 486, there is a one-cycle penalty for using a second or a multiplied register in the address, but the penalty goes away on the Pentium and Pentium Pro.

## Register Review

Although at first glance the registers appear to be equivalent, to some degree most of them retain some unique properties. Here is the register rundown:

ESP         The stack pointer. In the old 16-bit days, you couldn't address stack variables through it. In the new 32-bit days, you can use it to address parameters and variables on the stack. Unless you shut off all interrupts, you can't use this register to hold anything but the stack pointer.

EBP         By 16-bit convention, this register was usually used to address variables on the stack, since the SP register couldn't do it. It's still used that way—as a "stack frame pointer"—by most compilers, even though the ESP register is now generally adequate for the job. Assembly language programs can often "borrow" it for general use.

| ESI | A good general-purpose register. Its main "special" function is as a source data pointer for repeated string instructions, especially the `rep movs` block move instruction, which is still fairly useful. |
| --- | --- |
| EDI | A good general-purpose register. Its main "special" function is as a destination pointer for repeated string instructions, especially the `rep movs` block move instruction. |
| EDX | A good general-purpose register. It is also used in some multiplication, division, and port I/O operations. The Pentium cycle clock reports to this register. |
| ECX | A good general-purpose register. Its main "special" function is as a loop counter for repeated string instructions, especially the `rep movs` block move instruction. Its low byte also holds the shift count for shifts calculated at runtime. |
| EBX | A *great* general-purpose register. No important special functions are associated with it. |
| EAX | A good general-purpose register. It is also used in some multiplication, division, and port I/O operations. Its low two bytes have several other idiosyncratic uses from time to time. The Pentium cycle clock reports to this register. |
| AX, BX, CX, DX,SI, DI, BP, SP | Rarely worth using for the sake of efficiency. |
| BL, BH, CH, DL, DH | Good general-purpose byte registers, subject to the above 32-bit parent register considerations. |
| CL | Good general-purpose byte register. Holds the shift count for shifts calculated at runtime. |
| AH | Good general-purpose byte register. Acts as a transfer buffer for flag register information. |
| AL | Good general-purpose byte register. Also used for port I/O and binary-coded decimal operations. |

In summary, there are seven very usable general-purpose 32-bit registers, and eight very usable general-purpose 8-bit registers within them. Once in a while an instruction will require the use of one or more specific registers, in which case the efficient assembly language programmer may have to reshuffle register assignments to make just the right registers available at the right time.

## Basic Syntax

Here is a snippet of code that loads two long integers from memory, adds them, and deposits them back to a third location.

```
longarray dd ?
;          . . .

        mov     eax,[esi+ebx+8]     ;pick up first value
        mov     ecx,[edx]           ;pick up second value
        add     eax,ecx             ;add them
        mov     longarray,eax       ;store the result
```

This should look very similar to many other assembly languages, which all have opcode (for example, mov) and operand (for example, eax and [esi+ebx+8]) fields. The important twist to remember—and this is different from the way Motorola assemblers work—is that the destination of an operation's result is the *first* operand, not the second. Thus add eax,ecx puts the sum in EAX, not in ECX.

## Flags

There are seven "flag" bits that typically ever matter to a normal application. Of these seven, the direction flag which affects repetitive string operations can be set and cleared with special opcodes, but it is rarely examined directly. Although the 32-bit flags register contains many additional flag bits having to do with systems programming, only the remaining core six, which are important to applications, are shown in Figure 2-2.

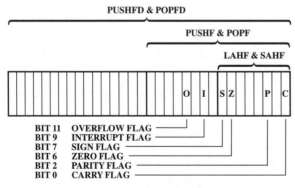

**Figure 2-2    The 32-Bit Flags Register**

A typical arithmetic operation, such as addition, affects five of the flags, as follows:

C (carry)      Viewing the two operands as *unsigned* integers, the Carry flag is set if the sum of the integers is too big to fit within an unsigned integer. For example, 0x90000000 plus 0x80000000 is 0x110000000, a value too big for 32 bits. The low 32 bits are recorded as the result, and the Carry flag is set.

O (overflow)   Viewing the two operands as *signed* integers, the Overflow flag is set if the sum of the integers is too big to fit within a signed integer. For example, 0x70000000 plus 0x60000000 is 0xd0000000, but the largest legal positive 32-bit signed value is 0x7fffffff. The 32-bit result is recorded as is, and the Overflow flag is set.

S (sign)       If the high bit of the resultant value is set, the Sign flag is set.

Z (zero)       If the result is zero, the Zero flag is set.

P (parity)     If the low *byte* of the result has an even number of bits set, the Parity flag is set. Note that even on 16- and 32-bit operations, it is only the low eight bits that affect this flag.

Bitwise logical operators such as `or` and `and` clear Carry and Overflow while setting the others according to the result. Shift operations usually leave Carry holding the last bit shifted out of an operand, Overflow in a sometimes-useful state, and S, Z, and P again set according to the result. Multiplication and division leave very little useful information in the flags.

The only other flag commonly inspected by applications is the I (interrupts enabled) flag. There is no instruction to directly test this flag, so the only way you can read it is by transfering a copy of the flags register to memory or another register and testing bit 9. If it is set, then the code is subject to interruption by interrupt routines, which come marauding through cyberspace anywhere from a few dozen (usually) to many thousands of times per second.

Most applications run with interrupts enabled simply because shutting them off for an extended period of time might mess other things up, like serial communications. Often, the operating system won't let you turn them off. But sometimes you can safely turn them off for short bursts of time without ill effects. In any event, whether or not a given stretch of code has the power to change its interrupt status, at times it is important to be able to read the status to know what's going on.

There are six instructions for reading and writing flags as a group. The bits they affect are shown in Figure 2-2. Not only are the 16-bit instructions `pushf` and popf (for pushing and popping flags) inefficient in a 32-bit environment, they can also cause the stack pointer, which should always be kept pointing to longword boundaries, to become misaligned, with major performance consequences. Pushing and popping should be done with the pushfd and popfd instructions. Once in a long while it's useful to transfer the low eight bits of the flags register to the AH register (the lahf instruction) for later restoration (the sahf instruction). There's a dangerous quirk to these last instructions in that the Overflow flag is not part of the transfer. This is a near-tragic omission, probably perpetuated in silicon from an ancestral flags register.

The most common way flags affect a running program is through the control of branching statements. The standard form of a branching opcode is jCC, where the CC is the particular condition tested, which may involve the states of more than one flag at the same time. The basic ten branches involving just one flag each, in both the set and not-set states, are

```
jc    jo    js    jz    jp
jnc   jno   jns   jnz   jnp
```

In addition to these one-flag opcodes, there are opcodes appropriate for signed and unsigned subtraction or comparison operations. (A comparison sets the same flags as a subtraction.) The *unsigned* comparisons are

| | | |
|---|---|---|
| ja | jump if above | same as jnbe |
| jae | jump if above or equal | same as jnb and jnc |
| jbe | jump if below or equal | same as jna |
| jb | jump if below | same as jnae and jc |

The *signed* comparisons are

| | | |
|---|---|---|
| jg | jump if greater than | same as jnle |
| jge | jump if greater than or equal to | same as jnl |
| jle | jump if less than or equal to | same as jng |
| jl | jump if less than | same as jnge |

Other opcode synonyms are

```
je    for   jz
jne   for   jnz
jpe   for   jp
jpo   for   jnp
```

In review, up to this point, the following code fragment should make sense:

```
                                        ;on entry, esi points
;         ...                           ;to a long integer array
          mov     ecx,100               ;load loop counter for 100
          mov     eax,0                 ;pre-zero accumulator
addlp:    mov     ebx,[esi]             ;load an integer
          add     eax,ebx               ;add it into the accumulator
          add     esi,4                 ;advance the pointer
          dec     ecx                   ;decrement the loop counter
          jnz     addlp                 ;if not zero, jump to addlp
;         ...                           ;exit loop here with sum of
                                        ;100 integers in eax
```

## The Floating-Point Unit

In the early days of the 80x86, heavy-duty floating-point arithmetic was done either by software routines building on the integer math abilities of the processor or by a separate chip, the floating-point coprocessor. When the 486 came out, the floating-point unit was built into the processor (except for a few low-end versions), and it's there in the Pentium and Pentium Pro, too. It migrated into the chip, where it still behaves like a distant cousin, communicating with the main processor through variables in memory instead of through direct register transfers.

The floating-point unit holds a stack of up to eight floating-point values with 80 bits of information each, even more than the 64 bits held in the usual double precision floating-point value. You can tell the floating-point unit to store or load values to or from memory in either long integer, single precision, double precision, or long double precision (80 bits) formats, but it keeps its internal stack in 80-bit floating point all the time.

Most floating-point operations involve operating on the item on the top of the stack and possibly on another, deeper stack entry. There are stack-manipulation instructions available to ensure that the stack can be correctly arranged for whatever operation you want. In addition to the usual addition, subtraction, multiplication, and division, there are many scientific functions available, including trigonometric, logarithmic, and exponential functions.

I got along for a dozen years without ever dealing with the floating-point unit. Until recently (especially since the advent of the Pentium), floating point was anathema to fast code, and there were often ways to skirt the edge of floating point with integer arithmetic games. But now floating-point arithmetic actually runs at speeds comparable to or better than the equivalent integer operations.

The floating-point unit has many complexities and subtleties. There are rounding and precision controls, representations for infinities and nonnumbers, and a special set of exception conditions and flags. Intel's processor documentation is the definitive source for a proper description, although other assembly language texts may describe it in more approachable ways. In this book, there are some learn-as-you-go examples in later chapters.

# The Instruction Set

There are about 210 basic operation codes (opcodes) in 80x86 assembly language, but only about 60 are useful in most optimized application code. And of those 60, only 26 make up the bread-and-butter RISC core of efficient Pentium computing.

In keeping with this chapter's theme of "forgetting," what follows is a categorized review of the opcodes with (hopefully) reassuring explanations for why you don't need to remember the vast majority of them most of the time.

## Floating-Point Instructions (79)

Intel pulled a mnemonic coup by ensuring that all floating-point opcodes—and *only* floating-point opcodes—begin with `f`. Thus `fadd`, `fsub`, `fmul`, and `fdiv` are the rather transparently labeled basic arithmetic operations, while `fld` and `fst` are the load and store operations that transfer values between memory and the floating-point stack. There are 73 other opcodes rounding out the list, but unless you're specifically trying to optimize floating-point math, you're unlikely to run across any of these opcodes. You can build entire operating systems without them.

## Inefficient Old Complex Instructions (13)

As mentioned earlier in the chapter, there are a number of old, inefficient legacy instructions left over from the early complex instruction set design of the 80x86 processor family. You still see them around in old code—which tends to die very hard. Although they do tend to be efficient in terms of space, if you're coding for speed, you're usually better off coming up with combinations of faster instructions that do the same thing. It's not necessary to *not* use them. But as a matter of personal style, I prefer to think I am "future-proofing" my code when I replace CISC instructions with RISC ones, even if they do cost a few extra bytes. (The tendency has been for CISC instructions to grow increasingly inefficient with successive processor generations.) Should you decide to replace them, suggested equivalents are given as follows.

First there's the "string" instruction family:

```
lods    stos    movs    cmps    scas
```

## Replace lods with

```
mov    reg,[esi]           ;reg is al, ax, or eax
lea    esi,[esi+size]      ;size is size of reg
                           ;(lea performs esi=esi+size)
```

## Replace stos with

```
mov    [edi],reg           ;reg is al, ax, or eax
lea    edi,[edi+size]      ;size is size of reg
```

## Replace movs with

```
mov    reg,[esi]           ;reg is a free register
mov    [edi],reg           ;move a value to destination
lea    esi,[esi+size]      ;size is size of reg
lea    edi,[edi+size]      ;size is size of reg
```

## Replace cmps with

```
mov    reg1,[esi]          ;reg1 is a free register
mov    reg2,[edi]          ;reg2 is a free register
lea    esi,[esi+size]      ;size is size of reg1, reg2
lea    edi,[edi+size]      ;size is size of reg1, reg2
cmp    reg1,reg2           ;do the compare
```

## Replace scas with

```
mov    reg1,[edi]          ;reg1 is a free register
lea    edi,[edi+size]      ;size is size of reg1
cmp    reg2,reg1           ;reg2 is al, ax, or eax
```

Then there's the loop family:

```
loop    loopz    loopnz
```

Because these instructions don't affect the flags, there is no truly convenient *exact* replacement for them, but the following replacements almost always work anyhow. Replace loop with

```
dec    ecx                 ;decrement the loop counter
jnz    looptop             ;if not zero, loop back
```

Replace `loopz` with

```
        jnz     done        ;exit if zero flag not set
        dec     ecx         ;decrement the loop counter
        jnz     looptop     ;if not zero, loop back
        inc     ecx         ;these instructions for ecx
done:   dec     ecx         ;adjustment might be skipped
```

Replace `loopnz` with

```
        jz      done        ;exit if zero flag set
        dec     ecx         ;decrement the loop counter
        jnz     looptop     ;if not zero, loop back
        inc     ecx         ;these instructions for ecx
done:   dec     ecx         ;adjustment might be skipped
```

Compilers used to use the following two instructions for entering and leaving a subroutine:

```
enter   leave
```

Many still use `leave`, which is not badly inefficient. Although there is a complex form of the `enter` instruction, you can usually replace the more common simple form of it with this:

```
        push    ebp             ;preserve old stack frame ptr
        mov     ebp,esp         ;set current stack frame ptr
        sub     esp,count       ;make room for local variables
```

The `leave` instruction is even simpler to replace:

```
        mov     esp,ebp         ;pop the local variables
        pop     ebp             ;pop the old stack frame
```

Finally, there are three isolated old complex instructions left:

```
xlat    jecxz   bound
```

If the top three bytes of the EAX register can be kept set to zero, then the old `xlat` (translate) instruction can be replaced with

```
        mov     al,[ebx+eax]    ;use [ebx] for translation
```

The `jecxz` instruction, like the `loop` instructions, is hard to replace exactly because it doesn't change the flags. But you can often get away with a flag-changing replacement anyhow:

```
test    ecx,ecx         ;see if ecx is zero
jz      somewhere       ;if so, branch
```

The array bounds checking instruction, `bound`, is actually still marginally efficient on the 486. On the Pentium and Pentium Pro it can be replaced with slightly faster but much larger code (not shown), if desired.

## Inefficient, Repetitive String Instructions (4)

There are actually more than four inefficient, repetitive string instructions, but there are only four that you generally ever see. They're still worth using from time to time for convenience or for compactness of code, but they can usually be replaced by loops—sometimes nontrivial loops—that run faster (markedly so on the Pentium).

| | |
|---|---|
| `rep stos` | Using ECX as a counter and EDI as a memory pointer, copies the contents of AL, AX, or EAX to successive memory locations, using EDI as the destination pointer. |
| `repe cmps` | Using ECX as an upper-limit counter, compares bytes, words, or longwords in the strings pointed to by ESI and EDI until a difference between the strings is found or ECX counts to zero. |
| `repe scas` | Scans the string pointed to by EDI until it finds a byte, word, or longword not matching AL, AX, or EAX respectively, or until ECX counts to zero. |
| `repne scas` | Scans the string pointed to by EDI until it finds a byte, word, or longword matching AL, AX, or EAX respectively, or until ECX counts to zero. |

The one repetitive string instruction that is often still efficient for speed (though not always) is `rep movs`, which is used for block memory moves.

## Systems Programming Instructions (22)

Some instructions are useful only if you're building an operating system and have to create the smoke-and-mirrors code that makes things so seemingly simple at the application level. Here are the names, without comment, of 22 such arcane instructions most mortals don't use:

```
arpl     clts    invd    invlpg   lar
lgdt     lidt    lldt    lmsw     lsl
ltr      rdmsr   rsm     sgdt     sidt
sldt     smsw    str     verr     verw
wbinvd   wrmsr
```

## Process Synchronization (8)

There are eight instructions that are mainly useful when you're trying to make sure that the processor you're programming doesn't get confused (or cause confusion) with or by another processor that's using the same memory—or even the same processor running a different task or an interrupt routine. If you're worried about other processors (including any form of direct memory access competition) or about coordinating multiple tasks, these are instructions to check out. Otherwise, you can fairly safely skip them.

```
btc   btr   bts   hlt   lock   cmpxchg   cmpxchg8b   xadd
```

## Segment Instructions (6)

The segment registers still lurk. Once in a long while, an application program has to deal with them. But for the most part, you can live without these five segment-loading instructions and the subroutine return instruction that switches to another segment.

```
lds    les    lfs    lgs    lss    retf
```

## Binary-Coded Decimal Instructions (6)

Once upon a time, perhaps before computers got really, really good at binary arithmetic, computer designers decided it would be good for computers to do arithmetic in the decimal system, as if they had ten fingers. So they cooked up a way to store the numbers zero through nine in four-bit units (while losing about 20 percent of the information content of a byte). That way, you could easily read out the decimal digits of a number just by looking at the bits. The legacy of this anthropomorphic twist is still with us, and there are still business applications that require computers to "count with their fingers," so to speak. As a result, there are instructions in many processor families, including the 80x86, that allow the processor to compute in the decimal number system.

I've never personally needed to use them. In case *you* do, here are the binary coded decimal opcodes:

```
aaa   aad   aam   aas   daa   das
```

# More Inefficient Old Instructions (12)

Though they are less used than the previous set of old complex instructions, the opcodes in this section should likewise be avoided in favor of speedier instruction combinations when speed is important. The instructions are

```
bt      bsf     bsr     xchg    cbw     cdq
cwd     cwde    movsx   movzx   pushad  popad
```

The three bit-testing instructions, `bt`, `bsf`, and `bsr`, use so many cycles that it's worth a good think as to whether there's a better way to get the job done (many times there is).

The instruction used to exchange registers, `xchg`, is not particularly efficient, and it can always be beaten for speed by three move (`mov`) instructions, using a spare register to temporarily hold a value.

The four instructions used to enlarge a smaller register into one or more larger registers by way of sign extension are actually still marginally efficient on the 486, and `cdq` and `cwde` appear to be adequately fast on the Pentium Pro. Use them there if you have to. On the Pentium and Pentium Pro, you can, if you like, perform the following replacements, as long as you don't have to preserve flags. Replace `cbw` with

```
cmp     al,80H          ;Carry set if AL positive
sbb     ah,ah           ;AH is -1 if AL positive
not     ah              ;invert the AH bits
```

Replace `cdq` with

```
mov     edx,eax         ;copy low bytes to high
sar     edx,31          ;shift sign down
```

There's no replacement for `cwd`, but it flirts with so many 16-bit registers you probably shouldn't be using it unless you're setting up for a 16-bit divide (which, as mentioned later, can still be a good idea).

Replace cwde with

```
shl     eax,16              ;shift left
sar     eax,16              ;pull it back right
```

Moving a small piece of data to a register that's bigger than the data item usually entails padding the upper part of the register, either with zeroes or with the sign extension of the data. There are two specific instructions to do this, movzx for zero extension and movsx for sign extension. These instructions are speedy on the Pentium Pro, but they run slow on the Pentium.

Replace, for instance

```
movzx   eax,bl              ;move byte BL to longword EAX
```

with

```
xor     eax,eax             ;pre-zero EAX
mov     al,bl               ;move byte BL
```

On the Pentium, if you don't need to preserve flags, you can replace

```
movsx   eax,bl              ;move BL signed to EAX
```

with

```
mov     al,bl               ;move BL
shl     eax,24              ;shift left
sar     eax,24              ;pull down sign bit
```

Finally, pushing and popping all registers with pushad and popad, while never a hallmark of highly optimized code, is now less efficient than the sum of the seven component pushes and pops. (The eighth push/pop of ESP is unnecessary.)

## Slow Mainstream Instructions (21)

This list includes instructions that are sometimes necessary in applications—and for which there generally are not faster alternatives available—but didn't make the cut for RISC-like speedup in the Pentium. When you need them, you need them, but they tend to cost at least a couple of cycles, if not considerably more. These instructions should be left out of tight inner loops, if possible.

The carry flag group:

```
clc   stc   cmc
```

These instructions clear, set, and toggle the carry flag, respectively. Using `cmp eax,eax` to clear the flag is a fast alternative to `clc` when the states of the other flags don't need to be preserved.

The interrupt flag pair:

```
cli   sti
```

These instructions clear and set the interrupt enable flag, respectively. Clearing disables interrupts. The ordinary application state is enabled (`sti`).

The direction flag pair:

```
cld   std
```

The direction flag controls the direction in which all the instructions starting with `rep` operate. After a `cld`, memory moves, scans, and fills advance from their starting positions, given in ESI and/or EDI, toward higher memory positions. After `std`, they descend through memory from their starting positions. The flag is usually kept clear by convention for normal operations and is set only for the less common operations that need it set.

The port I/O group:

```
in   out   ins   outs
```

These instructions input and output data to and from "ports." Ports occupy addresses in a 64K address space separate from the main memory address space. A lot of communication with peripheral cards and devices runs through ports. Applications may or may not have the privileges to issue these instructions, depending on operating system context.

The flag group:

```
pushfd   popfd   lahf   sahf
```

The first two are for pushing and popping the 32-bit flags register. They are remarkably slow on the Pentium (three and four cycles, respectively) and are to be avoided. An alternative is to use the last two instructions to transfer most of the important flags to the AH register and back, as mentioned previously. The latter strategy is subject to the restriction that the overflow flag is not preserved by `lahf` and `sahf`.

The interrupt entry and exit group:

```
int   into   iretd
```

The `int` instruction generates one of 256 possible software interrupts, much like a subroutine call, to what is usually part of the operating system. Under DOS, `int` `21H` was the standard way to communicate with DOS. The `into` instruction is just a special case interrupt that only executes if the overflow flag is set. It's mainly of use to compilers. And `iretd` returns from either software- or hardware-generated interrupts. Unless you're writing an interrupt routine or a compiler, the `int` instruction is the only one you're likely to encounter.

Two recently added instructions:

```
bswap   cpuid
```

The only exciting new instruction that came out with the advent of the 486 was `bswap`, which can reverse the order of bytes in a four-byte longword. This is particularly important when converting between longword integer values stored in "Intel format" (low byte first) and "Motorola format" (high byte first). Motorola format is used by many non-IBM-compatible computers, especially the Macintosh. Don't use `bswap` if you want backward compatibility with the 386.

The `cpuid` instruction is new with the Pentium. It identifies the processor, but the catch is that you have to first make sure that the processor is not a 486 or other predecessor form before executing the instruction. In any event, it's a non-time-critical instruction.

## Relatively Fast Mainstream Instructions (11)

There are 11 instructions that, though not single-cycle and pairable on the Pentium, are efficient workhorses in common application code.

The multiplication and division group:

```
mul    imul    div    idiv
```

These are the opcodes for signed and unsigned integer multiplication and division. The signed operands start with `i`. The `imul` instruction has forms that operate on any register, but the rest of the instructions expect that one operand and the result reside in EAX, or EAX *and* EDX, or some subregisters within these two. The 16-bit forms of the division instructions, when appropriate, represent one of the very few places in the instruction set where a 16-bit form handsomely beats the equivalent 32-bit form for speed. You can get values as large as 64 bits out of 32-bit multiplication, and you can likewise divide up to a 64-bit value. Division operations always leave a result and a remainder, useful for modulo arithmetic (the C operator `%`).

The two-register shifts:

`shld    shrd`

These instructions stand for "shift left double" and "shift right double." An ordinary register shift shifts in zeroes or sometimes ones. These double shifts shift in multiple bits from another register. Even though, at four cycles on the Pentium, these instructions seem a bit slow, they're still very useful when shifting through a bit stream such as you often encounter with compressed data. For example, `shld eax,ebx,9` shifts EAX left nine bits and fills its low nine bits with copies of the high nine bits of EBX.

Negativity:

`neg    not`

Just one gene away from being a part of the pairable RISC core of the Pentium, these fast operators, respectively, negate and perform bitwise inversion (the bitwise `not` operation) on their operand. In some cases, a `not eax`, for instance, can be accomplished faster with `xor eax,-1`. The `not` operator is unusual in that it doesn't affect the flags.

Subroutine return:

`retn`

The opcode `retn` stands for "return near," meaning return without changing the code segment register. Since a return is essentially an indirect jump with a stack increment thrown in on the side, it operates at the same speed as an indirect jump on the Pentium—two cycles.

Flag to register operation:

`setCC`

Like `jCC`, the generic form of the conditional jump instruction, `setCC` has many different forms, such as `setc` and `setnz`, for various condition codes. The instruction `setc dl` sets the DL register to 1 if Carry is set; otherwise it sets it to 0. It operates only on byte registers and memory locations. And even though it runs slower than the one cycle Intel documentation claims on the Pentium (it runs in two cycles), it's still a great little instruction that often beats the delays of branching logic necessary to do an equivalent flag-to-register transfer.

Block memory move:

```
rep movs
```

This is the last highly efficient old complex instruction. Copying memory is so fundamentally important that this instruction has been kept very fast, even through the RISC evolution to the Pentium instruction set. If you point at the block of memory you want to copy with ESI, point at the destination with EDI, and put a count of the number of longwords to copy in ECX (since copying by bytes or words is much less efficient), you can transfer up to about one longword per cycle. It burns quite a few cycles getting started, though, so there are better ways to copy just a handful of bytes. For very large block transfers, there are some faster options detailed in Chapter 10.

## Very Fast Mainstream Instructions (26)

They're fast in the 486, and in the Pentium they can execute in pairs in a single cycle (subject to certain pairing rules) when they operate on registers, giving an effective execution time of half a cycle each. They are similarly efficient on the Pentium Pro. They're the bread-and-butter operations of fast computing. In alphabetical order, with explanations, they are

adc    Add with Carry.

add    Add.

and    Bitwise and operation, like & in C.

call   Call a subroutine.

cmp    Compare; same as subtraction but only the flags get changed.

dec    Subtract 1 from something; no effect on the Carry flag.

inc    Add 1 to something; no effect on the Carry flag.

jCC    Conditional branch, as in jz outahere; CC is any condition code.

jmp    Unconditional jump or branch.

lea    Load Effective Address; if ESI contains 12345, then the instruction lea edi,[esi+11] puts 12356 in EDI.

mov    Move data from one place to another; a very common instruction.

nop    No Operation; do nothing. This instruction can actually be used to make some code run faster on the Pentium!

or      Bitwise or operation, like | in C.

pop     Pop something off the stack.

push    Push something onto the stack.

rcl     Rotate bits left through the Carry flag, as if the Carry flag were part of the register during the shift.

rcr     Rotate bits right through the Carry flag, as if the Carry flag were part of the register during the shift.

rol     Rotate bits left.

ror     Rotate bits right.

sar     Shift bits right arithmetically (with sign bit).

sbb     Subtract with borrow (Carry flag).

shl     Shift bits left.

shr     Shift bits right.

sub     Subtract.

test    Test; same as and except only the flags get changed.

xor     Exclusive Or; like ^ in C.

# Cycle-Counting Conventions

Counting cycles on assembly language code is an excellent way to predict performance. Throughout the rest of this book, I adopt the convention of annotating the number of cycles associated with a particular line of code, between semicolons at the beginning of its comment field, and putting summary information on lines with four semicolons in a row. Here is a loop as it would look, annotated for the 486:

```
lptop:  mov     eax,[esi+ecx] ; 2;get stream 1 bytes
        mov     ebx,[ebx+ecx] ; 2;get stream 2 bytes
        xor     eax,ebx       ; 1;xor them together
        mov     [edi+ecx],eax ; 2;save as stream 3
        add     ecx,4         ; 1;advance index
        jnz     lptop         ; 3;and loop
                              ;;;;11 cycles per loop
```

In this case, the best-case estimate of performance comes out to 11 cycles per loop. It would not be unusual, though, to find actual measured performance to be somewhat slower, especially if memory data sources are not in primary cache memory.

Here is the same loop, cycle-counted for the Pentium:

```
lptop:  mov     eax,[esi+ecx] ; 1;get stream 1 bytes
        mov     ebx,[ebx+ecx] ; 0;get stream 2 bytes
        xor     eax,ebx       ; 1;xor them together
        mov     [edi+ecx],eax ; 1;save as stream 3
        add     ecx,4         ; 0;advance index
        jnz     lptop         ; 1;and loop
                              ;;;;4 cycles per loop
                              ; 3;loop exit delay
```

In this case, some instructions are noted as costing zero cycles, because they execute in the same cycle as the preceding instruction. Especially on small, short loops, I often annotate the cycle cost of breaking out of the loop, which can be significant. (Usually it's four cycles to break out on the Pentium, but the unpaired final branch instruction in this example, as explained in Chapter 5, costs only three. The equivalent "cost" on the 486 is negative two cycles!)

Processor stall condition cycles, when predictable, get included with the cycle count of the instruction experiencing the stall. If a branch is expected to usually be taken, I generally annotate the branch-taken time. If a branch is expected to usually not be taken, then I annotate that way. If a branch is considered unpredictable, then I usually annotate the average performance figure expected. In reading through some of the code, it is not a simple matter of summing up the cycle count column to predict performance; rather, it's one of tracing through the expected path of execution to predict what will happen.

Loops of arbitrary complexity often have hidden sources of cycle loss, due to complexities of processor operation that are difficult to know or predict. But as a good rule of thumb, a properly cycle-counted loop operating on primary cache memory usually performs within 15 percent of prediction. Cycle counting is a very powerful predictive tool.

# Conclusion

Assembly language programming has benefited enormously from the transition to 32 bits. The old complexities of segment registers have largely been swept under the systems programming rug. And new addressing modes allow greater flexibility in the use of registers. The processor now handles two natural data sizes, the byte and the longword (four bytes).

Along the road from the original 8088 processor to the Pentium and the Pentium Pro, the instruction set has split into a RISC core and sets of infrequently used and legacy instructions that run more slowly. Many instructions are obsolete. Efficient coding now depends on using the fast core instructions to get things done.

# 3

# Structured Assembly Language

*Congress shall make no law . . . abridging . . .*
*the right of the people peaceably to assemble.*
—The First Amendment to the Constitution

Sometime around 1990, a very important innovation in 80x86 assembly language programming arrived on the scene. In fact, its arrival was so quiet that many experienced assembly language programmers know very little about it to this day. The innovation was the release of the MASM 6 assembler by Microsoft, with full-featured support for structured programming, much in the style of C. Its new features greatly enhanced the speed and accuracy of my own assembly language coding. In fact, I doubt that I would have attempted to write this book without it.

All the assembly language code accompanying this book was written using the C-style control structures of MASM 6 (where appropriate, of course). Although the control structures are considered "higher-level" tools, they can usually be used without the performance penalty often associated with higher level tools. Conversely, they make for wonderfully lucid code that can be read almost as easily as good C.

Although "inline" assemblers built into C compilers are very popular these days, they lack the generality of a good independently assembled module, which can be linked into just about anything. Hence the choice of stand-alone MASM 6 for this book. (Actually, I just enjoy structured assembly language so much that I would have put forth almost any excuse to use it!) This chapter is written to bring those who are at least knowledgeable about assembly language up to speed on structured assembly with MASM 6 and the particular form of mixed C and assembly language files on the accompanying CD-ROM.

MASM runs under DOS, Windows 95, and Windows NT, and as of this writing is on generation 6.11. Although the title and later parts of this chapter pertain particularly to the runtime structured controls of MASM 6, much of the rest of this chapter pertains to other assemblers as well.

# Conventional Assembly Language

Listing 3-1 shows a standard short 32-bit assembly language listing appropriate for use with the MASM assembler or a "work-alike." It contains a simple function that adds an input value to a stored sum and returns the new sum. It contains the following components:

| | |
|---|---|
| 1. `.486` | Enables all valid 486 instructions to be used. |
| 2. `.model flat` | Signals 32-bit flat model conventions (4GB address space). |
| 3. `_IL_DATA segment` | First declaration serves as data area prototype. |
| 4. `_IL_TEXT segment` | First declaration serves as code area prototype. |
| 5. `_IL_DATA segment` | Second (and later) declaration(s) hold actual data. |
| 6. `align 4` | A data alignment statement; power-of-2 alignments up to 256 are allowable in page-aligned segments. |
| 7. `val    dd    0` | An initialized longword (4-byte) variable. |
| 8. `_IL_TEXT segment` | Second (and later) declaration(s) hold functions, code. |
| 9. `AddToVal...` | Declaration of a C-callable function, publicly linkable, using near 32-bit calling and return conventions and taking one longword parameter called `addval`. |
| 10. body of function | Five lines of code, ending with a returned value in `eax`. |
| 11. `end` | Ends the source file. |

**Listing 3-1   A Short Assembly Language Program**

```
.486
.model flat
```

```
_IL_DATA segment page use32 public 'DATA'
_IL_DATA ends
_IL_TEXT segment page use32 public 'CODE'
_IL_TEXT ends

_IL_DATA segment
        align   4               ;find a longword boundary
val     dd      0               ;longword for summing
_IL_DATA ends

_IL_TEXT segment

AddToVal proc near C public, addval:dword
        mov     eax,val         ;fetch val to be added to
        mov     ecx,addval      ;and amount to add
        add     eax,ecx         ;do the addition
        mov     val,eax         ;store the result
        ret                     ;and return the value
AddToVal endp

_IL_TEXT ends
        end
```

## Listing 3-2    A Short C Program (Watcom)

```
#include <stdio.h>

#pragma aux MS_C "_*"                                   \
        parm caller []                                 \
        value struct float struct routine [eax] \
        modify [eax ecx edx es];


#pragma aux (MS_C) AddToVal;
long            AddToVal(long addval);

main(int argc, char **argv)
{
    int n, ret;

    for (n = 0; n < 5; n++)
        ret = AddToVal(n);
    printf("The sum of 0..4 is %d.\n", ret);
}
```

Listing 3-2 shows a short C program that can be linked with the assembly language routine shown in Listing 3-1. Note that the `pragma` statements are compiler-specific directives that are not necessarily portable between compilers. In this particular case, the Watcom C compiler requires the pragmas to be able to correctly pass information between C and assembly code. Other compilers might do so correctly by default.

Taken together, Listings 3-1 and 3-2 make up a complete working program. So far, so good.

# C and Assembly Language Interleaved

For those who like the convenience of embedding inline assembly language functions in their C source code, there *is* a way to use separately assembled assembly code while doing the same kind of thing. In fact, I've mixed C and assembly code in all the source files accompanying this book, giving them the file suffix `csm` to signify a mix of C and assembly. It's a great way to put related or equivalent C and assembly language versions of routines together in the same file. It is no doubt anathema by many coding standards, but it's quite convenient for many projects.

The key to mixing C and assembly language is the meaning of the semicolon character in the respective languages. Assembly language sees it as the start of a comment, while C sees it as an empty statement. A semicolon followed by `/*` looks like the start of a comment to C as well. The trick is to use this doubly commented start to embed each language's statements in the other's comment fields. (Assembly language has a `comment` operator that works much like `/*...*/` in C. It uses an arbitrary but presumably rare printable character to delimit a comment field.) Listing 3-3, inspired by the two previous separate listings, shows the typical form of the interleaved files accompanying this book.

### Listing 3-3   Combined C and Assembly Language Program

```
;/*`............ assembly language .....................
;
; Standard assembly language setup
;
        .486
        .model flat

_IL_DATA segment page use32 public 'DATA'
_IL_DATA ends
_IL_TEXT segment page use32 public 'CODE'
_IL_TEXT ends
```

```
   comment `.......... C language .......................*/
//
// Standard C language setup
//
#include <stdio.h>

#pragma aux MS_C "_*"                               \
        parm caller []                             \
        value struct float struct routine [eax]    \
        modify [eax ecx edx es];

;/*`............. assembly language ......................
;
; Assembly language function body
;
_IL_DATA segment

        align   4               ;find a longword boundary
val     dd      0               ;longword for summing

_IL_DATA ends

_IL_TEXT segment

AddToVal_A proc near C public, addval:dword
        mov     eax,val         ;fetch val to be added to
        mov     ecx,addval      ;and amount to add
        add     eax,ecx         ;do the addition
        mov     val,eax         ;store the result
        ret                     ;and return the value
AddToVal_A endp

_IL_TEXT ends

   comment `.......... C language .......................*/
//
// Assembly language function declaration for C use
//
#pragma aux (MS_C) AddToVal_A;
long            AddToVal_A(long addval);

;/*`............. assembly language ......................
   comment `.......... C language .......................*/
//
// C language version of same function
//
long
```

```
AddToVal_C(long addval)
{
    static long val = 0;

    return val += addval;
}

;/*`............. assembly language ......................
;
; End of assembly language portion of file
;
        end
 comment `......... C language .......................*/


long (*AddToVal)(long addval);      // function pointer

void
main(int argc, char **argv)
{
    int n, ret, addval = 5;

    if (argc < 3) {
        printf("usage: test num language\n"
                "where: num is a positive integer, and\n"
                "       language is C for C, or A for"
                  " assembly\n");
        return;
    }
    sscanf(argv[1], "%d", &addval);
    AddToVal = ((*argv[2] & ~0x20) == 'C') ?
                                    AddToVal_C : AddToVal_A;
    for (n = 0; n <= addval; n++)
        ret = AddToVal(n);
    printf("The sum of 0..%d is %d. (%s)\n", addval, ret,
            (AddToVal == AddToVal_C ? "C" : "assembly"));
}
```

This program, like most of the CSM files on the CD-ROM, illustrates the use of an interleaved file to put C and assembly language versions of routines side by side for easy comparison and alternative use. It is my convention to append _A to the names of assembly routines also implemented in C, and _C to their C counterparts implemented in assembly language. A function pointer with the same name, but without either suffix, can then easily be used to select between the two. Thus the main body of the program in Listing 3-3 selects between the two forms of the routine `AddToVal( )` as a function of user input, providing a good way to check that both are working properly.

# Calling and Returning

In my brief exposition of the simple assembly language routine shown in Listing 3-1, I glossed over the complexities of calling and returning from an assembly language function. MASM makes ample provision for setting up assembly language calls to take parameters and to set up local variables just like a C routine. For instance, consider this fragment:

```
routine proc near C public uses esi edi ebx, arg1:dword,
                                    arg2:dword, arg3:byte
        local   loc1:dword, loc2:dword
        local   loc3:byte
        .
        .
        .
        ret
routine endp
```

This is roughly equivalent to the following C routine:

```
routine(long arg1, long arg2, char arg3)
{
    long loc1, loc2;
    char loc3;
    .
    .
    .
    return;
}
```

And the code generated in either case would be either exactly, or equivalently, the following:

```
routine:push   ebp         ;save old stack frame pointer
        mov    ebp,esp      ;set up new stack frame ptr
        add    esp,-12      ;make room for 3 local vars
        push   esi          ;save specified registers
        push   edi          ;
```

```
        push    ebx             ;
        .
        .
        .
        pop     ebx             ;restore specified registers
        pop     edi             ;
        pop     esi             ;
        mov     esp,ebp         ;prepare to pop stack frame
        pop     ebp             ;pop old stack frame
        retn                    ;and return near
```

The last six instructions are all subsumed by the single `ret` statement in the original assembly language listing. In the context of a procedure such as this one, `ret` means "pop all saved registers, restore the old EBP register, and do a near return." All passed parameters are, by convention, referenced through the EBP register, known as the stack frame pointer. Thus, `arg1` is generally at `[EBP+8]`, `arg2` at `[EBP+12]`, `arg3` at `[EBP+16]`, and so forth, since by 32-bit convention, all parameters are stacked in units of four bytes or multiples thereof. Likewise, the local variables `loc1`, `loc2`, and `loc3` are at `[EBP-4]`, `[EBP-8]`, and `[EBP-12]`.

You don't have to use the built-in C/parameter/locals/entry/exit facilities. You actually can create slightly more efficient calling mechanisms for some routines, at the price of a significant amount of extra coding. But on the whole, I prefer the convenience of easy routine setup to the tedium of the alternative and would advise others to follow the same course. The speed penalty is usually insignificant if the body of the assembly language function is anything but trivially short.

## Register Modification Conventions

In the old days of 16-bit compilers and assembly modules, it was conventional for C to pass all its arguments (function call parameters) on the stack. The routine being called generally had to preserve the SI, DI, and BP registers. The rules changed slightly with the move to 32 bits. Now, the ESI, EDI, EBX, and EBP registers are preserved by convention. There are also competing calling conventions, which pass some of the arguments in registers and others on the stack; these expect different register preservation rules to be observed. For the purpose of the demonstration code in this book and on the CD-ROM, though, the rather universally accepted C-style stack argument passing rules and ESI/EDI/EBX/EBP preservation rules are observed. Parts of this convention are hardwired into MASM, and it's usually not worth bucking it for a handful of cycles and a loss of generality.

Note that if an assembly routine does not actually use a certain register that needs to be preserved, it need not be declared in the `uses` list and will not be pushed and popped on entry and exit.

Because the `rep movs` instruction is still very useful and common (not to mention some of the less speed-efficient `rep` instructions), and because it, incidentally, uses the ES segment register to locate its destination, there is a fly in the 32-bit flat-model ointment. In flat model, ES *should* be functionally the same as DS. In fact, though, it's dangerous to trust ES, especially if you're linking libraries with unknown conventions or quality control into your code. The safest thing to do when you need to guarantee the contents of ES is to push it on entry to the routine, load it with a copy of DS (via `push ds, pop es`), do the "reping," and restore it on exit. Less conservatively, you can omit save and restore if you're confident the calling routine had no expectation that ES would be preserved.

One final convention, also associated with the `rep` instructions, has to do with the setting of the direction flag. The direction flag controls whether the `rep` instructions march toward higher addresses or lower addresses from their starting point. After `cld`, `rep` increments. After `std`, `rep` decrements. Most of the time, programmers expect and want the `cld` state. Depending on whose version of the direction flag convention you listen to, it should either be preserved or, if modified, returned in the `cld` state by called routines. If a routine modifies the direction flag, then true preservation requires that the initial flag state be pushed and then popped on exit. As per the ES problem, this is the conservative solution. I generally prefer to simply always return the direction flag in the `cld` state if I've done anything to it in a routine. And I usually don't trust that it's in the `cld` state to begin with. In the environments in which I have programmed, this less conservative approach has worked fine, but other environments may require the more conservative approach.

# Data Structures

In C, it is customary to declare structures like this:

```
struct MyStruct {
    long wid;
    long bits;
};
```

A functionally equivalent structure can be declared in assembly language like this:

```
MyStruct        struct
wid             dd      ?
bits            dd      ?
MyStruct        ends
```

If, for instance, the ESI register points to such a structure, then an element of the structure can be accessed as in this example:

```
mov     eax,[esi].MyStruct.bits     ;pick up the bits field
```

There is no performance penalty for addressing a piece of data this way.

# Structured Assembly Language

One of the great assets of a language like C is its ability to make statements like these:

```
if (condition) {code_to_execute}
```

or    `while (condition) {code_to_execute}`

or    `do {code_to_execute} while (condition);`

MASM 6 (and, presumably, subsequent generations of MASM) gives the assembly language programmer similar constructs, which can greatly reduce dependence on code labels while increasing readability.

## The if Statement

Here is a simple if statement in C:

```
if (var1 < 7) var2++;
```

It would typically be written in ordinary assembly language as

```
        cmp     var1,7          ;compare variable to 7
        jnb     noinc           ;branch if not below
        inc     var2            ;increment the variable
noinc:                          ;label
```

But with structured assembly language, you can generate exactly the same code with

```
.if var1 < 7          ;compare and branch
   inc    var2        ;increment the variable
.endif                ;implicit end label
```

## The while **Statement**

Here is a simple while statement in C:

```
while (var & 0x80000000) var <<= 1;
```

In ordinary assembly language, it could be implemented as

```
        jmp    lptest        ;jump to bottom test
lptop:  shl    var,1         ;do the shift
lptest: test   var,80000000H ;test if done
        jb     lptop         ;branch if still going
```

But with structured assembly language, the same code is generated by

```
.while var & 80000000H
   shl   var,1
.endw
```

## The do . . . while **Statement**

Here is a simple do . . . while statement in C:

```
do {var >> 1;} while (!(var & 1));
```

Again, in common assembly language it would become

```
lptop:  shr    var,1         ;do the shift
        test   var,1         ;test if done
        jb     lptop         ;branch if still going
```

And with structured assembly language, the same code is

```
.repeat                   ;implicit loop top label
   shr    var,1           ;do the shift
.until var & 1            ;test and branch
```

## Life Without Labels

Labels are among the weakest features of assembly language. Generally speaking, a label in an assembly language listing is an open invitation to receive branches, jumps, and calls from far and wide. Just in looking at an assembly language listing full of labels, it is extremely difficult to know what points in the code may happen to reference a given label. In other words, conventional assembly language has a built-in tendency to look and sometimes behave like dreaded "spaghetti code."

It turns out, though, that most labels, even in heavily optimized code, are referenced only in the if/while/do-while patterns (plus a few straightforward variants), which can be accommodated by structured assembly language. In other words, most labels in even very efficient assembly language code can be omitted this way. My own label usage has gone down 80 to 90 percent, and the few labels that are left act as red flags indicating exceptions to C-style flow of control.

By indenting loops and conditionally executed code inside their control statements, it is possible to get the look and feel of good, readable C in the lion's share of good, efficient assembly language code. Structured assembly language has saved me an enormous amount of time and effort; that's why I chose to use it to write the code examples for this book. I strongly recommend it to anyone.

## Expression Evaluation

MASM's structured assembly language is capable of evaluating just about any expression that can be calculated just by looking at the flags and performing nondestructive tests on registers and memory. Nondestructive tests generally mean the `cmp` and `test` operations performed with immediates, registers, and memory locations. Consider the following conditional expression:

```
.if (!CARRY? && (eax <= ebx)) || (ecx & 7)
    .
    .
    .
.endif
```

This becomes

```
        jc      expr2       ;if Carry, check (ecx & 7)
        cmp     eax,ebx     ;compare registers
        jbe     body        ;branch and do it, maybe
expr2:  test    ecx,7       ;else check the 2nd condition
        je      skip        ;if it fails, skip
```

```
body:    .                              ;the conditional body
         .                              ;of code goes here
         .                              ;
skip:                                   ;.endif
```

The test, compare, and branch operations are among the fastest on the 486, Pentium, and Pentium Pro. With just a little practice, it is easy to predict exactly what code MASM will generate for a given expression, although feeding very complex expressions to the assembler leaves one feeling a little bit like one is surrendering to a compiler. Usually, simple and readily predictable expressions are all that's required. If, for efficiency's sake, you don't like the MASM-generated sequence, you are free to replace it with your own (using labels).

The C-style operators that can be used in expressions are

```
>    >=    <    <=    ==    !=    !    &&    ||    &
```

The flag status bit names, for use in expressions, are

```
CARRY?    ZERO?    SIGN?    PARITY?    OVERFLOW?
```

By default, comparison operations are unsigned. There is a cryptic way to force signed comparisons, for which one should consult the MASM manual. Some of the expressions you can write with these operators can't be evaluated in a nondestructive way (and therefore can't be evaluated at all by MASM), but the most common simple expressions evaluate just fine.

## Efficiency

There is a false supposition among many programmers that using structured assembly language will somehow severely degrade performance, so that they might as well be programming in C. There are several counterarguments to this notion.

First, as demonstrated in the previous section, it's not hard to know and evaluate what code you're going to get from a given statement. At the very least, you have the option to not use a structure if it actually does hurt performance. And if *it does* perform well, there is no apparent reason not to simplify the code, save a label or two, and use it.

Second, the most common assembly language loop takes the "repeat-until" form. In ordinary assembly language, that amounts to a label at the top and a conditional branch at the bottom, as in the following loop:

```
lptop:    .                              ;top of loop
          .                              ;body of loop
          .                              ;
```

```
        dec     ecx                     ;decrement a loop counter
        jnz     lptop                   ;branch to top
```

There is absolutely no difference between that loop and this:

```
        .repeat                         ;implicit loop top label
          .                             ;body of loop
          .                             ;
          .                             ;
         dec    ecx                     ;decrement a loop counter
        .until ZERO?                    ;branch to top
```

The latter code is easier to write and maintain, however.

Third, another argument used against structured assembly is that on the 486, especially, structured `if` statements that usually encounter the failure condition at runtime are better implemented by branching outside the control structure when true. In other words, consider the following piece of code:

```
        mov ecx,100
        .repeat
          .if ecx < 5
            inc eax
          .endif
          dec   ecx
        .until ZERO?
```

Since a branch taken is much slower than a branch not taken on the 486, and since the `if` condition usually branches over the `if` body in this loop, it could actually be more efficient on the 486 to write the following:

```
        mov     ecx,100
        .repeat
          cmp     ecx,5
          jb      doinc
incret:   dec     ecx
        .until ZERO?
          .
          .
          .


doinc:  inc     eax
        jmp     incret
```

It is true that on a 486 the latter is more efficient. On a Pentium, due to branch prediction logic, there is little or no difference. On a Pentium Pro, there might be a small delay associated with a branch taken, depending on the local instruction mix, but not nearly as severe a delay as the 486 penalty. So for the limited case of worrying about false `if`s inside critical loops optimized for 486 performance, and sometimes the Pentium Pro, there is a valid case for not using the `if` structure at times. In nearly all other cases, the structured assembly code works fine.

A fourth point to be made is that only a small part of the performance gain of assembly language over C can be traced to tight control stuctures. So even if there is a small performance loss involved in using structured assembly (which is not often the case), the big performance gains are usually elsewhere in the code, anyhow.

## Details

I've glossed over a few details. First, the `if` statement can have corresponding `else` and `elseif` statements associated with it. For instance, the following is legal code:

```
.if     eax == 1
  inc   ecx
.elseif eax == 2
  inc   edx
.elseif eax == 3
  inc   esi
.else
  inc   edi
.endif
```

It generates the code you would expect:

```
        cmp     eax,1
        jne     try2
        inc     ecx
        jmp     done
try2:   cmp     eax,2
        jne     try3
        inc     edx
        jmp     done
try3:   cmp     eax,3
        jne     doelse
        inc     esi
        jmp     done
doelse: inc     edi
done:
```

Another glossed-over detail is the `break` instruction used for breaking out of loops. It translates to a simple `jmp` instruction, which exits from a loop. For instance:

```
.repeat
  inc   esi
  .if esi > ebx
    mov esi,ebx
    .break
  .endif
  dec   ecx
.until ZERO?
```

translates to

```
lptop:  inc     esi
        cmp     esi,ebx
        jbe     esiok
        mov     esi,ebx
        jmp     done            ;.break
esiok:  dec     ecx
        jnz     lptop
done:
```

You can also do a `break if`, as in the following:

```
.repeat
  inc   esi
  .break .if esi > ebx
  dec   ecx
.until ZERO?
```

which translates to

```
lptop:  inc     esi
        cmp     esi,ebx         ;.if evaluation
        ja      done            ;.break out if above
        dec     ecx
        jnz     lptop
done:
```

There is also a `continue` and a `continue if` instruction, analogous with the C language `continue` command, which skips directly to the next loop condition evaluation instead of skipping out of the loop entirely. (I've rarely had a use for it, but `break` is pretty handy.)

# Debugging

Speaking from personal experience, a final benefit of structured assembly language is that it makes a good debugging tool for conventional assembly language. I've frequently found that the best way to debug conventional assembly language code is to revise it as structured assembly language code. Where the flow of control is fairly normal, labels disappear and structured controls appear. Where the flow of control doesn't fit into the structured controls, the labels remain. Very often, bugs in conventional assembly language programs are associated with branches to a wrong label or unusual entries to or exits from simple control structures. By revising code in structured assembly language and isolating the unusual branching exceptions, it is often possible to home in on otherwise difficult-to-find bugs. It's often as simple as asking, "Why does this label exist?"

# Conclusion

Structured assembly language programming for the 80x86 offers easier authoring, reading, and maintenance compared to regular assembly language code. It usually involves little or no performance penalty on Pentium processors. In any event, the option to use it or not use it at any particular point in one's code is entirely at the programmer's discretion. It brings many of the benefits of C to the assembly language level, without the drawbacks usually associated with compiled code.

# 4

# Optimizing
# the 486

*For now hath time made me his numbering clock;*
*My thoughts are minutes.*
*—Richard II, Shakespeare*

Like Richard II's numbering clock, the 486 is the simplest 80x86 processor for numbering clock cycles. And each "thought," or instruction, is often as little as one cycle—about 10 to 30 nanoseconds. It's the first noticeably RISC-like 80x86 processor.

In this chapter, we'll take a systematic look at what makes the 486 tick:

- The instruction set
- The cache
- The output FIFO (queue)
- Data and code alignment
- Cycle thieves and cycle savers

There are similarities and differences between code that is optimal for the 486 and code that is optimal for the Pentium and Pentium Pro. Even if you end up writing primarily for, say, the Pentium, it's often possible to massage your optimal code to be kind to the 486 at the same time. But, such necessity aside, understanding the 486 is also just a very good starting place for understanding the Pentium and Pentium Pro.

# The CH486.EXE Instruction Timing Program

Included on the CD-ROM accompanying this book is a program, CH486.EXE, that can be used on a 486 machine to time nearly all the instructions in the instruction set (except some system-level instructions and some floating-point instructions). It runs only under true DOS, not in a DOS "box" or window under Windows. You can select from a small menu of test runs (including tests of the main instruction set, alignment conditions, cache effects, and the floating-point unit) that dump test results to the screen. To save test results to a file, use indirection (`>filename`) on the command line when you run it.

All of the tests take a form like this:

```
>       mov     ebp,esp
        push    edx
<       mov     esp,ebp
```

In the above case, the test program would execute all three instructions 10,000 times, note the time, and then execute the first and last instructions (without the middle one) 10,000 times, again noting the time. It would then report the measured cycle time of the instruction (to the nearest hundredth of a cycle), based on the difference between the two runs. You can have multiple instructions in any or all of the three parts of the code test (pretest, test, and posttest).

The exhaustive instruction report takes 10 or 15 minutes to generate in full, but the others each take less than a minute. The result is just about as visually appealing as a page of stock quotes, but if that's what you're interested in, it can be fascinating.

Because I choose to do the timing without disabling interrupts or modifying the timer chip settings, once in a while a bad timing may show up as a result of a long interrupt hit. If you see what looks like a bogus number, especially one that is not approximately an integer value, try another run to check it. Most timings, if they are correct, have values within 0.1 of an integer. Some do not.

The results I got on my vintage 1992 33MHz 486 VEISA ALR machine are included for reference. Source code and a batch file to remake the program are also included. This is set up to expect Watcom C and may need slight modification for other compilers.

# The Instruction Set

The most striking thing about the instruction set is that the most common register-to-register operations are only one cycle, and so are memory fetches (from cache) and stores. So beware of multicycle instructions that run more slowly than equivalent sets of small instructions.

Table 4-1 shows a breakdown of the instruction set, from fastest instructions to slowest (excepting floating point). These are based on my own timings, which vary in some instances from Intel's published timing values. The instructions in boldface are the ones that I subjectively judge to be common candidates for application code inner loops. In other words, they're the ones I think of as frequently having a time-critical aspect. (This is to say, I can think of at least once when I put each of them in a tight loop.) The table is very abbreviated and does not explicitly list all the variations of all the instructions, but you can figure them out using these rules:

- Unless otherwise noted, instructions are referred to by their simplest form. That is, add refers to register-to-register forms of the add instruction, such as add edx,esi. If an instruction or group of instructions spaced closely together is followed by a note in parentheses, that note pertains to the preceding instruction or group.

- Add one cycle for an extra memory fetch. For instance, add ecx,memvar would take the basic one cycle, plus one cycle for the memory fetch, for a total of two cycles.

- Add one cycle for an extra memory store. For instance, inc memvar would take the basic one cycle, plus one cycle to fetch the original value from memory, plus one cycle to write it back to memory, for a total of three cycles.

- Add one cycle for performing a 16-bit operation, except in the case of segment register transfers. Thus, adc ax,bx takes a basic one cycle, plus another one cycle for being 16-bit, for a total of two cycles.

- Add one cycle if the instruction includes both an immediate value and a memory address offset. For instance, whereas add [esi+4],edx is a three-cycle instruction, as previously explained, add dword ptr [esi+4],100 takes four cycles. Likewise, add memvar,24 also takes four cycles (a directly addressed memory variable counts as an offset). But if there is no offset, as in add dword ptr [esi],123, there is no penalty. Note that immediate shift counts, such as that in shl memvar,3, count as immediate values for the purpose of this penalty.

- Add one cycle if the instruction uses either a two-register addressing mode (as in, for instance, `add ebx,[ebp + esi]`) or a multiplied register in the address (as in, for instance, `add ebx,memarray[ebx * 4]`). Only add one cycle even if both conditions are met.

- Where instructions don't obey the preceding rules (for instance, some of the shift operations do not), the various forms are explicitly listed in the table.

As an exercise in *inefficient* instruction coding, lets see how slow an instruction with a base cycle count of one can get:

| | | |
|---|---|---|
| 1 cycle: | add | `eax,ebx` |
| 2 cycles: | add | `eax,memvar32` |
| 3 cycles: | add | `memvar32,eax` |
| 4 cycles: | add | `memvar16,ax` |
| 5 cycles: | add | `memvar16,12345` |
| 6 cycles: | add | `memvar16[esi + ebx * 2],12345` |

And so it is that the fastest code tends to run in registers, reference memory sparingly, eschew 16-bit values, and avoid complex addressing modes.

| Table 4-1 | 486 Instruction Timings Sorted by Speed |
|---|---|
| 1 cycle | **add adc sub sbb and or xor cmp test lea**<br>**dec inc neg not mov pop push nop**<br>**jCC** (conditional branch *not* taken)<br>wait (1-3+ cycles) |
| 2 cycles | **rol ror sal sar shl shr** (reg,n form)<br>clc cld cmc stc std daa das bswap<br>sahf sldt smsw str |
| 3 cycles | **rol ror sal sar shl shr** (reg,cl or reg,1)<br>**rcl rcr** (reg,1) **shld shrd** (reg,reg,n)<br>**jCC** (conditional branch *taken*)<br>**jmp** (near) **call** (near)<br>**rep movs** (average time to do one move)<br>aaa aas cdq cwde push (ds, es, ss)<br>pushfd lahf xchg |
| 4 cycles | **shld shrd** (reg,reg,cl)<br>**setCC** (conditional byte set to memory)<br>**rep stos** (average time to do one store)<br>bt (reg,reg or reg,imm) cbw cwd<br>hlt invd movsx movzx  push (fs, gs)<br>mov (reg,segreg or mem,segreg) pushf<br>ror ror shl shr sar sal (mem,1 or mem,cl) |

| Table 4-1 (continued)    486 Instruction Timings Sorted by Speed | |
|---|---|
| 5 cycles | `rcl rcr` (mem,1) `xadd hlt xlat`<br>`rep lods` (average time to do one load)<br>**call** (near `reg`, near `mem`) **retn**<br>**jmp** (near `reg`, near `mem`) **retn** (immediate)<br>**setCC** (conditional byte set to register)<br>**rep scas** (average time to do one scan)<br>`leave lods stos cli sti  pop` (mem)<br>`rol ror shl shr sar sal` (mem,n form)<br>`shld shrd` (mem,reg,cl) `wbinvd`<br>`xadd` (mem,reg) |
| 6 cycles | `bsf` (6-19 cycles) `popfd scas`<br>`lock` (measured value, listed as 1 cycle)<br>`loop loopz loopnz` (branch not taken) |
| 7 cycles | **repe cmps** (average time to do one compare)<br>`bsr` (7-10 cycles) `btc btr bts movs bound`<br>`cmpxchg` (destination not loaded) `clts`<br>`loop` (branch taken) |
| 8 cycles | **rep stos** (startup overhead) `popf`<br>**repe scas** (startup overhead)<br>**repe cmps** (startup overhead)<br>`rep lods` (startup overhead)<br>`cmps mov` (fs,reg or fs,mem) `pop` (fs)<br>`rcl rcr` (reg,n form) |
| 9 cycles | `pop` (ds, es, ss) `popa popad`<br>`rcl rcr` (mem,cl) `bt` (mem,reg) `arpl`<br>`loopz loopnz` (branch taken) |
| 10 cycles | `btc btr bts` (mem,immediate) `lsl`<br>`mov` (to ds,es,gs,ss from reg or mem)<br>`pop` (gs) `sgdt sidt  xchg` (mem,reg) |
| 11 cycles | **rep movs** (startup overhead)<br>`lfs lar lgdt lidt lldt verr verw`<br>`cmpxchg` (destination loaded) |
| 12 cycles | `lds les lgs invlpg` |
| 13 cycles | **mul**    (al        by `reg or mem`,    13-18 cycles)<br>**mul**    (eax       by `reg or mem`,    13-42 cycles)<br>**imul**   (al        by `reg or mem`,    13-18 cycles)<br>**imul**   (eax       by `reg or mem`,    13-42 cycles)<br>**imul**   (reg8 by `immediate`,    13-18 cycles)<br>**imul**   (reg32 by `immediate`,    13-42 cycles)<br>**imul**   (reg8 by `reg,imm`,    13-18 cycles)<br>**imul**   (reg32 by `reg,imm`,    13-42 cycles)<br>`lss pusha pushad` |

| Table 4-1 (continued) | 486 Instruction Timings Sorted by Speed |
|---|---|
| 14 cycles | **mul** (ax      by reg or mem,   14-27 cycles)<br>**imul** (ax      by reg or mem,   14-27 cycles)<br>**imul** (reg16 by immediate,   14-27 cycles)<br>**imul** (reg16 by reg,imm,    14-27 cycles)<br>**imul** (reg8  by reg,       14-19 cycles)<br>**imul** (reg32 by reg,       14-43 cycles)<br>**imul** (reg8  by mem,imm,    14-19 cycles)<br>**imul** (reg32 by mem,imm,    14-43 cycles)<br>btc btr bts (mem,reg) aad enter lmsw |
| 15 cycles | **imul** (reg16 by reg,        15-28 cycles)<br>**imul** (reg16 by mem,imm,    15-28 cycles)<br>aam iret (15-36+ cycles) |
| 16 cycles | **div** (ax by reg8 or mem8) |
| 17 cycles | enter (arguments 0,1) |
| 18 cycles | retf (immediate) retf |
| 19 cycles | **idiv** (ax by reg8)<br>jmp (far) |
| 20 cycles | **idiv** (ax by mem8)<br>ltr |
| 22 cycles | call (far) |
| 25 cycles | **div** (dx:ax by reg16 or mem16) |
| 26 cycles | int (26-71+ cycles) |
| 28 cycles | **idiv** (dx:ax by reg16) |
| 29 cycles | **idiv** (dx:ax by mem16) |
| 37 cycles | **in** (al,dx) insb [reading a timer reg]<br>rep insb (average time to read one byte) |
| 38 cycles | **in** (al,immed) [reading a timer reg] |
| 39 cycles | **out** (dx,al) [writing a timer reg] |
| 40 cycles | **div** (edx:eax by reg32 or mem32)<br>**out** (immed,al) [writing a timer reg]<br>outsb |
| 43 cycles | **idiv** (edx:eax by reg32) |
| 44 cycles | **idiv** (edx:eax by mem32) |

One of the most important times to know is branch timing. A branch taken is three cycles, but it's just one cycle if not taken. Because of this one timing, fast 486 code tends to have fat loops that in one pass do the work of several iterations of smaller loops. The 486 likes to run through instructions in a straight line, without branching.

In some obscure corners of Intel's optimization literature, it is mentioned that instructions that are encoded into binary with a first byte value of 0fH (15 decimal) are considered to be "prefixed" by that byte and therefore take one cycle longer to execute than their published value (the exception to this rule being conditional branches with long displacements). This, it turns out, is why published timing values for `setCC`, `bswap`, `shld`, `shrd`, `movzx`, `movsx`, and a few other less common instructions usually take a cycle longer than is stated in the documentation. Of course, there's no way to ever issue the instructions without the "prefix" byte, so they might as well have called it the first byte of the opcode and published the correct timings. Perhaps at an early processor design stage the "prefix" was intended to have caused no delay.

## Instructions That Vary from Their Book Value

There are many discrepancies between the 1992 *Intel486 Microprocessor Family Programmer's Reference Manual* and the values I measured, even beyond the prefix byte issue. Most are one-cycle discrepancies on uncommon instructions. But some are worth making note of.

### pop

The happiest discrepancy is that the `pop reg` operation, although listed as four cycles in the book, actually takes just one cycle. I had actually sworn off pushing and popping the stack after reading Intel's discouraging timing value years ago, and I didn't realize for several years, until I read about it, that it was just a mistake. This just goes to show that it pays to measure. (As an aside, it turns out that there are good and reasonable ways to save registers on the stack without "popping" them back. I still avoid `push` and `pop` for code structural reasons.)

### loop

The unhappiest discrepancy—for those who believed the too-good-to-be-true documentation in the manual—is that a `loop` branch taken costs seven cycles, not the published two. Instead of being a faster way to loop than using a conditional branch, it's actually so much slower it's almost useless in optimized code. (I suspect that the discrepancy is the result of a transcription error.)

## bswap

The `bswap` instruction, which was introduced with the 486, runs in two cycles, not one. That's unfortunate in that this instruction, which converts longword byte order between Intel and Motorola formats (little-endian versus big-endian), could be used as a fast way to reach the high 16 bits of registers by swapping them down to the low part. But at two cycles, it's no more efficient than `rol eax,16`, the customary way to do it.

## shld and shrd

Another slight disappointment is that the `shld` and `shrd` instructions run one cycle slower than documented. These instructions are extraordinarily useful for bit-stream operations, allowing bits to be shifted from one register into another. They're often needed in compression and decompression algorithms.

## movsx and movzx

Both of these instructions take at minimum four cycles, not the documented three. The `movzx` instruction is slower than the two-instruction alternative, and `movsx` is only marginally efficient over the alternatives (by one cycle) when necessary.

## mul and imul

The integer multiplication instructions run more efficiently the smaller the absolute value of the "multiplier." You may ask, "Which of the two numbers being multiplied is the multiplier?" By Intel's convention, it's the value farthest to the right in the list of operands. If you take the highest nonzero bit position in the absolute value of the multiplier (from 0 to 31) and add 11, that's the number of cycles it should take to do a `mul` or `imul`, subject to a 13-cycle minimum. For instance, if the multiplier is 217 (in hex, D9), the highest bit set is in position 7, so the multiplication should take 18 cycles. Planning code so that the smaller absolute value is usually used as the multiplier can speed up 486 code. It makes no difference to the Pentium, but if you're writing code to run well on both processors, this is a principle to consider.

## Shifts and Rotations

There is an odd anomaly in the shift- and roll-class instructions. Historically, there were originally no instructions in the 8088 instruction set for shifting or rolling data by more than one bit at a time with an immediate shift count. In other words, `rol al,3` didn't always exist. Then, with the 286 processor, `rol al,3` and so on, became legal; as a side effect there were two ways to encode `rol al,1`—the old hardwired way, and the new way, with an immediate value field set to 1. Assemblers generally choose to encode `rol al,1` the old-fashioned way. Unfortunately, this is the slower way (three cycles versus two) on the 486. To get the faster version of `rol al,1`, you may have to examine the bytes used to encode `rol al,4`, `rol al,3`, and `rol al,2` to extrapolate how to encode `rol al,1` in its faster form. You'll end up with a `db . . .` data statement instead of a `rol al,1` statement, but it will execute faster.

Complicating matters further, the old-fashioned `rol al,1` instruction works better on the Pentium than the newer form of the instruction, which works better on the 486. This anomaly is limited to the rotation instructions `rol`, `ror`, `rcl`, and `rcr`. Sometimes you just can't entirely win in optimization.

One final note: the pessimistic variable-length timings given by Intel for the `rcr reg,n` and the `rcl reg,n` instructions seem to be wrong. They seem to execute at a flat eight cycles, but they're not very commonly used with shift values other than 1 anyhow.

### setCC

The `setCC` instruction, which came in with the 386, is a very handy way to set a byte to either 0 or –1 based on the condition of processor flags, *without* branching. On the 486, though, it's no faster at setting a register than a three-instruction equivalent sequence. Ironically, it *is* faster at setting a *memory* byte, and it has the odd distinction of being perhaps the only 486 instruction that operates faster to memory than to its own registers.

## Instructions That Are Much Slower Than Their Book Value

There are six instructions worth mentioning because they typically run much slower than their book value—not so much because the book values are wrong as because they don't tell the whole story.

### in and out

First, `in` and `out`, the port I/O operations, usually take much longer than their minimal book times of eight and ten cycles in protected mode with high privileges. These operations take closer to 40 cycles (or potentially much more) when they have to essentially handshake with external hardware like the timer chip registers I tested them on. Consider port operations potentially quite variable in duration, depending on what's on the other end.

### lock

Second, `lock`, the bus locking command that ensures, for instance, that no other processor or device can see a certain piece of data while you modify it, has to assert its authority on an external bus—and it generally takes longer than the one cycle listed to do it. In my tests it took about six cycles.

### xchg

Closely related to the `lock` instruction timing is the anomaly of the `xchg reg,mem` timing. It turns out that when exchanging a register with memory, the 486 *always* locks the bus, even if you didn't ask for it. It measures in at ten cycles, and it should generally be avoided in fast code.

### pusha and pushad

Logically, `pusha` and `pushad`, instructions that rapidly push eight registers onto the stack, could probably run in their alloted 11 book cycles, if only external memory could keep up. Chances are that anyone using these instructions isn't worrying much about speed, but these instructions are rather unique in their being able to clog up the data output queue of the processor (to be discussed later) by dumping eight items on it in rapid fire. They average, at minimum, a little over 13 cycles on the system I used for testing, but in the context of an already full output queue, they can take over twice as long.

## The rep Instructions

In Table 4-2, two figures are given for each `rep` instruction. One gives the "overhead time" to get such an instruction started, and the other gives the time for each additional item (`byte`, `word`, or `dword`) processed. The nonintegral timings in the cycles-per-item column are apparently due to complexities in the internal generation of repetitions by the processor.

| Table 4-2 String Instruction Timings on the 486 | | |
|---|---|---|
| | *Startup Cycles* | *Cycles per Item* |
| repe cmps | 8 | 7.6 |
| rep lods | 8 | 4.2 |
| rep movs | 11 | 3.3 |
| repe scas | 8 | 5.3 |
| rep stos | 8 | 4.1 |

These instructions are useful for processing large blocks of data all at once, but it's possible to write large software loops that run faster than all but the `rep movs` instruction (remember, on the 486, large loops can be faster than small ones, because of minimal branching overhead). They're great for the convenience. Note that large start-up times make these instructions particularly inefficient if you're only processing about half a dozen items or less. If you know you're going to copy one longword, spending 14 cycles on `rep movsd` makes much less sense than performing two moves in two cycles (if a register is available).

The most unusual `rep` instruction may be `rep lods`, which loads the accumulator repeatedly but does nothing more with the information. It turns out that it's handy, once in a very long while, for loading a large block of memory into cache so that subsequent instructions don't encounter delays (or so they *will* encounter delays if you fill the cache with unused memory). None of these instructions are particularly speed-worthy without their `rep` prefixes, either.

## Floating-Point Instructions

The floating-point unit is not the one-cycle speed demon of the main integer processor, and one major bottleneck impeding its use in time-critical code is the simple amount of time it takes to get data into and out of the floating-point registers. Remember, internally the floating-point system operates as a stack of up to eight floating-point numbers, and it takes a significant amount of time, usually, to put data on the stack or remove it to memory. There are no instructions that transfer numbers between the 486's integer registers and the floating-point stack, so memory mediates between the two.

An integer operation that reads memory, such as `add eax,mem`, costs an extra cycle over an equivalent operation, such as `add eax,edx`, that does not. But the floating-point unit generally imposes no penalty when fetching a floating-point operand from memory as part of an arithmetic operation. In fact, sometimes it actually *saves* cycles when an operand comes from memory. For instance, here is how `var3 = var1 * var2` could be calculated:

```
        fld     var1    ; 3;load var1 onto the stack
        fmul    var2    ;11;load and multiply times var2
        fstp    var3    ; 7;store to var3
                        ;;;;21 cycles total
                        ;;;;vars are all 32-bit floats
```

Note that for a simple multiplication calculation, loading and storing represents almost half the total time spent, even with `var2` getting a free ride into the floating-point unit.

Another big source of cycle loss is in converting between integer and floating-point formats. It's not uncommon to want integers as inputs and outputs for a function but to want floating-point calculations in between. The conversions are far from free.

## Floating-Point Loading and Storing

Table 4-3 shows the number of cycles required to load and store nonzero numbers to and from the floating-point stack in six different formats, three each of integer and floating-point. Two numbers separated by a forward slash represent, first, the maximum execution time if no other instructions overlap, and second, the minimum execution time if maximum overlap is achieved. For instance, loading a 16-bit integer with the `fild` instruction would cost 13 cycles if the very next instruction used the loaded value as an operand, but only 9 cycles if the next instruction didn't use it and burned up at least 4 cycles doing something else.

| Table 4-3 | Floating-Point Unit Load and Store Times | | | | | |
|---|---|---|---|---|---|---|
| Instructions | 16-bit integer | 32-bit integer | 64-bit integer | 32-bit float | 64-bit float | 80-bit float |
| fld / fild | 13/9 | 9/7 | 10/8 | 3 | 3 | 6 |
| fst / fist | 32 | 32 | 30 | 7 | 8 | 6 |

Note that storing to an integer format costs an approximate penalty of 25 cycles over a floating-point store. And loading an integer is about three times as expensive as loading a floating-point number.

A special case, not shown on the previous timing table, is that of storing the number 0 in either 32-bit or 64-bit floating-point format, which costs an ungodly 27 or 28 cycles respectively, so beware of tight loops outputting 0 frequently.

## Floating-Point Addition and Subtraction

Addition and subtraction are officially listed as having quite variable clock counts, depending on operand content, but I found them both clocking at eight cycles in the worst test case and four cycles when they were able to overlap execution with the following instruction. The execution times are the same whether operating entirely on the stack or drawing one operand from memory, except that an integer memory operand costs an extra 11 cycles (making its times 19/15).

## Floating-Point Multiplication

There are three inherent multiplication speeds on the 486 processor: 11/7 (multiplication by a 32-bit float), 14/10 (multiplication by a 64-bit float), and 16/12 (multiplication by an 80-bit float). At first I thought that the first two speeds only applied when using memory operands, but then, thanks to a bunch of timing anomalies, I noticed that the floating-point stack was sometimes exhibiting the 32-bit and 64-bit timings, even though it's an 80-bit stack. It turns out that if you load a 32-bit floating-point number onto the stack and don't modify it, you can use it indefinitely as the last operand in a multiplication, and the multiplication will proceed with 32-bit speed. The same is true of a 64-bit loaded value. As with addition, add 11 cycles if the memory operand is an integer.

## Floating-Point Division

Without reprogramming the floating-point unit's precision-control bits, there is just one main speed for division, 73/69, plus an optional 11 if the divisor is a memory integer. That's a long, long time. In fact, it's an order of magnitude slower than multiplication. But if you're willing to command the floating-point unit to operate below its default precision of full 80-bit values, you can get additional speed. Operating at 64-bit precision, it drops 11 cycles to 62/58. And at 32-bit floating-point precision, it drops all the way to 35/31.

## Floating-Point Precision Control

The `fldcw` instruction loads the floating-point unit's control word, and it fortunately takes only four cycles. So if you want to operate the floating-point unit at the highest possible precision except for an occasional floating-point division, it only costs eight cycles to change the precision before and after the division; this can still give a net 30-cycle gain on the division, despite the two precision changes. According to Intel documentation, changing the precision affects the operation of `fadd`, `fsub`, `fmul`, and `fsqrt` as well. It does not, however, change their timings on the 486 (`fsqrt` is 87/83).

## Floating-Point Flags

One last thing that slows the floating-point unit down is the fact that you can't directly branch based on its flag settings; you have to perform a sequence such as the following:

```
fnstsw  ax       ; 3;store flags in ax
sahf             ; 2;transfer flags to main flag reg
ja      founda   ; 1;branch statement
                 ;;;;6-cycle branch test
```

or, even better,

```
fnstsw   ax          ; 3;store flags in ax
test     ah,41H      ; 1;test Z and C flag bits
jz       founda      ; 1;branch statement, ja equivalent
                     ;;;;5-cycle branch test
```

Whereas the integer unit can execute a branch test in as little as one cycle, it takes at least five cycles to ferry the same sort of branching information over from the floating-point unit and act on it. On top of this, ordinary addition and subtraction don't even set the usual flags one would expect in the integer unit, such as Z, C, and S. You have to execute an explicit four-cycle fcom comparison instruction to set the flags so they can be transferred to the integer unit.

# The Cache

Perhaps the best way to understand how the 8K primary cache memory on board the 486 chip works is to look at a piece of code that defeats it. Remember, the idea of cache memory is to keep recently referenced areas of memory in a high-speed access state so that the 486 can get to it in a one-cycle fetch. Consider, then, this paradox.

This code runs fast:

```
.repeat                     ;   ;
   mov    eax,[esi+0000H]   ; 1;
   mov    eax,[esi+0800H]   ; 1;
   mov    eax,[esi+1000H]   ; 1;
   mov    eax,[esi+1800H]   ; 1;(+1 cycle for
   mov    eax,[esi+2010H]   ; 1;code fetch)
   dec    ecx               ; 1;
.until ZERO?                ; 3;
                            ;;;;11 cycles measured
```

But this code runs almost ten times slower!

```
.repeat                     ;   ;
   mov    eax,[esi+0000H]   ;19;
   mov    eax,[esi+0800H]   ;19;
   mov    eax,[esi+1000H]   ;19;
   mov    eax,[esi+1800H]   ;19;(+1 cycle for
   mov    eax,[esi+2000H]   ;19;code fetch)
```

```
        dec    ecx                ; 1;
    .until ZERO?                  ; 3;
                                  ;;;;101 cycles measured
```

The odd thing is that there is very little difference between the two. In fact, the only difference is the address of one of the load statements. What's happening?

# The Four-Way Principle

In technical jargon, the 8K cache memory on board the 486 is referred to as "four-way set associative with a cache line length of 16 bytes." The part about a cache line length of 16 bytes just means that the 8K of cache is broken up into 512 sixteen-byte pieces. Any time you read memory, the 486 first checks to see if one of the 512 sixteen-byte chunks has a copy of what you're looking for; if so, it returns it in just one cycle. Each 16-byte cache chunk is a copy of some 16-byte chunk of main memory, starting at an even 16-byte boundary (the low four bits of the address being zero).

If the memory read can't be satisfied by the cache, then the 486 picks one of the 512 sixteen-byte chunks to be a sacrificial lamb, throws out its contents, and loads it up with the sixteen-byte zone around the latest read operation. This way, if the processor wants to read the same spot again, or another spot nearby, it will have one-cycle access. The only downside to the transaction is that it has to toss out that old piece of cache information: what if it's needed again?

This is where the four-way principle comes in. It turns out that the 512 sixteen-byte cache lines are actually organized as 128 sets of four 16-byte cache lines. For any given memory address, there are exactly four cache lines (the set) that could possibly be used to hold it. The rule is that memory addresses that contend for the same little set of four cache lines are multiples of 2,048 bytes apart. So reading [esi+100H] will never, ever kick [esi+200H] out of cache. But it might kick [esi+834900H] out (2,048 is 800H, and 834900H – 100H is 834800H, which is a multiple of 800H). It could also kick [esi+110fH] out, because 110fH falls on the same chunk as 1100H (assuming esi is 16-byte aligned). So for any given set of four cache lines, there may be literally thousands of locations in memory that would map into them. The 486 uses a "least recently used" algorithm to decide which of the four to reuse when a new memory area is read. It kicks out the chunk that hasn't been read for the longest time and reuses it for the new data.

The explanation for the code paradox given at the beginning of this section is as follows: In one case the loop was reading all four cache lines in succession from one group and then performing the fifth read on another group. Nobody got kicked out of cache. But in the other case, by reading five locations contending for the same four cache lines, the least recently used algorithm was always kicking data out of cache just before it had to be read back in again. In effect, cache was totally defeated.

The moral of all of this is that the cache works well most of the time, but it can do some very strange things under special circumstances. Knowing how it's organized and how it operates helps in avoiding the pitfalls. The Pentium's cache is two-way set-associative, so it is even easier to trip up than the 486's.

## Cache Write-Through

The 486's primary cache is called a "write-through" cache, meaning that when the processor writes to a memory location, that write operation will write to main memory and also to any cache line that happens to have a copy of that chunk of memory. Writing to a location will not cause any cache line to be kicked out or a new one to be read in. Most 486 systems are configured so that all of the main memory may be cached; but some areas of the address space, such as the areas assigned to peripherals like the display adapter, are not cached, because their contents could change without the 486's cache knowing about it.

## Cache Miss Delays

On the test machine, reading from the primary cache always took one cycle, as expected. A typical read that missed the primary cache took 13 cycles, which would have been somewhat quicker if there had been a layer of secondary cache on the machine, but there wasn't. (The secondary cache, often between 128K and 512K, behaves similarly to the primary cache—it catches whatever falls through the cracks from the primary cache, responding faster than main memory.)

Yet, there's more to the story of cache misses. The first time the 486 tries to read data and finds that it's not in primary cache, it gets a 16-byte burst from either the main memory or the secondary cache system, to fill up a new primary cache line. The burst of 16 bytes comes in, four bytes at a time, over the 32-bit data bus, and the order of delivery of the bytes is generally such that the first 4-byte transfer contains the precise data the 486 was requesting. The instruction that requested the data completes before the remaining 12 bytes of the cache line have been fully transferred. But if the next instruction requests more data from the same cache—even the same exact bytes as before—it stalls until all 16 bytes have been delivered. So a cache miss sometimes affects more than one instruction. On the 486 I tested, back-to-back reads where the first one hit the 13-cycle penalty also incurred a 7-cycle penalty on the next instruction. So if you want to load two registers with the same memory value, which you suspect isn't in cache, then

```
mov     eax,[esi]   ;13;take a cache miss
mov     ebx,[esi]   ; 7;revisit the same miss
                    ;;;;20 cycles
```

is slower than

```
mov     eax,[esi]     ;13;take a cache miss
mov     ebx,eax       ; 1;don't touch that line again
                      ;;;;14 cycles
```

## Code and Data Cache Contention

Unlike the later Pentium and Pentium Pro, the 8K 486 cache is used for both code and data. That is, the 486 fetches instructions from the cache as well as data for those instructions. When writing time-critical inner loops, the amount of cache used up by the loops themselves is usually small in comparison with the 8K space. But because of the four-way set-associative way of managing cache, it's possible that some portion of the data you expect to be in cache may be systematically kicked out by the executable code itself. In fact, it's likely that from one compilation to the next during code development, code loops will shift in and out of alignment with key data addresses. This is not usually a major problem, and I've never personally seen it bring a program mysteriously to its knees, but it's something to keep in the back of one's mind should code timings ever start to wobble around mysteriously.

Of more direct importance to code planning, it's important to remember that for every 16 bytes of executable code fetched by the 486 from cache, the 486 has to spend one cache fetch cycle transferring that code into the bowels of the processor (the prefetch unit). Since it's "prefetching" the 16-byte chunk, it usually waits until it notices that there is no data read or write scheduled for the cache and then reads the 16 bytes of instructions without delaying computation. But if it doesn't spot a free cache cycle before the internal instruction queue gets dangerously low on instructions, it grabs a cache cycle and delays the computational unit for one cycle while doing so. The prefetch engine thus has to "come up for air" about every four or five instructions. Intel suggests that as a rule of thumb you assume that if four instructions in a row reference cache, you should expect the code prefetcher to take an extra cycle to grab instructions. As a corollary, for fast code, try to schedule gaps between short bursts (say, three instructions in a row) of memory reference instructions.

This code:

```
mov     eax,[esi+ 0]    ; 1;
mov     ebx,[esi+ 4]    ; 1;
mov     ecx,[esi+ 8]    ; 1;
mov     edx,[esi+12]    ; 2;assume prefetch delay
clc                     ; 2;
                        ;;;;7 cycles
```

is probably not as fast as this code:

```
mov     eax,[esi+ 0]     ; 1;
mov     ebx,[esi+ 4]     ; 1;
clc                      ; 2;
mov     ecx,[esi+ 8]     ; 1;
mov     edx,[esi+12]     ; 1;assume no prefetch delay
                         ;;;;6 cycles
```

# The 486 Output Queue

It may already have struck you as odd that if all writes to memory are actually written to main memory, they ought to take longer than just the one cycle described. The truth is, they do and they don't. What actually happens is that in one cycle, the 486 puts outgoing addresses and data in a little on-chip queue (also called a FIFO, for "first in, first out"). The queue is then emptied, at several cycles per data item, in due time. In my tests, it took about four cycles to empty a data item from the queue by writing it to memory. A data item destined for the ISA bus (for instance, data to a video card) takes much longer to write out. The queue is usually described as being four items deep. You can usually deposit five memory writes to it in successive cycles without encountering a delay, because the first write finishes before the last one is deposited. Going out to an ISA bus, however, you may get away with only four writes before encountering delays.

This little queue is a really, really great feature. If an inner loop averages not more than one write to memory every four cycles and doesn't bunch up its writes too much in one place, it gets the effect of one-cycle writes. When decompressing or otherwise processing graphics to go out to a display adapter, it's a great win to write a decompression/processing loop that about evenly matches the queue's data delivery speed. By overlapping necessary processing with the bus delays of graphics delivery, you can effectively get one-cycle data delivery over a bus that would otherwise waste dozens of cycles doing a simple block data transfer.

Finally, the pusha and pushad instructions, by putting eight items in the output queue in rapid succession, never quite make their book execution times, because they fill up this queue and have to wait while it empties.

# Data and Code Alignment

There's a magic statement in assembly language that can improve code performance without ever being executed. It's the `align` statement, and it's used to push code or data into address locations where it can operate or be operated upon most efficiently. The statement `align 4` means "make the next data or code statement that follows this statement fall on an address that's evenly divisible by 4." Likewise, `align 16` means "head for a 16-byte boundary." Some things just work better aligned on special boundaries.

## Integer Alignment

The 486 likes to address memory in 32-bit chunks. Its external bus to memory works this way, as does its internal path between registers and cache. But it can only request 32-bit chunks that lie on four-byte boundaries. If a word or longword crosses such a boundary, the processor has to issue two reads and then reconstruct the 16- or 32-bit value it was looking for from parts of both. As a result, it takes four cycles to read or write a value that crosses a four-byte boundary, instead of the usual one cycle. Listing 4-1 illustrates the use of the alignment statement and the effects of good and bad alignment.

### Listing 4-1    Aligned and Misaligned Reads

```
        align   4
var1    dd      1234
        db      0
var2    dd      5678
        .
        .
        .
        mov     eax,var1    ; 1;a 1-cycle aligned fetch
        mov     eax,var2    ; 4;a 4-cycle unaligned fetch
```

## Floating-Point Alignment

As one might expect, 32-bit floating-point values, like 32-bit integers, should seek out four-byte boundaries or else experience three-cycle penalties per reference. The larger 64- and 80-bit floating-point values work fine on 8-byte boundaries. Loading a 64-bit floating-point value at any other alignment incurs a three-cycle penalty, but it can be stored at a 4-byte boundary without penalty. At lesser alignments when storing, the penalty is six cycles. The penalties for reading and writing an 80-bit float with 1-byte alignment reaches seven and ten cycles, respectively.

### Rep Movsd **Move Alignment**

When moving large blocks of memory around with rep movsd, it is not always possible to longword-align both the source pointer and the destination pointer. For instance, you can't shift a block of memory by 23 bytes and have the source and destination pointers be multiples of 4, since the difference between the pointers has to be 23, which is not a multiple of 4. In such cases, you have the choice of aligning either the source or the destination pointer; but not both. Things work better if you align the destination pointer. The reason, apparently, is that while a misaligned source read costs three cycles, a misaligned write costs the same three and creates the added burden of placing two partial writes in the output queue instead of an aligned single write.

## Compiled Code Alignment

Compilers are usually pretty good about aligning global data on appropriate boundaries and local data on at least 4-byte boundaries on the stack. There are also structure alignment directives available to pad structures to meet alignment conditions.

## Code Alignment

Any time the 486 hits an instruction that modifies its instruction pointer, such as a branch taken or a call, return, or unconditional jump, it fetches the new incoming 16-byte cache line and spends a few cycles restarting its processing pipeline. If the first instruction it finds crosses into the next cache line, it has to abort, read in the second cache line, and restart the pipeline. As a result, branches and jumps that go to an instruction lying near the end of a cache line often experience a two-cycle delay (although I've seen it referred to as up to a three-cycle delay, and measured a one-cycle form at times). One way to avoid these delays is to use the align statement to put frequent branch destinations away from the end of the cache line. Although align 4 keeps some instructions safe, align 8 and align 16 work better. You can "execute through" the alignment padding, because it's just a bunch of no-ops, but it's not as elegant as designing code to avoid executing the padding.

Listing 4-2 shows an aligned loop preceded by some skipped padding (inside a never-executed conditional if body). As a rule of thumb, you should only align known time-critical loops, because alignment bulks up the code and thereby diminishes the effectiveness of the cache on a global scale.

### Listing 4-2   A Cache-Aligned Loop

```
.if 0                    ; 3;jump to loop start
  align 16               ;  ;padding
.endif                   ;  ;
.repeat                  ;  ;start of loop, aligned
  mov   [edi],eax        ; 1;
  inc   eax              ; 1;
  add   edi,4            ; 1;
  dec   ecx              ; 1;
.until ZERO?             ; 3;2-cycle penalty avoided
```

# Cycle Thieves and Cycle Savers

There is never a complete substitute for actually measuring code performance. Despite all attempts to predict actual loop cycles, the 486 often throws in an extra cycle (or, sometimes, even performs slightly faster than expected). There are, no doubt, many idiosyncratic 486 code behaviors that are not generally understood or documented. But herewith are three known cycle stealers and one oddity that saves cycles. Beyond these, you're on your own.

## Address Generation Interlock (AGI)

If you load or in any way modify a 32-bit register, you can't use it to address memory on the very next cycle. This code looks at first glance like it should take two cycles, but it ends up taking three due to what's called "address generation interlock" (a daunting term that just means the address register needs time to settle):

```
add   esi,4      ; 1;esi modified
mov   eax,[esi]  ; 2;1-cycle delay to use it
```

A very large percentage of the art of coding for the 486 is figuring out how to reorder instructions so that registers aren't used for addressing right after they're modified.

The `esp` register has a special relationship to the AGI problem. When you `push` and `pop`, you're implicitly changing `esp`, which is being used for stack addressing. But these instructions don't experience AGIs if executed back to back. If, however, you do something like add esp, 8, a push or pop as the next instruction would experience the one-cycle delay.

## Partial Registers

If you modify an 8- or 16-bit section of a 32-bit register, you can't execute an instruction that uses the contents of that 32-bit register on the next cycle:

```
mov     bl,0        ; 1;modify part of ebx
mov     eax,ebx     ; 2;1-cycle delay to use it
```

This particular delay goes away on the Pentium but comes roaring back with a vengeance on the Pentium Pro. Instead of a one-cycle delay, the Pentium Pro gets hit with a stall of at least seven cycles. So if you're writing code for the whole range of processors, be particularly wary of this stall.

## Byte Registers

This final way to lose cycles is a very odd phenomenon, one not mentioned in Intel's optimization literature. It was first brought to my attention in the book *The Zen of Code Optimization* by Michael Abrash. If you modify *any* 8-bit register and then use *any* 32-bit register to address memory exactly two cycles later, you get hit with a one-cycle stall.

This runs fine:

```
inc     bl          ; 1;modify a byte register
mov     eax,[esi]   ; 1;next cycle, [esi] works fine
mov     edx,ecx     ; 1;another instruction cycle
                    ;;;;3 cycles total
```

This doesn't:

```
inc     bl          ; 1;modify a byte register
mov     edx,ecx     ; 1;another instruction cycle
mov     eax,[esi]   ; 2;[esi] jams one cycle
                    ;;;;4 cycles total
```

## A Few Cycles Saved

Recall that there is a one-cycle penalty for operating on 16-bit values and one-cycle-slower-than-book-value timing on instructions that start with the byte 0fH (bswap, setCC, shld, shrd, and so on). Thus, there are times when the extra cycle doesn't get charged. If the preceeding instruction inherently takes more than one cycle or encounters its own stall condition, such as an AGI, the following instruction doesn't get charged the usual one-cycle penalty.

This code gets hit with the penalty:

```
mov     eax,ebx    ; 1;an ordinary instruction
mov     dx,cx      ; 2;a prefixed instruction
cmc                ; 2;a 2-cycle instruction
                   ;;;;5 cycles
```

This code doesn't encounter it:

```
mov     eax,ebx    ; 1;an ordinary instruction
cmc                ; 2;a 2-cycle instruction
mov     dx,cx      ; 1;a prefixed instruction
                   ;;;;4 cycles
```

# Conclusion

The 486 is a good first processor to learn in the 32-bit 80x86 family. On the one hand, it performs much like a Pentium without parallel instruction execution. On the other hand, its need for code alignment conditions and its susceptibility to the partial register stall make it seem akin to the Pentium Pro. As on the Pentium, the AGI stall is a major factor in code design. Knowing the 486 architecture is an important part of knowing how to create code that will run well across the broad 80x86 spectrum.

# References

Abrash, M. 1994. *Zen of Code Optimization*. Scottsdale, Ariz.: Coriolis Group Books. This book has good, detailed descriptions of 486 programming principles and nuances.

Intel Corporation. 1992. *Intel486 Microprocessor Family Programmer's Reference Manual*. Santa Clara, Calif.: Intel Corporation. Although the Intel manual contains the definitive description of the instruction set, its timing data has some inaccuracies.

# CHAPTER 5

# Optimizing the Pentium

*Double your pleasure, double your fun.*
*—The Doublemint Gum Slogan*

The distinguishing feature of the Pentium processor is its two parallel execution units, which often permit two instructions to be executed simultaneously, usually in a single processor clock cycle. The Pentium lends itself to manual optimization even more than the 486, because of the complexities of instruction ordering and the subtle interactions that affect timing.

In this chapter, we'll take a look at what's new and different about the Pentium architecture and how best to take advantage of it. The discussion includes

- Pentium features overview
- How instruction pairing works
- Branch prediction
- The instruction set
- The cache
- The output FIFO (queue)
- Data and code alignment
- Cycle thieves and cycle savers
- Instruction stream timing oddities

If anything, hand-optimized code on the Pentium tends to give even bigger performance wins than equivalent code on the 486. If you like brain teasers and chess puzzles, you can find plenty of equally interesting problems to solve on this processor.

# The CHPENT.BAT Instruction Timing Program

Included on the CD-ROM accompanying this book is a program, CHPENT.BAT, that can be used on a Pentium machine to time nearly all the instructions in the instruction set (except some system-level instructions and some floating-point instructions). It runs either under true DOS, or, with slightly less accuracy, in a DOS "box" or window under Windows. I have also included source code and the test results obtained on the test machine for comparison.

There is a new, almost undocumented (by Intel), instruction for reading a 64-bit cycle counting clock on the Pentium, and this is the timer used in the test code to establish timed values. Consequently, this program won't even function on a 486, but it establishes timings quickly on the Pentium.

# Pentium Features Overview

Four big-ticket items come to mind when one compares the Pentium and the 486:

1. The Pentium is capable of executing two instructions at a time.
2. The Pentium predicts branches and, when correct, executes them in a single cycle.
3. The Pentium has two separate 8K primary caches, one for data, the other for code.
4. The Pentium has a 64-bit bus to external memory, not just a 32-bit as on the 486.

First and most importantly, the "superscalar" execution of two instructions in parallel is a big win, to be covered in the next section. ("Superscalar" just means "more than one at a time.")

Branch prediction is, in most cases, another big win. Reducing the time it takes to decrement a loop counter and branch based on the results, from four cycles on the 486 to one cycle on the Pentium, leaves much less incentive to "unroll loops."

By adding a second 8K cache for the instruction stream and increasing the efficiency with which the 8K of code cache can be used (fewer address-related branching penalties), there is less of a problem with cache stalls and code/data competition. With two-way set-associative 32-bit cache lines, though, the likelihood of stumbling into a deadly three-way cache-line competition is slightly increased (as described later in this chapter).

The external 64-bit bus, cycle for cycle, doubles the byte transfer rate at which cache lines can be filled (although the cache lines now have twice as many bytes).

The rest is in the details.

# How Instruction Pairing Works

A conventional processor like the 486 reads and executes one instruction at a time, one after another. The Pentium tries its best to always read the next *two* instructions from the instruction stream and execute them simultaneously. As one might imagine, there are many situations, particularly when the result of the first instruction is needed by the second instruction, where simultaneous execution doesn't work. The Pentium detects those cases, backs off, and just executes one instruction, the first instruction of the two.

| Table 5-1 | Pairable Pentium Instructions |
|---|---|
| 1st or 2nd position | add sub and or xor cmp test (except immed) dec inc lea mov pop push nop |
| 1st position only | adc sbb sar shl shr sal rcl rcr rol ror (reg,1 form) |
| 2nd position only | call (near) jmp (near) jCC (conditional branch, taken or not) |

Table 5-1 shows all the instructions that can possibly pair with others. Some instructions, such as adc, can only pair if they are the first of the two instructions. Others, like jnz (a particular case of jCC), can only pair as the second of the two. And still others, like xor, can be in either position (or both). Although these instructions usually can even pair up in their two- or three-cycle forms, which operate on memory (such as add [esi],edx or xor al,[edi+1]), in efficient coding practice it is almost always the one-cycle register forms of the instructions, such as inc ebx, that are most useful.

Here is a four-instruction loop that usually executes in just two cycles, due to pairing:

```
lptop:  mov     [edi],eax   ; 1;this is pairable
        add     edi,4       ; 0;and this pairs with previous
```

```
        dec     ecx         ; 1;this is pairable
        jnz     lptop       ; 0;in 2nd position, this pairs
                            ;;;;2-cycle loop
```

If the add operation were adc instead, the loop would take longer:

```
lptop:  mov     [edi],eax   ; 1;this is pairable, but...
        adc     edi,4       ; 1;this can't take 2nd position
        dec     ecx         ; 0;this is pairable
        jnz     lptop       ; 1;nothing to pair with
                            ;;;;3-cycle loop
```

Note that because adc cannot be paired in the second position (to mov in the first position), the Pentium executes mov unpaired. Then adc and dec can pair, since adc can get first position, and jnz is left to execute unpaired.

## The Read-After-Write Pairing Exception

The main enemy of pairing in the Pentium is dependence, when the second instruction in a pair depends upon data produced by the first. This is referred to as the read-after-write problem. The following two instructions won't pair:

```
        mov     eax,[esi]   ;writes eax
        inc     eax         ;reads eax
```

The Pentium detects that the inc eax instruction has to read the register value written by the mov eax,[esi] instruction, and it thus refuses to pair them. (If it *did* actually execute them paired, it would probably try to increment the previous value of eax and then collide with the mov instruction writing to the eax register.) Unfortunately, it is the nature of a lot of computer code to tightly couple the output of one instruction to the input of the next. The art of Pentium programming has a lot to do with finding ways to arrange instruction sequences so that pairing isn't denied for this reason.

There are a couple of notable exceptions to the read-after-write problem. First, the flags generated by the first instruction of a pair are available to a paired branch instruction for branching on the same cycle. In other words, the following instructions pair, even though the second instruction depends on flag information generated by the first:

```
        dec     ecx         ;sets or clears Z flag
        jnz     lptop       ;branches based on the result
```

The other exception is the push and pop instructions, which implicitly modify the stack pointer (esp) register. The Pentium, hardwired to understand the effects of these instructions operating in pairs on esp, lets two pushes pair, and it lets two pops pair—but push and pop can't pair with each other.

## The Write-After-Write Pairing Exception

Another pairing illegality, called write-after-write, makes it impossible to pair any two instructions that both write to any part of the same 32-bit register. Thus, these instructions won't pair:

```
xor     eax,eax    ;writes the entire eax register
mov     al,[esi]   ;writes just one byte of eax
```

This restriction rarely cramps one's programming style, though, as it's fairly uncommon to do either partial or full register writes and overwrites back to back. It does have the nasty side effect, however, of making the following two instructions unpairable:

```
inc     dl         ;modify dl
mov     dh,5       ;modify dh, can't pair
```

Because the Pentium regards both instructions as writing to the larger register edx, it refuses to pair them—odd but true.

## Immediates with Displacements

There is a further exception to the pairing rules, for instructions that have both an immediate value and an address displacement, such as mov byte ptr [esi+1],7. These instructions won't pair. On the 486, the penalty for this combination is an extra cycle, but it's been reduced to simple nonpairing on the Pentium.

## Pairing Multicycle Instructions

Multicycle instructions with memory operands (like add [edi],eax, which takes three cycles to execute—one cycle to read from memory, one to add, and one to write the result back) are capable of pairing. But if you're after speed it rarely makes sense to use them, because they can often be broken into two or three simpler, one-cycle instructions that pair even more efficiently. Consider this code fragment:

```
add     [edi],eax      ; 3;a pairable 3-cycle op
mov     ebx,[edi+4]    ; 0;this instruction pairs
shl     ebx,2          ; 1;unpairable
and     ebx,1ffcH      ; 1;might pair with next
                       ;;;;5 cycles
```

Using just one free register (here, **edx**) and breaking the first instruction into three operations instead of one, the same code can run in three cycles instead of five:

```
mov     edx,[edi]      ; 1;pairable 1-cycle load
mov     ebx,[edi+4]    ; 0;pairable 1-cycle load
shl     ebx,2          ; 1;pairable 1-cycle shift
add     edx,eax        ; 0;pairable 1-cycle add
mov     [edi],edx      ; 1;pairable 1-cycle store
and     ebx,1ffcH      ; 0;pairable 1-cycle and
                       ;;;;3 cycles
```

Breaking up operations with memory operands into their component single-cycle pieces rarely hurts and often can help performance, with clever arrangement of the pieces.

Interestingly, if you try pairing two three-cycle instructions, the result is a five-cycle pair:

```
add     [edi],eax      ; 3;pairable
add     [edi+4],ebx    ; 2;pairable on 1 cycle
                       ;;;;5-cycle "pair"
```

The reason for this is that, to prevent an error in the situation where both instructions try to operate on the same memory location, the first instruction has to reach its write phase before the second instruction can start its read phase. Again, if you're sure the two instructions won't be operating on the same memory location, as in this example, you can decompose and rearrange for faster execution:

```
mov     ecx,[edi]      ; 1;paired reads
mov     edx,[edi+4]    ; 0;
add     ecx,eax        ; 1;paired adds
add     edx,ebx        ; 0;
mov     [edi],ecx      ; 1;paired writes
mov     [edi+4],edx    ; 0;
                       ;;;;3 cycles
```

Likewise, a three-cycle instruction (such as add [edi], eax) paired with a two-cycle instruction (such as add edx, [esi]) takes four cycles if the three-cycle version is the first of the pair; otherwise, if it falls in second place, they take three cycles. A pair of two-cycle instructions executes in two cycles.

## 16-Bit Instructions

Instructions that operate on 16-bit values, such as `add ax,bx`, start with a special prefix byte to indicate that they're 16-bit. These instructions can only pair as the first instruction of a two-instruction pair, and they also incur a one-cycle penalty for processing the prefix. Consequently, 16-bit instructions are to be avoided.

## U and V Pipes

Traditional explanations of Pentium pairing usually include references to the "U pipe" and the "V pipe." These are the official names of the first and second parallel instruction execution units. When two instructions are paired, the first is said to be executing in the U pipe, the second in the V pipe. Prefixed instructions are said to execute only in the U pipe. It's just a different terminology.

There are a couple of stall conditions that frequently arise and cause single-cycle delays: the familiar address generation interlock (AGI), which was present on the 486 as well, and occasional contention between paired memory transfers, which sometimes vie for the same path to memory. Technically, neither one of these changes the pairing patterns of the instructions, but they often do affect the way one chooses to pattern and pair instructions. Both are covered later in this chapter.

With the insignificant exception of pairable instructions with one-byte opcodes, Pentium instructions don't pair until the second time they are executed after being read into cache. This rarely has a significant effect on time-critical inner loops, which by their nature tend to execute repeatedly from cache.

## Branch Prediction

In a manner reminiscent of the way the Pentium handles cache memory, the Pentium also keeps track of 256 recent branch points in the code it's executing, along with the probable destination of those branches. Branch points include unconditional and indirect jumps, calls, and returns. But the most common event the Pentium tries to track is the conditional branch, such as `jnz`. Conditional branches are built to be fickle, and the Pentium uses a simple but effective strategy to psych them out.

There is a great little proverb that not only encompasses good advice on how not to be made a fool of but also describes, quite memorably, the philosophy behind branch prediction on the Pentium: "Fool me once, shame on you. Fool me twice, shame on me." Whenever the Pentium reaches a branch point that's recorded in its cache of branch information, it makes a prediction as to where execution will continue after the branch statement executes. It starts preliminary decoding of instructions at that point, even before the correctness of the prediction is known.

If the Pentium predicts the destination of a branch correctly, that guarantees that it will make the same prediction the next *two* times the branch is executed, even if it's wrong on the very next pass. Once it's been wrong twice in a row, it changes its prediction to whatever the latest branch destination actually was. In other words, the first time it gets fooled, it assumes the code was just temporarily doing something odd (the "shame on you" part) and sticks to its prediction. The second time it gets fooled, it abandons its old prediction and adopts a new one (the "shame on me" part).

This kind of prediction algorithm often works very well. The typical branch at the bottom of a loop gets predicted correctly all but the one time it is not taken and the loop terminates. Other branches, such as those involved in implementing `if` statements, also often tend to consistently branch the same way. It's the randomly unpredictable branch that causes trouble.

The penalty for a mispredicted branch is usually four cycles (or three if the branching instruction was not part of a pair). And so there is usually an inherent cost of four cycles involved in exiting from a loop. A branch that alternates on every pass between being taken and not being taken may be predicted correctly either half the time or not at all, depending on its initial branch history. If the branch is *ever* predicted correctly, it will continue to be predicted correctly half the time. If it is *never* predicted correctly, it will stay that way.

# The Instruction Set

Whereas the big deal with the 486 instruction set was the variety of one-cycle instructions that could get things done rapidly, on the Pentium, most of those instructions—plus a few more—are not only a single cycle but pairable as well, effectively making them *half-cycle* instructions.

Based on my own timings, Table 5-2 shows a breakdown of the instruction set from fastest instructions to slowest (except floating-point instructions). Instructions marked in boldface are those that I subjectively judge to be common candidates for application code inner loops. The table is very abbreviated and does not explicitly list all variations of all instructions, but you can figure them out using these rules, which are very similar to the corresponding 486 rules:

- Unless otherwise noted, instructions are referred to by their simplest form. That is, `add` refers to register-to-register forms of the `add` instruction, such as `add edx,esi`. If an instruction or group of instructions spaced closely together is followed by a note in parentheses, that note pertains to the preceding instruction or group.

- Add one cycle for an extra memory fetch. For instance, `add ecx,memvar` would take the basic one cycle, plus one cycle for the memory fetch, for a total of two cycles.

- Add one cycle for an extra memory store. For instance, `inc memvar` would take the basic one cycle, plus one cycle to fetch the original value from memory, plus one cycle to write it back to memory, for a total of three cycles.

- Add one cycle for performing a 16-bit operation, except in the case of segment register transfers. Thus `adc ax,bx` takes a basic one cycle, plus another one cycle for being 16-bit, for a total of two cycles.

- Where instructions don't obey the preceding rules (for instance, some of the shift operations do not), the various forms are explicitly listed in the table.

Two things that cost extra cycles on the 486 but no longer do so on the Pentium are address formation using two registers (or a multiplied register), and the use of a displacement and an immediate value in the same instruction. The latter prevents pairing on the Pentium, so it represents something like a half-cycle loss instead of a full-cycle loss.

As an exercise in *inefficient* instruction coding, here's how slow an instruction with a base cycle count of 1 can get:

| | | |
|---|---|---|
| 1 cycle: | add | eax,ebx |
| 2 cycles: | add | eax,memvar32 |
| 3 cycles: | add | memvar32,eax |
| 4 cycles: | add | memvar16,ax |

As with the 486, the fastest code tends to run in registers, reference memory sparingly, and avoid 16-bit values.

| Table 5-2    Pentium Instruction Timings Sorted by Speed | |
|---|---|
| half-cycle<br>1st or 2nd<br>position | **add sub and or xor cmp test** (except immed)<br>**dec inc lea mov pop push nop** |
| half-cycle<br>1st position | **adc sbb sar shl shr sal**<br>**rcl rcr rol ror** (reg, 1 form) |
| half-cycle<br>2nd position | **call** (near) **jmp** (near)<br>**jcc** (conditional branch, taken or not) |

| Table 5-2 (continued) | Pentium Instruction Timings Sorted by Speed |
|---|---|
| 1 cycle | **neg not rol ror** (immed) **test** (immed)<br>**rep movs** (time to move one item)<br>push (cs ds es ss) |
| 2 cycles | **jmp** (near reg, mem) **call** (near reg, mem)<br>**retn setCC** (conditionally set register)<br>clc cld cmc stc std cdq lahf sahf lods<br>bswap mov (reg, segreg) push (mem, fs, gs)<br>xchg (exchange reg with eax) |
| 3 cycles | **setCC** (conditionally set memory byte)<br>**retn** (immed)<br>aaa aas daa das cwd cwde jmp (far)<br>leave mov (segreg, reg except ss)<br>pop (mem, ds, es) pushfd stos<br>xchg (reg,reg)<br>rep lods (time to load one item) |
| 4 cycles | **rol ror sar sal shr shl** (by cl)<br>**repe cmps** (time to compare one pair)<br>**repe scas** (time to scan one item)<br>call (far) cbw into movs<br>movsx movzx (reg or mem) pop (fs, gs)<br>popfd pushf retf scas xlat<br>xadd (reg,reg) |
| 4.5 cycles | **rep stos** (time to store one item) |
| 5 cycles | **shld shrd** (reg by immed or cl)<br>**rep stos** (startup overhead)<br>rol ror sar sal shr shl (mem by cl)<br>bt (reg,reg reg,immed mem,immed)<br>cmps jecxz (not taken) popa popad popf<br>loop (taken) retf (immed) xadd (mem,reg) |
| 6 cycles | shld shrd (mem by immed or cl)<br>jecxz (taken) loop (branch not taken)<br>cmpxchg (no exchange) |
| 7 cycles | rcl rcr (reg by cl) cli bsf (7-43)<br>jcxz (taken) loopz loopnz (branch taken)<br>bound cmpxchg (exchange) |
| 8 cycles | rcl rcr (reg, immed) pop (ss) rdtsc<br>bsr (8-73) btc btr bts (reg,reg or immed)<br>loopz loopnz (branch not taken)<br>rep lods (startup overhead) |

| Table 5-2 (continued)    Pentium Instruction Timings Sorted by Speed | |
|---|---|
| 9 cycles | **mul** (reg32 or mem32)<br>**imul** (eax by reg32 or mem32; or mem32,immed;<br>reg32,reg32/mem32,immed)<br>**repe cmps** (startup overhead)<br>rcl rcr (mem,cl) mov (ss,reg) sti<br>btc btr bts (mem,immed) lock |
| 10 cycles | **imul** (reg32, reg32 or mem32)<br>**repe scas** (startup overhead)<br>rcl rcr (mem,immed) aad bt (mem,reg) |
| 11 cycles | **mul** (al by reg8 or mem8)<br>**imul** (al by reg8 or mem8)<br>enter (immed,0) xchg (reg,mem) |
| 13 cycles | **rep movs** (startup overhead) |
| 14 cycles | cpuid |
| 15 cycles | btc btr bts (mem,reg) |
| 17 cycles | **div** (ax by reg8 or mem8)<br>enter (immed,1) |
| 18 cycles | aam |
| 22 cycles | **idiv** (ax by reg8 or mem8) |
| 26 cycles | **div** (dx:ax by reg16 or mem16)<br>pusha pushad |
| 31 cycles | **idiv** (dx:ax by reg16 or mem16) |
| 41 cycles | **div** (edx:eax by reg32 or mem32) |
| 46 cycles | **idiv** (edx:eax by reg32 or mem32) |
| 66 cycles | **in** (al,dx) |
| 90 cycles | **out** (dx,al) |

One of the biggest changes from 486 timing is that correctly predicted branches execute, often paired, in a single cycle. This greatly increases the efficiency of small loops on the Pentium relative to the 486. A paradox occurs, though, if you ever construct what you think is a one-cycle loop like this:

```
.repeat         ;  ;
  dec   ecx     ; 1;count down
.until ZERO?    ; 0;branches back to the decrement
                ;;;;1 cycle predicted, 5 actual
```

This completely fools the prediction and fetch-ahead system, taking five cycles as if it were being perpetually mispredicted.

As with the 486, all instructions that start with an initial byte of 0fH (except conditional branches) generally take one cycle longer to execute than most published sources would indicate, because of the Intel fine print that regards 0fH as a prefix byte. These include `bswap`, `setCC`, `shld`, `shrd`, `movsx`, and `movzx`.

# New Instructions

There are two particularly important new instructions introduced with the Pentium, one for identifying the processor generation that's running the code, and the other (not very officially sanctioned for general use) for doing precise timings.

### rdtsc

There is a great new operation in the Pentium instruction set, `rdtsc`, that Intel has barely documented at all and that does not belong to the main instruction set that Intel will necessarily support on future processors. This instruction reads a 64-bit clock cycle count, which counts Pentium clock cycles since power-up, and puts the low 32 bits in `eax` and the high 32 bits in `edx`. It's excellent for doing fine timing in one pass through sections of code. It was used to perform most of the timings for this chapter.

If you have an assembler that doesn't support this instruction, you can use this macro instead:

```
rdtsc   macro
        db      0fH, 31H
        endm
```

One of the interesting findings one gets using this timer is that a stray cycle can hit any patch of code once in a while. Even `nop`, once in a very long time, will appear to take two cycles instead of one.

### cpuid

Another new instruction is the `cpuid` operation, which yields identifying information about the processor. Unfortunately, all processors prior to the Pentium lack this instruction, so it's necessary to first figure out that you're not running on a 386 or a 486 before issuing this instruction. An example of code that uses `cpuid` after first checking for earlier processor generations can be found in the source code for the CH486.EXE program that accompanied the previous chapter.

# Notable Instruction Timings

On the Pentium, instruction pairing is an important aspect of effective execution speed. Marked changes in instruction performance from the 486 to the Pentium are also worth noting, as they can markedly affect cross-processor code performance.

### rol and ror

The fastest way to swap the high and low halves of a 32-bit register is the one-cycle instruction `rol reg,16` (or `ror reg,16`). Contrary to what is stated in most documentation, this instruction behaves as a *nonpairable* instruction. It is a common candidate for tight inner loops, but without pairing it takes twice the effective time of a paired instruction. The closely related shift-by-immediate instructions, however, do pair, as do the one-bit rotations `rol reg,1` and `ror reg,1`.

### test

Another unfortunately nonpairable instruction is the "test immediate" instruction. The `test` instruction is just an `and` instruction that doesn't write out register results. Yet `and bl,3` is pairable, while `test bl,3` is not. (As an important exception to the rule, though, testing `al`, `ah`, `ax`, or `eax` *is* pairable.) This is just another little timing glitch to keep in mind when optimizing.

The `test` instruction also has increased importance on the Pentium for deciding whether or not a register is zero. Although both `and reg,reg` and `or reg,reg` can preserve a register while setting the Z flag state, using `test reg,reg` to do the same thing does not give the processor the impression that the register has been modified. This is often important in preventing processor stalls.

### Shifts and Rotations

On the 486, the `shift/rotate reg,immediate` instructions take two cycles, and `shift/rotate reg,cl` (shifting or rotating based on a counter in the `cl` register) takes three cycles. There is a modest speed difference between the two forms.

On the Pentium, `shift/rotate reg,immediate` drops to one cycle (or half a cycle if you are using a paired shift instruction), and `shift/rotate reg,cl` increases to four cycles. The speed difference between the two forms goes from 1.5:1 on the 486 to somewhere in the range 4:1 to 8:1 on the Pentium. Although I can't point to an individual algorithm that I chose to code differently on the Pentium than on the 486 (omitting, say, a shift by `cl`), I suspect the dramatic speed difference between the two forms has changed my selection of algorithms away from runtime-calculated shifts. Sometimes there is no substitute for a shift through `cl`, but the fact that it takes as much time to execute as eight paired instructions is a big incentive to find another way to get the same thing done.

Likewise, `shld` and `shrd`, at five cycles, are much slower than on the 486, even when shifted by an immediate amount. In fact, they're slow enough when shifted by an immediate amount to potentially justify a workaround using fast pairable instructions, as per the following:

```
shld    eax,ebx,27   ; 5;shift ebx bits into eax
shl     ebx,27       ; 1;prepare ebx for next shift
                     ;;;;6 cycles
```

This common instruction pair can be replaced with

```
shl     eax,27       ; 1;pairable slot open
rol     ebx,27       ; 1;not pairable
xor     eax,ebx      ; 1;pairable slot open
and     eax,not ((1 shl 27) - 1) ; 1;pairable open
xor     eax,ebx      ; 1;pairable slot open
and     ebx,not ((1 shl 27) - 1) ; 1;optional, pairable
                     ;;;;6 cycles with slots open
```

## mul and imul

When multiplying 32-bit quantities using either the `mul` or some forms of the `imul` instruction, the Pentium runs one cycle faster than book speed, at nine cycles per multiplication instead of ten. It's not an earthshaking increase in speed, but it's a pleasant surprise nonetheless.

## setCC

The `setCC` instruction, as on the 486, is a good way to set a byte to either 0 or 1, based on the condition of the processor flags, *without* branching. Since a fairly unpredictable branch costs approximately a two-cycle penalty on average (plus the original branch cycle), the `setCC` instruction can be faster in cases like the following:

```
mov     dl,0         ; 1;zero a flag register
.if CARRY?           ; 2;unpredictable branch
  mov   dl,1         ; 1;overwrite with 1
.endif               ;  ;
                     ;;;;3.5 cycles on average
```

The equivalent operation can be done with

```
setc    dl           ; 2;do it without branching
                     ;;;;2 cycles
```

With a more predictable branch condition, the former code might run faster.

# Instructions That Are Much Slower Than Their Book Value

Four of the six instructions that usually run slower than their book value on the 486 also do so on the Pentium, and for the same reasons.

### in and out

First, in and out, the port I/O operations, usually take much longer than their minimal book times of four and nine cycles in protected mode with high privileges. These operations take closer to 66 and 90 cycles, respectively (or potentially much more), when they have to essentially handshake with external hardware like the timer chip registers I tested them on. In another, more general way of looking at it, port I/O may cost somewhere in the ballpark of 0.5 to 1 microsecond, regardless of processor speed. This is not to say, though, that faster operations aren't possible. Consider port operations to be potentially quite variable in duration, depending on what's on the other end.

### lock

Second, lock, the bus-locking command that ensures, for instance, that no other processor or device can see a certain piece of data while you are modifying it, has to assert its authority on an external bus—and generally takes longer than the one cycle listed to do it. In my tests it took nine cycles.

### xchg

Closely related to the lock instruction timing is the anomaly of the xchg reg,mem timing. It turns out that when exchanging a register with memory, the Pentium, like the 486, *always* locks the bus, even if you don't ask for it. It measures in at 11 cycles, and it should generally be avoided in fast code.

### pusha and pushad

These two instructions used to clog the output queue on the 486, and they operated substantially slower than their book value. The Pentium uses a different caching strategy, depositing writes only to primary cache when possible, not directly to main memory. As a result, these instructions do operate at five cycles when pushing registers into a cached stack.

## The `rep` Instructions

In Table 5-3, there are two entries for each `rep` instruction. One entry gives the "overhead time" to get such an instruction started, and the other gives the time for each additional item (`byte`, `word`, or `dword`) processed. The table summarizes the results.

| Table 5-3 String Instruction Timings on the Pentium | | |
| --- | --- | --- |
| | *Startup Cycles* | *Cycles Per Item* |
| repe cmps | 9 | 4.0 |
| rep lods | 8 | 3.0 |
| rep movs | 13 | 1.1 |
| repe scas | 10 | 4.0 |
| rep stos | 5 | 4.5 |

These instructions are useful for processing large blocks of data all at once, but it's possible to write software loops that run faster than all of them (except the `rep movs` instruction when it's transferring memory from primary cache to primary cache). But they're great for the convenience. The large start-up times make these instructions particularly inefficient if you're only processing about half a dozen or less items. If you know you're going to copy one longword, spending 14 cycles on `rep movsd` makes much less sense than performing two moves in two (pairable) cycles.

## Floating-Point Instructions

The floating-point unit is respectably fast on the Pentium. Nevertheless, there is a major bottleneck that impedes its use in time-critical code—the amount of time it takes to get data into and out of the floating-point registers. Remember, internally the floating-point system operates as a stack of up to eight floating-point numbers, and it takes a significant amount of time, usually, to put data on the stack or remove it to memory. There are no instructions that transfer numbers between the Pentium's integer registers and the floating-point stack, so memory mediates between the two.

An integer operation that reads memory, such as `add eax,mem`, costs an extra cycle over an equivalent operation, such as `add eax,edx`, that does not. But the floating-point unit generally imposes no penalty when fetching a floating-point operand from memory as part of an arithmetic operation. In fact, sometimes it actually *saves* cycles when an operand comes from memory. For instance, here is how `var3 = var1 * var2` could be calculated:

```
fld     var1    ; 1;load var1 onto the stack
fmul    var2    ; 3;load and multiply times var2
fstp    var3    ; 3;store to var3
                ;;;;7 cycles total
                ;;;;vars are all 32-bit floats
```

Note that for a simple multiplication calculation, loading and storing represents half the total time spent (even more, by percentage, than on the 486, thanks to extremely fast multiplication), even with var2 getting a free ride into the floating-point unit.

And as with the 486, another big source of cycle loss is in converting between integer and floating-point formats. The conversions are far from free, and it's not uncommon to want integers as inputs and outputs for a function but to want floating-point calculations in between.

## Floating-Point Unit Loading and Storing

Table 5-4 shows the number of cycles required to load and store numbers to and from the floating-point stack in six different formats, three each of integer and floating-point. Two numbers separated by a forward slash represent, first, the maximum execution time if no other instructions overlap, and second, the minimum execution time if maximum overlap is achieved. For instance, loading a 16-bit integer with the fild instruction would cost three cycles if the very next instruction used the loaded value as an operand, but only one cycle if the next instruction didn't use it and burned up at least two cycles doing something else.

There is also a one-cycle delay between the time a floating-point value is ready for further computation (for example, the end of a three-cycle addition or multiplication) and the time it can be stored to external memory. So computations in a hurry for their results often pay three, not two, cycles for storage of the common floating-point forms.

| Table 5-4 Floating-Point Unit Load and Store Times | | | | | | |
|---|---|---|---|---|---|---|
| Instructions | 16-bit integer | 32-bit integer | 64-bit integer | 32-bit float | 64-bit float | 80-bit float |
| fld / fild | 3/1 | 3/1 | 3/1 | 1 | 1 | 3 |
| fst / fist | 6 | 6 | 6 | 2 | 2 | 3 |

Loading or storing an integer is about three times as expensive as loading or storing a floating-point number.

## Floating-Point Addition and Subtraction

You can issue a floating-point addition or subtraction operation on every cycle, but the results of the operation can't be used until three cycles have gone by (3/1 timing). Other instructions may proceed on the cycle after the add or subtract instruction is issued.

## Floating-Point Multiplication

Floating-point multiplication has the same timing parameters as floating-point addition and subtraction (1 cycle to issue, but 3 cycles before the results can be used—3/1 timing), except that multiplications are pipelined 2 cycles apart, meaning that in 100 cycles you can perform at most 50 multiplications.

## Floating-Point Division

Without reducing the floating-point unit's arithmetic precision, there is one main speed for division—39 cycles. This is a long, long time. In fact, it's long enough to perform about 39 additions or 19 multiplications, pipelined. But if you're willing to command the floating-point unit to operate below its default precision of full 80-bit values, you can get additional speed. Operating at 64-bit precision, it drops 6 cycles, to 33. (This precision is commonly used in programming environments such as Watcom's.) And at 32-bit floating-point precision, it drops all the way to 19 cycles. It only costs one cycle to issue a division, but it seems that at most one multiplication or addition may be issued in parallel with it. But you can generally perform ordinary Pentium integer operations other than multiplication and division in parallel with the division.

## Floating-Point Precision Control

The `fldcw` instruction loads the floating-point unit's control word, and it fortunately takes only two cycles. So if you want to operate the floating-point unit at the highest possible precision except for an occasional floating-point division, it only costs four cycles to change the precision before and after the division; this can still give a net 16-cycle gain on the division, despite the two precision changes.

## Floating-Point Flags

Branching based on floating-point flag settings is somewhat slower than branching off flags in the integer unit. About three cycles is the best you can usually do, as per this example:

```
fnstsw   ax        ; 2;store FP flags in ax
and      ah,41H    ; 1;test Z, C
jz       founda    ; 0;branch statement, ja equivalent
                   ;;;;3-cycle branch test
```

### The `fxch` Instruction

The `fxch` instruction, which exchanges the value at the top of the floating-point stack with another value in the stack, is the only instruction that can actually pair with another floating-point instruction (as the second of two floating-point instructions). In fact, it can only pair with some of the more common floating-point operations (specifically, `fld` [except with 80-bit form], `fadd`, `fsub`, `fmul`, `fdiv`, `fcom`, `fucom`, `ftst`, `fabs`, and `fch`) and it must also be followed by another floating-point operation for the parallelism to take effect.

Since most floating-point operations take the value on the top of the stack as an operand, the `fxch` instruction can allow the processor to operate, instead, on values from anywhere in the stack, without costing any extra cycles. The main practical difficulty, though, when coding floating-point sequences by hand is remembering what's been swapped to where.

In the code that follows, for instance, a constant value `st(3)`, is added to each of the top three stack values, taking only three cycles but permuting the order of the top three items on the stack in the process.

```
fadd    st,st(3)    ; 1;original stack order 0,1,2
fxch    st(1)       ; 0;new stack value order 1,0,2
fadd    st,st(3)    ; 1;
fxch    st(2)       ; 0;new stack value order 2,0,1
fadd    st,st(3)    ; 1;permuted stack order 2,0,1
                    ;;;;3 cycles (+ 2 to complete fadd)
```

# The Cache

The organization of cache memory on the Pentium is similar to that on the 486, but there are also some major differences. The first difference is that code and data have their own separate 8K caches. This means that inner loops are even more likely to stay in cache, and the data cache can be even more predictably devoted to data.

The second difference is that the data cache is "write-back" instead of "write-through." This means that if the processor writes to a location that is already in cache, it doesn't have to also write another copy to main memory. This helps keep the Pentium's output buffer from filling up and slowing down the processor.

The third difference is that both Pentium caches are organized as 128 pairs of 32-byte cache lines instead of 128 sets of four 16-byte cache lines. Most of the time, this organizational difference is transparent to the execution of the code. You can often service 8K of cached data just as well with the one scenario as with the other. (See the explanation in Chapter 4 of how cache lines are organized and work.)

As with the 486, a good way to understand how the 8K primary data cache memory on board the Pentium chip works is to look at a piece of code that defeats it. The idea behind cache memory is to keep recently referenced areas of memory in a high-speed, easy access state so that the processor can get to it in a one-cycle fetch. But there's a Pentium cache paradox. This code runs fast:

```
.repeat                      ;  ;
  mov    eax,[esi+0000H]     ; 1;
  mov    ebx,[esi+1004H]     ; 0;
  mov    eax,[esi+2020H]     ; 1;
  dec    ecx                 ; 0;
.until ZERO?                 ; 1;
                             ;;;;3 cycles measured
```

But this code runs over forty times slower!

```
.repeat                      ;  ;
  mov    eax,[esi+0000H]     ;42;
  mov    eax,[esi+1004H]     ;42;
  mov    eax,[esi+2000H]     ;42;
  dec    ecx                 ; 0;
.until ZERO?                 ; 1;
                             ;;;;127 cycles measured
```

On the 486, the equivalent paradox requires five read instructions, but here it takes only three. The difference is that the 486 is four-way set-associative, while the Pentium is only two-way set-associative.

## The Two-Way Principle

In technical jargon, the 8K data and code cache memory on board the Pentium is referred to as two-way set-associative with a cache line length of 32 bytes. The part about a cache line length of 32 bytes just means that the 8K of cache is broken up into 256 separate 32-byte pieces. Any time you read memory, the Pentium first checks to see if one of these 256 chunks has a copy of what you're looking for; if so, it returns it in just one cycle. Each 32-byte cache chunk is a copy of some 32-byte chunk of main memory, starting at an even 32-byte boundary (the low five bits of the address being zero).

If the memory read can't be satisfied by the cache, then the Pentium picks one of the 256 chunks to be sacrificed, throws out its contents (after first writing the contents back to main memory, possibly, if the cache line has been modified since it was read in), and loads it up with the 32-byte zone around the latest read operation.

This way, if the processor wants to read the same spot again, or another spot nearby, it will have one-cycle access. Everything works fine as long as the cache line that got tossed out is not likely to be needed again anytime soon.

This is where the two-way principle comes in. It turns out that the 256 separate 32-byte cache lines are actually organized as 128 pairs of 32-byte cache lines. For any given memory address, there are exactly two physical cache lines (the pair) that could possibly be used to hold it. The rule is that memory addresses that contend for the same pair of two cache lines are multiples of 4,096 bytes apart. So reading [esi+100H] will never, ever kick [esi+200H] out of cache. But it might kick [esi+834100H] out (since the two are a multiple of 1000H apart). It could also kick [esi+311fH] out, because 311fH falls on the same 32-byte chunk as 3100H (assuming esi is 32-byte aligned). So for any given pair of cache lines, there may be literally thousands of locations in memory that would map into them. The Pentium uses a "least recently used" algorithm to decide which of the two to reuse when a new memory area is read. It kicks out the chunk that hasn't been read or written for the longest time and reuses it for the new data.

The explanation for the code paradox given earlier in this section is as follows: In one case the loop was reading both cache lines in succession from one pair and then performing the third read on another group. Nobody got kicked out of cache. But in the other case, by reading three locations contending for the same two cache lines, the least recently used algorithm was always kicking data out of cache just before it had to be read back in again. In effect, cache was totally defeated.

## Avoiding the Two-Way Trap

Here's an example of how easy it is to get burned by the two-way set associative architecture. The example routine shown in Listing 5-1 is very likely to "thrash the cache," much the way the earlier example code did. You can imagine that it uses a mask buffer to apply a graphic object from another buffer onto a background given in yet another buffer. In graphics applications such scenarios are not uncommon, and buffer sizes in multiples of 64K are not uncommon either.

The way the buffers are declared in C, they will most likely be aligned one after another at 64K intervals through memory (a multiple of 4,096 or 4K, the magic cache line pair spacing!). With every iteration of the loop, all three buffers get read, each at exactly the same offset. This code will probably run very slow as a result, because at least two, and possibly three, cache line fills will have to take place on every pass through the loop. (Note, though, that even without alignment problems, you would expect to read in new cache lines on every eighth iteration as you pass from one cache line pair's domain to another.) Problems like this are less common on the 486, because it requires an equivalent five-buffer operation to produce the same paradox.

**Listing 5-1    A Pentium Cache-Thrashing Routine**

```
unsigned long objectbuf[0x4000];
unsigned long maskbuf[0x4000];
unsigned long picturebuf[0x4000];

void
ApplyObject()
{
    int n;

    for (n = 0; n < 0x4000; n++)
        picturebuf[n] = (picturebuf[n] & ~maskbuf[n]) |
                        (objectbuf[n] & maskbuf[n]);
}
```

This problem can be avoided by ensuring that at least one of the three buffers is slightly offset from the multiple-of-4,096 spacing. Perhaps the easiest way to convince the compiler to do so would be to declare 0x4008 elements in each array, just never making use of the last 32 bytes (eight longwords) that are just there for spacing.

## A Cache Write-Back Paradox

If the Pentium tries to write to memory and finds that there is no cache line available to write to, it writes to main memory by depositing the write request in the output queue going to main memory. If the output queue gets backed up, the Pentium stalls momentarily. So if you ever have a tight loop that repeatedly writes a memory location without reading it (as in keeping an old pointer in case you need to back up and use it due to an error condition), it might actually run faster if, just once at the very beginning, you read that write location. That will force it into the cache, where it can be written directly, without taking the chance of stalling on an output to memory.

## The Eight Parallel Paths into Data Cache Memory

You might have wondered how it is possible for two instructions that access memory to pair up and execute in a single cycle without competing for the bus to memory. The answer is that there are actually eight 32-bit buses connecting the processor's registers to cache memory. When two memory transfers are issued simultaneously, they can both complete in just one cycle, if and only if they don't happen to need to use the same bus into the cache.

There is an elegant correspondence between the size of 32-byte cache lines and the organization of the eight 32-bit (4-byte) buses available for memory transfer. As it turns out, one of the buses communicates only with the lowest 4 bytes of any and all cache lines. Another services the next 4 bytes, and so on. So it's the position of data within the eight 4-byte zones of a 32-byte cache line that determines which of the eight buses will be used for a transfer.

Another way of looking at things is that two transfers to and/or from memory can execute simultaneously, if and only if bits 2 through 4 of the two addresses are not the same. The following two instructions can execute simultaneously:

```
mov     al,[esi]     ; 1;read a byte
mov     bl,[esi+7]   ; 0;use a different bus
```

The following two instructions, with addresses pointing a multiple of 32 bytes apart, cannot execute simultaneously (although, technically speaking, they do pair and subsequently stall on bus contention):

```
mov     al,[esi]      ; 1;read a byte
mov     bl,[esi+96]   ; 1;hit a memory bus stall
```

And if esi is longword-aligned, even the following stalls:

```
mov     al,[esi]      ; 1;read a byte
mov     bl,[esi+3]    ; 1;stall on the same bus
```

If all memory references were random, you would expect paired memory references to stall only about one-eighth of the time. But memory references are rarely random, and predictable bus stalls, thanks to multiple-of-32 spacings and data items packed in the same longword, are not uncommon.

## Cache Miss Delays

When the Pentium tries to read a value from memory and can't find it in the cache, it tosses out an existing cache line of 32 bytes (possibly involving writing it back to memory) and reads in a new one. If there is a secondary cache on the machine, there is a good chance the refill will come from there. On the test machine, a simple cache miss like this usually caused a six-cycle delay. But the process of reading in a cache line in its entirety seemed to take about 13 cycles. In other words, you could read the first value from a cache line in seven cycles (1 + 6), but any subsequent reads from the same cache line had to wait about another seven cycles before they could execute. For this reason, it actually pays, sometimes, to plan code that references new cache lines just once and then does other productive things for a few cycles before reading anything else from the cache line.

There is some pipelining involved in the filling of cache lines, and so it's possible to initiate a new cache line fill about every 9 cycles, even though the complete filling process takes about 13.

Also, on the test machine, if you didn't hit either primary or secondary cache and therefore had to fill up from main memory, the delay was about 16 cycles for the first value read and an additional 12 cycles before a second read could be made on the same cache line.

The Pentium keeps an internal quick reference list of 4K physical memory pages that it knows how to address quickly. It's called a page table cache, and if your program throws out a reference to an address that isn't on one of those pages, the processor has to go out to tables in memory to find it. This may cause a delay of up to about 48 cycles, followed by another 12 for the remainder of the line to become available.

In my tests with Watcom C and the DOS4GW DOS extender—which may have different properties than other 32-bit environments—the Pentium's page table cache behaved as if it was holding information on 48 data pages (4K each) at one time. This may be an implementation-specific number, as specs on the Pentium indicate that more entries are available. There also seemed to be a savings if a new 4K page reference fell within a 32K zone that included another known page. This may be a system-specific feature of the test hardware. Table 5-5 shows the chart I use when estimating cache miss delays. It's possible to have a value in the secondary cache, and even one in the primary cache, without having a valid entry for it in the page table cache. Even though this is a slightly unusual situation, it also has its own timing characteristics, as shown in the table.

As an example of how to use the table, if you expect a given instruction to miss both the primary and the secondary cache but to land on a known page, you could expect these timings:

```
        mov     al,[esi]    ;17;initial hit costs 17
        mov     cl,bl       ; 0;this pairs, no penalty

    or

        mov     al,[esi]    ;17;initial hit costs 17
        mov     bl,[esi+4]  ;12;second hit takes penalty

    or

        mov     al,[esi]    ;17;initial hit costs 17
        mov     cl,bl       ; 0;this pairs, no penalty
        clc                 ; 2;do something else
        mov     bl,[esi+4]  ; 9;hit remainder of the delay
```

| Table 5-5 | Cache Miss Delay Times | | | | |
|---|---|---|---|---|---|
| 1st ref. cost | 2nd ref. delay | Found in primary cache | Found in secondary cache | Found in 32K zone | Found in page tables |
| 1 | 0 | Yes | Yes | Yes | Yes |
| 7 | 7 | No | Yes | Yes | Yes |
| 17 | 12 | No | No | Yes | Yes |
| 48 | 12 | No | No | No | No |
| 21 | 0 | Yes | Yes | Yes | No |
| 27 | 8 | No | Yes | Yes | No |
| 36 | 12 | No | No | Yes | No |

These timings may seem arcane, but knowing how to take advantage of the natural availability times of cache lines can sometimes make for measurable (if not always large) differences in performance.

# The Pentium Output Queue

Like the 486, the Pentium maintains a little FIFO (first in, first out) or queue of items that need to be written to memory. Since, on the Pentium, writes that hit cache don't go to main memory (unlike on the 486, which sends all writes to memory), there is often less of a bottleneck at this point on the Pentium. Any write that doesn't hit cache gets deposited in the queue for execution whenever the Pentium can get to it. Whereas the 486 keeps a single queue of four items, the Pentium keeps two queues of two items each, one for the "U pipe" (instructions executed solo or in the first pairing position) and one for the "V pipe" (instructions executed in the second pairing position).

It takes about four cycles to actually execute a write once it's put in the queue. So if an inner loop is expected to issue two noncached writes per iteration, it will be limited to about an eight-cycle loop, because that's as fast as the queue can be emptied. And if you ever have to dump four items to noncached memory in rapid succession as part of a larger loop (which, for argument's sake, takes over 16 cycles to execute anyhow), it pays to make sure that two are written from the U pipe (first position) and the other two are written from the V pipe (second position); otherwise, one of the pipe's queues will fill up and stall execution.

The `pusha` and `pushad` instructions may behave remarkably differently, from one invocation to the next, depending upon whether or not the stack area into which the registers are pushed is already in cache. If it *is* in cache, they take just the five book cycles they're supposed to take. Otherwise, they pile eight writes onto presumably just one queue (probably the U pipe's) and take 26 cycles. It could actually be faster, depending upon alignment, to read a 32-byte cache line in from the stack first and then execute the writes at top speed.

# Data and Code Alignment

As previously mentioned in connection with the 486, the assembly language `align` statement can work runtime wonders without ever being executed itself. It's used to push code or data into address locations where it can operate or be operated upon most efficiently. The statement `align 4` means "make the next data or code statement that follows this statement fall on an address that's evenly divisible by 4." Likewise, `align 16` means "head for a 16-byte boundary." Some things just work better aligned on special boundaries.

## Integer Alignment

The Pentium, although it has an external 64-bit bus, likes to address cache memory in 32-bit chunks, as per the eight 32-bit bus system. But it can only request 32-bit chunks that lie on 4-byte boundaries. If a word or longword crosses such a boundary, the processor has to issue two reads and then reconstruct the 16- or 32-bit value it was looking for from parts of both. As a result, it takes four cycles to read or write a value that crosses a 4-byte boundary, just as on the 486, instead of the usual one cycle. Listing 5-2 illustrates the use of the alignment statement and the effects of good and bad alignment.

### Listing 5-2   Aligned and Misaligned Reads

```
        align   4
var1    dd      1234
        db      0
var2    dd      5678
        .
        .
        .
        mov     eax,var1    ; 1;a 1-cycle aligned fetch
        mov     eax,var2    ; 4;a 4-cycle unaligned fetch
```

## Floating-Point Alignment

As one might expect, 32-bit floating-point values, like 32-bit integers, should seek out 4-byte boundaries or else experience three-cycle penalties per reference. The larger 64-bit floating-point values work fine on 8-byte boundaries. And the 10-byte, 80-bit floating-point form requires a 16-byte boundary to work efficiently. Loading a 64-bit floating-point value at any other alignment incurs a three-cycle penalty. Misaligning an 80-bit value costs a read penalty of at least six cycles, and this goes up to nine cycles if it's at a modulo-8-plus-7 address and is forced to span three quadwords.

## `rep movsd` Move Alignment

When moving large blocks of memory around with `rep movsd`, it is not always possible to longword-align both the source pointer and the destination pointer. For instance, you can't shift a block of memory by 23 bytes and have the source and destination pointers be multiples of 4 (because the difference between the pointers has to be 23, which is not a multiple of 4). In such cases, you have the choice of aligning either the source or the destination pointer, but not both. Things work better if you align the destination pointer. Even if you're just moving from cache to cache, there is a one-cycle-higher penalty per write operation than there is for misaligned reads. When the move destination is not in cache, the penalty gets even worse for a misaligned destination address, because the output queue apparently gets clogged with fragmentary write requests.

## Compiled Code Alignment

Compilers are usually pretty good about aligning global data on appropriate boundaries and local data on at least 4-byte boundaries on the stack. There are also structure alignment directives available to pad structures to meet alignment conditions.

## Code Alignment

The good news about Pentium code alignment is that, unlike on the 486, the alignment of branch destination addresses makes very little difference to execution speed. There is enough resilience and foresight built into the instruction prefetcher, which speculatively fetches past branches, that a branch to an instruction near the end of a cache line is not likely to cause a stall. Code that needs to run well on a 486 as well as a Pentium can be aligned with little penalty to the Pentium other than the increased bulk of the code.

# Cycle Thieves and Cycle Savers

If the 486 is occasionally guilty of producing unexpected loop timings, the Pentium is probably even more guilty. Write a 20-line loop and, as often as not, an idiosyncratic extra cycle may creep in due to instruction interactions unknown and perhaps unknowable. It's a very complex chip and can be forgiven the occasional timing glitch for all its other efficiencies. The Pentium still has forms of a couple of the timing idiosyncrasies that first appeared in the 486. Others have gone away.

## Address Generation Interlock (AGI)

On the 486, if you load a register on one cycle and use it to address memory on the next cycle, you incur a one-cycle delay. This rule is exactly the same for the Pentium, but there is a funny twist to it, due to pairing of instructions. The following code experiences an "address generation interlock" (that is, a one-cycle stall due to loading an address register and using it on the next cycle), even though there are two instructions between the load and the usage:

```
.repeat              ;  ;
  add    esi,4        ; 1;<- modify esi here
  mov    eax,ebx      ; 0;this is the same cycle
  shl    ebx,1        ; 1;this is the next cycle
  mov    [esi],eax    ; 1;<- AGI stall hits
  dec    ecx          ; 1;and loop
.until ZERO?          ; 0;
                      ;;;;4-cycle loop
```

In my experience, the most common challenge in writing Pentium code is in finding ways to put useful instructions in between a register load or modification and its subsequent use to address memory. In a context where all instructions are successfully paired for maximum efficiency, either two or three instructions (depending upon pairing alignment) must sit between the register load or modification and the addressing instruction just to prevent them from executing on back-to-back cycles.

The `esp` register has a special relationship to the AGI problem. When you `push` and `pop`, you're implicitly changing `esp`, which is being used for stack addressing. But these instructions don't experience AGIs if executed back to back. If, however, you do something like add esp, 8, a push or pop as the next instruction would experience the one-cycle delay.

## Partial Registers

On the 486, if you modify an 8- or 16-bit section of a 32-bit register, you can't execute an instruction that uses the contents of that 32-bit register on the next cycle. This particular delay is not there on the Pentium. But it's back in spades on the Pentium Pro, as explained in Chapter 6. Instead of a one-cycle delay, the Pentium Pro gets hit with a stall of at least seven cycles. So if you expect your code to migrate to the Pentium Pro, beware of this stall condition.

## A Few Cycles Saved

The Pentium takes advantage of essentially the same cycle savings, by instruction overlap, that the 486 does, as follows. Recall that there is a one-cycle penalty for operating on 16-bit values and a one-cycle-slower-than-book-value timing on instructions that start with the byte 0fH (bswap, setCC, shld, shrd, and so on). Thus, there are times when the extra cycle doesn't get charged. If the preceding instruction execution inherently takes more than one cycle or encounters its own stall condition, such as an AGI, the following instruction doesn't get charged the usual one-cycle penalty.

This code illustrates how a prefixed 16-bit instruction can benefit from an AGI stall:

```
        mov     ecx,ebx     ; 1;load ecx
        mov     edx,[ecx]   ; 2;an AGI stall
        mov     ax,bx       ; 1;no 16-bit penalty here
        add     ebx,4       ; 0;and it's even pairable!
```

## Instruction Stream Timing Oddities

There are two particularly odd things worth mentioning about the way a stream of Pentium instructions works. First, the nop instruction, which does nothing but burn up a pairable instruction slot, is often useful for speeding up code by forcing pairing patterns. And second, it's possible for minor shifts in the pairing sequence to have a major impact on performance.

Here's an example of a nop instruction that actually saves cycles. This loop runs in five cycles, due to an AGI stall:

```
.repeat                 ;   ;
    add     esi,4       ; 1;<- modify esi here
    mov     eax,ebx     ; 0;this is the same cycle
    shl     ebx,1       ; 1;this is the next cycle
    mov     [esi],eax   ; 1;<- AGI stall hits
    inc     ebx         ; 1;
    dec     ecx         ; 0;and loop
.until ZERO?            ; 1;
                        ;;;;5-cycle loop
```

The same loop with a judiciously inserted nop executes one cycle faster:

```
.repeat                 ;   ;
    add     esi,4       ; 1;<- modify esi here
    mov     eax,ebx     ; 0;this is the same cycle
    shl     ebx,1       ; 1;this is the next cycle
    nop                 ; 0;pairs and does nothing
    mov     [esi],eax   ; 1;no AGI stall this time
    inc     ebx         ; 0;this pairs
    dec     ecx         ; 1;and loop
.until ZERO?            ; 0;this
                        ;;;;4-cycle loop
```

As a rule of thumb, if an instruction that is scheduled to execute in the V pipe (second position of a pair) will cause an AGI delay, there is a good possibility (depending on the pairing of the code that follows) that if you delay its execution until the next cycle with a nop, you can actually gain a cycle. Unfortunately, though, the 486 will generally incur a one-cycle delay from the very nop that gives a one-cycle acceleration to the Pentium. In this case, you can't have it both ways.

The Pentium does know enough to not pair an instruction that writes a register with a following instruction that reads it, but it doesn't know not to pair instructions that are going to contend for the same bus into cache memory. As a result, a slight change in pairing sequence can make these bus delays appear and disappear. Here's a loop that experiences two delays due to contention for the same one-out-of-eight memory bus into cache:

```
.repeat                 ;   ;
    mov     eax,[esi]       ; 1;read a value
    mov     ebx,[esi+32]    ; 1;bus jam delay
    mov     [esi+16],eax    ; 1;write a value
    mov     [esi+48],ebx    ; 1;bus jam delay
```

```
    add    esi,4              ; 1;advance pointer
    dec    ecx                ; 0;this pairs
.until ZERO?                  ; 1;and loop
                              ;;;;6-cycle loop
```

All the instructions are pairable, so the Pentium just starts at the top of the loop and works its way down. But by shifting pairing positions by one instruction, the two bus contentions disappear:

```
.repeat                       ; ;
    nop                       ; 1;
    mov    eax,[esi]          ; 0;read a value
    mov    ebx,[esi+32]       ; 1;no bus jam delay
    mov    [esi+16],eax       ; 0;write a value
    mov    [esi+48],ebx       ; 1;no bus jam delay
    add    esi,4              ; 0;advance pointer
    dec    ecx                ; 1;this pairs
.until ZERO?                  ; 0;and loop
                              ;;;;4-cycle loop
```

If there were ten bus contention cycles in the loop, it could just as easily have been shortened by ten cycles in the same shift.

# Conclusion

The Pentium is a complex chip, and there are more simultaneous variables to work with when optimizing for the Pentium than there are for the 486. Optimal Pentium code is not necessarily the same as optimal 486 code, but there are instances in which one can try to appease both. The efficient use of single-cycle paired instructions—if you avoid stall conditions like AGIs and cache memory bus contention—is the answer to most coding problems. And with a Pentium, a good programmer can take performance where compilers dare not tread.

# References

Intel Corporation. 1993. *Pentium Processor User's Manual. Volume 3: Architecture and Programming Manual.* Santa Clara, Calif.: Intel Corporation.

Intel Corporation. October 1995. *Application Note AP-526, Optimizations For Intel's 32-Bit Processors.* Santa Clara, Calif.: Intel Corporation.

Oddly, the main Pentium programming manual from Intel has little information on pairing rules—which this chapter does cover—but covers the rest of the instruction set exhaustively. The application note covers both Pentium and Pentium Pro optimizations. As of this writing, it is available for free at Intel's Web site, www.intel.com.

# Optimizing the Pentium Pro

> *There is nothing more difficult to take in hand,*
> *more perilous to conduct, or more uncertain in its success,*
> *than to take the lead in the introduction of a new order of things.*
> —The Prince, *Machiavelli*

The Pentium Pro chip, first manufactured in late 1995, marks a radical architectural departure from its predecessors. In a nutshell, the Pentium Pro reads and guesses its way through the instruction stream, looking for opportunities to execute things out of the "natural" order in which they were written and trying to do its own, on-the-fly optimal instruction sequencing. As a result, it's not always easy to predict just how long a given piece of code will take to run, but the chances are good that it will run fast.

In this chapter we'll take a look at the various aspects of the Pentium Pro that affect execution speed and can help predict performance:

- Dynamic execution
- Micro-ops
- New instructions
- Instruction set timing
- The floating-point unit
- The cache
- Data and code alignment
- The partial register stall
- Branch prediction
- Optimization summary

**123**

Not all Pentium code runs well naturally on the Pentium Pro, but with a little bit of careful tuning, almost all Pentium code can run as well, or significantly better, on the Pentium Pro as on the Pentium.

# The CHPPRO.EXE Instruction Timing Program

On the CD-ROM accompanying this book are source code, executable code, and the results of two timing runs on a 200 MHz Pentium Pro system. It is basically the same program used to time the 486, adapted slightly for the Pentium Pro. The raw instruction timings it produces should be taken with a grain of salt because instruction timings on the Pentium Pro are very sensitive to the code context in which they are run. Thus some instructions appear to execute in no time flat, while others may even produce *negative* timings. Others exhibit the effects of odd stall conditions, especially an odd carry flag–related stall that appears to be the product of the artificiality of the test loop. It is not always easy to tell just what the numbers represent.

Most of the Pentium Pro–specific tests are in the stall condition report, which in fact contains more than just stall tests.

# Dynamic Execution

"Dynamic execution" is the phrase Intel coined to describe the workings of the Pentium Pro. It means, in effect, "you can't count cycles very well anymore, because instruction ordering is out of your direct control." This is not entirely bad, but it's disconcerting when the processor manual set makes literally no mention of instruction timings. Fortunately, though, Intel did publish the somewhat obscure *Application Note AP-526*, which does give some insights into the timing of things and which served as the basis for much of what is in this chapter.

The Pentium Pro is said to operate a 12-stage pipeline for instruction execution. This simply means that in any given processor cycle there may be a dozen separate processing steps taken on perhaps a dozen separate instructions at various phases of completion. The more stages there are in the "pipeline," the more net work can get done in a single cycle. Older processors have fewer stages in their pipelines and thus get correspondingly less work done per cycle. The downside to a long pipeline is that unpredictable branching tends to defeat it. For instance, the pipeline stage that fetches instructions for future execution needs to guess where the program will flow to at branch points—often several cycles before the branches are computed. If it guesses right, everything keeps flowing just fine. If it guesses wrong, it may take many cycles to get itself restarted on the right track. The Pentium Pro is designed to be superb at guessing branch destinations, so the pipeline usually flows along with few interruptions.

Partway through the pipeline, the Pentium Pro converts the assembly language instructions it receives into "micro-ops," which are the primitive units of execution that actually get things done. The bread-and-butter assembly language instructions (mov, add, inc, jCC, and so on) usually translate into a single micro-op, but others translate into two, three, four, or more. (And at least one does not translate into a micro-op at all, but instead affects register assignments.) These micro-ops are then set adrift, so to speak, in an execution pool, where they may be executed in a different order than that in which they entered. If a micro-op gets hung up waiting for a slow cache-missed piece of data to arrive, others, such as an unrelated register-to-register addition, can proceed.

Due to the legacy of its predecessors, the Pentium Pro is *very* short on general-purpose registers. Modern RISC processors generally have two to four times as many, or more. But hidden at the core of the Pentium Pro is a set of 40 general-purpose registers that it uses for executing its micro-ops. To see how the micro-ops can make use of these registers, consider the following code fragment:

```
mov     eax,[esi]      ;   ;pick up a value
inc     eax            ;   ;increment it
mov     [esi],eax      ;   ;store it
mov     eax,[esi+4]    ;   ;pick up another value
inc     eax            ;   ;increment it
mov     [esi+4],eax    ;   ;store it
```

In an ordinary processor, the last three instructions would have to wait for the first three to complete before starting their execution. But the Pentium Pro can figure out that the last three instructions don't have to be performed using literally the same **eax** register as the first three instructions. So it picks one of its 40 registers from the register pool and uses it for the last three instructions. This is known as register renaming, and it basically occurs every time a register is loaded or cleared to zero. Every time you load a fresh new value into a register, you can think of it as operating under a new logical identity. The code above, renamed, may look to the Pentium Pro like the following:

```
mov     eax1,[esi]     ;   ;pick up a value
inc     eax1           ;   ;increment it
mov     [esi],eax1     ;   ;store it
```

```
mov     eax2,[esi+4]  ;  ;pick up another value
inc     eax2          ;  ;increment it
mov     [esi+4],eax2  ;  ;store it
```

Note that the last three instructions may complete before the first three, although the Pentium Pro makes it a strict rule to perform writes to memory in the original order, so the write to memory in the sixth instruction remains pending until the write to memory in the third instruction completes.

The Pentium Pro even goes so far as to execute micro-ops before it is sure they represent the correct instructions past a branch. It won't write the results back to memory or to permanent register data until it is sure they are the correct instructions to be executed. If it executes the wrong micro-ops for a while, it just tosses them out and restarts with the correct ones. This is called speculative execution, and since branches are usually predicted correctly, it usually works well.

The Pentium Pro micro-ops get "retired" or "engraved in stone" in their original program order so that the illusion of in-order program execution is maintained, even though there was a very out-of-order middle phase that the code went through.

This, in brief, is what "dynamic execution" is about. It's about a processor that does its own instruction sequencing and guessing while maintaining the illusion that it is just executing instructions in linear sequence. To make clear the point that the programmer is no longer in firm control of loop execution speeds, consider the paradoxical timings of the loops shown in Listing 6-1. Sometimes it is actually possible to add instructions to a loop and see a net loss of cycles. This indicates that the dynamic execution scheduler may be doing some idiosyncratic, heuristic things, which don't always work out ideally.

## Listing 6-1   Paradoxical Loop Timings

```
.repeat         ;  ;this loop takes 7 cycles
  mul edx       ;  ;
  inc esi       ;  ;
  inc edi       ;  ;
  dec ebx       ;  ;
.until ZERO?    ;  ;

.repeat         ;  ;this loop takes 6 cycles
  mul edx       ;  ;despite the fact that it
  inc esi       ;  ;contains 2 more instructions
  inc edi       ;  ;than the 7-cycle loop
  inc esi       ;  ;
  inc edi       ;  ;
  dec ebx       ;  ;
.until ZERO?    ;  ;
```

# Micro-ops

The closest thing to countable cycles on the Pentium Pro are the countable micro-ops issued for each instruction. There are three significant points at which they can be counted:

- At creation
- At execution
- At destruction (retirement)

There are three parallel engines for creating micro-ops from assembly language instructions. Two of the engines can only handle simple assembly language instructions that translate to exactly one micro-op. The third engine handles all the more complex instructions—those that translate to multiple micro-ops. It can issue as many micro-ops as necessary and put out up to four of them in one cycle. Thus the translation from assembly language to micro-ops can proceed at three assembly language instructions per cycle, providing that two of the three are simple instructions and that the fourth requires no more than four micro-ops.

If complex instructions get bunched up together, the simple instruction translators go idle. So to prevent pipeline starvation, it's better to pattern code so that simple and complex instructions are mixed, whenever you are given the choice of mixing or not mixing. Any instruction involving a store to memory ranks as a complex instruction, so rapid sequences of stores are candidates for interleaving.

Micro-ops are retired, in order, at a constant rate of three per cycle, providing they are done and available for retirement. If the micro-op creation engines can keep cranking them out at an average of about three per cycle, the retirement unit can accept the final results at about the same rate. What's left is for the out-of-order processing in the middle to keep up.

Figure 6-1 shows the five parallel execution units in which micro-ops get executed. Although Intel documentation mentions the existence of a sixth, it consistently draws only these five boxes. In any event, these five units serve well enough to understand what's basically going on.

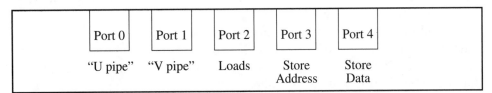

**Figure 6-1    The Five Micro-op Execution Units**

The twin execution units of the older Pentium processor, known as the U pipe and the V pipe, are still there inside the Pentium Pro, albeit in modified form. Just like in the Pentium, there are two execution units that are both capable of performing most simple instructions. The one known as Port 0, analogous to the U pipe, also handles floating-point instructions, shifts, and various other instructions not handled by the V pipe. Likewise, Port 1, analogous to the V pipe, handles conditional branching. All fetches from memory are implemented as orders to Port 2, the loading unit. And all writes to memory require two orders, one each to the store address and the store data ports.

These five micro-op execution units should be thought of as a parallel arsenal of tools that can, in a single cycle, perform one memory fetch, one memory store, and two computational operations. Because of the rate limit on micro-op retirement, you can only sustain an ongoing average of three micro-op operations per cycle, but that is a reasonable number to expect as long as the load and store traffic is not unusually high.

Consider the instruction `inc eax`. This is a simple instruction that translates into a micro-op that means "add 1 to `eax`." It can be sent to either Port 0 or Port 1 for execution. The instruction `adc eax,7` translates to two micro-ops that mean, roughly, "add carry to `eax`" and "add 7 to `eax`." Both of these instructions can execute in either pipe. Thus, at the micro-op level the `adc` instruction takes up more pipeline time than it does on the Pentium—a small loss amidst a larger win. The instruction `inc dword ptr [esi]` translates to a whopping four micro-op instructions: one to load the data, one to perform the increment, one to generate the store address, and one to deliver the data to be stored.

It may seem odd that there need be only one micro-op to load data but two to store it. But it makes sense when you think about the legacy of AGIs—the delay between calculating an address and actually using it to reference memory. When storing to memory, it makes sense to issue one instruction to calculate the address well in advance of the need for it, and another instruction to supply the data at a later time, if necessary, when the address has presumably advanced to execution stage. Since the data is always in a ready state for loading, only one instruction is needed for loads.

Because loads and stores can occur in parallel with computations, they can sometimes seem to be "free." But as a general rule, storing to memory is more likely to cause a slowdown than is reading from memory.

Not all micro-ops execute in a single cycle. Some, like division or a floating-point square root calculation, can tie up Port 0 (the U pipe) for dozens of cycles. But, unlike the Pentium in the case of integer division, Port 1 (the V pipe) can continue executing instructions all the while.

The Pentium Pro dynamically decides which instruction will execute on which port, and when. Micro-ops that get hung up waiting for data to arrive from a load operation may see others pass them by into the execution units, but sooner or later the data comes in and they get issued, and in the end it all works out as originally planned.

# New Instructions

There are three important new instructions on the Pentium Pro that speak directly to execution efficiency needs:

- cmovCC—conditional integer move
- fcmovCC—conditional floating-point move
- fcomi—floating-point comparison, directly into the EFLAGS register

The first instruction, cmovCC (where CC is a condition code, like ge, c, and so on), moves a word or longword from memory or a register into a given register, if and only if the particular condition code is true. This is a two-micro-op instruction, and it can save a lot of time over a branching situation if the condition code is difficult to predict and hence would cause major branching delays. Intel warns that this instruction may not be available on all flavors of the Pentium Pro and advises using the cpuid instruction to check for its presence.

The second instruction, fcmovCC, is the floating-point equivalent of cmovCC; it performs a replacement of the contents of the top of the floating-point stack, based on a condition code. As with the previous instruction, Intel does not promise to implement it on all Pentium Pros.

The third instruction, fcomi, and its variants finally provide a way to compare floating-point numbers and directly set the main flags register according to the results. It used to take a couple of extra instructions to communicate the flags. This instruction, unlike the previous two, appears to be a permanent instruction set addition across the Pentium Pro product line. It takes just one micro-op.

# Instruction Set Timing

There is no one right way to try to count cycles on the Pentium Pro. Micro-ops tell only part of the story. For instance, the `lods` instruction appears to be a nearly free way to load a register, but in actual tests it seems to cost a cycle more than an equivalent pair of load-and-increment instructions. I don't know why, but I suspect it's tied in with all the reasons that the `lods` instruction is inefficient on the 486 and the Pentium. As a general rule, if it's a bad idea to use it on the Pentium, don't trust it on the Pentium Pro without proof to the contrary.

Table 6-1 shows many, but not all, of the micro-op instruction timings as they relate to throughput through ports 0 and 1 (which I have dubbed the U pipe and the V pipe, respectively, due to their similarity to the pipes of the same name on the Pentium). Remember, any instruction requiring a load from memory has another micro-op issued to handle the load, and a store costs two extra micro-ops. Since loads and stores are sometimes free (done in parallel with computation), they are not explicitly shown in the accounting of Table 6-1. Nevertheless, they should be kept in mind as potential causes of slowdowns. Table 6-1 is provided to help predict performance when the rate-limiting factor is the speed of execution of the U and V pipes. For many well-sculpted inner loops, this may be the case.

| Table 6-1 Common Instruction-Timing Information | |
|---|---|
| "free" memory transfers: | `mov movzx movsx fld fst lods stos` |
| 1 half cycle, either pipe: | `add sub and or xor cmp test inc dec not neg`<br>`push pop mov movzx movsx (reg-to-reg) call`<br>`clc stc cmc lahf sahf bt setCC bswap nop`<br>`cbw cwde scas fldcw` |
| 1 half cycle, U pipe: | `shl shr sal sar rol ror lea btc btr bts`<br>`cwd cdq fcom fucom ftst fldz fld1 fnop`<br>`fabs ffree fincstp fdecstp fnstsw (to mem)`<br>`fld (STi)`<br>`fadd fsub`  (3-cycle wait for completion)<br>`fist fxam`  (3-cycle wait for completion)<br>`fldpi`  (3-cycle wait for completion)<br>`fldl2t`  (3-cycle wait for completion)<br>`fldl2e`  (3-cycle wait for completion)<br>`fldlg2`  (3-cycle wait for completion)<br>`fldln2`  (3-cycle wait for completion)<br>`imul`  (4-cycle wait for completion)<br>`fmul`  (5-cycle wait for completion) |

| Table 6-1 (continued) | Common Instruction-Timing Information |
|---|---|
| 1 half cycle, V pipe: | `jCC jmp` (near or reg) `aas daa das` |
| 2 half cycles, either pipe: | `adc sbb leave fwait` |
| 2 half cycles, at least 1 in U pipe: | `rcl rcr shld shrd cmovCC fld` (80-bit) `ffreep fcompp fucompp fchs fcmovCC` `fild` (3-cycle wait for completion) |
| 2 half cycles, at least 1 in V pipe: | `jcxz jecxz bsf bsr` |
| 3 half cycles, either pipe: | `xchg fnclex` |
| 3 half cycles, at least 1 in U pipe: | `fnstsw` (to ax) `int` `aad` (4-cycle wait for completion) `mul imul` (times ax or eax) (4-cycle wait) |
| 3 half cycles, at least 1 in V pipe: | `retn` |
| 4 half cycles, either pipe: | `cld std xadd xlat` |
| 18 cycles: | `fdiv` 32-bit |
| 20 cycles: | `div idiv` 8-bit |
| 23 cycles: | `div idiv` 16-bit |
| 29 cycles: | `fsqrt` 32-bit |
| 32 cycles: | `fdiv` 64-bit |
| 38 cycles: | `fdiv` 80-bit |
| 39 cycles: | `div idiv` 32-bit |
| 58 cycles: | `fsqrt` 64-bit |
| 69 cycles: | `fsqrt` 80-bit |

Instructions not shown in Table 6-1 may require more than four micro-ops. These instructions have not been further described by Intel. The instruction test runs given on the CD-ROM include nearly the entire instruction set, but the timings shown there should be interpreted cautiously, as timings can shift with the execution environment.

# Speedups

There are a number of instructions that run faster, cycle for cycle, on the Pentium Pro than on the Pentium.

## Memory References

The first that come to mind are loads and stores to and from memory. Sometimes they're practically free, especially the loads. On a Pentium, for instance, if you wrote a loop that repeatedly used a calculated bitmask to operate on a register, the masking operation would run faster this way:

```
and     ebx,edx       ;  ;mask ebx using edx
```

than this way:

```
and     ebx,[esp+12]  ;  ;mask ebx using memory
```

On the Pentium Pro, the two operations are likely to run at the same speed, because the memory fetch may get done in parallel with other operations. In fact, the latter code has the side benefit of freeing up a processor register. As a general rule, assembly language operations that have operands of the form reg,mem, in which a memory variable operates on a register, are often as efficient as the equivalent reg,reg forms.

If you repeatedly load a register with a constant value held in another register (as in mov eax,ebx), the code will probably run faster if you load the register from a memory location (as in mov eax,[esp+12]), since a register-to-register transfer takes one micro-op in the U or V pipe, but a load from memory takes none.

The floating-point operations fld and fst are likewise done in parallel with calculations. On the Pentium Pro, cache memory, in combination with register renaming, effectively extends the register space of the processor.

### movzx and movsx

The instructions movzx and movsx, which are only marginally efficient, if at all, on the 486 and the Pentium, appear to be fast and appropriate ways to sign- and zero-extend on the Pentium Pro.

## Calculated Shifts

Only slightly less spectacular than the free memory transfers, the calculated shift operations that use the cl register for a shift count seem to be genuinely fast now, about as fast as the shift-by-immediate operations. On the Pentium, operations like shl edx,cl took an exceedingly long four unpaired cycles. On the Pentium Pro, they appear to cost less than a cycle. And the double shifts, shld and shrd, are nearly as fast as well. This bodes well for bitstream operations like Huffman compression that use calculated shifts intensively.

## Multiplication

Integer multiplication is fast on the Pentium Pro. Although the multiplication instructions that have to use the `eax` register, or a portion of it, by default take about a cycle longer than those that don't, most integer multiplications complete in just four cycles. It generally takes just one micro-op in the U pipe to initiate a multiplication, after which the U pipe may continue executing other micro-ops while the mutiplication occurs in parallel. In principle, a multiplication instruction may be issued on every cycle. The only catch is that the processor may stall if it has to wait for multiplication results in order to proceed with calculations. The V pipe continues executing instructions all the while, of course. Effectively, integer multiplication on the Pentium Pro is about triple the speed of a Pentium, cycle for cycle.

## Division

The cycle counts for integer division are marginally faster than the Pentium's, and division operations essentially shut down the U pipe until they complete. But the saving grace of integer division on the Pentium is that the V pipe doesn't get shut down. You can crank literally dozens of micro-ops through the V pipe while the U pipe is executing one big divide. Of course, if a critical U pipe instruction, on which V pipe instructions depend, comes along during a division, it just has to wait. Planning loops with division operations mixed with a lot of nondependent potential V pipe operations is one of the more interesting challenges in programming for the Pentium Pro. (And then, of course, you hope the instruction scheduler sees things your way as well.)

## Prefixed Opcodes

It appears that prefixed opcodes—such as 16-bit instruction overrides, which usually cause a one-cycle stall on the Pentium—usually dissolve somewhere in the pipeline and don't often affect performance. This is not to say that 16-bit instructions are a particularly good idea on the Pentium Pro, but they do appear to be less harmful than on the Pentium.

# Slowdowns

A few things got relatively slower on the Pentium Pro.

### adc and sbb

On the Pentium, `adc` and `sbb` each take half a cycle in the U pipe. But when translated to micro-ops, they each take two operations, effectively a full cycle. It's not a very bad hit, but it's worth noting.

## Block Memory Moves

Cache-to-cache memory movement is significantly slower, cycle for cycle, on the Pentium Pro than on the Pentium. On a Pentium, it takes about 1.1 cycles to move an aligned longword with the `rep movsd` instruction. On the Pentium Pro, the figure is about 1.8 cycles. It ostensibly takes three micro-ops to move a doubleword from one place in memory to another (one for the load, and two for the store). According to theory, the chip should be able to handle that in a single cycle, but apparently something else is going on to slow things down.

It turns out that memory can be copied from one place in primary cache to another at an even faster rate of 1.6 cycles per longword using a simple loop that does eight loads and eight stores each time through the loop.

## FMUL Latency

On the Pentium, it only takes three cycles to execute a floating-point multiplication. On the Pentium Pro, it takes five cycles. On both processors, other instructions can overlap the execution of the multiplication, and both processors can initiate a multiplication every other cycle. Because the Pentium Pro can spawn duplicate registers and let them float around in the execution pool while executing other instructions and waiting for them to complete, many applications may not notice the extra delay. But some algorithms that feed multiplication results back into further multiplications will see a delay. As of this writing, the top speed production chips for both the Pentium and the Pentium Pro run at 200 MHz. At least on some floating-point tests, the Pentium may run faster.

# The Floating-Point Unit

Most of the secrets of floating-point execution have already been mentioned in the preceeding section, but to review and expand:

- Addition and subtraction each take three cycles, and one such operation can be issued on every cycle in the U pipe. This is very similar to Pentium timing.

- Multiplication takes five cycles, and one such operation can be issued on every other cycle in the U pipe. The Pentium multiplies in three cycles.

- Division ties up the U pipe for extended periods of time. The time it takes to divide is a function of the precision requested, but in any precision, division by a power of 2 takes just eight cycles. The Pentium, cycle for cycle, runs slightly slower.

# The Cache

One very remarkable thing about the Pentium Pro is that it comes not only with an on-chip primary cache but also with a secondary cache housed in the same packaging. At present, secondary cache sizes of 256K and 512K are available. The primary cache is very similar to the Pentium's: 8K each for code and data. In future chips, especially those employing MMX technology (the multimedia extensions), the primary cache sizes will double, to 16K each (and so, too, on the Pentium).

The primary and secondary caches are very tightly coupled; the primary cache is actually able to communicate multiple pending requests to the secondary cache at the same time. The "minimum delay" for missing the primary cache is three cycles, but the delay may be masked by parallel execution. The "minimum delay" for missing the secondary cache as well is 14 cycles, a bit harder to mask.

On the Pentium, both code and data caches are two-way set-associative, as explained in Chapter 5. On the Pentium Pro, the code cache is four-way set-associative, meaning that it is less likely than the Pentium to encounter critical pieces of code tossing other critical pieces of code out of cache. The data cache is still two-way set-associative, and both caches operate on 32-byte cache lines.

As on the Pentium, there are essentially eight 32-bit buses into cache memory, one for each longword position in a cache line. Whereas the Pentium can opt to read or write on any two of them in a given cycle, the Pentium Pro can do at most one read and at most one write. The read and write can't use the same bus. But, of course, the programmer has little direct control over how the Pentium Pro decides to schedule operations to and from the cache.

If the Pentium Pro writes to a location that is not already in cache, it reads it into cache first (along with the rest of a 32-byte cache line) and then writes to it. This strategy avoids some of the pitfalls the Pentium hits by writing repeatedly to locations in main memory and stalling on the output queue (FIFO) delay.

Note that if the Pentium Pro reads a cache line into cache and then writes to it, it is then obligated to write out the cache line when its cache spot gets replaced by a newer cache line. So sometimes it pays to have the Pentium Pro check to see if a value it is about to write into a cache line is already there; if it is, the write can be skipped, and the cache line won't have to be written back to memory—perhaps saving cycles in the long run. On rare occasions, avoiding redundant writes like this can pay off.

The great thing about the cache on the Pentium Pro is that, due to parallel operations, accessing cache can be as fast as (or faster than!) using registers for many purposes.

# Data and Code Alignment

The Pentium Pro resembles the 486 with respect to code alignment. Even though cache lines are 32 bytes long, there is an internal 16-byte constriction in the cache line processing. Thus, if you branch to a point near the end of a 16-byte chunk of code, the processor may not see a full instruction, and it may stall. In fact, I have observed a one-cycle stall when a branch lands very close to the end of a 16-byte chunk of memory. Therefore, as with the 486, frequent branch destinations, especially those in inner loops, may be aligned modulo 8 or 16 to make sure they don't unnecessarily slow down the code. The Pentium did not require such alignment.

Data alignment is still important on the Pentium Pro, but the effects of misaligned stalls may be at least partially masked by parallel execution. When using `rep movsd`, it is still better to misalign the source pointer than to misalign the destination pointer. In general, following the Pentium's rules for data alignment is appropriate on the Pentium Pro.

# The Partial Register Stall

One of the most unfortunate differences between the Pentium and the Pentium Pro has to do with the "partial register stall." On a Pentium, these two instructions can execute on successive cycles:

```
mov     dl,7    ;  ;load a byte register
mov     ebx,edx ;  ;move dl inside edx
```

On a Pentium Pro, however, they would be separated by at least seven cycles. Writing to a little register and then using the big register, of which it is a part, for anything causes a horrendous stall. But there is a special case fix, as follows:

```
xor     edx,edx ;  ;zero the register, 1st cycle
mov     dl,7    ;  ;load a byte register, 2nd cycle
mov     ebx,edx ;  ;move dl inside edx, 3rd cycle
```

On the Pentium, you can set up a register to point to a page-aligned table, load the low byte, and use the whole thing as an address into the table two cycles later. That option is gone on the Pentium Pro. The best you can do is to zero a register with `xor reg,reg` or `sub reg,reg`, then load the low byte (or low word), in which case the Pentium Pro has no problem understanding what's going on.

Whereas on the Pentium, you can use a single register to load an index byte and index into an aligned table, the Pentium Pro takes two registers (one zeroed, except for the loaded byte, the other holding the table pointer) to do the same job in a reasonable time.

You can clear a register just once and then modify the low byte and move the register or use it in address calculations and continue modifying the low byte and moving and addressing. A register will remember that it has had its upper parts cleared—until an interrupt hits, uses the same register, and makes the processor forget that the register's high bytes are cleared.

It is a shame to have to clear a register every time you want to load or modify the low byte and subsequently use the entire register. In practice, you don't have to. It is sufficient to clear the register in question about once every few hundred microseconds or so (assuming interrupts run much less frequently), as long as the only part of the register that you modify is the low byte. You can add to it, decrement it, shift it, negate it, or `xor` it, but as long as you only operate on the low byte, the full register remains ready for use.

You can't get around the problem by writing a byte to memory and then reading it back in a longword. The pipelined logic of the chip imposes a similar stall for going that route.

Everything stated about the low byte of a register is also true of operations on the low word of a register. I have also seen the claim in some Intel documentation that writing to a large register (such as `eax`) and then reading its high byte register (in this case, `ah`) causes a stall, but the tests I have run do not confirm this.

# Branch Prediction

If the Pentium's branch prediction is good, the Pentium Pro's branch prediction is great. Because of the long execution pipeline, there is more riding on accurate branch prediction with the Pentium Pro, where a mispredicted branch is said to typically cost 10 to 15 cycles (versus four on the Pentium). The Pentium Pro keeps more branch history information and does a much better job of predicting patterns of taken and not-taken branches in its cache of 512 such entries.

On the Pentium Pro, even correctly predicted branches can cost a cycle in some cases. At some level of its pipeline, the Pentium Pro appears to make a guess about branch outcome without consulting the main branch prediction logic. It guesses that any backwards branch will be taken and any forward branch will not be. Sometimes this simplistic guesswork results in a one-cycle (or less) delay when the guess fails. Sometimes the delay gets masked by other activities. In any event, for really tight inner loops, it's best to make sure, if possible, that the most common path traversed is via backwards branches taken and forward branches ignored.

Branches taken, even when correctly predicted, interrupt the instruction fetching part of the pipeline for one cycle. Usually this delay gets lost in the subsequent pipelining, but not always. The shortest loop you can have, as a result, is two cycles. Unconditional jumps operate with the same constraint.

The very special case of predicting the destination of a return instruction (`ret`) is handled by an on-chip internal stack of return addresses. Whenever a `call` instruction is executed, the return address is pushed not only into a stack in the primary cache but also into a stack somewhere in the vicinity of the branch prediction logic. That way, whenever the prediction logic encounters a return instruction, it "guesses" that the return instruction will branch to the return address on the top of its internal stack. The Pentium chip predicts return addresses very poorly when a routine is called from more than one place in succession. That problem has largely been fixed on the Pentium Pro, with its return address stack.

## Optimization Summary

In approximate order of importance, the things to remember when optimizing for the Pentium Pro include the following:

- Avoid the partial register stall. Try not to write `dl` and then read `edx`, for instance, unless `edx` has been previously cleared using either `xor` or `sub`.

- Try to make branching as predictable as possible, and use `setCC`, `cmovCC`, and `fcmovCC` whenever possible to replace the need for hard-to-predict branches.

- Try to sculpt inner loops with backwards branches most often taken and forward branches most often not taken.

- Use `opcode reg,mem` operations liberally to free up registers at little or no cost to performance.

- Try to use multi-micro-op instructions sparingly, as they clog up the system and can only be processed at a maximum rate of one per cycle.

- Calculate memory register pointers and index registers well in advance of use, because the Pentium AGI problem is still there just below the surface (but the Pentium Pro out-of-order logic helps minimize the AGI's impact).

- Align the most frequently hit branch targets away from the end of 16-byte segments of memory, preferably at addresses modulo 8 or 16.

- Avoid pushing return addresses directly onto the stack instead of letting the `call` instruction do it, as the chip's return address branch prediction logic will be defeated.

- Avoid writing a byte or word to memory and then immediately reading back the longword that contains it, as this causes a stall.

- If you've modified a byte register but no longer care about it or the larger register's contents of which it is a part and you are about to call a routine that will push the register to save it, do an `xor reg,reg` to save cycles on the subsequent push operation (a process known as "cleansing" the register).

- Avoid unnecessary zeroing (cleansing, via `xor reg,reg`) of registers inside tight loops when the effect of zeroing outside the loop every few hundred microseconds can be expected to last until the next interrupt hits.

- In some algorithms, avoid writing redundant data (the same data that is already in memory) to memory, to avoid having to write cache lines back to main memory.

- Use integer multiplication in most circumstances where shifting and adding would have been used for a quick calculation on the Pentium.

# Conclusion

The Pentium Pro is a rather amazing piece of computing machinery that breaks with the tradition of letting the programmer control the smallest details of execution. Now the processor controls the details and the programmer provides hints and broad brush strokes. Nonintegral loop timings, like $12\frac{2}{3}$ cycles, are common because the processor may make different sequencing decisions from one pass through the loop to the next.

At its core, the Pentium Pro has two execution units very much like the two execution units in the Pentium. And as a general rule, good tight Pentium code should run well on the Pentium Pro. It may get a boost from the nearly free transfers of data to and from memory.

The Pentium Pro encounters frequent instances of paradoxical timing, where adding an instruction actually decreases a loop's execution time. Accordingly, if you really want to be sure a loop is running at its best, you need to measure it, and if it seems to be running longer than necessary, modify it until something breaks loose and it starts running faster. (This is not a satisfying way to go about computing, but it works.)

Whereas on the 486 and the Pentium the art of inner loop timing was largely predictive, on the Pentium Pro it is a mix of prediction and measurement, a new ball game that promises to keep assembly language interesting for years to come.

# References

Intel Corporation. 1996. *Pentium Pro Family Developer's Manual. Volume 2: Programmer's Reference Manual.* Santa Clara, Calif.: Intel Corporation. There is literally no instruction-timing information in the developer's manual, but it otherwise contains a full description of the instruction set.

Intel Corporation. October 1995. *Application Note AP-526, Optimizations For Intel's 32-Bit Processors.* Santa Clara, Calif.: Intel Corporation. This note covers both Pentium and Pentium Pro optimizations and includes timing information at the micro-op level. As of this writing, it is available at Intel's Web site, www.intel.com.

# 7

## Achieving Speed

> *Be good.*
> *If you can't be good, be careful.*
> *If you can't be careful, be quick.*
> —*Richard Brill*

There is a natural tension between conventional "good" code and code that runs at top speed. The simplest way to code an algorithm is very rarely the fastest, and the fastest is often judged much more risky to implement and maintain. And then there are the gray areas in between. This chapter takes a look at what *can* be done to attain speed, leaving the question of what *should* be done to the reader's judgment and the contexts of individual problems.

Touching on both C and assembly language approaches, this chapter covers

- When and where to speed code up
- Rethinking algorithms
- The special advantages of assembly language
- Data and stack alignment
- Running on seven registers
- Table-driven code
- Unrolling loops
- Loop counter efficiencies
- Minimizing pointer increments
- Jump tables
- Coiled loops
- Tandem loops

- Prefetching into cache
- Setting flags
- Fast multiplication
- Rethinking in assembly language

# When and Where to Speed Code Up

It is often said that only 5 or 10 percent of the code in a typical program is likely to be time-critical. By this it is meant that usually only a small fraction of the code determines its execution speed. And quite often, depending on the application, the speed is acceptable on the first attempt, without any tweaking. Indeed, many pieces of software that performed like dogs just a few years ago seem like models of efficiency thanks only to the fact that they're running on faster hardware now. Time has been kind to slow-running code.

Yet sometimes speed (or, rather, the lack of it) is a problem. Sometimes this is discovered after the fact, such as when you switch on a new program for the first time and find out it runs slowly. Sometimes it is anticipated, such as in designing real-time video compression and decompression software. Throughout most of my own programming experience with digital video and video games, the latter has been the case. If you're programming a graphics engine, speed translates into the power to get more and more things done in a given amount of time, so you know up front that speed is a goal. Other situations may call for the use of a code profiler to tell you where—in what routines—the processor is spending its time. The more complex a piece of code, or the more authors it has had, the more likely it is that a code profiler will point out the culpable code. Most integrated development environments include a profiling tool these days.

To the extent that you find yourself developing routines that may be used in a wide variety of future contexts as yet unknown, you have a natural need to optimize. Many routines that are not time-critical in one context may be extremely time-critical in another. And if you can't anticipate that a routine will not become a bottleneck, you might as well prepare it, within reason, for the worst. Reusable library routines are perpetual candidates for efficient coding.

It is often the case that speeding up one code bottleneck will just shift the bottleneck (albeit a now faster bottleneck) to another section of code. Many times I have squeezed an inner loop to top performance only to find that the next outer loop around it has become the new bottleneck. And tightening that one up may shift the burden out to the next level. Or the burden may shift to another part of the system entirely. Fast code begets the need for even more fast code. Even if only 5 or 10 percent of the code was originally responsible for determining execution speed, sometimes the optimization process draws in a much higher percentage before it's all done.

As anecdotal evidence, when I started writing the 6502 assembler mentioned in the preface, it was built around the speed of the symbol lookup loop, which made it appear possible to write an assembler 100 times faster than the only other such assembler on the market. But to keep that kind of speed, I had to optimize virtually everything else in the system—expression evaluation, code generation, text parsing, macros, and so on. In the end, it achieved its 100-to-1 win over the competition, and remains to this day five times faster than any PC-based assembler I've tested. Less than 1 percent of the code represented the most critical inner loop, but it took virtually *all* the code to keep the big win.

# Rethinking Algorithms

Almost by definition, optimization implies changing or rearranging algorithms. After all, if you don't change it, it won't run faster. Much of the remainder of this chapter is devoted to specific techniques for rearranging algorithms for speed. But there is a limit to how well cookbook techniques can be applied to the infinite range of algorithmic problems. Often it ultimately comes down to a simple battle of wits, not unlike a chess game, between the programmer's brain and the processor's instruction set.

Just as there are natural limits to the compressibility of various sorts of data (a full-screen photographic image compressed to 100 bytes will look unacceptable), there are limits to the speed of algorithms. One can think of these limits as the algorithms' time-compression dimension. For instance, you can't expect to ever decompress a JPEG image at a rate of five cycles per pixel when a multiplication costs more than that and it takes more than one multiplication per pixel to do the decompression. If you can strip an algorithm down to its minimum necessary operations (which, unfortunately, are not always obvious) and sum up their execution times, even before arranging them as functional code, you may get a sense of the speed limit you're facing.

As an example of rethought code, consider the routine in Listing 7-1, which counts words found in a buffer somewhere in memory. It does so by counting all the alphanumeric characters that immediately follow nonalphanumerics (indicating the start of a word). Although it is good that the alphabetic comparisons are done in an order such that the probable most common lowercase letters will be detected quickly, the whole chain of logical comparisons chews up significant cycles at assembly language level, especially when it encounters blank space and fails all comparisons. In testing, this code executed on a Pentium at about 23 cycles per byte. But the speed limit is nine times faster, as will be shown.

### Listing 7-1 Unoptimized Word Counting

```
int
WordCount1(unsigned char *p, int size)
{
    int inword = 0, inprev, count = 0;
    while (size--) {
        inprev = inword;
        inword = ((*p >= 'a') && (*p <= 'z')) ||
                 ((*p >= 'A') && (*p <= 'Z')) ||
                 ((*p >= '0') && (*p <= '9')) ||
                 (*p == '\'');
        count += inword && !inprev;  //check start of word
        p++;
    }
    return count;
}
```

Listing 7-2 shows a faster version that uses a table lookup to determine whether one is inside a word or not. The table, not shown, performs the same function as the former chain of comparisons, but it does so quite efficiently. The execution time here has dropped to about 18 cycles per character.

### Listing 7-2 Table-Driven Word Counting

```
int
WordCount2(unsigned char *p, int size)
{
    int inword = 0, inprev, count = 0;
    while (size--) {
        inprev = inword;
        inword = alphatable[*p++];   //external lookup tbl
        count += inword && !inprev;  //check start of word
    }
    return count;
}
```

Listing 7-3 shows the same function, rethought and implemented without any pointer increments. Furthermore, the preincrement of the loop counter may save a cycle at assembly level over the alternative postincrement. The timing drops further, to 14 cycles per character.

### Listing 7-3   Word Counting Without Pointer Increments

```
int
WordCount3(unsigned char *p, int size)
{
    int inword = 0, inprev, count = 0;
    p   +=  size;
    size = -size - 1;
    while (++size) {
        inprev = inword;
        inword = alphatable[p[size]]; //external lookup tbl
        count += inword && !inprev;   //check start of word
    }
    return count;
}
```

Listing 7-4 shows the same function reimplemented with bitwise logical operators generating the 1 or 0 to add to the count. These tend to run faster than the general logical operators && and !. The cycle count per character is now down to approximately 11 cycles, from an original 23. The code already runs twice as fast!

Believe it or not, there are still more things that can be done in C, and others in assembly, that can reduce the execution time of this loop to about 2.6 cycles (or even less on data already in cache) on a Pentium. Subsequent sections of this chapter will detail the other steps.

Rethinking algorithms is often not so much a matter of having one big "eureka" moment as it is a matter of layering on technique after technique until an irreducible core of code stares you in the face, defying you to do anything else to improve it. Sometimes, as in the case of the two-cycle solution to the word count problem, you can be pretty sure you've reached the limit.

### Listing 7-4   Word Counting with Bitwise Logical Operations

```
int
WordCount4(unsigned char *p, int size)
{
    int inword = 0, inprev, count = 0;
    p   +=  size;
    size = -size - 1;
    while (++size) {
        inprev = inword;
```

```
        inword = alphatable[p[size]];  //external lookup tbl
        count += inword & (inprev ^ 1);//check start of word
    }
    return count;
}
```

# The Special Advantages
# of Assembly Language

The ultimate optimization of the `WordCount()` function for the Pentium is not possible in C. As will be seen in the final solution, you need to use the `adc` (add with carry) operation at assembly language level to pull off the two-cycle loop. Unfortunately, C does not have any mechanism to express the "add with carry" notion. In fact, C has no way at all to express branching based directly on processor flags. This is just one of the advantages assembly language will always have over C, no matter how good the compiler.

The `rol` and `ror` (rotate left and right) instructions have no equivalent in the C syntax. Thus in assembly language you can swap high and low halves of a 32-bit register in a single cycle while C is still puzzling through shifts. And whereas you can address byte and word sections of a larger 32-bit register with ease in assembly language, it is virtually impossible with any compiler I know of to get C to operate on, say, just the low byte of a 32-bit value in a register. This piece of code, a four-cycle piece of cake in assembly language, turns into a monstrosity in C:

```
        add     esi,ebx     ; 1;a normal 32-bit add
        adc     eax,edi     ; 1;C can't do adc easily
        jc      exception   ; 0;C can't branch on flags easily
        rol     eax,16      ; 1;C can't rotate easily
        mov     bh,al       ; 1;C can't do subregisters easily
```

As it turns out, many of the performance gains that assembly language can achieve over C are a result of the added types of operations for which C has no direct expression.

The bottom line is that assembly language can not only turn on a dime and be hand-packed better than compiled C, it can perform primitive operations outside the scope of C. So it's always good to keep the assembly language superset in mind when running out of improvements to an algorithm implemented in C.

# Data and Stack Alignment

As mentioned in Chapters 4 through 6, data alignment is critical to good performance. C compilers generally know enough about intelligent alignment to place global and static data at appropriate memory positions: 2-byte boundaries for 16-bit values, 4-byte boundaries for 32-bit values, 8-byte boundaries for 64-bit values such as doubles. In assembly language, it is often necessary to force such alignments for static data using the `align 4` and `align 8` directives.

But what about the "automatic" variables, the ones that are created when a routine is entered, and destroyed upon exit? These live on the stack, and the stack is usually, at best, guaranteed to be 4-byte-aligned. In fact, the stack can be aligned even worse. I once used a compiler that generated code that had an annoying habit of exhibiting default 4-byte stack alignment when it ran under its associated debugger but only 2-byte alignment when it ran unobserved. I was getting crazy timings due to the delays of accessing 4-byte local variables on the 2-byte-aligned stack, and the evidence disappeared under the debugger. The fact is, 4-byte stack alignment is important to get and to keep. Generally speaking, C routines are smart enough to always push and pop and allocate stack space in multiples of 4 bytes. An assembly language routine that calls other routines must be careful to avoid pushing 16-bit values (like `ax` instead of `eax`) onto the stack, for this dooms all subsequently called routines to 2-byte alignment and automatic variable access time delays.

If you don't trust that an assembly routine will always be called with good stack alignment, you can force the matter with code like this:

```
start:  push    ebp             ;usually save ebp
        mov     ebp,esp         ;ebp locates passed parameters
        and     esp,not 3       ;4-byte align (or "not 7")
        sub     esp,40          ;for instance, 40-byte chunk
        ...                     ;body goes here
        mov     esp,ebp         ;get old esp back
        pop     ebp             ;get old ebp back
        retn                    ;and exit
```

The passed parameters may still be misaligned, but the chunk of storage allocated on the stack can have as high an alignment as desired.

Floating-point doubles generally have about a 50-50 chance of being aligned correctly or incorrectly as automatic variables, even when 4-byte stack alignment is observed. If you want to ensure an aligned array, instead of doing this:

```
routine()
{
    double array[40];
    ...
    printf("%f", array[12]); // access may be misaligned
}
```

try this instead:

```
routine()
{
    double ar[40 + 1], *array;
    array = (double *)(((int)&ar[1]) & ~7);
    ...
    printf("%f", array[12]); // access is 8-byte aligned
}
```

There may or may not be significant extra overhead incurred for using the pointer in the latter case, but it still may be less than the misalignment penalty.

Finally, sometimes you want to align data at an address with a lot of zeroes in the low bits. C doesn't support such notions directly, and assembly language generally only supports up to "page" alignments, which in this case refers to a 256-byte page, not a 4K physical page of processor memory. In assembly language, a 256-byte table aligned on a 256-byte boundary can be accessed by loading a 32-bit register with a pointer to the table and then just changing the low byte of the register to point to different table elements. (And since you can multiply the register by 2, 4, or 8, you can also use it to access tables up to 2,048 bytes in size.) The two-cycle solution to the WordCount() loop makes use of this technique.

If you're given a pointer to a free area of memory and wish to align it to the next highest address with, say, the low N bits set to zero, you can use an expression like this:

```
ptr = (char *)((((int)ptr) + ((1 << N)-1)) & ~((1 << N)-1));
```

# Running on Seven Registers

There are eight 32-bit general registers in the 80x86 architecture. Of these, the esp register is dedicated to pointing to the stack, and it's next to impossible to use it for any other kind of data or pointer. That leaves seven registers free. But all C compilers that I have seen use the ebp register as a "stack frame pointer," meaning, a stack pointer that doesn't move around when you push and pop. Passed parameters and automatic variables on the stack are usually accessed through ebp, and whenever you write inline assembly code and reference variables, chances are that you're secretly using the ebp register to locate them. Even the MASM assembler has built-in logic to access parameters and variables through ebp. The tragedy of it all is, now that esp can be used as a base pointer for referencing the stack (a new feature of the 32-bit instruction set), you often don't really need to tie up the ebp register with redundant duties.

The 80x86 family of processors is considered register-impoverished in this day of RISC processors, where 16 registers is considered skimpy. Reclaiming the ebp register for general use often makes a big difference in algorithm performance. In fact, I make it a habit to free it up and use it almost any time I start working on an assembly routine of any complexity.

### Listing 7-5 Freeing EBP for General Use

```
locvar1 textequ <dword ptr [esp+0]>
locvar2 textequ <dword ptr [esp+4]>
dblvar  textequ <qword ptr [esp+8]>
parm1a  textequ <dword ptr [esp+16]>
parm2a  textequ <dword ptr [esp+20]>
espsave textequ <dword ptr [esp+24]>
espsub  textequ <28>

aroutine proc near public C uses esi edi ebx ebp,
                                parm1:dword, parm2:dword
        mov     eax,esp         ;preserve esp
        and     esp,not 7       ;optional 8-byte alignment
        sub     esp,espsub      ;clear to use 28 bytes
        mov     espsave,eax     ;save the old esp for exit
        mov     eax,parm1       ;load up stack parameters
        mov     ebx,parm2       ;through ebp
        mov     parm1a,eax      ;store them again through
        mov     parm2a,ebx      ;the esp register
        ...                     ;body goes here, trash ebp
        mov     esp,espsave     ;get the old esp back
        ret                     ;and exit

aroutine endp
```

Listing 7-5 shows how to reclaim the ebp register for use in assembly language. The idea behind the code is to set up a data area sufficient to hold all the variables and parameters the routine will need to run, and address it off the esp register. Passed parameters can be transferred into this area if so desired. (In this case, parm1, and parm2 are fetched through the ebp register and stored through esp under the similar names `parm1a` and `parm2a`.) In the body of the code, the `ebp` register can be used freely, since it isn't needed to address anything on the stack. At the end, it gets restored by the implicit magic of the `ret` statement in conjunction with the `uses ebp` statement, which causes `ebp` to be automatically pushed on entry and popped on exit. In inline assembly language, you would have to explicitly push and pop `ebp`.

Note that everything works fine until the body of the routine starts pushing things onto the stack. Then it gets tricky to remember where things are, relative to the stack pointer. The solution is usually to preallocate space for the items that would otherwise be pushed. It takes no longer to store and fetch to memory off the `esp` pointer than it does to push and pop. Except for rather uncommon recursive routines, almost any algorithm can afford to preallocate enough stack memory so that it doesn't have to push and pop. And so the stack pointer can double as a stack frame pointer, and the `ebp` register can be used for other things.

There is one unusual danger in using the `ebp` register. As part of the segment register legacy, both `esp` and `ebp` "see memory" through the `SS` segment register when they are used as memory pointers. All the other registers use `DS` by default. In true flat-model code that's not normally a problem, but in some closely related models that are almost but not quite identical, the `SS` segment may be set up to throw out a hardware trap if the stack descends below where it thinks the lower limit of the stack should be. This detection of stack overflow is actually a valuable protection to have. But it has the nasty side effect of throwing traps out whenever the `ebp` register is used to access nonstack data outside the allowed stack area. Thus code that uses `ebp` in one context without difficulty may crash the program in an only slightly different context. For this reason, it's a good habit to arrange your register usage to avoid addressing memory other than the stack through `ebp`. This will prevent your code from crashing when someone makes a subtle code environment change. The two-cycle solution to the `WordCount()` loop, given later in this chapter, makes use of `ebp`.

# Table-Driven Code

One of the most common ways to speed up a given computation is to turn it into a table lookup. For instance, the first optimization to the WordCount routine, already shown in Listing 7-2, was a lookup using a byte index into a table of 256 bytes. It was faster to do the lookup than to do a chain of comparisons to determine if the character belonged to a word or not.

But big tables can be very bad. If you build a 1-megabyte table and reference it in a fairly random manner, expect an average cache delay of nearly 50 cycles per reference. That's enough time to do plenty of computing, so you might as well spend 40 cycles calculating a value instead of looking it up in a really giant table.

Sometimes the access pattern of, say, a 64K table is nonrandom enough that it behaves almost as if it were always in the primary cache. Suppose, for instance, that you were to implement the WordCount algorithm with a 64K table indexed by successive pairs of characters (the method of choice for the 386). Since most text consists of lowercase alphabetics, most of the table hits would occur in a $26 \times 26$ zone within the $256 \times 256$ table—and that small zone can fit into the primary cache quite nicely. Nonrandom access patterns can sometimes be the saving grace of big tables, but in general, as total table sizes accessed by an inner loop exceed 8K, beware of slowdowns.

# Unrolling Loops

Unrolling a loop just means repeating the body of a loop several times in a row so that the looping logic overhead (usually a decrement followed by a conditional branch) only has to run once at the end of the repetitions instead of once per loop.

### Listing 7-6    Word Counting with an Unrolled Loop

```
int
WordCount5(unsigned char *p, int size)
{
    int words = 0, thischar = 0, prevchar;
    p += size;
    size = -size;
    while (size <= -4) {
        prevchar = thischar;
        thischar = IL_WCTable[p[count +  0]];
        words += thischar & (1 ^ prevchar);
        prevchar = thischar;
        thischar = IL_WCTable[p[count +  1]];
        words += thischar & (1 ^ prevchar);
        prevchar = thischar;
        thischar = IL_WCTable[p[count +  2]];
        words += thischar & (1 ^ prevchar);
        prevchar = thischar;
        thischar = IL_WCTable[p[count +  3]];
        words += thischar & (1 ^ prevchar);
```

```
        count += 4;
    }
    size--;
    while (++size) {
        prevchar = thischar;
        thischar = IL_WCTable[p[size]];
        words += thischar & (1 ^ prevchar);
    }
    return words;
}
```

Listing 7-6 shows the WordCount routine with its inner loop unrolled four times. In practice, you often want to unroll many more times in a row; when I tested this routine with 16 loops unrolled in a row, the number of cycles per character processed dropped from about 11 to just over 8.

There is often a limit to the amount of loop unrolling that is beneficial, especially if the loop is not likely to be in cache when it is started up. If you completely unroll a loop so that it never goes back to its beginning and it has to be read into the cache, it will almost certainly run worse than if you never unrolled it at all. Loops benefit greatly from running in cache, so if unrolling causes a large percentage of a loop's time to be spent on its first pass being read into the cache, it may be counterproductive. If a completely unrolled loop is expected to stay in cache from one execution to the next, there's no problem (except, possibly, with the other pieces of code that are being elbowed out of the cache by a massive unrolled loop).

Sometimes, when the number of iterations of a loop is not known up front, you still have to test for loop termination on every unrolled copy, as in expanding this:

```
.repeat
  shl   eax,1
.until CARRY?
```

to this:

```
shl   eax,1
jc    done
shl   eax,1
jc    done
shl   eax,1
jc    done
...
```

On a Pentium this usually buys you nothing, because branches taken and branches not taken take about the same amount of time. But on the 486, it's a win. (Ironically, though, this particular example, because it's a deadly one-cycle loop on the Pentium that actually executes in five, works much better unrolled there as well. Loops longer than one cycle behave more conventionally on the Pentium.)

As a side effect of unrolling a loop, it may be possible to save a few cycles through code rearrangement. For instance, the code in Listing 7-6 executes the statement `prevchar = thischar` in every unrolled iteration, which translates to one move operation per iteration. But by alternately assigning the `thischar` value to two different variables, essentially reversing their roles, there is no need to perform the move operation in order to preserve the past value. The code to implement this simplification is shown in Listing 7-7. It reduces the per-character execution time from eight cycles to seven.

### Listing 7-7    Word Counting with a Pair of Reversing Variables

```
int
IL_WordCount6(unsigned char *p, int count)
{
    int words = 0, thischar = 0, prevchar;
    p += count;
    count = -count;
    while (count <= -4) {
        prevchar = IL_WCTable[p[count +  0]];
        words += prevchar & (1 ^ thischar);
        thischar = IL_WCTable[p[count +  1]];
        words += thischar & (1 ^ prevchar);
        prevchar = IL_WCTable[p[count +  2]];
        words += prevchar & (1 ^ thischar);
        thischar = IL_WCTable[p[count +  3]];
        words += thischar & (1 ^ prevchar);
        count += 4;
    }
    count--;
    while (++count) {
        prevchar = thischar;
        thischar = IL_WCTable[p[count]];
        words += thischar & (1 ^ prevchar);
    }
    return words;
}
```

# Loop Counter Efficiency

One of the most common loop controls in C programming is the postdecremented counter:

```
while (cnt--)
```

But the *pre*decremented counter usually runs faster when compiled:

```
while (--cnt)
```

A predecremented counter corresponds directly to a decrement-and-branch sequence in assembly language (two instructions, one cycle). But a postdecrement corresponds to at least three instructions at assembly language level (usually a test instruction, an `lea` that decrements without changing the flags, and the branch—three instructions, 1.5 cycles) and often four.

Making subtle changes in loop logic to allow for predecrement (or preincrement) tests for loop completion often shaves a cycle off a Pentium loop and usually even more off a 486 loop.

A typical `for` loop looks like this:

```
for (n = 0; n < 100; n++)
```

This is fine if the value of n is actually used for something in the associated loop. But if n is nothing but a pure loop counter, this is usually faster:

```
for (n = 100 + 1; --n;)
```

Note that n must be assigned a value one greater than the number of iterations desired for the predecrement to work. This form is likely to save a cycle per loop. It has the disadvantage of being a less readable loop control than the original, and you really have to ask yourself if you want a cycle that badly.

The `WordCount()` optimization includes a switch to a preincremented counter.

# Minimizing Pointer Increments

Very often, a loop has not only a loop counter but also pointers internal to the body of the loop that increment with every loop iteration. Often there is a potential savings in using the loop counter as an array index off the unmoving original pointer value instead. As a case in point, consider this loop:

```
for (n = 0; n < 100; n++)
    *p++ = *q++;
```

In compiled assembly language, this code might look like this, assuming the pointers are operating on longwords:

```
        .repeat                 ;  ;
            mov     eax,[esi]   ; 1;fetch off pointer q
            add     esi,4       ; 0;increment q
            mov     [edi],eax   ; 1;store off pointer p
            add     edi,4       ; 0;increment p
            inc     edx         ; 1;increment n
        .until edx >= 100       ; 1;check if done
                                ;;;;4 cycles
```

By changing the C code to this, though, you may be able to save a cycle:

```
for (n = 0; n < 100; n++)
    p[n] = q[n];
```

This can translate to more efficient assembly code on the Pentium, where there is no penalty for addressing through two registers:

```
        .repeat                      ;  ;
            mov     eax,[esi+edx*4]  ; 1;fetch off q and n
            mov     [edi+edx*4],eax  ; 1;store off p and n
            inc     edx              ; 0;increment n
        .until edx >= 100            ; 1;check if done
                                     ;;;;3 cycles
```

Of course, this efficiency will only be realized in a C program if the compiler is agreeable to writing the more efficient code. If a pointer is associated with an object size other than one, two, four, or eight bytes—the index register multiples a Pentium supports—then it is probably better to increment the pointer than to force a difficult indexing situation.

# Jump Tables

A jump table is just an array of executable addresses. The C language only permits you to construct tables of function addresses, but in assembly language you are not constrained to "calling" the executable address. You can simply jump to it, and it need not be a function entry point.

Here is a simple assembly language loop that could be used to advance a pointer through text "white space" until a nonblank character is found:

```
vectbl  dd      33 dup (offset white)      ;  ;ASCII 32 and
        dd      (256-33) dup (offset notwh) ;  ;below is white
        .
        .
        .
        xor     eax,eax                    ;  ;clean for indexing
white:  mov     al,[esi]                   ; 1;fetch character
        inc     esi                        ; 0;advance pointer
        jmp     vectbl[eax*4]              ; 3;jump via table
                                           ;;;;4-cycle loop
notwh:                                     ;  ;non-white here
```

In the early days of the 80x86 family, especially on the 8088, jump tables were more often a good speed solution than they are today. Note that the jump table in the previous example takes up 1K of memory. That's one-eighth the size of the primary cache. Unless the table is used intensively, there's a good chance it won't be in the cache when it's needed, adding memory delays to the loop. In the days of the 8088 there was no cache, so in an odd way the entire address space performed like cache, which is to say it performed at top speed. Back then, jump tables didn't push other things out of prime memory locations. And the instruction pipelining that we enjoy today wasn't around then. If a jump through a jump table on a Pentium or Pentium Pro finds a different execution address from one use to the next, then there will be a four-cycle or greater delay due to misprediction of the jump address. On the 8088, with no prediction or pipelining, there are no such delays.

Although jump tables no longer have all the appeal they once had, they remain the best way to make a large multi-way branching decision off a few bits of information (usually less than about ten bits). Sometimes compilers implement the `switch` statement by making a jump table of the various case value execution addresses. This only works, though, when the case values are clustered fairly closely together; otherwise the table would be prohibitively big.

# Coiled Loops

Sometimes it's not possible to construct a simple inner loop with fully paired instructions and no stall conditions, such as AGIs. Listing 7-8 shows an example, drawn from Chapter 14, of an inner loop that, in its uncoiled form takes eight cycles, due to an AGI on its third instruction that can't execute until the second cycle after the first instruction executes. The numbers 1 through 7 in the comment field indicate the natural order of the instructions.

The solution to this kind of problem is to overlap the end of one loop with the beginning of the next, in effect "coiling" the loop code upon itself. The lower part of Listing 7-8 shows the same seven instructions, reordered so that the same work gets done but taking three passes through the loop to do it. If you follow the instructions in sequence from 1 through 7 in the coiled loop, you should be able to confirm that the same processing gets done, but the AGI is avoided and the code runs a cycle faster.

## Listing 7-8 Original and Coiled Versions of a Loop

```
;                 mov al,[esi]                 ; 1;1-get encode val
;                 inc esi                      ; 0;2-advance byte ptr
;                 mov ecx,[ebx+eax*8].IL_HuffEncode.wid ;<- AGI hits
;                                              ; 2;3-get bit width
;                 mov edx,[ebx+eax*8].IL_HuffEncode.bits
;                                              ; 0;4-get code bits
;                 sub edi,ecx                  ; 1;5-enough room?
;                 jc  out_of_loop              ; 0;6-no -> exit
;                 shrd ebp,edx,cl              ; 4;7-shift bits in
;                                              ;;;;8 cycles as is
;
;

        .repeat                                ; ;
          shrd ebp,edx,cl                      ; 4;7-shift bits in
          mov ecx,[ebx+eax*8].IL_HuffEncode.wid
                                               ; 1;3-get bit width
          mov edx,[ebx+eax*8].IL_HuffEncode.bits
                                               ; 0;4-get code bits
          mov al,[esi]                         ; 1;1-get encode val
          inc esi                              ; 0;2-advance byte ptr
          sub edi,ecx                          ; 1;5-enough room?
        .until CARRY?                          ; 0;6-yes -> branch
                                               ;;;;7 cycles
```

Coiling a loop can be tricky headwork. It's easy to get confused as to which pass the data in a given register is in. The best way I've found to keep things straight when writing this kind of code is to write it uncoiled with the instruction steps numbered, as shown in the listing, and then try to coil them with the order numbers still in place.

The other problem associated with coiled loops is in writing the correct entry and exit code. In the example in Listing 7-8, it would be appropriate to lead into the loop with the execution of the first six steps of the loop, since the loop starts with instruction 7. The exit condition of this particular loop usually leads to a loop reentry after dumping 32 bits of output and refreshing the ebp register, but final exit involves executing instruction 7 from one loop and instructions 3 through 7 from the next iteration of the loop.

If you encounter an uncoiled loop with AGI delays and/or several unpaired instructions, there is a good chance that coiling can improve performance.

# Tandem Loops

The Pentium has two parallel execution units—two "pipes"—which can each execute one instruction on each cycle. Sometimes, though, you find yourself with an inner loop in which many instructions cannot be paired, due to dependence on the result of the previous instruction. Rather than suffer many wasted execution slots, it is sometimes possible to run two copies of a loop, essentially side by side in tandem, if one iteration of the loop doesn't depend on the results of the other.

Listing 7-9 shows a tandem loop drawn from the code in Chapter 15. Many of the instructions from one loop are paired with their exact counterparts from the duplicate tandem loop. The loops use different registers, and at one point they check to see whether they need to execute some special case code when operating on the same data object. There is just enough difference between the loops, in terms of registers used and data offsets applied, to have them operate on independent pieces of data.

### Listing 7-9    A Tandem Sorting Loop

```
    .repeat                  ;  ;
      xor eax,eax            ; 1;clear out regs for
      xor ebx,ebx            ; 0;indexing
      mov al,[esi+ebp]       ; 1;pick up sort bytes
      mov bl,[esi+ebp+1]     ;.5;bus bank contention half
                             ;  ;the time
```

```
.if eax == ebx          ; 1;check for same byte value
  mov edx,[esp+eax*4]   ; 1;get pointer for next spot
  add edx,2*4           ; 1;advance it 2 positions
  mov ebx,[edi+ebp*4+4] ; 0;pick up record pointer 2
  mov [esp+eax*4],edx   ; 1;store advanced spot ptr
  mov eax,[edi+ebp*4+0] ; 0;pick up record pointer 1
  mov [edx-4],eax       ; 1;store sorted record ptr 1
  mov [edx],ebx         ; 0;store sorted record ptr 2
.else                   ; 1;
  mov ecx,[esp+eax*4]   ; 1;get pointer for spot 1
  mov edx,[esp+ebx*4]   ; 0;get pointer for spot 2
  add ecx,4             ; 1;advance it 1 position
  add edx,4             ; 0;advance it 1 position
  mov [esp+eax*4],ecx   ; 1;store spot pointer 1
  mov [esp+ebx*4],edx   ; 0;store spot pointer 2
  mov eax,[edi+ebp*4+0] ; 1;pick up record pointer 1
  mov ebx,[edi+ebp*4+4] ; 0;pick up record pointer 2
  mov [ecx],eax         ; 1;store sorted record ptr 1
  mov [edx],ebx         ; 0;store sorted record ptr 2
.endif                  ; ;
add ebp,2               ; 1;advance by 2 sort bytes
.until ZERO?            ; 0;and loop
                        ;;;;9.5 cycles + branch
                        ;;;;misprediction
                        ;;;;5 cycles per rec approx.
```

The MMX instruction set extensions, described in Chapter 9, lend themselves well to tandem loops—especially *staggered* tandem loops (meaning that the two loops don't start or end in the same place). Listing 7-10 shows some MMX code with the two loop start positions noted. Just as it's helpful to annotate the instruction order in coiled loops, it helps to annotate the loop identities of the instructions in tandem loops, especially when they are running staggered. Here, loops 1 and 2 are marked with a 1 or 2 in the comment field.

MMX instructions can pair, but only one instruction of a pair can access memory or use certain processor features. That is why staggering tandem loops works. Memory access and resource usage can be distributed more efficiently. (This is more fully explained in Chapter 9.)

## Listing 7-10   Tandem, Staggered MMX Loops

```
.repeat                        ; ;
  movq    [edi+ecx*2-16],mm3  ; 1;2
  movq    mm2,mm0             ; 0;1
  movq    [edi+ecx*2-8],mm5   ; 1;2
  pmullw  mm0,mm1             ; 0;1
```

```
        movq        mm3,[esi+ecx+8]      ; 1;2 <- loop 2 start
        pmulhw      mm1,mm2              ; 0;1
        movq        mm4,[edx+ecx+8]      ; 1;2
        movq        mm5,mm3              ; 0;2
        pmullw      mm3,mm4              ; 1;2
        movq        mm2,mm0              ; 0;1
        pmulhw      mm4,mm5              ; 1;2
        punpcklwd   mm0,mm1              ; 0;1
        movq        mm5,mm3              ; 2;2 <- pmullw stall
        punpckhwd   mm2,mm1              ; 0;1
        movq        [edi+ecx*2],mm0      ; 1;1
        punpcklwd   mm3,mm4              ; 0;2
        movq        [edi+ecx*2+8],mm2    ; 1;1
        punpckhwd   mm5,mm4              ; 0;2
        movq        mm0,[esi+ecx+16]     ; 1;1 <- loop 1 start
        add         ecx,16               ; 0;
        movq        mm1,[edx+ecx+16]     ; 1;1
    .until ZERO?                         ; 0;
                                         ;;;;12 cycles
```

# Prefetching into Cache

There is an old saying that banks only loan cash to people who prove they don't need it. Similarly, cache performs best when you don't need it badly. By this I mean that it's OK to ask for something that's not in the cache, but if you come back quickly and ask for another part of the same cache line, or even something that is not in the cache, you can be penalized.

Suppose you read a memory location that is not in the primary cache but *is* in the secondary cache. This takes about seven cycles, but at the end of that seven cycles, the 32-byte cache line arriving in the primary cache from the secondary cache still has about seven cycles to go before it's entirely read in and ready for continued one-cycle access. No matter what, you have to wait at least the seven extra cycles before reading the same cache line again—even if you're trying to read the same value that was read in with the original cache miss. If you "go back to the well" before then, you hit delays. For the best cache effect, it is best to plan, when possible, to put seven cycles or more between the first reference to a new cache line and the second reference.

The following code calculates a fast checksum on a million-element array, and it does so fairly efficiently, with an unrolled loop and a loop counter that doubles as an array index:

```
for (n = 0, sum = 0; n < 1000000; n += 8) {
/*    garb = array[n +16]; */
    sum += array[n + 0];
    sum += array[n + 1];
    sum += array[n + 2];
    sum += array[n + 3];
    sum += array[n + 4];
    sum += array[n + 5];
    sum += array[n + 6];
    sum += array[n + 7];
}
```

If the comment delimiters are removed from the "do-nothing" second line of code, though, the function runs 25 percent faster! It runs faster because the `garb` read is encountering all the cache misses, instead of the summing instructions. It brings memory into the cache well in advance of the need for it, so that by the time it is needed by the other instructions it is completely ready for one-cycle access in the primary cache. Without that statement, a summing instruction would encounter a cache miss, and the next summing instruction, because it occurs within a very few cycles of the previous one and references the same cache line, would encounter the residual delay. Reading ahead prevents the need for the loop to suffer the residual cache line delay. But you do have to be careful in the development of professional code that the prefetcher instruction doesn't read past the end of the array and generate a protection fault.

In Chapter 10, there is an algorithm that uses this principle to perform memory-to-memory block moves up to 20 percent faster than the processor's `rep movsd` block-move instruction. And there is another example in Chapter 14, where an unused instruction slot, when given over to prefetching, speeds up the code.

# Setting Flags

There are five flags that are set by most arithmetic and logical operations. Usually only one of them is important at any given time; *which* one depends on the context in which it is being used. But sometimes there are situations in which you want to control and pay attention to the states of several flags at a time. You may want to perform a test that tells you whether or not to exit a loop based on the carry flag, but you may also want the same test to set or clear the state of another flag—perhaps the sign flag—to indicate more information about why the loop was exited.

In Chapter 14 there is an example of this two-flags-at-once technique in the Huffman decompression loop. As each value is decompressed, the number of bits associated with that decompressed value is subtracted from the number of bits available in a register. When the carry flag is set as a result, that means either that the bit count went below zero or that a special huge number was subtracted to signal the end of the data. If the bit count was exhausted, you would expect the sign flag to be set. But if the huge number (greater than 0x80000020) was the culprit, the sign flag would be clear. Thus a single test tells not only whether an exit condition occurred (carry flag set), but also why (sign bit set means bit exhaustion; sign bit clear means end of data). Situations like this frequently arise, wherein a single instruction can generate more than one flag's worth of useful information.

Suppose you want to pick up a byte from a text stream and set flags to tell whether or not the byte is white space, whether it is numeric or alphabetic, and whether it is uppercase or lowercase. Believe it or not, this can be done with a single table lookup and one addition operation. The following code can set the C, S, P, and Z flags to carry all the above information:

```
xor     eax,eax       ;  ;clean out the register
mov     al,[esi]      ;  ;pick up a byte
inc     esi           ;  ;and advance pointer
mov     al,[ebx+eax]  ;  ;translate the byte
add     al,al         ;  ;set 4 meaningful flags
              ;  ;Z set means white space
              ;  ;S set means numeric
              ;  ;C set means alphabetic
              ;  ;P set means upper case
```

Of course, you have to pick the translation table values correctly. Under this scenario, for instance, Q could translate to the number 0x83. Since 0x83 plus 0x83 equals 6 in byte arithmetic, Z is not set (since this isn't white space), S is not set (since it isn't numeric), C is set (since it is alphabetic), and P is set (since there are an even number of bits in the number 6 and since it represents uppercase). In effect, you get four discriminations for the price of one. Such flag games are often associated with table entries like this, which can be manipulated at design time to give just the right effects.

# Fast Multiplication

On the Pentium processor, integer multiplication is fairly slow, about ten cycles. But you can perform overlapped shifts and additions at the rate of one per cycle. So, if you know in advance that you will be multiplying by a fixed integer, it may be faster to perform shift-and-add arithmetic to accomplish a multiplication than to use the multiplication instruction. Sometimes the `lea` instruction is also useful (as in `lea eax,[eax+eax*4]` to achieve multiplication by 5), but it may suffer from the AGI problem. In preparing Chapter 17 (JPEG), I needed to find fast ways to multiply by four different constants. I ended up preparing four macros to handle the four cases. Each macro made use of two otherwise unused registers to perform the shift operations—an ideal case. Here is one of the macros:

```
mul473  macro   reg, t1, t2      ;  ;multiply by binary 111011001
        mov     t1,reg           ; 1;
        mov     t2,reg           ; 0;
        shl     t2,4             ; 1;
        lea     reg,[reg+reg*8]  ; 0;0...1001
        shl     t1,6             ; 1;
        add     reg,t2           ; 0;0...11001
        shl     t2,5             ; 1;
        sub     reg,t1           ; 0;1...111111011001
        add     reg,t2           ; 1;0...000111011001
        endm                     ;;;;5 cycles
```

Note that a mix of techniques is used here to generate multiplication by 473. There are three shifts, one `lea`, two additions, and one subtraction. The subtraction operation is useful in sections of the multiplier where there are several bits set in a row. The net effect is a multiplication in nine instructions that runs twice as fast as a one-instruction integer multiplication. This kind of multiplication is actually efficient, in terms of time, up to about 16 bits in the multiplier, and even more if there are big contiguous runs of 1's and 0's in the value.

# Rethinking in Assembly Language

The `WordCount()` function described earlier in this chapter descended from 23 cycles to 7 in C using some of the techniques just described, but for further improvement, rethinking and reworking in assembly language are required. Revisiting Listing 7-4, the line of code that advances the word count value can be reworked to run faster in assembly language thanks to the `adc` operation, which is not available in C. Here is the original C form:

```
count += inword & (inprev ^ 1);//check start of word
```

Note that this code requires three operations to advance the count, `+=`, `&`, and `^`. But since `inword` and `inprev` are both one-bit values, the same calculation can be performed in assembly language with these two instructions:

```
        cmp bl,al                 ;  ;bl holds inprev
        adc ecx,0                 ;  ;al holds inword
                                  ;  ;ecx holds count
```

Listing 7-11 shows `WordCount()` implemented with a central four-instruction sequence or "loop" per character. This code improves on the C performance, dropping the per-character time from seven cycles to about five. But there are still two unpaired instructions and an AGI stall in each loop, slowing it down by as much as two cycles per character.

### Listing 7-11 `WordCount()` in Assembly Language with `adc` Logic

```
IL_WordCount7 proc near C public uses esi edi ebx ebp,
                              txtptr:dword, siz:dword
        mov     esi,txtptr
        mov     edi,siz
        add     esi,edi
        neg     edi
        lea     eax,IL_WCTable
        lea     ebx,IL_WCTable
        xor     ecx,ecx
        .while edi & 1fH
          mov   al,bl
          mov   bl,[esi+edi]
          mov   bl,[ebx]
          cmp   al,bl
          adc   ecx,0
          inc   edi
        .endw
        .if edi
          .repeat
ofst       =    0
           rept 16
           mov  al,[esi+edi+ofst]      ; 0;fetch byte
           mov  al,[eax]               ; 2;translate it
           cmp  bl,al                  ; 1;compare
           adc  ecx,0                  ; 1;and add
           mov  bl,[esi+edi+ofst+1]
           mov  bl,[ebx]
           cmp  al,bl
           adc  ecx,0
ofst       =    ofst + 2
           endm
           add edi,32
          .until ZERO?
        .endif
```

```
        mov     eax,ecx
        ret

IL_WordCount7 endp
```

To achieve full instruction pairing and remove the AGI stall, it is necessary to coil the loop's logic. Listing 7-12 shows a faster assembly language solution, with a central repeated macro containing four variants of the four-instruction loop coiled together. The instructions are commented with two-letter codes like 3b, meaning "third instruction of the b loop". It helps to use these comment fields to trace the execution of the four copies of the four-instruction loop. Tracing the execution should not only confirm that the loops work as advertised but also that there are no longer any AGIs or unpaired instructions. When tested on a very large text file (measured in megabytes), this code runs in about 2.9 cycles per character processed. Even though the loop's theoretical speed limit appears to be 2.0 cycles per character, memory delays due to cache misses account for most of the remaining 0.9 cycles.

## Listing 7-12  WordCount() in Coiled Assembly Language

```
IL_WordCount8 proc near C public uses esi edi ebx ebp,
                                txtptr:dword, siz:dword
        mov     esi,txtptr
        mov     edi,siz
        add     esi,edi
        neg     edi
        lea     eax,IL_WCTable
        lea     ebx,IL_WCTable
        lea     ecx,IL_WCTable
        lea     edx,IL_WCTable
        xor     ebp,ebp
        .while edi & 1fH
          mov     al,dl
          mov     dl,[esi+edi]
          mov     dl,[edx]
          cmp     al,dl
          adc     ebp,0
          inc     edi
        .endw
        mov     cl,dl
        .if edi
          mov     al,[esi+edi]            ; 0;1a
          .repeat
ofst        =    0
          rept 8
```

```
                mov bl,[esi+edi+ofst+1]      ; 1;1b
                cmp cl,dl                    ; 0;3d
                adc ebp,0                    ; 1;4d
                mov al,[eax]                 ; 0;2a
                mov bl,[ebx]                 ; 1;2b
                cmp dl,al                    ; 0;3a
                adc ebp,0                    ; 1;4a
                mov cl,[esi+edi+ofst+2]      ; 0;1c
                mov dl,[esi+edi+ofst+3]      ; 1;1d
                cmp al,bl                    ; 0;3b
                adc ebp,0                    ; 1;4b
                mov cl,[ecx]                 ; 0;2c
                mov dl,[edx]                 ; 1;2d
                cmp bl,cl                    ; 0;3c
                adc ebp,0                    ; 1;4c
                mov al,[esi+edi+ofst+4]      ; 0;1a
ofst            =    ofst + 4
                endm
;               mov bl,[esi+edi+70]          ;prefetch disabled
                add edi,32
              .until ZERO?
              cmp    cl,dl                   ; 0;3d
              adc    ebp,0                   ; 1;4d
            .endif
          mov      eax,ebp
          ret

IL_WordCount8 endp
```

Near the end of Listing 7-12 is a commented-out instruction with the notation "prefetch disabled." It would at first appear that if the instruction were allowed to execute, it would do nothing logically useful and perhaps add a cycle to the first outer loop. But in fact, when this instruction is enabled, it speeds execution up by 10 percent, from 2.9 cycles to 2.6 cycles. This is an example of how prefetching a cache line before you need to reference it repeatedly can boost performance. The `mov bl,[esi+edi+70]` does nothing more than start a cache line on its way into memory before the inner loop starts referencing it repeatedly at approximately two-cycle intervals. As described earlier in this chapter, that prevents residual second-read delays.

And so the `WordCount()` optimization odyssey comes to an apparent end on the Pentium. It appears that the basic fetch-translate-compare-add set of loop instructions is about as minimal as you can get, and when they run in pairs at an effective half-cycle each, they're running at the speed limit. Cache prefetching is the final touch. From beginning to end, these optimizations bring a nine-fold performance improvement.

But the Pentium Pro is a different story. The optimal Pentium solution is far from optimal on the Pentium Pro. Because of the partial register-stall condition that the Pentium Pro suffers, the optimal Pentium solution runs at seven cycles on the Pentium Pro. To fix it, I had to

1. Scavenge the use of a register to hold the translation table pointer

2. Prezero the 32-bit registers into which bytes were read

3. Repeatedly refresh the prezeroing of the registers so that when interrupts destroy the processor's knowledge of the prezeroed register states, the inefficiency doesn't last long

**Listing 7-13  The `WordCount()` Solution for the Pentium Pro**

```
IL_WordCount10 proc near C public uses esi edi ebx ebp,
                                 txtptr:dword,siz:dword
        mov     esi,txtptr
        mov     edi,siz
        add     esi,edi
        neg     edi
        lea     eax,IL_WCTable
        lea     ebx,IL_WCTable
        lea     ecx,IL_WCTable
        lea     edx,IL_WCTable
        xor     ebp,ebp
        .while edi & 1fH
          mov   al,dl
          mov   dl,[esi+edi]
          mov   dl,[edx]
          cmp   al,dl
          adc   ebp,0
          inc   edi
        .endw
        mov     cl,dl
        .if edi
          push  esi
          push  esi
          push  esi
          add   esi,edi
          lea   edi,IL_WCTable
          xor   eax,eax
          xor   ebx,ebx
          xor   ecx,ecx
          xor   edx,edx
          mov   al,[esi]              ; 0;1a
          .repeat
```

```
ofst          =   0
          rept 8
          mov bl,[esi+ofst+1]       ; 1;1b
          cmp cl,dl                 ; 0;3d
          adc ebp,0                 ; 1;4d
          mov al,[eax+edi]          ; 0;2a
          mov bl,[ebx+edi]          ; 1;2b
          cmp dl,al                 ; 0;3a
          adc ebp,0                 ; 1;4a
          mov cl,[esi+ofst+2]       ; 0;1c
          mov dl,[esi+ofst+3]       ; 1;1d
          cmp al,bl                 ; 0;3b
          adc ebp,0                 ; 1;4b
          mov cl,[ecx+edi]          ; 0;2c
          mov dl,[edx+edi]          ; 1;2d
          cmp bl,cl                 ; 0;3c
          adc ebp,0                 ; 1;4c
          mov al,[esi+ofst+4]       ; 0;1a
ofst          =   ofst + 4
          endm
          mov [esp+4],ecx
          mov [esp+8],edx
          xor eax,eax
          xor ebx,ebx
          xor ecx,ecx
          xor edx,edx
          mov cl,[esp+4]
          mov dl,[esp+8]
          mov al,[esi+ofst]
          add esi,32
          cmp esi,[esp]
         .until ZERO?
          cmp   cl,dl               ; 0;3d
          adc   ebp,0               ; 1;4d
          add   esp,12
         .endif
        mov     eax,ebp
        ret

IL_WordCount10 endp
```

Listing 7-13 shows the reworked Pentium Pro code. It runs slightly slower on the Pentium (about 10 percent) than does the optimal Pentium code. But compared with optimal Pentium code, it runs twice as fast on the Pentium Pro, at about 3.7 cycles per character. Why 3.7 instead of 2.6? The Pentium Pro I was testing on runs at 200 MHz, but the cache line delivery times from main memory were, I believe, running at about the same rate, in terms of absolute time, as on a 100 MHz Pentium. In other words, a cache line miss that took, say, 17 cycles to arrive from main memory on the Pentium took in the vicinity of 30 cycles on the Pentium Pro. The Pentium Pro therefore exhibited a longer cycle count, due to relatively longer cache delays. It actually ran at a speed equivalent to 1.9 cycles per character on the Pentium.

And so ends the `WordCount()` optimization story. . . until the next processor arrives.

# Conclusion

The first line of performance defense is always the selection of a good algorithm and appropriate data structures. But, given a good general algorithm, the next step is usually to find and perfect the inner loops.

Many things can systematically be done to minimize C loop execution time. You can replace logic with tables, unroll loops, make the loop counter double as array indexes, and even prefetch memory into the cache. Going beyond C, into assembly language, you can make use of instructions not available in C (like `adc`), use jump tables, structure data so that multiple useful flags can be set by single operations, do fast fixed-value multiplications, and coil loops or run tandem loops in parallel. The techniques presented in this chapter are not exhaustive, but they are among the more important and common ones available.

The `WordCount()` problem reaches its performance limit at two cycles per character processed. Its solution is the kind of code you can walk away from, satisfied that the limit has been nearly enough reached. But more complex problems rarely come to such clean conclusions. The possibility of a better solution, of reducing a problem to its minimum yet fastest-running essence, always begs the question, "What if . . ." And *that* is the enduring fascination of code optimization.

# C Performance

## 8

*It was a grade.*
—Apocryphal origin of the name
of the C programming language

Actually, C deserves an A, which stands for assembly. Among the "higher-level" computer languages of the world, C is one of the closest to the assembly language level of control. Many C statements translate into only one or two instructions at assembly language level, and so it's not hard to think of code in bilingual terms—writing in C and thinking about the assembly translation, or conversely writing in assembly and thinking C.

In writing the code to accompany this book, I wrote many routines in two versions, C and assembly, and there was rarely any difficulty in translation. There just aren't many things you can do in assembly language that don't have close cousins in C. Here and there, C is a little clumsier because of its generality, but on the whole, there is more convergence than divergence between the languages.

This chapter focuses not so much on how to optimize C as on how to equate C and assembly language thinking and so think about optimizing in the context of both. The three main topics are

- How C statements translate into assembly language
- Compiler optimization switch behaviors
- Predicting C performance

Without writing so much as a line of assembly code, you can scope out performance problems with an accuracy rarely mentioned in high-level language texts.

**171**

# How C Statements Translate into Assembly Language

There are remarkably few keywords in the C language that actually do anything at runtime. Of the 27 keywords actually used in the original specification, only 10 arguably generate code. Most of the remainder generate data structures or other information that the compiler uses to decide how to translate the other ten keywords (plus, of course, the symbolic operators). Since there are so many of them, it's worth taking a look first at what all those data structures are doing to the environment.

## C Data Structures

In the universe of 32-bit PC computing, the following keywords usually correspond to the data sizes shown:

- char    1 byte
- short   2 bytes
- int     4 bytes
- long    4 bytes
- float   4 bytes
- double  8 bytes

In 16-bit days, an "int" was two bytes, but any self-respecting 32-bit environment these days defines it as synonymous with "long." The "long double" type may be implemented in some environments as a ten-byte value, but in the Watcom environment in which I tested, it was still eight bytes.

Proper data alignment, as previously discussed, is very important to good code performance. Any good compiler will do an excellent job of aligning these data types on appropriate boundaries: chars anywhere, shorts on two-byte boundaries, longs and floats on four-byte boundaries, and *global or static* doubles on eight-byte boundaries. The one alignment condition a compiler will likely not be able to handle, though, is the automatic double variable, which is usually consigned an arbitrary four-byte aligned position on the stack.

Backing up a little, in the C universe there are two worlds in which the compiler places data structures: the global-static world and the automatic-stack world. If a variable is global, it has a single address in memory that lasts forever. The compiler has no trouble placing doubles at eight-byte alignments in fixed memory. The other world is that of the automatic and passed parameter variables on the stack. Consider the following simple routine:

```
double globalvar;

double
AddToGlobal(double paramvar)
{
    double autovar;
    autovar = paramvar + globalvar;
    return autovar;
}
```

At runtime, pushing, popping, calling, and returning are all transacted on the stack in four-byte units. The variable `paramvar` gets pushed onto the stack before `AddToGlobal()` is called. Then one of the first things `AddToGlobal()` does is to clear some stack space for the variable `autovar`. The stack is not naturally eight-byte-aligned, and it turns out that the pain of doing things differently at run-time to get doubles into their natural alignment is rarely worth the hassle. (When it *is* important, you can handle it in assembly language.) But the point to be made is that storage on the stack is a little different than storage in global memory. If the stack ever loses its basic four-byte alignment, it can slow down access to many variables besides the doubles.

In the preceding routine, code to address the three variables would look something like this:

```
fld     qword ptr [534068H] ;   ;fetch absolute globalvar
fld     qword ptr [ebp+8]   ;   ;fetch stack paramvar
fld     qword ptr [ebp-8]   ;   ;fetch stack autovar
```

Note that passed parameters and automatic variables are usually addressed through the `ebp` register on the stack. The global variable just has an absolute address. Automatic variables, if not initialized, contain whatever junk happened to be on the stack when the routine was called. Some of the worst instabilities in C programming can occur when uninitialized automatic variables are accidentally used. A program can sit in a tight loop for hours, calling a simple routine again and again, only to have it crash mysteriously on the zillionth call because an interrupt left just the right junk on the stack to cause the crash.

C structures made with the `struct` directive combine simpler data types into a compound data type. Consider the following structure:

```
struct foo {
    long    longvar1;
    char    charvar;
    long    longvar2;
}
```

By default, C compilers usually make this a nine-byte structure with the `char` sandwiched in the middle between the two longs. If the first long is four-byte-aligned, the second one is not, and vice versa. Usually, compiler switches will allow you to force internal four-byte alignment on both longs if you wish. This adds three unused bytes right after the `charvar` in the middle, but at least it allows both longs to be four-byte-aligned if the entire structure is. In my own coding, I prefer to design structures that naturally give the best possible alignment to all elements, even if that means putting in unused dummy variables in the structure, like this:

```
struct foo {
    long    longvar1;
    char    charvar;
    char    padding1;    // this achieves 2-byte alignment
    short   padding2;    // this achieves 4-byte alignment
    long    longvar2;
}
```

This may be considered bad practice in some coding circles, but I generally find it helpful to know structures that deserve good alignment *get* good alignment, regardless of compiler switch settings.

When a structure like this is placed on the stack as an automatic variable or parameter, it is generally given four-byte alignment.

Unions just allow multiple data structures to share the same space. Whether in global memory or on the stack, enough space has to be allocated to hold the largest member of the union. On the stack they are generally four-byte-aligned, just like structures.

Arrays pack their elements into a contiguous block of memory. If the size of the elements is a multiple of four bytes, then all elements will generally be given four-byte alignment. If the size of an individual element is, say, seven bytes, then only one array element in four will happen to have four-byte alignment. When an array has multiple indices, as in `arrayobject[row][column]`, items that differ only in the rightmost index value are closer together in memory than items differing in the index value farther to the left. In the particular example given in the previous sentence, successive column entries would be next to each other in memory, and row entries would be separated by as many data items as there are columns. When given the choice, inner loops that iterate over a rightmost index value usually run faster than equivalent routines iterating over other index values, since memory generally responds better when accesses fall close together. Random access to array elements usually runs fastest when the array element size is a power of 2. That way the index value can just be shifted to give an offset into the array, instead of undergoing a more lengthy multiplication step.

# C Keywords in Action

The C code-generating words are not far above the assembly language level. Here they are in increasing order of complexity.

### Else, Case, and Default

These three words usually serve as little more than labels inside compiled executable code. An `else` statement usually just labels the branch destination for a preceding `if` statement's failure test. It's just a place to go to. Similarly, `case` and `default` set up destination labels for the switch statement.

### Do

The `do` keyword really means "don't jump to the `while` test at the end of the loop." It's a tag that lets the compiler know that it doesn't need to run a conditional test the first time it enters a loop. Usually this means that the code preceding the loop just "falls through" into the loop.

### Goto, Break, and Continue

These statements generally just turn into `jmp` instructions. A `goto` jumps wherever you tell it to within a function. A `break` jumps to an instruction outside an enclosing `while/do-while/for` loop. And a `continue` jumps straight over remaining loop interior code to the loop condition code.

### Return

A `return` statement just cleans up, restores some registers, and leaves, as in this representative piece of code:

```
mov     eax,retval    ;  ;load up return value
pop     esi           ;  ;pop a saved register
pop     edi           ;  ;pop a saved register
pop     ebx           ;  ;pop a saved register
mov     esp,ebp       ;  ;release automatic vars
pop     ebp           ;  ;pop old stack frame
retn                  ;  ;and return
```

Actual return code may vary from case to case, but it's fairly mundane and straight-forward.

## If

An `if` statement boils down to a conditional branch. Once its argument is evaluated, it becomes a `jc` or a `jz` or some other such statement that skips the body of the conditional code if the condition fails. A simple `if (var > 3)` statement may translate to

```
        mov     eax,var       ;  ;fetch the variable
        cmp     eax,3         ;  ;compare it
        jle     past_the_body ;  ;branch on failure
```

## While

A statement like `while (arg != endval)` may be translated in one of these ways:

```
whloop: mov     eax,arg       ;  ;fetch arg
        mov     edx,endval    ;  ;fetch endval
        cmp     eax,edx       ;  ;compare
        je      endwh         ;  ;maybe exit
;                             ;  ;
;body of while goes here      ;  ;
;                             ;  ;
        jmp     whloop        ;  ;go back to test
endwh:                        ;  ;exit here
```

or...

```
        jmp     wheval        ;  ;
whloop:                       ;  ;
;                             ;  ;
;body of while goes here      ;  ;
;                             ;  ;
wheval: mov     eax,arg       ;  ;fetch arg
        mov     edx,endval    ;  ;fetch endval
        cmp     eax,edx       ;  ;compare
        jne     whloop        ;  ;maybe loop
```

The latter translation usually runs a little faster (half a cycle per loop, on average) than the former. The `do-while` form is the same as the latter code, without the initial jump to the evaluation code.

## For

The `for` statement is like a macro for doing convenient `while` statements. The statement `for (expression1; expression2; expression3)` is exactly the same as

```
expression1;
while (expression2) {
    // body of for goes here
    expression3;
}
```

The `while` code inside the `for` code is the same as any other `while` code. One real-time danger often overlooked in C programming is that both the second and third expressions in a `for` statement become part of the loop. Consider this statement:

```
for (n = 0; n < strlen(arg); n++) {}
```

Since `strlen(arg)` is actually inside the loop, this loop may run very slowly, making a string measuring call on every iteration. What may be more appropriate, as well as being consistent with the original intention, is

```
for (n = 0, m = strlen(arg); n < m; n++) {}
```

## Switch

The `switch` statement is the C statement for which it is most difficult to confidently predict actual code. I have seen it implemented in three different ways, as follows:

1. *As a* `repne scasd` *scan of case values.* The first time I looked at compiled `switch` code, I found that it had made a memory array of all the case values associated with the `switch` statement. It used the `repne scasd` statement to scan for a match. When it found the match, it noted its position in the array and then used the same array index to locate a jump vector associated with that label in another table. This scheme rewarded case statements early in the list with faster execution than those later in the list.

2. *As a jump table indexed by case value.* When all the case statement values are small and close together, the compiler can afford to make a jump table (so that, for instance, case 27 vectors off through jump table entry 27). This scheme rewards the practice of keeping case statements contiguous in their values. In other words, cases limited to, say, cases 1, 2, 3, 4, and 5 would get to directly index a jump table, while cases 1,000, 2,000, 3,000, 4,000, and 5,000 would have to be dealt with some other way.

3. *As a binary comparison tree.* Another way compilers can deal with case statements, especially when option 2 isn't practical, is by creating a binary decision tree in code. As per the case above, it might first compare the switch value to 3,000. If it finds a match, it executes the appropriate code. If the value is greater than 3,000, then it only has to discriminate between 4,000 and 5,000. If it is lower, then the decision is between 1,000 and 2,000. This scheme is most rewarding to large case lists, especially those biased toward a small subset of the case statements (in which case branch prediction logic will help execution considerably).

If you don't know what your compiler is thinking, a good way to hedge your bet for best performance is to put the most commonly executed case statements at the top of the case list (in case the compiler is using the first scheme, or, even worse, a serial chain of `if`-like comparisons) and use small, contiguous numbers for the case values (to promote scheme 2, which is usually the fastest).

## C Operators

Most of the rest of the operators in C have simple assembly language correlates. In cases where the values being operated upon are held in registers, the code generated by C operators often looks like this:

```
mov    eax,[esi+8]   ;   ;a = b->c
mov    eax,[esi]     ;   ;a = *b
lea    eax,[esi+8]   ;   ;a = &b->c
neg    eax           ;   ;a = -a
not    eax           ;   ;a = ~a
inc    eax           ;   ;a++
dec    eax           ;   ;a--
imul   eax,ebx       ;   ;a * b
idiv   ebx           ;   ;a / b  (result in eax)
idiv   ebx           ;   ;a % b  (result in edx)
add    eax,ebx       ;   ;a + b
sub    eax,ebx       ;   ;a - b
sar    eax,cl        ;   ;a >> b
shl    eax,cl        ;   ;a << b
and    eax,ebx       ;   ;a & b
xor    eax,ebx       ;   ;a ^ b
or     eax,ebx       ;   ;a | b
```

The operators that can generate a logical 0 or a logical 1, such as `!=`, are often just used for branching, without actually ever generating a 0 or 1. For instance, `if (a != b) c = d;` may be translated like this:

```
            cmp     eax,ebx         ;   ;compare
            je      skipit          ;   ;branch on failure
            mov     ecx,edx         ;   ;success code
skipit:                             ;   ;common end point
```

If, instead, you wrote a = (b != c), you might get this code:

```
            xor     eax,eax         ;   ;clear the register to 0
            cmp     ecx,edx         ;   ;compare
            je      skipit          ;   ;branch on failure
            inc     eax             ;   ;record a 1
skipit:                             ;   ;common end point
```

A chain of logical ands, such as if (a && b && c), always evaluates left to right and opts for an early out whenever possible:

```
            test    eax,eax         ;   ;if (a)...
            je      skipit          ;   ;failure exit
            test    ebx,ebx         ;   ;if (b)...
            je      skipit          ;   ;failure exit
            test    ecx,ecx         ;   ;if (c)...
            je      skipit          ;   ;failure exit
;                                   ;   ;
;conditional body here              ;   ;
;                                   ;   ;
skipit:                             ;   ;common end point
```

A chain of logical ors, such as if (a || b || c), always evaluates left to right and opts for an early execution whenever possible:

```
            test    eax,eax         ;   ;if (a)...
            jne     doit            ;   ;success entry
            test    ebx,ebx         ;   ;if (b)...
            jne     doit            ;   ;success entry
            test    ecx,ecx         ;   ;if (c)...
            je      skipit          ;   ;failure exit
doit:                               ;   ;
;                                   ;   ;
;conditional body here              ;   ;
;                                   ;   ;
skipit:                             ;   ;common end point
```

When values are held in memory instead of registers, more data movement instructions and more cycles are involved. But the essence of most C operators is usually just an opcode or two and a few memory movements.

## C Functions

When you invoke a C function like `foo(a, b, c)`, what you usually get is code to push `c`, `b`, and `a` onto the stack in the reverse order from the way they were listed as function parameters. By pushing parameters in reverse order, they appear on the stack as if they were in their original, unreversed order. That is, the first parameter will be at a lower address than the second, and so forth. This reverse order of evaluation is not guaranteed by the C language specification, so in general it's not safe to pass parameters to a function when the parameters are sensitive to the order of evaluation. Calling a function like `foo(arg++, arg++, arg++)` may not do what you expect. You should *expect* `foo(arg+2, arg+1, arg)`, not `foo(arg, arg+1, arg+2)`, but you shouldn't *count* on it. Some compilers implement parameter passing via a mix of registers and stack locations, and their order of evaluation is even more questionable.

After pushing all the parameters (or stuffing some in registers), the callee function is called. When the function returns, C adjusts the stack to remove all the previously passed parameters.

Here is how `foo(var1, var2, var3)` might look at assembly language level:

```
        push    var3        ;   ;third var
        push    var2        ;   ;second var
        push    var1        ;   ;first var
        call    foo         ;   ;call the function
        add     esp,12      ;   ;pop 3*4 off the stack
```

Functions usually return values in the `eax` register.

Translation from C into assembly language is often straightforward and understandable. Optimizing compilers sometimes reorder instructions for the best execution, making it a little harder to trace the flow, but compiled code is nevertheless usually fairly easy to follow with respect to the original C code.

# Compiler Optimization Switch Behaviors

With any given compiler, there are usually a variety of optimization switch options. And unless you're very focused on a certain aspect of performance, you usually just want to say, "Give me the max" and forget about it. Most compilers come with something like a give-me-the-max switch, or at least some give-me-the-max directions.

Here are some of the components of what "give-me-the-max" means. These may be individually selectable options in any given environment.

1. *Expanding small functions inline.* Rather than spend time stacking parameters and calling and returning from a function call, just put the function code inline. You can end up with dozens of separate copies of a commonly called routine this way, but the program may run faster if the copies are mainly located in looped code that stays in the cache from one execution to the next. This may bulk up the code, but it may run significantly faster.

2. *Loop unrolling.* Another way to add bulk (and possibly speed) is to let the compiler unroll loops—several copies of the loop body in a row. Presumably it will have enough sense to unroll mainly the small loops, when possible, and leave the big ones alone.

3. *Removing loop-invariant code from the loop.* For instance, if the compiler noticed that you used the expression a = b * c inside the loop but never modified b or c, it could do the multiplication temp = b * c before entering the loop and then just perform a much faster a = temp inside the loop.

4. *The space/speed switch.* Compilers often have some sort of general switch that can be thrown to favor speed over space, or vice versa. Choosing space as the priority may, for instance, enable some of the time-inefficient instructions, like lodsb, that were once fast but now have virtue only in their smallness. For my own personal use, I always prefer the speed switch. But as my gigabyte hard drive shrinks under the onslaught of hundreds of megabytes of others' code libraries, I can see the virtue of compiling small code when it is expected to be rarely used and is not time-critical.

5. *Code reordering.* When debugging code and looking through the generated assembly, it often helps if all the code associated with a given line is in the same place. Giving the compiler permission to shuffle instructions around so that they no longer seem to be associated in the original order is not as harrowing a thing as it sounds. To the extent that I have dealt with reordered code, it still looks pretty familiar, and the occasional surprise instruction often just suggests a good optimization.

6. *Allowing inexact floating-point division through multiplication.* If you have the expression a = b/3.0 in your code, it will take about 50 cycles to execute. The expression a = b*0.333333333, however, produces nearly identical results and costs less than ten cycles. At the level of the least significant bits, there may be a minute difference between the evaluations of these two expressions. Usually it's OK to let this multiplication-for-division substitution take place.

7. *Relaxing alias checking.* If you're not careful and just leave this optimization on all the time, sooner or later it may introduce a bug. This switch is basically a contract between the programmer and the compiler that says, "I promise that I will never pass a pointer to a global variable to a routine that also uses that global variable by direct reference." The compiler won't know if you're lying, but your code could fail if you are. The problem is that the optimized code would like to be able to keep variables in registers, and if it picks up and operates on two copies of the same variable (the global copy and the pointed-to copy) without knowing that it's really the same variable, one copy can end up erroneously overwriting the other. It's an extremely rare piece of code that would ever experience that problem, but it *can* happen.

There are no doubt other optimization options available from compiler to compiler, but these are among the most common ones.

# Predicting C Performance

Here is a quick-and-easy way to estimate how fast an inner loop written in C will run on a Pentium:

1. Count the number of separate variable names and C keywords used in the loop.
2. Add to that the number of multiplications, times 10.
3. Add to that the number of divisions, times 50.
4. The resultant number should be somewhere in the ballpark of the number of cycles required to execute the loop.

For the purposes of counting cycles, words connected by a dot operator (.) should be counted as one large single word. The expression a = b.c.d only counts as two variables. If certain sections of code are expected to be skipped regularly, they should be omitted from the count.

This formula works best in the context of integer arithmetic. The more complex the loop, the more likely the variable count number should be multiplied by 1.5 or 2, since more variables means more traffic to and from memory, perhaps including cache misses. With the exception of multiplication and division (and modulo, which is equivalent to division), it doesn't matter much which specific operations are connecting the variables.

Floating-point arithmetic, especially conversions between integer and floating-point formats, can complicate matters. For each integer-to-floating-point conversion, add 5. And for each floating-point-to-integer conversion, add 100, at least in the Watcom environment. The floating-point unit normally rounds its results to the value most nearly correct. But when it converts from floating-point format to a C integer, it must "chop" to the integer value closer to zero. Reprogramming the floating-point unit to do this, then doing it, and then reprogramming the floating-point unit to round to the nearest value can cost up to 100 cycles. If C accepted the round-to-the-nearest-integer philosophy, it could all be over within five cycles or so of overhead.

Here is a working example:

```
for (n = 0; n < 100; n++) {
    d += ar[n & 3];
}
```

On the first line, n = 0 doesn't count, because it's outside the loop. But n and 100 and n (from the n++ expression) count. On the second line, d, ar, n, and 3 count. That's a total of seven items with no multiplications and no divisions. So seven cycles is the predicted execution time; on a 100 MHz machine that would mean 14 million loop executions per second (100,000,000/7). My actual measured execution time, compiled with full optimizations on, was six cycles. Not bad for a rule of thumb.

## Conclusion

C and assembly language are cousins. It is not difficult to think and write bilingually when coding in one langage or the other. The facilities of structured assembly language bring the two languages even closer together. Optimizing compilers go a long way toward making C execution speed competitive with assembly language's speed. A simple rule of thumb allows you to approximately equate words in a C loop with cycles at execution time on the Pentium.

# MMX

*Two, four, [six,] eight. Who do we appreciate?*
*—Common cheer, in apparent anticipation of MMX parallelism*

In early 1996, Intel announced the first major architectural extension of the 80x86 instruction set since the introduction of 32-bit registers and their associated instructions with the 386. Called MMX, the eight new 64-bit registers and their associated instruction set are to be grafted onto future Pentium and Pentium Pro processors. Although the term "MMX" appears to have been inspired by the expression "multimedia extensions," Intel claims that it doesn't stand for anything in particular. But whatever the name does or doesn't mean, it's a major boost to the processor's power—particularly with regard to multimedia applications!

As of this writing, in mid 1996, the chips aren't out. But a fair amount of detailed documentation is. This chapter is a preliminary look at what the new chips should have to offer. In particular, this chapter looks at

- General processor enhancements
- The MMX registers
- The MMX instructions
- MMX instruction timing and pairing
- Software emulation of MMX

The presence or absence of MMX can be detected using information returned by the `cpuid` instruction (which was new with the Pentium). And if software doesn't find MMX, it needs fast inner loops to even come close to making up for its absence.

---

# General Processor Enhancements

Almost overlooked in the celebration of the new MMX features is the fact that Pentium Pros and, especially, Pentiums produced with MMX will have several significant improvements to their general architecture that will benefit general program execution.

## 16K Primary Cache

The first great and general gift of MMX is a 16K primary data and code cache. Each cache line is still 32 bytes, but instead of the former, slightly dangerous two-way set-associative structure (where just three memory references in a cycle can produce worst-case cache behavior), the cache is four-way set-associative. This not only means that there's a lot more cache to go around but also that it's much less likely that situations will arise where cache lines get thrown out just before they're needed (although, in truth, this was a rather rare occurrence on the Pentium anyhow). Having the extra 8K is just a great thing.

## Faster Instructions (0FH Prefix)

The following common instructions (plus some uncommon ones) should run one cycle faster on a Pentium with MMX, because, the claim is made, instructions with the 0FH prefix are no longer penalized one cycle by this "prefix":

- `bswap`
- `setCC`
- `shld`
- `shrd`
- `movsx`
- `movzx`

This doubles the speed of `bswap` and `setCC` and makes them much more attractive in inner loops.

## 16-Bit Instructions More Pairable

It used to be that instructions that operated on 16-bit data had to execute in the U pipe (the first position in a pair). On a Pentium with MMX, 16-bit instructions can also occupy the second position, in the V pipe. It is not entirely clear from the documentation what the performance penalty is for pairing two 16-bit instructions, or, for that matter, pairing a 16-bit instruction in the V pipe. My best guess, subject to verification, is that there's a one-cycle penalty for each 16-bit instruction.

## Pairable Immediate/Displacement Instructions

On a regular Pentium, this instruction is not pairable, because it contains both an immediate value and a displacement:

```
mov     byte ptr [edi+7],99
```

On a Pentium with MMX, however, it can be placed in the first position of a pair, and hence in the U pipe. In effect, this particular instruction's effective speed is thereby doubled from one cycle to half a cycle (when paired with another half-cycle instruction).

## Merged Write Buffers

On the Pentium, there is a two-deep write buffer, or queue, associated with each "pipe." If you have to do four writes in rapid succession to noncached memory, the best way to do so is to issue two of them from the U pipe and the other two from the V pipe. If they all come from, say, the U pipe, the queue will jam up and the processor will be delayed, even though the V pipe write buffer is empty. Basically, the right hand can't help out the left, even if it does know what it's doing.

On the Pentium with MMX, however, the two separate write buffers have been merged into a single, four-deep write buffer. Now you don't have to worry about which pipe is writing to memory.

## Return Stack Buffer

The return stack buffer, which made its debut in the Pentium Pro, is also present in Pentiums with MMX. Consider the following routine:

```
int
Add3()
{
    int ret;
    ret  = NextByte();
    ret += NextByte();
    ret += NextByte();
    return ret;
}
```

A regular Pentium would try in vain to predict the return address of the `NextByte()` routine. Because there are three separate invocations and three separate return addresses, the branch table prediction mechanism would get totally confused and guess wrong every time. (A Pentium thinks of a `ret` instruction as a form of a branch.)

On a Pentium with MMX, the processor actually keeps a limited list of stacked return addresses inside the chip, as well as on the external stack in memory. So when it sees a `ret`, it doesn't have to rely on the branch predictor but references the internal stack instead, for a near-perfect prediction. The routine shown above will execute about a dozen cycles faster under MMX.

## Faster Cache Delivery

On both the 486 and the Pentium, there is a marked delay between the time a given cache miss completes and the time another reference to the same cache line can complete. A typical scenario would be

```
        mov     al,[esi+0]      ; 7;primary cache miss
        mov     bl,[esi+4]      ; 7;same-line delay
                                ;;;;14 cycles
```

The claim is made that on processors with MMX, cache line data will be available for a second hit (and beyond) as soon as it arrives in the cache line, and you don't have to wait until the cache line is full anymore. If this is really true, then the preceding code should execute more like this under MMX:

```
        mov     al,[esi+0]      ; 9;primary cache miss
        mov     bl,[esi+4]      ; 0;no delay in same 8 bytes
                                ;;;;9 cycles
```

The difference in the timing of the first instruction is due to the reported larger delay associated with a cache miss under MMX.

If your cache miss hits somewhere in the first eight bytes of a cache line, then the cache line will be delivered in eight-byte chunks from low to high. If it hits in the top eight bytes, then it delivers in high-to-low order. This way, applications that reference data serially in memory, whether from low address to high or the other way around, will get data delivered in the order in which it will most likely be needed. If it's really true, this will be a significant boon to applications that rip through memory very quickly.

## Some Minuses

The delay for a primary cache miss usually measures in at about six cycles on the Pentium (plus the normal one cycle for a memory reference). On a Pentium with MMX, it is claimed to be eight. And it's ten on a Pentium Pro with MMX. So a cache miss is a little more expensive. On the plus side, with 16K of data cache and 16K of code cache, you should be missing much less often.

If, on an MMX chip, you have two back-to-back branching statements and they both end in the same four-byte-aligned, four-byte chunk of memory, the second branch will probably be mispredicted. If, as is usually the case, the branches are short and take up only two bytes, then there's about a 50-50 chance that back-to-back branches will have this problem in any given instance. The best, but very awkward, solution is to force the second branch to be a six-byte-long branch instead (with a 32-bit offset rather than 8-bit). It takes four more bytes, but it executes in the same time. This is, frankly, hard to do with some assemblers. MASM likes to optimize branch sizes, so you could end up putting the branch in with data statements. It may be easier to put a pairable no-op such as `mov ebx,ebx` in between them for spacing. It will only end up costing a cycle on the Pentium if the branch mispredicts.

# The MMX Registers

The eight 64-bit MMX registers correspond exactly to the stack of eight floating-point registers available in the floating-point unit. In fact, they correspond so exactly that if you read an MMX register that hasn't been initialized, you'll see the mantissa of the last floating-point number stored there. And if you don't take the proper precautions, you can make the floating-point unit rather sick by interspersing MMX instructions with floating-point instructions, since they use the same register bits.

Generally speaking, the floating-point instructions and the MMX instructions should be used in separate groups of instructions, because it takes a reported "up to 50 cycles" to revert from MMX code to floating-point code. Floating-point instructions and MMX instructions cannot be freely intermixed.

Each of the eight MMX registers, named `mm0` through `mm7`, can be thought of and treated in one of three basic ways during the execution of any individual instruction:

- An MMX register can be eight independent 8-bit bytes.
- An MMX register can be four independent 16-bit words.
- An MMX register can be two independent 32-bit doublewords.

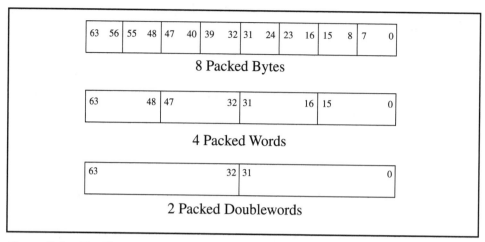

**Figure 9-1    The Three Ways MMX Registers Can Be Used**

These are illustrated in Figure 9-1. The powerful aspect of MMX is that it can operate, usually in a single cycle, on all the independent units in a register in parallel, performing a variety of logical, arithmetic, and housekeeping operations.

As an illustration of just how much MMX can do in a single cycle, consider the following two instructions, which can pair together and add 16 individual bytes to 16 other individual bytes in just one cycle:

```
paddb    mm0,mm1    ; 1;packed add mm1 to mm0
paddb    mm2,mm3    ; 0;packed add mm3 to mm2
                    ;;;;1 cycle
```

That's an order of magnitude faster than the main integer processor can do the same thing.

When you want to revert to using floating-point instructions, you have to issue an `emms` instruction to make the registers safe once again for floating-point operations.

# The MMX Instructions

In some ways, the MMX instructions are reminiscent of the floating-point instruction set. They don't set the processor's flags, or indeed any flags. There is no performance penalty for fetching one operand from memory instead of from an MMX register. You can only generate arithmetic or logical results in registers, not in memory operands. And you can't store a computational result back to memory until the second cycle after its computation. But other than these similarities, there is a much different—and very fast—integer machine under the hood.

## Data Movement Instructions

The main data movement instruction is `movq`, which transfers quadwords (eight bytes) between MMX registers and memory as well as between two MMX registers. Another data movement instruction, `movd`, transfers doublewords back and forth between the low halves of MMX registers and the processor's own 32-bit registers (like `ebx`).

## Packing and Unpacking Instructions

Suppose you had a large array of signed words that you wanted to convert to signed bytes instead. You would probably want a word with value 300 to be converted to a byte of value 127, the largest possible signed byte. Likewise, −144 should become −128. Well, MMX is good at pulling off this kind of transformation. It has instructions for packing words into bytes with or without saturation (signed or unsigned), which is the process of setting a smaller data item to its largest or smallest possible value when it can't adequately represent the larger data item it came from.

The three basic packing instructions are

- `packssdw`  Pack with signed saturation, dwords to words
- `packsswb`  Pack with signed saturation, words to bytes
- `packuswb`  Pack with unsigned saturation, words to bytes

To pack eight signed words located at `[esi]` into eight signed bytes in register mm0, you would do this:

```
movq     mm0,[esi]     ;  ;load 4 words into mm0
packsswb mm0,[esi+8]   ;  ;pack with 4 words in mem
```

When unpacking the same data (the reverse process), you might expect to have a signed and an unsigned unpack instruction. But you don't. Instead, you take two MMX registers and then intermix them into one register, using either the four high bytes of both registers or the four low bytes of both registers. The eight bytes in the destination register thus come alternately from one source register and then the other. If you want to do sign extension, one of the operands has to be precalculated to hold sign extension bytes.

The unpacking instructions, which operate on bytes, words, and doublewords to produce words, doublewords, and quadwords, respectively, are

- `punpcklbw`   Unpack from low halves, bytes to words
- `punpckhbw`   Unpack from high halves, bytes to words
- `punpcklwd`   Unpack from low halves, words to doublewords
- `punpckhwd`   Unpack from high halves, words to doublewords
- `punpckldq`   Unpack from low halves, doublewords to quadwords
- `punpckhdq`   Unpack from high halves, doublewords to quadwords

Here is how you would zero-extend eight bytes in `mm0` into eight words in `mm0` and `mm1`, assuming `quadzero` is a zero quadword memory variable:

```
movq        mm1,mm0       ;  ;copy the register
punpcklbw   mm0,quadzero  ;  ;expand 4 low bytes
punpckhbw   mm1,quadzero  ;  ;expand 4 high bytes
```

## Addition and Subtraction

Addition and subtraction come with the option of value saturation, much like the way the packing instructions saturate packed values. If you add two MMX registers via byte-wise addition, you can choose no saturation option (values wrap) or saturation according to either signed or unsigned arithmetic. The addition operations are

- `paddb`    Add by bytes, ignoring overflows (wraps)
- `paddsb`   Add by bytes, signed bytes with saturation
- `paddusb`  Add by bytes, unsigned bytes with saturation
- `paddw`    Add by words, ignoring overflows (wraps)
- `paddsw`   Add by words, signed words with saturation
- `paddusw`  Add by words, unsigned words with saturation
- `paddd`    Add by doublewords, ignoring overflows

There are subtraction operations exactly equivalent to each of the addition operations.

## Bitwise Logical Operations

There are four 64-bit bitwise logical operators. There is no distinction between byte, word, doubleword, and quadword forms, because a bitwise operator works the same way regardless. The operators are

- pand     A 64-bit and operation
- por      A 64-bit or operation
- pxor    A 64-bit xor operation
- pnand   Inverts the bits of the destination, then does a 64-bit and

Sometimes you may want to combine two quadwords into a single quadword, using a mask of bits to indicate which of the two quadwords the corresponding bit comes from. To do this, you and the mask with one quadword and then invert the bits of the mask (logical not) and and it with the other one; then you or the two intermediates together. The pnand operation is specifically there to serve the invert-and-and function in one step.

## Mask-Making Instructions

Suppose you have some sort of graphic image stored in memory at one byte per pixel, and you want the bytes with value 211 in the image to be transparent when you overlay the image on a bitmap. Let [esi] be the pointer to a piece of the image, let [edi] be the pointer to the area where you would like to overlay it, and let mmx211 be a memory quadword filled with bytes of value 211. Then this sequence would perform the overlay with transparency:

```
movq    mm0,[esi]   ;   ;fetch image to overlay
movq    mm1,[edi]   ;   ;fetch background
movq    mm2,mmx211  ;   ;fetch bytes for mask test
pcmpeqb mm2,mm0     ;   ;make transparent spots 0ffH
pand    mm1,mm2     ;   ;mask only visible background
pnand   mm2,mm0     ;   ;mask only visible image
por     mm1,mm2     ;   ;combine background and image
movq    [edi],mm1   ;   ;and store the result
```

The comparison instruction in this case put 0ffH in any byte position that matched exactly in both operands, or zero otherwise. There is another comparison operation that deposits 0ffH if the byte in a given position in the first operand is greater than the byte in the second operand at that position, according to signed arithmetic. These instructions can operate on bytes, words, or doublewords. There are six forms:

- pcmpeqb   Compare by bytes. If equal, set byte to 0ffH; otherwise, set to 0
- pcmpeqw   Compare by words. If equal, set word to 0ffffH; otherwise, set to 0
- pcmpeqd   Compare by dwords. If equal, set dword to 0ffffffffH; otherwise, set to 0
- pcmpgtb   Compare by bytes. If greater than, set byte to 0ffH; otherwise, set to 0
- pcmpgtw   Compare by words. If greater than, set word to 0ffffH; otherwise, set to 0
- pcmpgtd   Compare by dwords. If greater than, set dword to 0ffffffffH; otherwise, set to 0

## Shifting

Although there is no 64-bit addition instruction in MMX, there *is* a pair of 64-bit shifts. On the other hand, there are no shifts that operate on bytes. Although the missing byte shifts are to be slightly mourned, the full 64-bit shift is useful for coping with data that doesn't lie on natural eight-byte boundaries.

Here are the shift operations:

- psllw   Shift left logical by words
- pslld   Shift left logical by doublewords
- psslq   Shift left logical by quadwords
- psrlw   Shift right logical by words
- psrld   Shift right logical by doublewords
- psrlq   Shift right logical by quadwords
- psraw   Shift right arithmetic by words
- psrad   Shift right by doublewords

The amount of the shift can be specified as an immediate value:

```
psllw   mm0,7   ;   ;shift each word by 7
```

Or the amount(s) can be read from another quadword:

```
psllw   mm0,mm1 ;  ;shift by mm1 amounts
```

Note that in the preceding example, `mm1` could possibly contain four different values in its four component words, in which case the four words of `mm0` would each be shifted by a different amount.

## Multiplication

All MMX multiplication is based on the notion of multiplying the four signed words of one quadword by the four signed words of another quadword. Of course, multiplying two 16-bit values gives a 32-bit value, so the three result options are as follows: take the low 16 bits of all four results; take the high 16 bits of all four results; or take two 32-bit sums of the results of two pairs of multiplications.

The instructions are

- `pmulhw`    Multiply and return the high word
- `pmullw`    Multiply and return the low word
- `pmaddwd`   Multiply and return two doubleword multiplication sums

Compared to conventional integer multiplication, the MMX forms are blazingly fast.

# MMX Instruction Timing and Pairing

MMX instructions are fast. Other than the `emms` instruction—which ends an MMX session (and is implied to take up to 50 cycles)—and the multiplication instructions, all the MMX instructions take just one cycle, and most are pairable. The multiplication instructions take three cycles to complete, but because they are heavily pipelined, you can issue a multiplication instruction on every cycle, and as long as you don't try to read the results until three cycles later, you won't encounter a stall.

Besides the typical Pentium pairing constraints (no read or write after write, and so on), the biggest single constraint on paired instructions is that only the first instruction of a pair (the one in the U pipe) can read or write to memory or to a processor 32-bit register. Less inhibiting, you can't issue two multiplication instructions in the same cycle, and you can't issue two pack/unpack/shift instructions in the same cycle (whereas packing and unpacking are really types of shift operations and presumably use the shifter's engine). And finally, an MMX instruction can pair with a regular processor instruction as long as that regular instruction doesn't access memory. For instance, `add edx,esi` would pair with an MMX instruction just fine.

According to Intel's documentation, if you write to video memory over a PCI bus, you are likely to see a performance improvement writing from the MMX registers over writing the same data with 32-bit writes. And if you're doing a large memory-to-memory copy (not in a cache), you might do well to write a loop that loads and stores 64 bits at a time. On some Pentiums, they say, a performance gain of up to 30 percent has been seen. (This is comparable to the performance gain seen when using the floating-point unit to do memory transfers, as described in Chapter 10.)

One final thing to remember about MMX timing, already mentioned, is that an MMX register isn't ready to be written to memory for an extra cycle after its last computation completes.

# Software Emulation of MMX

If software is to be built that can opt to use MMX if present—or perform equivalent actions if it is not—the first question that comes to mind is, "How much faster is MMX-enabled code than work-alike code on, say, a Pentium?" It depends on what you're doing.

## Packing with Signed Saturation

First consider the problem of packing an array of words into bytes using signed saturation, represented by this MMX code:

```
movq     mm0,[esi]       ; 1;load 4 words
packsswb mm0,[esi+8]     ; 1;pack with 4 more words
movq     [edi],mm0       ; 1;store
                         ;;;;3 cycles
```

Listing 9-1 shows the fastest equivalent Pentium code I could think of to do the same thing. At 24 cycles, it takes eight times longer. The 64K table should not be a cache miss problem unless the data is very badly behaved and much of it is wildly out of the saturation range.

**Listing 9-1    Pentium Equivalent of MMX** `packsswb`

```
;on entry:
;        ebx - pointer to 64K saturation table
;        ecx - 0
;        edx - 0
;        esi - source pointer
;        edi - destination pointer
;
         mov    cx,[esi+6]       ; 2;pick up 4th word
         mov    dx,[esi+4]       ; 2;pick up 3rd word
         mov    ah,[ecx+ebx]     ; 1;saturate 4th byte
         mov    cx,[esi+2]       ; 2;pick up 2nd word
         mov    al,[edx+ebx]     ; 0;saturate 3rd byte
         mov    dx,[esi+0]       ; 2;pick up 1st word
         shl    eax,16           ; 1;boost al,ah up 16 bits
         mov    ah,[ecx+ebx]     ; 1;saturate 2nd byte
         mov    cx,[esi+14]      ; 2;pick up 8th word
         mov    al,[edx+ebx]     ; 0;saturate 1st byte
         mov    dx,[esi+12]      ; 2;pick up 7th word
         mov    [edi],eax        ; 0;store 4 saturated bytes
         mov    ah,[ecx+ebx]     ; 1;saturate 8th byte
         mov    cx,[esi+10]      ; 2;pick up 6th word
         mov    al,[edx+ebx]     ; 0;saturate 7th byte
         mov    dx,[esi+8]       ; 2;pick up 5th word
         shl    eax,16           ; 1;boost al,ah up 16 bits
         mov    ah,[ecx+ebx]     ; 1;saturate 6th byte
         mov    al,[edx+ebx]     ; 1;saturate 5th byte
         mov    [edi],eax        ; 1;store 4 saturated bytes
                                 ;;;;24 cycles
```

# Packing with Unsigned Saturation

Unsigned saturation can run about twice as fast on a Pentium if there are few bytes to be saturated. If you're willing to use an algorithm that modifies the source array in order to gain a few cycles, you can write an MMX instruction equivalent for `packuswb` in 13 cycles. Listing 9-2 shows the first half of the algorithm. The second half repeats eight bytes higher and saves a cycle by overlapping with the first half.

**Listing 9-2    Unsigned Saturation of Four Bytes, as in `packuswb`**

```
;on entry:
;        ebp - 0ff00ff00H
;        esi - source pointer
;        edi - destination pointer

        mov     eax,[esi+0]             ; 1;get first 2 words
        mov     ebx,[esi+4]             ; 0;get second 2 words
        .if eax & ebp                   ; 1;check for saturation
          .if eax & 0ff00H              ;   ;maybe saturate byte 1
            mov al,0ffH                 ;   ;
          .endif                        ;   ;
          .if eax & 0ff000000H          ;   ;maybe saturate byte 2
            mov byte ptr [esi+2],0ffH   ;   ;modify source!
          .endif                        ;   ;
        .endif                          ;   ;
        .if ebx & ebp                   ; 1;check for saturation
          .if ebx & 0ff00H              ;   ;maybe saturate 3
            mov bl,0ffH                 ;   ;
          .endif                        ;   ;
          .if ebx & 0ff000000H          ;   ;maybe saturate 4
            mov byte ptr [esi+6],0ffH   ;   ;modify source!
          .endif                        ;   ;
        .endif                          ;   ;
        and     eax,0ffffH              ; 1;clear top of eax
        mov     bh,[esi+6]              ; 0;bx has byte pair
        shl     ebx,16                  ; 1;ebx ready for or
        mov     ah,[esi+2]              ; 0;ax has byte pair
        or      eax,ebx                 ; 1;compose 4 bytes
        mov     [edi],eax               ; 1;and deposit
                                        ;;;;7 cycles
```

# Multiplication

Pipelined parallel multiplication is obviously a large win. It takes a Pentium 44 cycles to execute four 16-bit signed multiplication instructions, whereas MMX can cut the effective cost down to half a cycle if the instruction is paired and the results are not accessed for three cycles. You can multiply the elements of two memory word arrays into a third word array using MMX at an overall cost approaching 0.75 cycles per array element (assuming reasonably large arrays in the primary cache and overlapped load-multiply-store sequences). In fact, multiplication is so fast in this instance that it can be rate-limited at perhaps half its top speed if the arrays aren't in cache. The best a raw Pentium can do, in contrast, is about 15 cycles per element, although it can deliver full 32-bit results.

Performing 16-bit array multiplication with 32-bit results is actually a very interesting optimization problem. The following sequence of instructions multiplies two quadwords to *produce* two quadwords:

```
movq       mm0,[esi]      ;  ;fetch from input array 1
movq       mm1,[edx]      ;  ;fetch from input array 2
movq       mm2,mm0        ;  ;copy array 1 data
pmullw     mm0,mm1        ;  ;multiply low into mm0
pmulhw     mm1,mm2        ;  ;multiply high into mm1
movq       mm2,mm0        ;  ;duplicate low result
punpcklwd  mm0,mm1        ;  ;unpack low quadword
punpckhwd  mm2,mm1        ;  ;unpack high quadword
movq       [edi],mm0      ;  ;store 2 low doublewords
movq       [edi+8],mm2    ;  ;store 2 high doublewords
```

The tricky part about optimizing code like this is in obeying all the special constraints, like one memory operation per cycle, the three-cycle wait for multiplications to complete, and the one-cycle delay before unloading results to memory. Code like this is a perfect candidate for tandem loops.

Listing 9-3 shows an example of a high-efficiency loop that produces a 32-bit array from two input 16-bit arrays. Not shown (and not even written) is the entry and exit code, both of which are tedious problems in and of themselves. The two instructions of loop overhead are nestled in between otherwise unpaired MMX instructions, and there is only one stall cycle, due to a multiplication result that was read early. The end result is what appears to be a 12-cycle loop that produces eight 32-bit results. That's 1.5 cycles per result, a clean factor of 10 faster than a plain Pentium.

### Listing 9-3    16 × 16 → 32-Bit Multiplication Inner Loop

```
.repeat                          ;  ;
  movq      [edi+ecx*2-16],mm3   ; 1;2
  movq      mm2,mm0              ; 0;1
  movq      [edi+ecx*2-8],mm5    ; 1;2
  pmullw    mm0,mm1              ; 0;1
  movq      mm3,[esi+ecx+8]      ; 1;2 <- loop 2 start
  pmulhw    mm1,mm2              ; 0;1
  movq      mm4,[edx+ecx+8]      ; 1;2
  movq      mm5,mm3              ; 0;2
  pmullw    mm3,mm4              ; 1;2
  movq      mm2,mm0              ; 0;1
  pmulhw    mm4,mm5              ; 1;2
  punpcklwd mm0,mm1             ; 0;1
  movq      mm5,mm3              ; 2;2 <- pmullw stall
  punpckhwd mm2,mm1             ; 0;1
```

```
        movq      [edi+ecx*2],mm0      ; 1;1
        punpcklwd mm3,mm4              ; 0;2
        movq      [edi+ecx*2+8],mm2    ; 1;1
        punpckhwd mm5,mm4              ; 0;2
        movq      mm0,[esi+ecx+16]     ; 1;1 <- loop 1 start
        add       ecx,16               ; 0;
        movq      mm1,[edx+ecx+16]     ; 1;1
    .until ZERO?                       ; 0;
                                       ;;;;12 cycles
```

## Overlaying Graphics

A very common procedure in graphic animation is to overlay one graphic on top of another. Typically both objects are stored as bitmaps, and there is one unique "color" in the graphic image that indicates transparency. For this example, assume the bitmaps consist of one byte per pixel (the very common 256-color-lookup screen mode) and that the transparent "color" is any byte in the object that has a value of zero. Furthermore, assume that the alignment of the graphic object in memory is different from what its alignment will be when it is overlaid. This is a reasonable general assumption, since smooth animation often requires placing objects at every possible alignment.

Listing 9-4 shows a reasonable Pentium solution to the problem. It is natural to want to align the reads and writes of the background data on doubleword boundaries, but this generally means that corresponding doubleword reads from the object being overlaid will probably not be doubleword-aligned. There is a strong disincentive to read the object data a doubleword at a time at arbitrary alignment, as this will generally cause a three-cycle delay. (To be honest, though, if there is a high probability that doublewords will be consistently transparent or opaque while reading through the data, there are somewhat more efficient solutions that do take the three-cycle penalty.) Randomly mixed transparent and opaque bytes, though, will do quite well with the loop in Listing 9-4, which if further unrolled will average, at best, about three cycles per pixel but will run closer to four or five if branch misprediction becomes frequent (due to frequent transparent-to-opaque changes).

### Listing 9-4    A Pentium Graphic Overlay Loop

```
    .repeat                 ; ;
      mov   eax,[edi+ecx]   ; 1;pick up background
      mov   bl,[esi+ecx+0]  ; 0;
      .if bl                ; 1;decide about 1st byte
        mov al,bl           ; 1;overlay it
      .endif                ; ;
```

```
        mov     bl,[esi+ecx+1]  ; 0;
        .if bl                  ; 1;decide about 2nd byte
          mov   ah,bl           ; 1;overlay it
        .endif                  ; ;
        mov     bl,[esi+ecx+2]  ; 0;
        rol     eax,16          ; 1;
        .if bl                  ; 1;decide about 3rd byte
          mov   al,bl           ; 1;overlay it
        .endif                  ; ;
        mov     bl,[esi+ecx+3]  ; 0;
        .if bl                  ; 1;decide about 4th byte
          mov   ah,bl           ; 1;overlay it
        .endif                  ; ;
        rol     eax,16          ; 1;
        mov     [edi+ecx],eax   ; 1;deposit overlayed data
        add     ecx,4           ; 0;advance counter/pointer
    .until ZERO?                ; 1;and loop
                                ;;;;13 cycles
```

Now, how fast is MMX? The MMX is so fast that a three-cycle penalty for a misaligned read is much more troublesome than it would be in the Pentium loop. The object of the loop design, therefore, is to read both the object bitmap and the background bitmap along quadword-aligned boundaries and use internal shifts to register the data correctly. Listing 9-5 shows the basic loop sequence that achieves this.

## Listing 9-5  Overlaying an Image with Transparency

```
on entry:
;       mm7 - contains 0
;       mm6 - contains amount by which to shift left
;       mm5 - contains amount by which to shift right
;       esi - points to aligned object data
;       edi - points to aligned background data

        movq    mm0,[esi]       ;  ;fetch 8 pixels of sprite
        movq    mm2,mm0         ;  ;and make a copy
        psllq   mm2,mm6         ;  ;shift both left
        psrlq   mm0,mm5         ;  ;and right
        por     mm2,mm1         ;  ;build shifted qword
        movq    mm3,mm7         ;  ;copy a qword of zeroes
        pcmpeqb mm3,mm2         ;  ;make a transparency mask
        pnand   mm3,[edi]       ;  ;mask against background
        por     mm3,mm2         ;  ;combine fgnd,bgnd
        movq    [edx],mm3       ;  ;and output it
```

By interleaving two copies of the loop, it is possible to get complete pairing and a tandem loop that can be unrolled at ten cycles per tandem (double) iteration, as shown in Listing 9-6.

### Listing 9-6    Fast Image Overlay Loop

```
        .repeat                  ;  ;
          movq    mm0,[esi+ecx]    ; 1;1 <- loop 1 start
          por     mm4,mm0          ; 0;2
          movq    [edx+ecx-16],mm3 ; 1;1
          movq    mm3,mm7          ; 0;2
          pcmpeqb mm3,mm4          ; 1;2
          movq    mm2,mm0          ; 0;1
          pnand   mm3,[edi+ecx]    ; 1;2
          psllq   mm2,mm6          ; 0;1
          por     mm3,mm4          ; 1;2
          psrlq   mm0,mm5          ; 0;1
          movq    mm1,[esi+ecx+8]  ; 1;2 <- loop 2 start
          por     mm2,mm1          ; 0;1
          movq    [edx+ecx],mm3    ; 1;2
          movq    mm3,mm7          ; 0;1
          movq    mm4,mm1          ; 1;2
          pcmpeqb mm3,mm2          ; 0;1
          pnand   mm3,[edi+ecx]    ; 1;1
          psllq   mm4,mm6          ; 0;2
          psrlq   mm1,mm5          ; 1;2
          por     mm3,mm2          ; 0;1
          add     ecx,16           ; 1;
        .until ZERO?               ; 0;
                                   ;;;;11 cycles
```

In just over five cycles per eight bytes, the MMX performs the overlay in about 0.7 cycles per byte, despite the work of shifting to achieve alignment. This is typically about four to five times faster than the Pentium-only class of solutions. Parallelism *does* make a difference.

# Conclusion

The MMX enhancements to the Pentium and Pentium Pro appear to be able to speed up various multimedia-related operations by a factor of five to ten over base Pentium performance. Put another way, if software that is heavily dependent on

MMX to achieve high performance has to run on an ordinary Pentium or Pentium Pro in emulation, then it may end up running several times slower.

It's a good bet that many, if not most, optimized MMX processing loops will really be two loops operating in tandem to achieve instruction pairing. In many instances the eight MMX registers are just enough to supply two sets of registers for two parallel loops.

# References

Intel Corporation. March 1996. *Intel Architecture MMX Technology Developer's Manual.* Santa Clara, Calif.: Intel Corporation. The developer's manual gives optimization advice and practical code examples.

Intel Corporation. March 1996. *Intel Architecture MMX Technology Programmer's Reference Manual.* Santa Clara, Calif.: Intel Corporation. The instructions are fully specified in the programmer's manual.

# Practice

# CHAPTER 10

## Moving Memory

*We make moving better.*
—*Slogan, North American Van Lines*

At first glance, it would seem that moving memory efficiently is as easy as falling off a log. After all, the `rep movsd` instruction is the processor's own built-in, optimized way to move memory from one place to another. So how can it be beaten? The answer has to do with the fact that there are usually three layers of memory—two caches and the main memory—and this affects the dynamics of data movement. The `rep movsd` instruction is most efficient in some, but not all, combinations of source and destination layers. And it also depends on which processor you're using. Sometimes software loops can do better.

The speed of large block transfers of memory is occasionally important to software performance, but the principles *behind* fast block transfers affect many algorithms. And so it is that a survey of the microscopic complexity of that most mundane of operations, the "bit blit," is the topic of this chapter.

This chapter looks at four ways to beat the ordinary C library `memcpy()` function, which is generally implemented with the `rep movsd` instruction at the assembly language level:

| | |
|---|---|
| 1. `IL_MemCopyAlignedRepMovsd()` | A best-alignment-seeking function |
| 2. `IL_MemCopyLoadStoreLoop()` | A surprise winner on the Pentium Pro |
| 3. `IL_MemCopyToSecondaryCache()` | Good on the Pentium when the destination memory is already in the secondary cache |

4. `IL_MemCopyToMainMemory()`     Great on the Pentium, especially when the main memory is involved

# The CHMEM.EXE Program

The CD-ROM accompanying this book contains a copy of both the source and executable code for the program CHMEM.EXE, which was used to generate most of the timing information for this chapter. You can run it on a Pentium or Pentium Pro in a DOS environment to generate your own statistics for comparison.

# Alignment, the First Rule

Proper data alignment has been stressed in earlier chapters. Nowhere is its importance more obvious than in block memory transfers, where every fetch and store, if misaligned, can create a problem. At a minimum, it is desirable for all fetches and all stores to be done in doublewords aligned on doubleword (four-byte) boundaries. And if a choice must be made between loading aligned values and storing aligned values, storing is the better option.

There are no guarantees as to how the `memcpy()` function is implemented in any given C library. I found out empirically under Watcom C that that particular `memcpy()` makes no attempt to align its destination pointer with a doubleword boundary. Whatever pointer alignment is passed to it as a destination is used with `rep movsd` to do the bulk of the transfer. This is fine if the destination is always properly aligned, but it slows things by a factor of about 2 or more if it isn't. Table 10-1 shows the difference between transfer speeds with source and destination both aligned and those with them both misaligned. L1 is an abbreviation for the level 1, or primary, cache. L2 is an abbreviation for the level 2, or secondary, cache. These measurements were made on the test system, a 100 MHz Pentium, but the same virtue of alignment pertains to the 486 and Pentium Pro as well.

| Table 10-1  Aligned and Misaligned `memcpy()` Performance | |
|---|---|
| `memcpy()` (`rep movsd`, *aligned*) | |
| L1 to L1: | 0.28 cycles/byte |
| L1 to L2: | 1.15 cycles/byte |
| L2 to L1: | 0.82 cycles/byte |
| L2 to L2: | 1.52 cycles/byte |
| main to L2: | 1.89 cycles/byte |
| L2 to main: | 1.46 cycles/byte |
| main to L1: | 1.17 cycles/byte |
| L1to main: | 1.15 cycles/byte |
| main to main: | 2.05 cycles/byte |
| `memcpy()` (`rep movsd`, *misaligned*) | |
| L1 to L1: | 1.52 cycles/byte |
| L1 to L2: | 2.27 cycles/byte |
| L2 to L1: | 1.87 cycles/byte |
| L2 to L2: | 2.66 cycles/byte |
| main to L2: | 2.97 cycles/byte |
| L2 to main: | 2.60 cycles/byte |
| main to L1: | 2.25 cycles/byte |
| L1 to main: | 2.30 cycles/byte |
| main to main: | 3.19 cycles/byte |

In this and subsequent timing tables, a copy destination of, say, L2 does not mean that the data is only being copied to L2. Rather, it means that the destination of the copy is memory that is already in L2 (but not in L1) as unmodified cache lines that, initially, don't need to be written back to memory if they are replaced with other data. A source or destination of main is not in either cache. Note that copying to L2 is statistically just about like copying to main memory, since the Pentium, not finding the destination in L1, resorts to using its write queue (output FIFO) in either case.

A simple improvement over unaligned `memcpy()` is the `IL_MemCopy-AlignedRepMovsd_A()` function, which ensures that the destination of `rep movsd` is doubleword-aligned. Its best-case performance is virtually the same as the best case for `memcpy()`. But its worst-case performance, when passed two unaligned pointers, is much better. Table 10-2 shows the worst-case performance of the function `IL_MemCopyAlignedRepMovsd_A()`. It limits or eliminates misalignment damage by executing this little loop just before the main `rep movsd` transfer:

```
.while (edi & 3) && ecx
   movsb
   dec      ecx
.endw
```

If no alignment problem exists in the first place, this extra code costs only about two cycles (assuming it's cached) per call—and a single misalignment fix can save thousands to millions of cycles in a single call, depending on the size of the transfer.

| Table 10-2   Worst-Case Move Performance, Destination Aligned | |
|---|---|
| IL_MemCopyAlignedRepMovsd_A() | |
| L1 to L1: | 1.05 cycles/byte |
| L1 to L2: | 1.16 cycles/byte |
| L2 to L1: | 1.38 cycles/byte |
| L2 to L2: | 1.56 cycles/byte |
| main to L2: | 1.90 cycles/byte |
| L2 to main: | 1.52 cycles/byte |
| main to L1: | 1.85 cycles/byte |
| L1 to main: | 1.18 cycles/byte |
| Main to main: | 2.09 cycles/byte |

The same effect can be obtained with the following C function:

```
void MemCopyAligned(void *dest, void *source, unsigned long count)
{
    while ((((long)dest) & 3) && count) {
        *(char *)dest = *(char *)source;
        dest   = (void *)(((char *)dest   ) + 1);
        source = (void *)(((char *)source) + 1);
        count--;
    }
    memcpy(dest, source, count);
}
```

If you're absolutely sure that the destination address of your block move is doubleword-aligned, then just about any `memcpy()` function will do. But if in doubt, it pays to force the alignment.

# The Copy Loop Paradox of the Pentium Pro

Simple cycle counting would predict that a series of one-cycle loads and stores in a big unrolled loop on the 486 could beat its measured `rep movsd` timing of 3.3 cycles per doubleword transfer. But, in fact, thanks to code fetches and delays in decoding successive long instructions, `rep movsd` is the faster option.

On the Pentium, `rep movsd` from primary cache to primary cache costs just 1.1 cycles per doubleword. If there were no looping overhead or other delays, a series of load and store instructions should be able to achieve nearly 1.0 cycles, but in practice it performs no better than `rep movsd`.

So what should happen on the Pentium Pro? Theoretically, it's hard to tell, except to guess that `rep movsd` *ought* to still win. But in fact, particularly in L1-to-L1 copies, it doesn't. On the Pentium Pro, `rep movsd` from primary cache to primary cache takes a whopping 1.8 cycles per doubleword. A loop with eight load-store pairs does the same job in just under 1.6 cycles, a measured 14 percent speed improvement. And a Pentium can do the equivalent in 1.1 cycles. Apparently the `rep` mechanism on the Pentium Pro throws in some overhead cycles. The loop solution appears to generate three micro-ops per cycle, one for a load and two for a store, which should be able to be executed in a single cycle as well. But in fact it runs at about two-thirds that speed. Cache-to-cache transfer is apparently not a Pentium Pro strong point.

### Listing 10-1   A Fast Pentium Pro Memory Transfer Loop

```
.repeat                        ;  ;
  mov eax,[esi+ecx+0*4]        ; 1;
  mov ebx,[esi+ecx+1*4]        ; 0;
  mov [edi+ecx+0*4],eax        ; 1;
  mov [edi+ecx+1*4],ebx        ; 0;
  mov eax,[esi+ecx+2*4]        ; 1;
  mov ebx,[esi+ecx+3*4]        ; 0;
  mov [edi+ecx+2*4],eax        ; 1;
  mov [edi+ecx+3*4],ebx        ; 0;
  mov eax,[esi+ecx+4*4]        ; 1;
  mov ebx,[esi+ecx+5*4]        ; 0;
  mov [edi+ecx+4*4],eax        ; 1;
  mov [edi+ecx+5*4],ebx        ; 0;
  mov eax,[esi+ecx+6*4]        ; 1;
  mov ebx,[esi+ecx+7*4]        ; 0;
  mov [edi+ecx+6*4],eax        ; 1;
  mov [edi+ecx+7*4],ebx        ; 0;
  add ecx,32                   ; 1;
.until ZERO?                   ; 0;
                               ;;;;9 cycles for 32 bytes
                               ;;;;actual, 13 cycles
```

Listing 10-1 shows a load-store loop appropriate for efficient execution on the Pentium Pro. This is the inner loop of the `IL_MemCopyLoadStoreLoop_A()` function. It exhibits one particularly noteworthy optimization when it's run on the Pentium. Note that both loads and stores are done in pairs. If loads and stores were interleaved one after the other, all Pentium instruction execution pairs would consist of one load and one store. It is possible that the relative alignments of the loads and stores could be such that all instruction pairs would encounter a one-cycle stall contending for access to cache. But it is guaranteed, in the particular case of the loop shown in Listing 10-1, that paired loads and paired stores will never encounter such collisions. So by forcing instructions to pair this way, you guarantee that cache bus contention won't be a problem, no matter what the memory pointer values are.

Avoiding cache bus (alias bank) contention is one of the finer, but not unimportant, points of loop optimization.

# A Pentium Read-Before-Write Speedup

Whenever the Pentium writes to a memory location that is not in the primary cache, it deposits the write request in an output write queue (FIFO). This queue is often the bottleneck determining copy speed. In some cases, especially where the destination memory is already in the secondary cache, it pays to first force a cache line to be read into primary cache, then fill it up at top speed, and then let the cache management system write it back out in a line burst when that cache line gets replaced by a newer one. This effect also shows some benefit when the destination is in main memory, but to a lesser degree than when the secondary cache is the target.

This read-before-write strategy is implemented in the `IL_MemCopyTo-SecondaryCache_A()` function with the inner loop shown in Listing 10-2. This function is also set up to minimize the delay often encountered when reading a new cache line for a second time soon after the first read of that cache line. Although the function advances through memory from low addresses toward high addresses, its inner loop processes 32-byte groups from high address to low address with an alignment such that the first of the eight reads always comes from a different (and presumably new) cache line than the other seven, which come from a cache line read in on the previous pass through the loop. This design ensures that the time gap between first and second reads of a new cache line is sufficient, so that the second read encounters little or no delay.

The instruction mov eax,[edi+ecx+28+32] forces destination cache lines into the primary cache in advance of their use. Because the instruction speculatively reads 60 bytes ahead of the current register pointers, care must be taken to terminate the loop before this instruction reads past the end of the destination data area, potentially causing a protection error or page fault. The IL_MemCopyToSecondaryCache_A() function does take this precaution.

This memory movement function works to best advantage when the destination memory is already in the secondary cache but not in the primary cache. This is not an uncommon situation, as the secondary cache is usually dozens of times larger than the primary cache, and at 256K or 512K, there is room for the large critical memory buffers that are likely to be the recipients of block moves.

## Listing 10-2    A Read-Before-Write Pentium Loop

```
                                        ;  ;do moves from
        .repeat                         ;  ;high to low
          mov   eax,[esi+ecx+7*4]       ; 1;<-- this read likely
          mov   [edi+ecx+7*4],eax       ; 1;to miss cache
          mov   eax,[esi+ecx+6*4]       ; 0;
          mov   [edi+ecx+6*4],eax       ; 1;
          mov   eax,[esi+ecx+5*4]       ; 0;
          mov   [edi+ecx+5*4],eax       ; 1;
          mov   eax,[esi+ecx+4*4]       ; 0;
          mov   [edi+ecx+4*4],eax       ; 1;
          mov   eax,[edi+ecx+28+32]     ; 0;<-- throw in a
          mov   eax,[esi+ecx+3*4]       ; 1;destination read
          mov   [edi+ecx+3*4],eax       ; 1;
          mov   eax,[esi+ecx+2*4]       ; 0;
          mov   [edi+ecx+2*4],eax       ; 1;
          mov   eax,[esi+ecx+1*4]       ; 0;
          mov   [edi+ecx+1*4],eax       ; 1;
          mov   eax,[esi+ecx+0*4]       ; 0;
          mov   [edi+ecx+0*4],eax       ; 1;
          add   ecx,32                  ; 0;count up
        .until ZERO?                    ; 1;until zero
                                        ;;;;11 cycles
                                        ;;;;+ 2 cache misses
```

| Table 10-3 Read-Before-Write Function Performance | |
|---|---|
| `IL_MemCopyToSecondaryCache_A()` | |
| L1 to L1: | 0.40 cycles/byte |
| L1 to L2: | 0.88 cycles/byte |
| L2 to L1: | 0.84 cycles/byte |
| L2 to L2: | 1.17 cycles/byte |
| main to L2: | 1.48 cycles/byte |
| L2 to main: | 1.39 cycles/byte |
| main to L1: | 0.98 cycles/byte |
| L1 to main: | 1.09 cycles/byte |
| main to main: | 1.82 cycles/byte |

Table 10-3 shows the performance of `IL_MemCopyToSecondary-Cache_A()`. Comparing it to Table 10-1, it is apparent that, although in some situations it performs worse than `rep movsd`, it performs about 30 percent better when L2 is the destination and 5 percent to 12 percent better when main memory is the destination. Transfers from main memory to L1 are made faster by 19 percent thanks to the delayed second read on new cache lines.

This function works well on the Pentium whenever both source and destination share the same doubleword alignment. But if you can arrange for quadword (eight-byte) alignment instead, there is a still better way to transfer memory on a Pentium.

## Moving with the Floating-Point Unit

The fastest general way I know of to move noncached memory from one place to another on a Pentium is, surprisingly, through the floating-point unit. Ordinarily, it takes eight four-byte writes to transfer a cache line from one place to another. But if memory is treated as an array of eight-byte double floating-point values, then the same transfer can be done in four eight-byte writes. When the destination memory is not already in the primary cache, the processor's output queue has to handle all the memory write traffic. Instead of having to handle eight doubleword requests, it needs to handle only half that number—and since that's often the bottleneck in the transfer, things go a lot faster as a result.

## Listing 10-3  A Fast Floating-Point Memory Transfer Loop

```
                mov   ebp,7ff80000H              ;1;bits to test
                mov   ebx,7ff00000H              ;0;bits to check for
                mov   edx,[edi+ecx+0*8+4]        ;0;preload edx
                .repeat                          ; ;
                  mov  al,[esi+ecx+63]           ;1;pre-read into cache
                                                 ; ;
fldfstp macro    num, reg1, reg2                 ; ;
         fld    qword ptr [esi+ecx+num*8]        ;1;load a quadword
         mov    reg2,[esi+ecx+num*8+8+4]         ;1;do an advance fetch
         and    reg1,ebp                         ;0;check a 12-bit zone
         fstp   qword ptr [edi+ecx+num*8]        ;2;store the quadword
         .if reg1 == ebx                         ;1;if zone fails test
           mov reg1,[esi+ecx+num*8+4]            ; ;patch the zone
           mov [edi+ecx+num*8+4],reg1            ; ;
         .endif                                  ; ;
         endm                                    ;;;;5 cycles per transfer
                                                 ; ;
                fldfstp 0, edx, eax              ;5;
                fldfstp 1, eax, edx              ;5;
                fldfstp 2, edx, eax              ;5;
                fldfstp 3, eax, edx              ;5;
                add   ecx,32                     ;1;
                .until ZERO?                     ;0;
                                                 ;;;;22 cycles per 32 bytes
```

There is a minor complication involved in using the floating-point unit to move memory. There are some rare bit patterns that the floating-point unit insists upon modifying between read and write operations. If you were transfering a megabyte of random data using floating-point double-precision reads and writes, you could expect about 30 "zero" bits to be changed to ones. Fortunately, there *is* a workaround.

Listing 10-3 shows the inner loop that accomplishes the transfer, complete with watchdog code that checks for the offending bit pattern and corrects the output write if necessary. The extra cycles taken for watching the data stream usually don't delay the algorithm much, if at all, because the bottleneck is still the output write queue. The instruction mov al,[esi+ecx+63] at the top of the loop prefetches cache lines and so adds significantly to loop performance.

| Table 10-4 Floating-Point Memory Transfer Performance | |
|---|---|
| `IL_MemCopyToMainMemory_A()` *(8-byte aligned)* | |
| L1 to L1: | 0.77 cycles/byte |
| L1 to L2: | 0.77 cycles/byte |
| L2 to L1: | 1.00 cycles/byte |
| L2 to L2: | 1.06 cycles/byte |
| main to L2: | 1.24 cycles/byte |
| L2 to main: | 1.00 cycles/byte |
| main to L1: | 1.27 cycles/byte |
| L1 to main: | 0.77 cycles/byte |
| main to main: | 1.49 cycles/byte |
| `IL_MemCopyToMainMemory_A()` *(4-byte aligned)* | |
| L1 to L1: | 0.77 cycles/byte |
| L1 to L2: | 0.78 cycles/byte |
| L2 to L1: | 1.02 cycles/byte |
| L2 to L2: | 1.06 cycles/byte |
| main to L2: | 1.24 cycles/byte |
| L2 to main: | 1.00 cycles/byte |
| main to L1: | 1.33 cycles/byte |
| L1 to main: | 0.78 cycles/byte |
| main to main: | 1.81 cycles/byte |

Table 10-4 shows the performance figures for `IL_MemCopyToMain-Memory()`, so named because it is particularly good at copying to main memory. For very large block transfers that involve little cached memory, it represents a speed improvement of about one-third over `rep movsd`. From main memory to L2 memory, it's about 52 percent faster. From L2 to either L2 or main, it's nearly 50 percent faster. And from L1 to either L2 or main, it's also 50 percent faster. In fact, the only measurements on which it loses out to `IL_MemCopyToSecondary-Cache()` as the best alternative to `rep movsd` is copying from main memory or L2 to L1. There, the delay between first and second cache line reads, implemented in `IL_MemCopyToSecondaryCache()`, makes the performance difference.

`IL_MemCopyToMainMemory_A()` is perhaps the fastest way on a Pentium to copy bulk memory from one place to another, unless the destination of the move is already in the primary cache. On the 486 and Pentium Pro, however, `rep movsd` is faster.

# Conclusion

For all the apparent simplicity of the task of moving memory quickly from one place to another, a variety of approaches may be taken, depending on the processor and the levels of memory involved in the transfer. On the Pentium, large copies through the floating-point unit are often most efficient. When L1 is the transfer destination but not the source, a software loop that carefully times its source data cache hits can sometimes be a good alternative. The `rep movsd` instruction is unassailable for L1-to-L1 moves on the Pentium, but even it can lose out to a simple software loop on the Pentium Pro.

# 11

# Random Numbers and Primes

*Anyone who considers arithmetical methods of producing random digits is, of course, in a state of sin.*

*—John von Neumann*

The need for random numbers arises fairly frequently in computing. In the course of working up example code for this book, I frequently called upon random numbers to run simulations. In fact, that's how this chapter got started. And in a separate randomness-related matter, while working on a communications problem recently, I was faced with the interesting problem of simulating a variable, random bit error rate. The problem to be solved was, "How fast can you generate a bit stream with a certain given percentage of 1s randomly arranged in the stream?" The best practical answer I found, after researching this chapter, was slightly over three cycles per bit on a Pentium—fast enough, in principle, to be used to simulate errors on 4 megabytes of signal data per second on a Pentium-100. But speed isn't everything in random numbers. This chapter takes a performance-oriented look at a variety of ways to generate the unpredictable.

There are a lot of ways to generate "random" numbers on a computer—all of them flawed to one degree or another. The good news is that you can generate nearly 10 million pretty good 32-bit numbers per second. The so-so news is that better bit mixing and mashing might bring that count down to a few hundred thousand per second. The bad news is that you can spend serious clock time exercising disk drives and asynchronous bus transfers (which have slightly random, analog timings) if you're looking for a divinely inspired random bit—but the times you really need to do this may be mercifully rare.

# The Algorithms

There are eight random number routines presented in this chapter. These are also given in assembly language, C, and executable forms on the CD-ROM accompanying this book. Each one returns a single 32-bit value each time it is called. In order of speed, they are as follows:

| Name | Cycles | Routine | Recommendation |
|------|--------|---------|----------------|
| r250 | 10 | IL_R250Random | very good, fast |
| simple | 14 | IL_SimpleRandom | not great |
| standard | 16 | IL_StandardRandom | OK |
| mix | 24 | IL_MixRandom | very good |
| hash | 172 | IL_HashRandom | very good |
| shift32 | 233 | IL_Shift32Random | not great |
| combined | 473 | IL_CombinedRandom | great |
| seed | 10,000 | IL_PickRandomSeed | great for seeds |

The original descriptions of most of these algorithms have, of course, been published elsewhere. Please see the reference list at the end of this chapter to see who ultimately deserves credit.

There are three other related routines mentioned in this chapter and given on the CD-ROM:

1. `IL_RandomChiSquareTest`  Tests randomness validity
2. `IL_PiByMonteCarlo`  Finds 3.14159. . . using random numbers
3. `IL_FindPrimes`  Finds millions of prime numbers

I've implemented one version of the statistical "chi square" test, which can be used to check the randomness of random number sequences. Partly as a test, but more as a demonstration of the elegance of random integration, I've included a routine that finds pi by successive approximation using random numbers, two multiplies, and three additions. And since random numbers and primes often tread each other's turf—and since Eratosthenes' sieve is a classic algorithm and computer benchmark—I close the chapter with a fast way to find primes up to nine digits.

# On the CD-ROM

This chapter's demonstration program is CHRANDM.EXE. There are six main ways to invoke it and have it do something interesting:

1. `chrandm random`      Prints numbers from a given generator
2. `chrandm graph`       Shows a 2-D progressive random point graph
3. `chrandm chart`       Generates a .BMP file snapshot of graph
4. `chrandm chisquare`   Runs a progressive test on a generator
5. `chrandm pi`          Finds pi with a generator
6. `chrandm primes`      Finds primes in a given range

If you just want to generate a bunch of 32-bit decimal random numbers in a text file, choose `chrandm random` and pick your generator and seed. For something more interesting, try `chrandm graph`. This lets you pick a seed and generator and watch it fill in a $256 \times 256$ graph of points found with successive calls to the generator. Each point is derived from two successive calls to the generator and uses only the low eight bits from each value as coordinates. Check out the suspicious behavior of the `simple` and `shift32` algorithms. A good random generator should "look" random; if it doesn't, it's not.

The `chrandm chart` option is much like the `graph` option, except that it calculates its graph or chart off screen (running quicker that way), stops after a fixed number of iterations, displays its result, and writes out a .BMP file to disk. (I used this feature to prepare illustrations for this chapter.) If you don't want the .BMP, name the file NUL. There's a very gratifying way to visually check a generator after it has generated half a million points. There should be about 30 "holes" left in the $256 \times 256$ graph of points plotted. Like the exception that proves the rule, seeing 20 to 40 survivor dots is a very good sign.

The chi square test, as implemented on the CD-ROM, is much more limited in scope than the name "chi square" implies. Basically all this one does is check to see if a few hundred thousand 16-bit "halves" of the 32-bit random values really "look" random. It generates a statistic more or less equivalent to whether or not the set of values is within about a standard deviation of what it would expect. About 15 percent of the time it's outside the deviation limit, and about 85 percent it's inside—if it's a good generator. The test runs progressively, and it can take hours for a generator to home in on 15. But all of the generators I've recommended report in the range of about 10 to 22 after a few minutes of running and settle at 15 or 16 after about ten hours. Watch how fast the "simple" generator fails.

You can test a random number generator with a rigged problem when you know the results it *should* get. For instance, if you take two random numbers between 0 and 1, square them, and add them, the result should be less than 1 a large fraction of the time, to the tune of the ratio of pi over 4. (Imagine a circle of radius 1 inside a square for the derivation.) The first three digits of pi pop out very quickly, and you can get the first seven digits of pi in an overnight run with a good generator. To the extent that a random run stabilizes away from true pi, some flaw may be showing.

An old computer benchmark standard—and an even older Greek's idea—is Eratosthenes' sieve, a terribly efficient way to exhaustively hunt down prime numbers under about ten digits. If you need to find a bunch of primes, use `chrandm primes`. Specify a range to hunt in, and it will respond ASAP.

A speed note: the `seed` algorithm is much slower than the other random generators. You may experience much longer delays between output cycles when the seed algorithm is used for serial random number generation instead of as the one-shot "seed" it was designed to be. Also, the prime sieve may take a few minutes when searching for nine- or ten-digit numbers.

# Random Number Theory

Randomness and computers are odd bedfellows. On the one hand, a random stream of bits should look like so many transistors gone mad, flipping coins to set their every state. On the other hand, the sequence should be completely predictable and repeatable with respect to the underlying algorithm generating the stream. We always seem to want it both ways.

## Chi Square and Graphic Inspection

Broadly speaking, there are two ways random number sequences fail (although, at a deeper level, they're often the same problem). First, there may be subtle tendencies for bits or bit groups within (say) a 32-bit number to correlate. Perhaps bit 3 and bit 22 tend be the same more than half the time—or odd parity numbers outpace even ones. Second, there may be correlations between successive numbers—such as an odd-even train or the reappearance of numbers with their bits shifted from one sample to the next. Chi square testing helps spot the first; graphic inspection of the data helps with the second. There are many other, more sophisticated tests one could apply that are beyond the scope of this book. These are accessible through the references at the end of the chapter. Real-world tests that make use of the sequences tend to reveal even more flaws; hence the quest for ever better random numbers.

## Combining Randoms

Although it is possible to consider forms of randomness in which bits are set to 1s and 0s in ratios like 70:30 or 89:11, the most natural way to deal with random bits is as 50:50 propositions. Heads it's a 1; tails it's 0. A good 32-bit random number is just the composition of 32 one-bit random numbers.

It's hard to hurt a random number, at least with the `xor` operation (or sometimes `add` or `sub`). If you take two random numbers from different and philosophically unrelated generators and "exclusive-or" (`xor`) them together, the resultant number is almost always *more* random than either of its predecessors. Just as every voice in a crowd makes each other voice harder to hear, every random value tossed into the mix makes it harder to see the pattern within. (But two closely related randoms can exhibit the equivalent of destructive wave interference—making it, paradoxically, a little bit easier to hear in the crowd.)

## Shuffles

One very effective way to fight correlations between numbers in a series is to "shuffle" them as they are output. Imagine that before starting to output numbers from a given generator to an application, you fill up a 256-entry array with its first 256 output values. Then whenever the application needs a random number, you use a second generator to pick a random index into the array and return that array value to the application. The first generator then refills the used array slot with a new random value. The same numbers still come out, but in a locally mixed-up order. If a generator looks good on chi square but graphs funny or otherwise misbehaves, a shuffle might do it a world of good.

## Random Number Ranges

Thirty-two bits is not everyone's cup of tea. Suppose you want a number in the range 0 to 11. The classic way to get it is

```
num = ((unsigned long)rand()) % 12;
```

There are two drawbacks to this approach. First, it introduces a tiny bias related to the fact that $2^{32}$ is not a multiple of 12. It may be negligible in this instance (depending on the application), but it's an enormous error, for instance, when the range is 0 to 3 billion. The other problem is that the modulo operator pulls a 41-or-more-cycle division (`div`) operation. That's a lot longer than it may take to generate the random number in the first place. Both problems are solved with the following code instead:

```
do {
    num = rand() & 0xf;
} while (num >= 12);
```

By masking only as many bits as necessary, you first limit the number to the next highest power of 2 above the desired ceiling. Then you retry, if the number is still above the ceiling, and keep retrying until it's in range. A good random generator will typically average 1.5 calls to get a non-power-of-2 random number; the worst-case average is 2 calls when the upper limit is one more than a power of 2. This procedure is actually theoretically sound (safer than modulo arithmetic), and it tends to run faster than the modulo procedure with several of the fast generators in this chapter.

## Floating-Point Numbers and Double Precision

What if you don't want integers? Sometimes you want a floating-point number, and the usual way to express it is as a value between 0 and 1. (But if you want another range, that's always easy to get with a single multiplication.) The usual way cited to convert a random 32-bit integer to a value in the range 0 to 1 is

```
numdbl = ((unsigned long)rand()) / (double)0xffffffff;
```

This is fine if your application can tolerate an occasional exact 0 and 1. But some-times it's preferable to never see an exact 1 or 0, for reasons having to do with the vanishingly small probability of seeing the exact endpoint of a continuous range. In such case, use

```
numdbl = ((unsigned long)rand())
                    * (1 / (0x10000 * (double)0x10000))
                    + (1 / (0x20000 * (double)0x10000));
```

The ugly-looking divisors are an awkward workaround to express 0x100000000 and 0x200000000, which are too big for 32 bits but well within the range of dou-bles. Fortunately, the ugliness works itself out at compile time, and it runs without undue delay.

Remember that `float` values only keep 24 bits of precision, so you toss away essentially the bottom byte of 32-bit values when turned into floats. Doubles, on the other hand, keep 53 bits of precision. So if you want a double randomized to the max, try this:

```
numdbl = ((unsigned long)rand())
                    * (1 / (0x10000 * (double)0x10000))
                    + ((unsigned long)rand() & 0xfffff800)
                    * (1 /((0x10000 * (double)0x10000)
                    * (0x10000 * (double)0x10000)));
```

The masking value 0xfffff800 is used to clip off unwanted low bits that *could* possibly be recorded in the double and bias the randomness. (For instance, *not* clipping the bits would make the value 0 about two thousand times more rare than it should be in 53 random bits.) The resultant double never reaches exact 1.0 but *may* reach exact 0. If exact 0 is problematic, just screen it out and ask for another number.

## Seeds

You have to start somewhere. Every random number generator that creates a reproducible sequence of numbers must have a "state" involving a set of bits that determine all subsequent output. Historically, many generators have used a single 32-bit (or even 16-bit!) seed. That is the case with the `simple`, `standard`, and `shift32` generators treated here. The `hash` generator uses two 32-bit seeds. And `r250` and `mix` both use arrays of 32-bit integers (of sizes 250 and 92, respectively). After each number is generated, the "seed" or "state" changes. The generators that use arrays of integers are usually initialized by yet another generator, presumably one that requires a simpler seed. And so it is that the array-based generators actually draw from a large reservoir of randomness and don't have to work very hard to churn out good-looking bits; hence their efficiency.

Getting a good first random seed to start a sequence is not easy. It's that very first seed value that determines everything else. But where does *it* come from? Usually it's some function of the clock time on the computer. But the standard C clock—if that's what you use—only ticks once per second. What if you want a bunch of nonreproducible seed values all at once, a series you are very unlikely to ever see or reproduce again? At the risk of being pilloried for using a largely undocumented Pentium instruction, I've included a very good "seed picker" function. It's described later in the chapter.

## Integration

It may not be obvious, but random numbers can be very useful in evaluating complex functions that defy simple, formulaic answers. Suppose you have a mathematical function that looks like an amoeba when graphed in two dimensions. The function simply tells you, given any pair of X and Y coordinates, whether that particular point is "inside" the amoeba or "outside" of it. And when you draw the graph of all the "inside" points, this amoeba pops out.

Now suppose you want to find the surface area of the amoeba. Just draw a rectangle around it (of *known* area) and pick random points within that rectangle. The amoeba's surface area is approximated by

```
(rectangle area) * (inside points) / (all points)
```

And the more random points you pick, the better the estimate. In fact, with virtually perfect random numbers, you can drive the precision arbitrarily high (but still limited to a few dozen bits, since each bit of achieved precision costs about twice as much as the bit before; you can wait weeks, months, and years for an extra few bits).

As an example for this chapter, I chose the unit circle. (Not a typical amoeba, but perhaps an amoeba's ego ideal.) It integrates well and quickly to several decimal places. The technique works just as effectively in three and more dimensions. Note that it is the impartiality of randomness—with no bias to either overestimate or underestimate—that actually makes random numbers superior to systematic grid-like evaluation methods. They're the ultimate sequestered jury.

## The Cryptographic Link

Suppose you had a billion bytes of pure-as-the-driven-snow random data. Now take any program, message, database, or other recognizable collection of digital goods and `xor` it against the random data. The result: perfectly encrypted programs, messages, databases, and so on. Randomness doesn't decrease, and the resulting bits are pure noise to everyone who doesn't possess the original random sequence. So if you can design a great random number generator with an impossible-to-guess starting state (say, 100 bits or more defining the starting state or key of the generator), you can encrypt messages by `xor`-ing the message with the random numbers, and only those with the key and another copy of the random number generator can decrypt it by `xor`-ing it back. (Remember, the `xor` operation is its own inverse—so data becomes noise with the first `xor` and then becomes data again with the second `xor`.)

Some cryptographic systems are based on just this principle—generating a string of random numbers and `xor`-ing it against a message. The `RC4` algorithm popular in Internet traffic is one such. There's a note later in the chapter about code breaking and security.

## Extreme Randomness

There are statistical applications in this world that tax the limits of any algorithmically generated series of random numbers. Or, at least, there are statisticians wise enough to distrust any algorithmically generated series of numbers. While working on this chapter, I looked for a good general way to get really, really random seed bits, statistically balanced halfway between 1 and 0. The best I could do was to force some disk activity, read the processor's 64-bit, ten-nanosecond cycle clock, and use the value's parity. But that's a *very* time-consuming way to crank out bytes, about 10 million times slower than r250. And I suspect a good statistician wouldn't trust it, anyhow. They tend to prefer the randomness of nuclear decay and thermal noise to anything cybergenic.

For those interested in extreme randomness that is not generated by a computer but is computer-readable, there is at least one company advertising a PC device to convert thermal noise into virtually perfect random bits. It's slower than any of the generators discussed in this chapter, but the quality is presumably very high. (Look for the initials QNG on the Web or try the URL http://rainbow.rmii.com/~comscire/QNGADINT.html. This is not an endorsement.)

# Random Numbers in Practice

Herewith are several ways to get random.

## IL_StandardRandom()

This routine is a 32-bit variant of the most common rand() routine in C libraries. An ANSI C document defining C library standards gave, in essence, the following suggestion for a random number generator:

```
random_num = ((seed = seed * 1103515245 + 12345) >> 16) & 0x7fff;
```

A lot of C libraries, though not required to use it, have chosen to do so. Perhaps because it is so widespread, this seems to be the most reviled random number routine around. By default, it's the one that fails people first. But one of the worst things about it is that it only returns 15 bits. Here in IL_StandardRandom(), I've extended it to 32 bits. It behaves well on the simple chi square test I've used, and it plots random dot patterns that are visually indiscernible from ostensibly

better generators. It's also very fast, running at about two-thirds the speed of
`IL_R250Random()`, and can generate over 5 million values per second. It's at
least OK for many purposes.

Listing 11-1 shows the assembly and C versions of `IL_StandardRandom()`.
Note that the C version is *much* slower because C can't make use of the 64-bit intermediates generated by 32-bit integer multiplication.

### Listing 11-1  StandardRandom Function in C and Assembly Language

```
extern unsigned long IL_StandardRandom_seed;

long
IL_StandardRandom_C()
{
    unsigned long lo, hi, ll, lh, hh, hl;

    lo = IL_StandardRandom_seed & 0xffff;
    hi = IL_StandardRandom_seed >> 16;
    IL_StandardRandom_seed =
                    IL_StandardRandom_seed * IL_RMULT + 12345;
    ll = lo * (IL_RMULT  & 0xffff);
    lh = lo * (IL_RMULT >> 16     );
    hl = hi * (IL_RMULT  & 0xffff);
    hh = hi * (IL_RMULT >> 16     );
    return ((ll + 12345) >> 16) + lh + hl + (hh << 16);
}
```

```
;long IL_StandardRandom_A()
;
;Returns a pseudo-random 32-bit number.
;
IL_StandardRandom_A proc near C public      ; 0;
        mov     eax,IL_StandardRandom_seed  ; 1;get last base
        mov     edx,1103515245              ; 0;& multiplier
        mul     edx                         ; 9;do multiply
        shl     edx,16                      ; 1;ready high 16
        add     eax,12345                   ; 0;fixd addition
        adc     edx,0ffffH                  ; 1;carry to high
        mov     IL_StandardRandom_seed,eax  ; 0;record latest
        shr     eax,16                      ; 1;toss low 16
        and     edx,0ffff0000H              ; 0;mask high 16
        or      eax,edx                     ; 1;combine hi lo
        ret                                 ; 2;and return it
IL_StandardRandom_A endp                    ;;;;16 cycles
```

IL_StandardRandom() will repeat its numeric sequence only after $2^{32}$ (about 4 billion) calls.

## IL_SimpleRandom()

Encouraged by the not-terrible performance of IL_StandardRandom(), I tried the "simplest possible" multiply-and-add generator mentioned in *Numerical Recipes in C* (see the References section) as a "quick and dirty" technique, shown in Listing 11-2.

**Listing 11-2** SimpleRandom **Function in C and Assembly Language**

```
extern unsigned long IL_SimpleRandom_seed;

long
IL_SimpleRandom_C()
{
    return IL_SimpleRandom_seed =
                (IL_SimpleRandom_seed * 1664525) + 1013904223;
}



;long IL_SimpleRandom_A()
;
;Returns a pseudo-random 32-bit number.
;
IL_SimpleRandom_A proc near C public          ; 0;
        mov     eax,IL_SimpleRandom_seed      ; 1;get last base
        mov     edx,1664525                   ; 0;& multiplier
        mul     edx                           ; 9;do multiply
        add     eax,1013904223                ; 1;add const
        mov     IL_SimpleRandom_seed,eax      ; 1;record latest
        ret                                   ; 2;return it
IL_SimpleRandom_A endp                        ;;;;14 cycles
```

Unfortunately, the low bits of the returned values tend to be *very* predictable. Bit 0 simply alternates between 0 and 1 with each call. (It's interesting to consider why randomness concentrates in the middle bits of multiplication results and is very poor toward the extremes.) The C implementation is a lot faster than that for IL_StandardRandom(), but in assembly language the speed gain is hardly noticeable.

If all you want to do is generate a floating-point number with 20 or so bits of pretty good randomness, it's probably fine. But the low bit problems make it flunk chi square and graph tests. Use only with considerable caution.

IL_SimpleRandom() will repeat its numeric sequence only after $2^{32}$ (about 4 billion) calls.

## IL_Shift32Random()

Here's another way to cycle through about 4 billion different numbers with a simple algorithm. I do not recommend IL_Shift32Random for general use, though, because there are significant correlations between successive returned values. The algorithm is presented here as background for IL_MixRandom(), which relies on such "shift register" class functions, and as an illustration of the disparity between efficient C and assembly implementations.

Here's what's happening in IL_Shift32Random(). Take any initial 32-bit value, xor six of its bits from certain positions together, and put the resultant bit back into the value at another certain position. Then rotate the whole 32 bits one position. That's the procedure to generate one "random" bit. Repeat 31 more times to get a full new 32-bit value. This algorithm is usually cited as being good at generating fairly random bits taken individually, but not so good at making complete numbers. It repeats after $2^{32}-1$ calls (about 4 billion).

The classic and necessary way to implement this algorithm in C is with a lot of shift and xor operations, as seen in the C code below. But there's an elegant way to skip the sound and the fury in assembly language. The processor parity flag (which C knows nothing about) is really just a multibit xor machine, so with a single test instruction, assembly language can achieve what takes C five shifts and five xors to do. What a win! And then you can turn the flag into the new bit with the rare but effective setpo instruction; it's more efficient than branching on the flag. Yet for all this efficiency, it still runs slowly, at about 4 percent of the speed of IL_R250Random().

Listing 11-3 shows both the C and assembly language versions.

### Listing 11-3   Shift32 Random Function in C and Assembly Language

```
extern unsigned long IL_Shift32Random_seed;

long
IL_Shift32Random_C()
{
    unsigned long n, bit, temp;

    temp = IL_Shift32Random_seed;
    for (n = 0; n < 32; n++) {
        bit = ((temp >> 0) ^ (temp >> 1) ^ (temp >> 2) ^
                (temp >> 3) ^ (temp >> 5) ^ (temp >> 7)) & 1;
```

```
            temp = (((temp >> 1) | (temp << 31)) & ~1) | bit;
        }
    IL_Shift32Random_seed = temp;

    return temp;
}


;long IL_Shift32Random_A()
;
;Returns a pseudo-random 32-bit number.
;
IL_Shift32Random_A proc near C public          ; 0;
        mov     eax,IL_Shift32Random_seed      ; 1;get old seed
        mov     edx,0                          ; 0;
        mov     ecx,32                         ; 1;32-bit count
        .repeat                                ;  ;
          test  al,10101111b                   ; 1;check bits
          setpo dl                             ; 2;odd parity=1
          ror   eax,1                          ; 1;rotate right
          and   al,not 1                       ; 1;clear bit
          or    eax,edx                        ; 1;and modify
          dec   ecx                            ; 1;done?
        .until ZERO?                           ; 0;no -> loop
                                               ;;;;7 cycle loop
                                               ; 4;
        mov     IL_Shift32Random_seed,eax      ; 1;save value
        ret                                    ; 2;and return it
IL_Shift32Random_A endp                        ;;;;233 cycles
```

## IL_MixRandom()

A big part of the inefficiency of `IL_Shift32Random()` was due to the fact that the inner loop and all of its 32-bit operations were being used to generate a single bit, not a whole 32-bit value. But this kind of problem lends itself well to processing bits 32 at a time. Instead of operating on a single 32-bit value, suppose you have an array of thirty-two 32-bit values. Here's the trick: Don't think of the 32-bit "shift register" values as being laid out left to right in the bits of the array words. Think of all the bits at bit position 0 in the 32 array words as constituting the "shift register." And think the same for bit positions 1, 2, 3, and so on. When you look at it this way, you can simultaneously solve 32 "shift register" problems, one in each bit position, using the same five `xor` operations that `IL_Shift32Random` used on just one bit. This is a win.

There's another win in the fact that the 32 bits are generally uncorrelated, so the integers produced in sequence have much better random qualities. Still, if you follow a single bit position through a few dozen iterations, patterns may show.

But `IL_Shift32Random()` isn't the only fish in the sea. There are similar sequences for other lengths of bit strings. In particular, `IL_MixRandom()` incorporates a 32-bit, 31-bit, and 29-bit "shift register" sequence, `xor`ing the results together. This has the twin salutary effects of better randomizing the bit patterns and increasing the time until the sequence repeats from 30 minutes (of continuous calling) to about 37 trillion years.

At 24 cycles per invocation, this sequence is fast. The assembly language implementation given here gets a good bit of its speed from keeping duplicate copies of every array entry so it doesn't have to worry about time-consuming checks to avoid indexing past the end of the array. The array entries don't actually shift positions; the base for indexing into the array does.

This generator needs a big 2,944-bit (92-longword) initial state or "seed." Practically speaking, it takes another random number generator to initialize this generator. So I've provided the function `IL_MixRandomSeed(long (*rand)())`. To seed, for instance, using `IL_StandardRandom`, do this:

```
IL_MixRandomSeed(Il_StandardRandom);
```

There are a couple of straightforward gotchas to watch out for when seeding, and `IL_MixRandomSeed()` prevents them both. First, you don't want all the bits in any of the virtual "shift registers" to be 0. That's the one value the algorithm can't tolerate, because it gets stuck there. Also, you don't want any two of the virtual shift registers to have identical contents. That would lead to identical bits always coming out at two positions in the 32-bit output value. If you give `IL_MixRandomSeed()` a really horrible generator to work with, it could hang up, unable to make a seed satisfying these criteria. But no self-respecting generator will cause problems.

Running at about half the speed of `IL_R250Random()`, this routine makes a good code contender. It takes a little less storage space than `IL_R250Random()`. It does nine `xor`s, compared to the one in `IL_R250Random()`, so I suspect it may pass some statistical tests the latter routine might have trouble with. For better or worse, in statistics and in health, its code is given in Listing 11-4.

### Listing 11-4  MixRandom Function in C and Assembly Language

```
struct IL_MixRandom_struct {
    long trseed32[32*2];
    long trseed31[31*2];
    long trseed29[29*2];
    long ptr32;
```

```
        long ptr31;
        long ptr29;
};

long
IL_MixRandom_C()
{
        int n;
        long sum, temp, i32, i31, i29, *iptr;
        struct IL_MixRandom_struct *p;

        p       = (struct IL_MixRandom_struct *)&IL_MixRandom_seeds;
        i32     = ((p->ptr32 >> 2) + 1) &  0x1f;
        if ((i31 =  (p->ptr31 >> 2) + 1) ==   31)
            i31 = 0;
        if ((i29 =  (p->ptr29 >> 2) + 1) ==   29)
            i29 = 0;
        p->ptr32 = i32 << 2;
        p->ptr31 = i31 << 2;
        p->ptr29 = i29 << 2;

        iptr    = &p->trseed32[i32];
        temp    = iptr[31] ^ iptr[6] ^ iptr[4] ^ iptr[2] ^ iptr[1]
                                                         ^ iptr[0];
        iptr[0] = iptr[32] = temp;
        sum     = temp;

        iptr    = &p->trseed31[i31];
        temp    = iptr[30] ^ iptr[2];
        iptr[0] = iptr[31] = temp;
        sum     ^= temp;

        iptr    = &p->trseed29[i29];
        temp    = iptr[28] ^ iptr[1];
        iptr[0] = iptr[29] = temp;
        sum     ^= temp;

        return sum;
}



;long IL_MixRandom_A()
;
;Returns a pseudo-random 32-bit number.
;
IL_MixRandom_A proc near C public uses ebx esi  ; 1;
                                                ;  ;
```

```
        mov     edx,ptr32                       ; 1;ring of 32
        mov     esi,ptr31                       ; 0;ring of 31
        add     edx,4                           ; 1;advance
        add     esi,4                           ; 0;pointers
        .if esi == 31*4                         ; 1;wrap at 31
          mov   esi,0                           ; ;
        .endif                                  ; ;
        mov     ptr31,esi                       ; 1;set new ptr31
        and     edx,7cH                         ; 0;modulo-32 edx
                                                ; ;
        mov     ebx,trseed31[esi+30*4]          ; 1;ptr31 group
        mov     ecx,trseed31[esi+ 2*4]          ; 0;
        xor     ebx,ecx                         ; 1;
        mov     ptr32,edx                       ; 0;fill 1/2 cyc
        mov     trseed31[esi+ 0*4],ebx          ; 1;set results
        mov     trseed31[esi+31*4],ebx          ; 0;
                                                ; ;
        mov     eax,trseed32[edx+31*4]          ; 1;ptr32 group
        mov     ecx,trseed32[edx+ 6*4]          ; 0;
        xor     eax,ecx                         ; 1;
        mov     ecx,trseed32[edx+ 4*4]          ; 0;
        xor     eax,ecx                         ; 1;
        mov     ecx,trseed32[edx+ 2*4]          ; 0;
        xor     eax,ecx                         ; 1;
        mov     ecx,trseed32[edx+ 1*4]          ; 0;
        xor     eax,ecx                         ; 1;
        mov     ecx,trseed32[edx+ 0*4]          ; 0;
        xor     eax,ecx                         ; 1;
        mov     esi,ptr29                       ; 0;fill 1/2 cyc
        mov     trseed32[edx+ 0*4],eax          ; 1;beware bus
                                                ; ;collision!
        add     esi,4                           ; 0;fill 1/2 cyc
        mov     trseed32[edx+32*4],eax          ; 1;
        xor     eax,ebx                         ; 0;has xor sum
                                                ; ;
        .if esi == 29*4                         ; 1;wrap at 29
          mov   esi,0                           ; ;
        .endif                                  ; ;
        mov     ebx,trseed29[esi+28*4]          ; 1;ptr29 group
        mov     ecx,trseed29[esi+ 1*4]          ; 0;
        xor     ebx,ecx                         ; 1;
        mov     ptr29,esi                       ; 0;fill 1/2 cyc
        mov     trseed29[esi+ 0*4],ebx          ; 1;
        mov     trseed29[esi+29*4],ebx          ; 0;
        xor     eax,ebx                         ; 1;final result
        ret                                     ; 3;return it
IL_MixRandom_A endp                             ;;;;24 cycles
```

## IL_R250Random()

The algorithm known as r250 is presently enjoying a lot of much-deserved popularity. It's practically the fastest possible good random number generator, and it produces pretty good numbers for most purposes. However, and with no slight intended, r250 consists of little more than a well-placed xor between two array elements.

Like IL_MixRandom(), IL_R250Random() uses an array of 32-bit values as its "permutation pool" from which to xor new values into existence. In fact, it uses 250 such values; hence the name. It keeps an index into the array and increments it after each call. When it reaches 249, it increments to zero. It keeps a second index value that works the same way but initializes it 103 positions ahead of the first index. All IL_R250Random() does, then, is pick up the value at the second index, xor it into the value at the first index, increment both indexes (modulo 250), and return the new value at the first index. It's simple and effective.

In the code in Listing 11-5, I implemented the index increment logic as a table in order to shave a cycle of execution time when running in primary cache (and make it run 9 percent faster). This is one of those possibly counterproductive optimizations that can bite back if the tables get knocked out of cache a lot between calls; but if that's happening, the random routine isn't taking a very big slice of the processor pie anyhow. So I left the 250-byte wraparound index table in for the extra little kick it can give tight loops.

Like IL_MixRandom(), it requires a small army of bytes to initialize the array before start-up. You can initialize IL_R250Random() with, for instance, IL_StandardRandom() with this statement:

```
IL_R250RandomSeed(IL_StandardRandom);
```

Also like IL_MixRandom(), IL_R250Random() needs to ensure that no two 250-bit slices of the array are identical and that none is zero. Although the odds that either would occur are virtually nil when using any decent random number generator to do the initialization, there is a little bit of binary violence committed in the setup routine so as to easily guarantee that neither condition occurs. The truly digitally paranoid could add additional tests to guarantee that the patterns produced in one bit position do not closely lag and duplicate another bit position. But again, the odds are astronomical against it.

IL_R250Random() is a very efficient way to produce good random numbers. And it won't repeat its sequence within $10^{50}$ times the age of the universe (seriously!).

## Listing 11-5    `R250Random` **Function in C and Assembly Language**

```c
extern unsigned long IL_R250RandomIndex1;
extern unsigned long IL_R250RandomIndex2;
extern unsigned long IL_R250Table[];
extern unsigned char IL_R250IncrementTable[];

long
IL_R250Random_C()
{
    long ret;

    ret = (IL_R250Table[IL_R250RandomIndex1] ^=
           IL_R250Table[IL_R250RandomIndex2]);
    IL_R250RandomIndex1 =
                 IL_R250IncrementTable[IL_R250RandomIndex1];
    IL_R250RandomIndex2 =
                 IL_R250IncrementTable[IL_R250RandomIndex2];
    return ret;
}
```

```asm
IL_R250RandomIndex1    dd        0
IL_R250RandomIndex2    dd        103
;...
;long IL_R250Random_A()
;
;Returns a pseudo-random 32-bit number.
;
IL_R250Random_A proc near C public uses ebx      ; 1;
        nop                                       ; 0;for alignment
        mov     edx,IL_R250RandomIndex1           ; 1;get index 1
        mov     ecx,IL_R250RandomIndex2           ; 0;get index 2
        mov     eax,IL_R250Table[edx*4]           ; 2;get @ index 1
        mov     ebx,IL_R250Table[ecx*4]           ; 0;get @ index 2
        xor     eax,ebx                           ; 1;xor result
        mov     cl,IL_R250IncrementTable[ecx]     ; 0;inc/loop ecx
        mov     IL_R250Table[edx*4],eax           ; 1;save result
        mov     dl,IL_R250IncrementTable[edx]     ; 0;inc/loop edx
        mov     IL_R250RandomIndex1,edx           ; 1;new index 1
        mov     IL_R250RandomIndex2,ecx           ; 0;new index 2
        ret                                       ; 3;and return
IL_R250Random_A endp                              ;;;;10 cycles
```

## IL_HashRandom()

Isn't there anything better than a few xors, a shift, an add, and a multiply to achieve randomness? Of course there is. There are plenty of more complex generator proposals out there. Hunt for keywords "random numbers" on the Internet, and you'll get a nice variety of offerings. The Web has several good reference pages devoted to the topic. And the more highly regarded routines tend to have even more xors, shifts, adds, and multiplies than the routines discussed so far.

Listing 11-6 shows a good one, derived originally from *Numerical Recipes in C* (see the References). It's 17 times slower than R250 but presumably makes up for it with randomness qualities that please professional statisticians. Note that its inner loop spends most of its time on three multiplies amid xors and shifts, a bit inversion (not), and two additions. It is suggested that the loop run 4 times to thoroughly mash the bits, but I've set it up so that it can be run from 2 to 20 times at the whim of the user (using the variable IL_HashRandom_reps); it defaults to 4.

This generator takes *two* 32-bit seeds, leaves one constant from call to call, and increments the other by one after each call. This is a great feature. It means that if you want to see what the millionth value to be generated in a sequence is, you can just plug in the index number 1,000,000 (or original_seed + 1000000, more properly) and see it. All the other random number generators discussed in this chapter force you to generate 999,999 intermediate values you don't want, if all you want to do is see the millionth. This is very handy if you ever want to "back up" and see what the generator spit out a while back, even though you just noticed its effect much later.

I chose this generator to be an important part of the IL_PickRandomSeed() routine because of its excellent mixing of 64 bits into 32.

### Listing 11-6   HashRandom **Function in C and Assembly Language**

```
extern unsigned long IL_HashRandom_seed;
extern unsigned long IL_HashRandom_index;
extern unsigned long IL_HashRandom_reps;

long
IL_HashRandom_C()
{
    static long xormix1[] = {
                0xbaa96887, 0x1e17d32c, 0x03bcdc3c, 0x0f33d1b2,
                0x76a6491d, 0xc570d85d, 0xe382b1e3, 0x78db4362,
                0x7439a9d4, 0x9cea8ac5, 0x89537c5c, 0x2588f55d,
                0x415b5e1d, 0x216e3d95, 0x85c662e7, 0x5e8ab368,
                0x3ea5cc8c, 0xd26a0f74, 0xf3a9222b, 0x48aad7e4};
```

```
        static long xormix2[] = {
                0x4b0f3b58, 0xe874f0c3, 0x6955c5a6, 0x55a7ca46,
                0x4d9a9d86, 0xfe28a195, 0xb1ca7865, 0x6b235751,
                0x9a997a61, 0xaa6e95c8, 0xaaa98ee1, 0x5af9154c,
                0xfc8e2263, 0x390f5e8c, 0x58ffd802, 0xac0a5eba,
                0xac4874f6, 0xa9df0913, 0x86be4c74, 0xed2c123b};

    unsigned long hiword, loword, hihold, temp, itmpl, itmph, i;

    loword = IL_HashRandom_seed;
    hiword = IL_HashRandom_index++;
    for (i = 0; i < IL_HashRandom_reps; i++) {
        hihold = hiword;
                                        // save hiword for later
        temp   = hihold ^  xormix1[i];
                                        // mix up bits of hiword
        itmpl  = temp   &  0xffff;
                                        // decompose to hi & lo
        itmph  = temp   >> 16;
                                        // 16-bit words
        temp   = itmpl * itmpl + ~(itmph * itmph);
                                        // do a multiplicative mix
        temp   = (temp >> 16) | (temp << 16);
                                        // swap hi and lo halves
        hiword = loword ^ ((temp ^ xormix2[i]) + itmpl * itmph);
                                        // loword mix
        loword = hihold;        // old hiword is loword
    }
    return hiword;
}


;long IL_HashRandom_A()
;
;Returns a pseudo-random 32-bit number.
;
IL_HashRandom_A proc near C public uses esi ebx ; 1;
        mov     eax,IL_HashRandom_seed          ; 1;install seeds
        mov     ebx,IL_HashRandom_index         ; 0;
        mov     loword,eax                      ; 1;
        mov     hiword,ebx                      ; 0;
        inc     ebx                             ; 1;advance index
        mov     ecx,IL_HashRandom_reps          ; 0;loop count
        mov     IL_HashRandom_index,ebx         ; 1;set next idx
        mov     esi,0                           ; 0;
        .repeat                                 ; ;
```

```
        mov     eax,hiword          ; 1;get both hi
        mov     ebx,loword          ; 0;and lo words
        mov     loword,eax          ; 1;switch hi/lo
        mov     edx,xormix1[esi]    ; 0;get XOR mask
        xor     eax,edx             ; 1;hit hiword
        mov     hiword,ebx          ; 0;switch lo/hi
        mov     ebx,eax             ; 1;copy old
        and     eax,0ffffH          ; 0;lo 16 bits
        shr     ebx,16              ; 1;hi 16 bits lo
        mov     edx,eax             ; 0;lo 16 bits
        imul    edx,ebx             ; 9;lo*hi in edx
        imul    eax,eax             ; 9;lo*lo in eax
        imul    ebx,ebx             ; 9;hi*hi in ebx
        not     ebx                 ; 1;~(hi * hi)
        add     eax,ebx             ; 1;lo*lo+
                                    ;  ;      ~(hi*hi)

        mov     ebx,xormix2[esi]    ; 0;get XOR mask
        rol     eax,16              ; 1;do word swap
        add     esi,4               ; 0;advance ptr
        xor     eax,ebx             ; 1;apply mask
        add     eax,edx             ; 1;+ lo * hi
        mov     ebx,hiword          ; 0;get old
        xor     eax,ebx             ; 1;xor it in
        mov     hiword,eax          ; 1;make hiword
        dec     ecx                 ; 0;done yet?
    .until ZERO?                    ; 1;no -> loop
                                    ;;;;40 cycle loop
                                    ; 4;

        ret                         ; 3;return hiword
                                    ;;;;172 cycles
IL_HashRandom_A endp                ;;;;for 4 loops
```

## IL_CombinedRandom()

As mentioned earlier in this chapter, random numbers tend to get even better when logically mixed. The IL_CombinedRandom() function mixes all six generators covered so far. Since individual algorithm weaknesses tend to not be propagated as much as their strengths, it's not unreasonable to include the "weak" IL_SimpleRandom() and IL_Shift32Random() generators. They still bring something to the party.

A call to this function, shown in Listing 11-7, takes a little less than 500 cycles, if the cache is kind. That's 200,000 possibly excellent (depending on the purpose, of course) 32-bit values per second. And that's not bad.

**Listing 11-7** `CombinedRandom` **Function in C and Assembly Language**

```
long
IL_CombinedRandom()
{
    return     IL_R250Random()              //  10 cycles
           ^ IL_SimpleRandom()              //  14 cycles
           ^ IL_StandardRandom()            //  16 cycles
           ^ IL_MixRandom()                 //  24 cycles
           ^ IL_HashRandom()                // 172 cycles
           ^ IL_Shift32Random();            // 233 cycles
}
```

# IL_PickRandomSeed()

Every random number generator covered so far runs its course from an initial state or "seed." The array-based algorithms get bootstrapped by yet other generators, which in turn depend on one or two initial 32-bit seed values. So where do the seeds come from?

Random seeds are often derived from the computer system's clock at the time the question is asked. But the standard C library clock only ticks once per second. What if you want two arbitrary seeds? I constructed a seed picker that works on Pentiums and up, based on the mostly undocumented cycle clock built into the chip. The Pentium returns a 64-bit time value, measured since its last reset, in units of approximately ten nanoseconds (for a 100 MHz Pentium). And the C library returns a 32-bit count of the seconds since the start of 1970. (In 2106 there'll be chaos.) I xor the C time bits in reverse order into the high 32 bits of the Pentium clock, which aren't very variable, then feed low-Pentium and high-Pentium-plus-C-clock through `IL_HashRandom()` to pick the seed. You're virtually guaranteed to never get the same value twice in a row, because it's impossible for the chip clock to not advance between calls. This function is shown in Listing 11-8.

This generator is slow in this particular implementation because the `time()` function in the C library is dreadfully slow, taking up over 90 percent of the 10,000 or so cycles this call takes. But even at this rate, you can still generate 10,000 values per second. That's not bad for many purposes. The simple checks I've run indicate it's a pretty good random number stream generator in its own right.

A final word of caution: if you run this function on a pre-Pentium 80x86 chip, it will probably crash, as the processor won't understand the Pentium timer instruction.

**Listing 11-8**   RandomSeed **Function in C and Assembly Language**

```
long
IL_PickRandomSeed()
{
    unsigned long t, lo, hi;

    t  = time(NULL);                      // get C time
    lo = IL_ReadPentiumClock_A(&hi);      // get processor time
    for (n = 0; n < 32; n++)              // combine C time bits
        hi ^= ((t & (1 << (31 - n))) != 0) // with processor hi
                                << n; //
    IL_HashRandom_seed  = hi;              // assign new values
    IL_HashRandom_index = lo;
    IL_HashRandom_reps  = 4;
    return IL_HashRandom();                // about 10,000 cycles
}



;long IL_ReadPentiumClock_A(unsigned long *hi)
;
;Returns low longword of processor clock and optionally the high
;longword if "hi" is non-null.
;
IL_ReadPentiumClock_A proc near C public, hi:dword ; 2;
        mov     ecx,hi                      ; 1;
        rdtsc                               ; 8;0fH, 31H
        .if ecx                             ; 1;if not null
          mov   [ecx],edx                   ; 1;deposit hi
        .endif                              ;  ;
        ret                                 ; 3;
IL_ReadPentiumClock_A endp                  ;;;;16 cycles
```

## IL_RandomChiSquareTest()

Listing 11-9 shows a quick and dirty version of "chi square" testing I devised per a suggestion in *Algorithms in C* (see the References). Although it doesn't do justice to the generality of chi square testing, here's what it does do: Given a random number routine to test, IL_RandomChiSquareTest() calls the routine 640,000 times. It breaks each 32-bit number it receives into a high half and a low half and keeps separate tallies of how many of each high value and each low value it sees. (In other words, there are 128,000 longwords acting as counters keeping track of all the high and low 16-bit values.) The bins should average ten counts each, but due to statistical variation, you should see a range of values. The sum of the squares of the counts ought to be a little more than the sum of the same number of squares of the average value, 10. (This is related to the fact that $(n-1)^2+(n+1)^2 > 2 * (n)^2$ for positive $n$. It's easy to check.) The function checks to see if the sum is elevated enough to make statistical sense.

The return value is not the chi square statistic itself but a kind of standard deviation function that ranges between +1.0 and −1.0 most of the time, if the generator behaves well. In fact, empirical testing shows that all the generators given in this chapter, with the exception of `IL_SimpleRandom()`, fall into the +/−1.0 range 84 to 85 percent of the time when tested for several hours. Within a few minutes' testing there is, of course, more variability, but they all do converge.

There is a sample test program on the accompanying CD-ROM. It lets you pick, seed, and run this test repeatedly on the random routine of your choice. The statistic it produces is the percentage of the time that `IL_RandomChiSquareTest()` returns a value outside the +/−1.0 deviation range. A good generator should start bouncing around between 10 and 22 percent within a minute or two and asymptotically approach 15 or 16 percent.

There are much more sophisticated tests available, but this one has the dual virtues of being fast and straightforward. To speed execution up, I took the liberty of keeping twin 128,000-entry arrays, one in bytes, the other in longwords. To keep things running at least in secondary cache memory (the primary cache, at 8K, is too small to help randomly access these arrays), I did the accounting in the byte arrays until a byte should overflow, at which point I recorded 256 hits in the corresponding longword array position. At the end, I summed the byte array into the longword array to make everything add up right. It obfuscated the code a bit, but it speeded up the test significantly.

### Listing 11-9    A Form of Chi Square Validity Test

```
double
IL_RandomChiSquareTest(long (*rand)())
{
    unsigned long *ar, n, l, lo, hi;
    unsigned char *p;
    double sqrsum, chisqr, dev, norm;

    ar = calloc(2 * 0x10000, 5);
    if (!ar)
        return 999999.0;                          // flags failure
    p  = (unsigned char *)(ar + 2 * 0x10000);
    for (n = 0; n < 10 * 0x10000; n++) {
        l  = rand();
        lo = l & 0xffff;
```

```
        hi = (l >> 16) | 0x10000;
        if (!++p[lo])
            ar[lo] += 0x100;
        if (!++p[hi])
            ar[hi] += 0x100;
    }
    for (n = 0; n < 2 * 0x10000; n++)
        ar[n] += p[n];
    for (n = 0, sqrsum = 0; n < 2 * 0x10000; n++)
        sqrsum += ar[n] * (double)ar[n];
    free(ar);
    chisqr = ((2 * 0x10000 * sqrsum) / (2 * 10 * 0x10000))
                                    - 2 * 10 * 0x10000;
    dev    = chisqr - 2 * 0x10000;
    norm   = 2 * sqrt(2 * 0x10000);
    return dev / norm;
}
```

# Chrandm Chart: Statistical Snapshots

One of the most satisfying things you can do with a random number generator is check its randomness graphically. The CHRANDM.EXE program on the accompanying CD-ROM has a chart subfunction that allows you to see two-dimensional graphs of the points plotted by using the low byte of successive calls to the random number generator of your choice. One of the most telling tests you can give a generator is to ask it to plot half a million random points on a 256 × 256 grid. Statistically speaking, the generator should cover all but about 30 points, and those 30 or so (20 to 40, to be gracious) should "look" random.

Figure 11-1 shows some half-million-point charts generated by the routines in this chapter. The weak ones are easy to spot.

## IL_PiByMonteCarlo()

What would random numbers be without a good application? As promised earlier in this chapter, here's an elegant little function that does a "Monte Carlo" integration on a circle to calculate pi. If you think of each 32-bit value as a fractional number between 0 and 1, it's just taking them in pairs and seeing if the sum of their squares is greater than 1. If it is, then the random point lies outside the unit radius circle but still inside its bounding square. Knowing the $\pi R^2$ formula and the area of the square, we can find pi. With a fast random number generator, you can squeeze out the first seven digits in an overnight run—*if* it's well behaved. (The first three digits pop out in no time.) Listing 11-10 shows the code to do this.

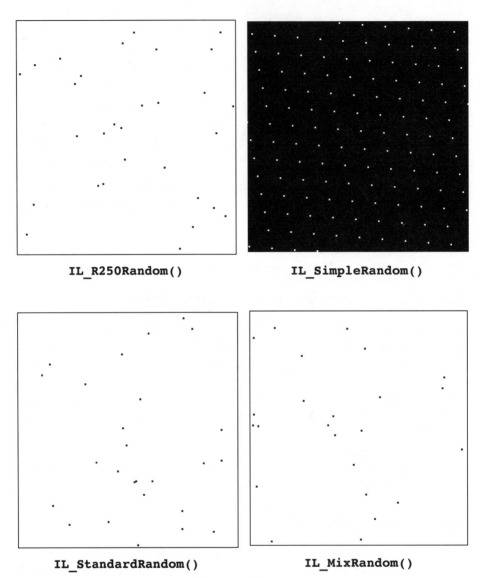

IL_R250Random()          IL_SimpleRandom()

IL_StandardRandom()          IL_MixRandom()

Figure 11-1   Random Number Generator Graph Test Results

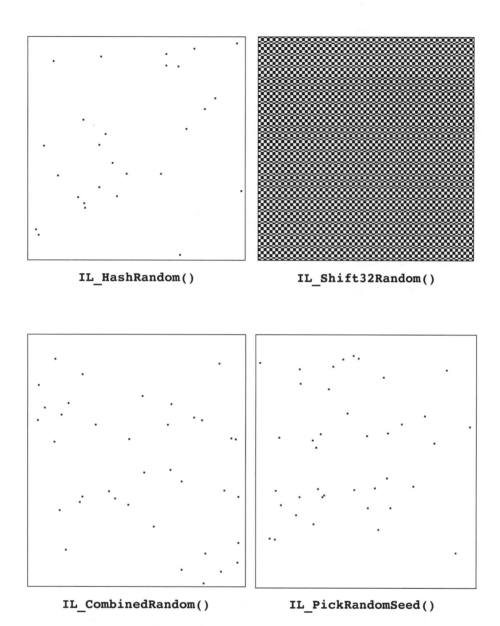

IL_HashRandom()

IL_Shift32Random()

IL_CombinedRandom()

IL_PickRandomSeed()

Figure 11-1 (Continued)   Random Number Generator Graph Test Results

The formula for the volume of a sphere is $\dfrac{4\pi R^3}{3}$ . Knowing this, it's possible to devise a similar routine to do a three-dimensional integration to find pi as well. I'm leaving this problem as an invitation to the interested reader.

### Listing 11-10   Code to Find Pi by Monte Carlo

```
double outside = 0.0, total = 0.0, pi;
long (*rand)();

while (!kbhit()) {
    outside += IL_PiByMonteCarlo_A(rand, 1000000);
    total   += 1000000;
    pi = 4 * (total - outside) / total;   // pi*R*R    where R == 1
}


;unsigned long IL_PiByMonteCarlo(long (*rand)(),
;                                               unsigned long tests)
;
;Returns number of 2-D test points found outside the unit circle
;out of "tests" point tests.
;
IL_PiByMonteCarlo_A proc near C public uses ebx esi edi,
                                rand:dword, tests:dword
                                          ; 3;
        mov     ecx,tests                 ; 1;
        mov     esi,rand                  ; 0;
        push    ebp                       ; 1;save ebp
        push    ecx                       ; 0;stack tests
        mov     ebp,0                     ; 1;ebp is countr
        .repeat                           ;  ;
          mov     [esp],ecx               ; 1;save counter
          call    esi                     ;*0;get a rand
          mul     eax                     ; 9;square it
          mov     ebx,eax                 ; 1;save all
          mov     edi,edx                 ; 0;64 bits
          call    esi                     ;*1;get a rand
          mul     eax                     ; 9;square it
          add     ebx,eax                 ; 1;sum lo
          mov     ecx,[esp]               ; 0;loop counter
          adc     edi,edx                 ; 1;sum hi
          adc     ebp,0                   ; 1;carry to ebp
          dec     ecx                     ; 0;done?
        .until ZERO?                      ; 1;no -> loop
                                          ;;;;25 cycles
                                          ;;;;+ 2 rands
```

```
        mov      eax,ebp                        ; 1;
        pop      ebx                            ; 0;stack discard
        pop      ebp                            ; 1;get ebp back
        ret                                     ; 4;
IL_PiByMonteCarlo_A endp                        ;  ;
```

# An Encryption Problem

In researching this chapter I ran across an interesting random number problem with political implications on the Internet. It seems the United States government won't, as of this writing, allow U.S. companies to export "strong" encryption software for use on the Internet, the theory being that it's important to maintain the ability to "wiretap" breakably encrypted messages to catch international crooks and protect the border. So the government only certifies suitably weak codes for export.

One such code is known as RC4-40. The "RC" is believed to stand for "Ron's code," after its inventor. The "-40" stands for its 40-bit (5-byte) key or seed value. And the first "4" probably means Ron has at least three other coding schemes on tap. (He surely has many more, as he's a well-respected cryptographer.) The RC4 algorithm can use "seed" values up to 2,048 bits, but the government decided that exportable versions had to be limited to 40 bits so they could break them at will. The fuss started when someone used a hundred powerful workstation computers over eight days to break a public challenge message encrypted with RC4-40.

The RC4 algorithm is simple to implement and readily available on the Internet. It's just a fast random number generator with a couple of additions, an `xor`, and a great shuffle. If you have a thousand-byte message to encode, you just crank out a thousand random bytes and `xor` them into the message. Only someone with the same 40-bit key can produce the same random sequence, and so decrypt the message, with another giant `xor`.

The "brute force" way to break an encrypted message is to just try every possible 40-bit key until you find one that works. The security in RC4 is partly that it takes a considerable number of cycles, at least a thousand, to sort of hash the key up into a 256-byte table before decryption can begin. In fact, when breaking the code, that's where almost all the processing power goes, since most decryption attempts can be rejected as garbage after inspecting just a few bytes of the message (presuming you know at least something about the expected form of the message; you have to know *something* about the message form beforehand to distinguish noise from the real thing).

The minimal inner loop for hashing up the 40-bit key runs in four cycles on the Pentium. It has to be executed 256 times for each key. A Pentium-100 can generate all the key tables in less than five months. Allowing a little extra time to test (and usually quickly reject) decoded message attempts, it could take six months to try them all. But on average, the solution will pop out halfway through an exhaustive search. So, in practice, a Pentium-100 would typically have the power to break RC4-40 messages in three months.

To console those worried about security, it was stated that it takes 64 "MIP years" (millions of instructions per second for a year) to break RC4-40. It sounds like a lot of years, until you realize that a Pentium-100 can execute 200 MIP years in a year. In fact, a Pentium can do it in 40 to 45 "Pentium MIP years," or about three months. A dozen Pentiums can break one message per week.

The moral of this story is that MIP years aren't what they used to be, and a Pentium is a formidable machine when programmed efficiently. All it takes is extrapolation from a little four-cycle inner loop to put things in perspective.

## The Prime Sieve of Eratosthenes

Although it may not be obvious from the examples given so far, prime numbers are often involved in randomness problems. For instance, to convert a large and possibly nonrandom number series to a smaller, somewhat more random number series, it's generally appropriate to pick a smaller prime number and use the values of the large numbers modulo the prime:

```
small_semi_random_number = large_number % prime;
```

For example, if you wanted to convert the ASCII text in this chapter to smaller, more random byte values (as if for use in a hashing algorithm), the prime number 31 would serve a lot better than 32. It's a matter of avoiding as many "resonant" frequencies of repetition in the data as possible.

Extremely large primes—in the hundreds of digits—are critical to the operation of some of the most secure encryption systems in existence. Public key cryptography, wherein everyone can know how to encrypt a message to someone but only the receiver knows how to decrypt it, is based on long primes. The somewhat controversial PGP public key system is a case in point. ("PGP" stands for Pretty Good Privacy.)

The longest prime known as of this writing is a string of 1,257,787 one-bits. It actually takes 150K of memory and about a millisecond of the `rep stosd` instruction to write it to RAM. As it turns out, most of the largest primes known are long strings of 1s because such numbers are the easiest to test for primality.

There is an old algorithm, known to the ancient Greeks, for efficiently finding all primes between 0 and a given upper bound—for practical purposes, up to about ten digits or a little more, depending on memory constraints. Known as the sieve of Eratosthenes (because it's a sieving process that lets primes pass through successive trials), it used to be commonly cited as a computer benchmark.

Here's how it works. If you want to find all the primes between 0 and 100, set up a 100-element array and initialize every value to 1. Starting the search with the number 2 and proceeding to higher indexes, look to see if that element of the array is a 1. If it is, then the number is prime, and you must zero out all values at multiples of this index. Thus the number 2 will pass, but it will knock out all the remaining even values from consideration. The number 3 will pass, but 6, 9, 12, 15, and so on will be knocked out. The number 4, already zeroed, doesn't pass. But 5 does, and so forth. When you have thus checked through all the indexes up to the square root of the number of entries in the array, all the 1s in the array represent primes.

These days, thanks to cache memory, large-scale application of the sieve isn't a very important benchmark. The ability to hop quickly through huge arrays says less about the processor than about its slowest form of random memory access. Nevertheless, I have implemented it in near-fastest-possible assembly and C for the fascination and utility of generating moderately large primes. The implementation given here, based on the routine IL_PrimeSieve(), can find 26,355,868 primes below 500,000,000 in two minutes (two minutes and forty-five seconds in C) with 32 megabytes of memory.

The full routine is given on the CD-ROM, but the core is the ten-line macro shown in Listing 11-11. It skips through an array of bits representing odd integers, zeroing the multiples of a prime when it discovers that they haven't previously been zeroed. By only zeroing bits that are not already zero, the algorithm avoids writing to many otherwise unmodified cache lines so that when the cache lines are discarded from cache, they need not be written back to memory. This can decrease the number of cache lines written back to memory by an order of magnitude, and it saves a lot of time. The macro is a bit cryptic, and it's best understood in the context of the big inline repetitions in the code on the CD-ROM. But it's also virtually the fastest way to find primes, and if the sieve ever comes back into favor, it's a great way to make a Pentium perform. Listing 11-12 gives the equivalent core routine to cast out multiples of primes, written in C.

## Listing 11-11    The Inner Loop Macro of Eratosthenes' Sieve

```
incmac  macro   bitnum, carry, reg1, reg2, jxx, dest
        mov     al,[reg1]               ; 1;pick up byte to clear
        lea     reg2,[reg1+ecx+carry] ; 0;generate next ptr
        it al & (1 shl bitnum)          ; 1;stop unneeded writes
            and    al,not (1 shl bitnum); 1;clear the bit
            mov    [reg1],al             ; 1;store processed byte
        .endif                          ; ;
        dec     edx                     ; 1;check if done...
        jxx     dest                    ; 0;branch out or loop
        endm                            ;;;;3 cycles if no write
```

**Listing 11-12    A Portion of Eratosthenes' Sieve in C**

```
long
IL_PrimeSieve_C(unsigned char *arrayptr, unsigned long arraybits,
                                          unsigned long prime)
{
    unsigned long index;

    if (!(prime & 1))                      // reject evens outright
        return 0;
    index = prime >> 1;
    if (!(arrayptr[index >> 3] & (1 << (index & 7))))
        return 0;                          // reject non-primes
    while (index < arraybits) {            // mark prime multiples
        arrayptr[index >> 3] &= ~(1 << (index & 7));
        index += prime;
    }
    return 1;                              // and return success
}
```

You can use the CHRANDM.EXE program on the CD-ROM to generate primes with the optimized sieve.

As a final challenge, left for the ambitious reader, I considered the problem of how to run the sieve with memory bits representing only integers that are *not* multiples of 2, 3, 5, 7, or 11. My previous implementation only made the trivial simplification of eliminating even values. But it turns out you can more than double your search range by eliminating the next four primes as well. What I believe to be an efficient inner loop to solve the problem (in around a dozen cycles per loop) is given on the CD-ROM in the "Eratosthenes" section of the CHRANDM.CSM code.

# Conclusion

There are many ways to generate random numbers. Unlike most other areas of computer science, there is no one agreed-upon algorithm to do the job, since an algorithm is inherently a nonrandom procedure. The best you can do is to come very close. Picking a random seed is a difficult problem in itself, one that can sometimes make or break the utility of all the pseudorandom numbers subsequently generated.

The R250 algorithm is, for many purposes, the fastest, simplest way to get the job done. The weighted random bitstream problem posed at the beginning of this chapter reduces to just over three cycles per bit when optimized, unrolled R250 is employed.

# References

Knuth, D. E. 1968. Seminumerical Algorithms. *The Art of Computer Programming.* Vol. 2: *Seminumerical Algorithms.* Reading, Mass.: Addison-Wesley. Devotes 177 pages to the topic of random numbers, with an emphasis on randomness testing.

Maier, W. L. May 1991. "A Fast Pseudo Random Number Generator." *Dr. Dobb's Journal.* Discusses the R250 algorithm.

Press, W. H., Teukolsky, S. A., Vetterling, W. T., and Flannery, B. P. 1988. *Numerical Recipes in C.* Cambridge, England: Cambridge University Press. Has a lot of good practical suggestions and examples beyond what I've presented; the original source of the Hash algorithm, as I call it.

Schneier, B. Feb. 1992. "Pseudo-Random Sequence Generator for 32-Bit CPUs." *Dr. Dobb's Journal.* Concerns shift register algorithms (such as `Shift32` and `Mix`, given in this chapter).

Sedgewick, R. 1990. *Algorithms in C.* Reading, Mass.: Addison-Wesley. This author makes the suggestions behind the chi square test in this chapter.

Another good source of information is the Internet. On the World Wide Web, there are quite a few prime and random number information sites, which can easily be found by asking Web index programs for "random numbers" or "prime numbers" sites. To find the really large primes, use the keyword "Mersenne." The Mersenne primes are the really long strings of one-bits.

# 12

---

# Linked Lists
# and Trees

*I think that I shall never see a poem lovely as a tree.*
*—Joyce Kilmer, rhyming about the wooden*
*inspirations of computer science*

Just as atoms are the deceptively simple building blocks of complex compounds, so too are the fundamental links of lists and trees the building blocks of myriad compound structures. This chapter takes a look first at the spectrum of list and tree structures and then at the timing implications of various operations commonly performed on linked lists and trees.

## Nodes in a Nutshell

Whether you want to make a linked list—which is really just a very special kind of tree—or some kind of more general tree structure, the node is the data structure with which you build. A link is just a little node.

Although a purist can argue that indirect and implicit pointers can be part of a node, the typical form for a linked list or tree node, as I have most commonly known them, is as shown in Listing 12-1. A node is a bag of pointers pointing to other nodes. Depending upon how the pointers are set up, a set of nodes can be a list, a tree, or just a peculiar tangle of references.

### Listing 12-1    A Node Contains at Least One Pointer

```
struct node {
    struct node *pointer1;    // always have at least 1 pointer
    struct node *pointer2;    // second pointer optional
    struct node *pointer3;    // etc.
            .
            .
            .
    // other data besides node pointers may go here
}
```

In both linked lists and trees, there is a natural sense of direction—two directions, in fact. A list can be read from beginning to end, and likewise from end to beginning. So, too, one can follow the nodes of a tree either from a common "trunk" out to an individual "leaf" or from leaf to trunk. Nodes can have pointers oriented in either or both directions in relation to other nodes.

Listings 12-2 and 12-3 show, respectively, a typical unidirectional link and a bidirectional link. Bidirectional links are useful for "backing up" through a list, typically when you are trying to delete a link.

### Listing 12-2    A Simple Link or Node

```
struct node {
    struct node *next;    // points to next node in the list
    int         data;     // dummy data
}
```

### Listing 12-3    A Bidirectional Link or Node

```
struct node {
    struct node *next;    // points to next node in the list
    struct node *back;    // points to previous list node
    int         data;     // dummy data
}
```

You can make one form of tree—one that can only be followed from leaf to trunk—using the simple links of linked lists. If you take several lists that start out separate but join one another somewhere down the chain, then all the lists share the same end point. Looked at from the opposite direction, the common end is the "trunk," or beginning of a tree structure, with each separate linked list starting point being a "leaf."

More common forms of trees use multiple pointers. The best-known form, the binary tree, uses either two or three pointers, depending on whether or not the tree can be "unclimbed" starting from any node. Listing 12-4 shows a root-to-leaf-only form, and Listing 12-5 shows the bidirectional form.

### Listing 12-4   A Simple Binary Tree Node

```
struct node {
    struct node *left;      // points to "left" branch node
    struct node *right;     // points to "right" branch node
    int         data;       // dummy data
}
```

### Listing 12-5   A Bidirectional Binary Tree Node

```
struct node {
    struct node *left;      // points to "left" branch node
    struct node *right;     // points to "right" branch node
    struct node *parent;    // points to "parent" node
    int         data;       // dummy data
}
```

Binary trees are perhaps the most common trees found in computing, because it's such a natural thing for computers to make binary (two-way) decisions. As often as not, one pointer is followed for a "less than" decision and the other for the opposite, "greater than or equal to" decision.

Beyond binary trees lie ternary, quad, penta, hex, septa, oct and beyond trees. The prefixes are just pointer counts and do not include the optional pointer to the parent node. A ternary tree can be used, for instance, to hold "less than," "greater than," and "equal to" branches. A quadtree node can be used to break down two-dimensional squares into their four quadrants, with a different node pointer assigned to each quadrant. And likewise, an octree node, with eight pointers, is a convenient way to break down a cube into eight subcubes, each half as tall, wide, and deep. (Think of cutting a cube in half in each dimension so that each of its eight original corners is part of a new smaller cube.)

Listing 12-6 shows an octree node that might be used for subdividing space into ever smaller cubes. If you want to find the smallest cube that contains, say, the point at the XYZ coordinate [17, 34, 22] and the first node has its x, y, and z center coordinates set at [20, 30, 40], you're left (17 < 20), up (34 > 30), and near (22 < 40) relative to the center. So just follow the left-up-near pointer to the next node and repeat.

## Listing 12-6    An Octree Node for Partitioning Cubes

```
struct node {
    struct node *XYZ;        // right-up-near   sub-cube
    struct node *XYz;        // right-up-far    sub-cube
    struct node *XyZ;        // right-down-near sub-cube
    struct node *Xyz;        // right-down-far  sub-cube
    struct node *xYZ;        // left-up-near    sub-cube
    struct node *xYz;        // left-up-far     sub-cube
    struct node *xyZ;        // left-down-near  sub-cube
    struct node *xyz;        // left-down-far   sub-cube
    struct node *parent;     // parent cube
    int          x;          // x position of cube center
    int          y;          // y position of cube center
    int          z;          // z position of cube center
    int          data;    // dummy data
}
```

There is no one right way to begin or end lists and trees, but there certainly are options. If you want to keep a linked list of ten items, you might choose to use 10 nodes or 11 or 12, depending on whether or not you want to start and/or end the list with dummy nodes, or even link the tail to a dummy head.

The reasons for using dummy heads and tails on lists are well covered in many algorithm books, but here is my summary: A dummy head node makes the next node, the *real* first node, just like the rest of the valid nodes by giving it a predecessor node. Code that operates on the pointers binding nodes to their predecessors won't generally work on the first valid link unless you do this. A dummy tail node serves the same type of function for the last valid node, and if it points to itself, you won't ever "fall off" the end of the list, and you won't have to deal with an invalid node pointer (such as the null pointer), causing problems at the end of a list. Sometimes it even makes sense to use the same node as head and tail.

The classic way to end a stream of pointers is to use a null pointer to mean "nothing there." As mentioned in the last paragraph, that's not always the best solution with lists. It's a common solution with trees. But so, too, is it fairly common to store a couple of bits in a node that indicates whether left and right pointers (a binary tree, in this case) are pointing to other nodes, are pointing to some other object that makes up the leaf termination, or aren't really pointers at all, but some kind of leaf data.

When you combine the variety of termination strategies with the variety of tree and list structures, including directionality, and then add in a wide variety of uses, from language parsing to compression dictionaries to memory management schemes, there are a bewildering array of possible implementations of routines to operate on lists and trees. The remainder of this chapter looks at a few representative, straightforward ones that illustrate some of the speed issues.

## Speed Issues

Every once in a while, the speed with which you can scan through a linked list looking for something may be a critical factor. As a general rule, scanning a long list is just about the last thing you would want to do when cycles are scarce, and there are often ways to design faster access to whatever you're looking for. But sometimes there is no alternative to the list. When that happens, consider these guidelines:

- Make sure all link pointers are longword-aligned.
- If links are evenly spaced throughout memory, as in an array, avoid spacings that are multiples of a large power of 2 (such as 64, 128, 256, and so on—and 96, for instance, isn't very good either). Powers of 2, plus or minus 8, work well.
- Keep the links localized to one or a very few areas of memory, if possible.
- If possible, practical, and necessary in the context, keep links and data to be scanned for in an array separate from the rest of the data associated with the link—which may be kept in another array.

The first guideline is fairly obvious and should be an automatic impulse if you've read this far. Aligned data can be read faster.

The second guideline is based on an architectural subtlety of Intel's primary cache structure. Pentium cache can hold, at most, two values (in this case, pointers) whose locations in memory have the same low address bits at positions 5 through 12. Translation: pointers spaced 4,096 bytes apart compete for the same four slots in the cache. If you had an array of one thousand 4,096-byte records linked in a list, not more than two of the links could be in the cache at once. If the records were 4,064 bytes long, 256 would have a shot at the cache, since pointer addresses would be staggered better through the address space. (The 32-byte cache line "chunkiness" prevents this number from being higher.)

The third guideline is related to the fact that chains of pointers can, in principle, jump through memory so randomly that they completely baffle all the hardware mechanisms meant to enhance memory access speed. The Pentium processor keeps a list of typically fewer than sixty-four 4K memory pages that have been recently accessed. If, in running down a list of 100 links, it encounters 90 different pages, there will be a lot of "page thrashing," costing 20 to 40 cycles per page miss. This situation can come about if links are allocated over time in a program environment that is doing a lot of other allocating as well.

If you ever want to demonstrate some of the worst behavior of a computer running virtual memory, you can do it with linked lists. In fact, common implementations of the C library `malloc()` memory allocation function have been known to bring mighty computers to their knees. `Malloc()` is often implemented using one big linked list to connect all "free" memory fragments throughout a memory pool of, potentially, many megabytes. Whenever a new memory chunk is requested, `malloc()` runs through the list looking for a big enough chunk. As if it weren't bad enough that the free fragment list may thrash the page tables, the run down the list may visit so many memory pages that the computer has to run virtual memory page swaps to disk just to get from one end of the list to the other. And a page swap costs about 10,000 times more than a page miss! If a typical `malloc()` or equivalent list procedure makes the red disk light flicker, you might be seeing a sign of scattered links.

The final guideline is a desperation optimization measure. Suppose you need to repeatedly search a list of, say, 32-byte records for a certain integer index field. If the records all exist in a single array, then at most 256 link pointers can sit in the primary cache simultaneously (the cache chunkiness effect). But if you create a separate-but-parallel array of 8-byte records, four bytes for the pointer and four bytes for the integer index, you can fit up to 1,024 link pointers with index data into the cache. This can make a performance difference when there are many links to repeatedly process. Once you locate a given "minilink," you can deduce what its array position is and then locate the remainder of the record in the larger parallel array. It's not a pretty sight, but it works.

Tree speed issues are similar to linked list issues. But since traveling through a tree usually involves making logical decisions about which pointer to follow, tree travel is just a little bit slower. The three guidelines mentioned above for links apply as well for tree nodes.

# Inner Loops

So how fast do lists and trees go? Of course, it depends on what you're doing with them, but here's a look at

- Running down a linked list looking for a data value—2 cycles per link, best-case

- Running down a binary tree looking for a data value—6 cycles per node, best-case
- Running all over every node in a tree (known properly as "traversing the tree")—about 12 cycles per node, best-case

It's worth remembering that nodes and their pointers have a way of defying cache memory. Byte for byte, links and nodes tend to see less cache benefit than almost any other type of data structure. Whereas a primary cache miss normally costs seven cycles, the next miss can't "begin" until an additional several cycles have passed. So, when traversing a list or tree and rapidly generating cache misses, instead of seeing, say, 2 or 7 cycles per node, one can easily see 10 cycles per node, or 20 cycles if secondary cache misses too, or 60 cycles if the processor is really clueless about an address, or 3 million cycles if the next node is swapped out to disk.

# Linked List Searching

How fast can a linked list be searched for a given data value match? In just over two cycles per link, *if* you're running down a long list in primary cache, and degrading to 10 cycles per link running from pure secondary cache.

Listing 12-7 shows the slightly odd way to run through a list fast in assembly language, assuming the list is terminated with a dummy link pointing to itself. By rotating pointing duties among three registers, it is possible to blaze down the list and still keep a record of the pointer to the link previous to the one that is ultimately found. In case you want to subsequently detach the link from the list, you need to keep that backup pointer. The algorithm avoids wasting time checking for the end-of-list condition by letting the main loop iterate through three links for every one check for the end condition. Since the end condition harmlessly perpetuates itself until it can be detected, no harm is done.

### Listing 12-7   Fast Two-Cycle Linked List Search

```
;Enter this loop with the following registers loaded:
;
;eax - data value to be searched for
;esi - points to first link to check
;ebx - points to previous link, possibly dummy header link
;ecx - points to dummy end link which points to self
;
```

```
;The first link of the list and the last should both be
;dummies, and the last one should point to itself

        .repeat
          mov   edi,[esi].link.next      ; 1;do first link
          mov   edx,[esi].link.val       ; 0;
          .if eax == edx                 ; 1;
            mov edi,ebx                  ;  ;
            jmp found                    ;  ;
          .endif                         ;  ;
          mov   ebx,[edi].link.next      ; 1;do second link
          mov   edx,[edi].link.val       ; 0;
          .if eax == edx                 ; 1;
            xchg  esi,edi                ;  ;
            jmp found                    ;  ;
          .endif                         ;  ;
          mov   esi,[ebx].link.next      ; 1;do third link
          mov   edx,[ebx].link.val       ; 0;
          .if eax == edx                 ; 1;
            mov   esi,ebx                ;  ;
            jmp found                    ;  ;
          .endif                         ;  ;
        .until edi == ecx                ; 1;check end condition
                                         ;;;;2.33 cycles/link
;
;code falls through here if value not found
;
;       ...


found:
;
;When it arrives here, the following registers are set:
;
;esi - points to the "found" link
;edi - points to the previous link
;
;       ...
```

Listing 12-8 shows an equivalent C loop, which may execute in about five cycles per link if it compiles efficiently. It is no doubt possible to "psych out" some compilers and make them write C code that is two-cycle efficient, but that's tantamount to writing compiler-specific assembly language in C, and best done behind closed doors.

### Listing 12-8   A Relatively Fast C Linked List Search

```
link *prev, *present, *endlist;
int   val, searchval;

//start out with 'present' pointing to dummy first link,
//'endlist' pointing to dummy last link, and searchval set

while (present != endlist)
    if ((present = (prev = present)->next)->val == searchval)
        break;

if (present != endlist) {
//      ... found
} else {
//      ... not found
}
```

# Binary Tree Searching

Binary trees have many uses, but one of the more common ones has to do with serving as an indexing system. You can compare a string or numeric value against strings and numeric values stored in the data fields of nodes. After each comparison, then, you can decide whether to continue to the "less than" or the "greater than or equal to" child node. (Sometimes, as in the next example, you may want to quit the search on an equality condition.) Ultimately you either find an exact match or you run out of nodes; in the latter case you may have the option of adding the new unmatched value to the binary tree "dictionary" as a new node, right at the point where the search ended.

Listing 12-9 shows a fast, approximately seven-cycle way to advance from node to node on a binary search for an integer value match. If you were absolutely assured, going in, that an exact match would be found, you could even shorten the loop one cycle by discarding the node termination (null pointer) checks, making it a six-cycle procedure. The code as shown is suitable for adding new node entries to the tree in that there are three exit points, one each for "found," "add as left child," and "add as right child."

If you're willing to take advantage of fixed adjacent positioning of child pointers within a node structure, there is also a way, demonstrated in Chapter 13, to do a six-cycle search node descent while still checking for a "not found" condition.

## Listing 12-9    Indexing Through a Binary Tree

```
;Enter with esi pointing to the base node of the tree
;and eax holding the match value
;
        .repeat                        ;  ;
          .repeat                      ;  ;
            test esi,esi               ; 1;assure valid ptr
            je  exitright              ; 0;else
            mov edi,[esi].node.right   ; 1;load esi node data
            mov eax,[esi].node.data    ; 0;
            mov ebx,esi                ; 1;backup the pointer
            mov esi,[esi].node.left    ; 0;
          .until eax >= edx            ; 3;loop down right side
          .break .if ZERO?             ; 1;done? yes -> exit
          .repeat                      ;  ;
            test edi,edi               ; 1;
            je  exitleft               ; 0;
            mov esi,[edi].node.left    ; 1;load edi node data
            mov eax,[edi].node.data    ; 0;
            mov ebx,edi                ; 1;backup the pointer
            mov edi,[edi].node.right   ; 0;
          .until eax <= edx            ; 3;loop down left side
        .until ZERO?                   ; 1;
                                       ;;;;approx 7 / node
;
;Falls through here with pointer to exact match node in ebx
;
;          ...

exitright:
;Arrives here with ebx pointing to potential parent node and
;the match value a candidate for right child node insertion
;
;          ...

exitleft:
;Arrives here with ebx pointing to potential parent node and
;the match value a candidate for left child node insertion
;
;          ...
```

Binary tree nodes tend to be 16 or more bytes in size, so there's an upper limit of about 512 of them in primary cache at any one time. That's enough for a fully populated symmetric binary tree eight levels deep. (Symmetric means right and left nodes exist at all levels down to the leaves—eight decisions deep in this case.) You can find a random value, therefore, in approximately 75 cycles, allowing for eight node decisions and a little start-up and exit overhead.

You might actually get similar performance on much larger trees if some search values are much more common than others. The common paths would stay in the cache. You can go to a depth of up to 13 levels running random lookups mostly in the secondary cache, but beyond about the seventh or eighth node depth level (since the first few node levels tend to stay in cache), the node time triples to about 21 cycles per node, since back-to-back read operations on a not-in-cache node incur the full 14-cycle penalty for filling a cache line.

Listing 12-10 shows a C routine equivalent to the assembly language routine in Listing 12-9. Depending on the quality of compiler optimizations, it may run from several times slower to nearly as fast.

### Listing 12-10    Indexing Through a Binary Tree in C

```
while (nodeptr->val != searchval) {
    while (nodeptr->val < searchval)
        if (!(nodeptr = (backup = nodeptr)->right))
            goto exitright;
    while (nodeptr->val > searchval)
        if (!(nodeptr = nodeptr->left))
            goto exitleft;
}

// Falls through here with exact match on node at nodeptr
//
//      ...


exitright:

// Arrives here with potential parent for right child in backup
//
//      ...


exitleft:

// Arrives here with potential parent for left child in backup
//
//      ...
```

# Traversing a Binary Tree

Perhaps the most common question asked by prospective employers on programming tests is, "How would you write a routine to traverse a binary tree?" A good answer, written in C, is shown in Listing 12-11.

Traversing is just a matter of visiting all the nodes, and you might want to do so to generate a list of all nodes or to look for nodes containing certain data not directly indexed by the node connection rules. If, say, you were printing out data values found in the nodes, there are three positions in the traverse() routine where you might choose to do the printing, as shown in the listing. Choosing any one of the three will print the entire list, but the order of output will be different according to position. For instance, "in-order" printing of a binary parse tree (a tree used to analyze expressions in computer languages) can produce fairly readable code as output, but choosing "preorder" or "postorder" printing would scramble things.

Traversing a tree without doing anything with the nodes visited is a bit like flying around the world without landing. But some useful routines do execute at or near raw traversal speed. For instance, simply counting the nodes in a tree may run as fast as raw traversal because the increment instruction may occupy an empty instruction pairing slot. The search for a particular data value runs not much slower.

### Listing 12-11 Binary Tree Traversal in C

```
void
traverse(node *nodeptr)
{
    // optional "pre-order"  operation on *nodeptr goes here

    if (nodeptr->left)
        traverse(nodeptr->left);

    // optional "in-order"   operation on *nodeptr goes here

    if (nodeptr->right)
        traverse(nodeptr->right);

    // optional "post-order" operation on *nodeptr goes here
}
```

It is very often true that recursive routines—routines that call themselves to get things done—run slower than alternative, nonrecursive routines. The overhead of parameter passing, register preservation, stack frame setup, and stack frame cleanup usually make the recursive call inefficient. But optimized assembly language can relieve many of these inefficiencies.

Listing 12-12 shows an optimized, recursive assembly language equivalent of the code in Listing 12-11. It certainly runs a good bit faster than any compiled code I could imagine coming out of Listing 12-11. And, to my surprise, it appears to run as fast as a fast nonrecursive traversal relying on parent node pointers for reverse flow through the tree. (Translation: I thought I had found a really good, esoteric, nonrecursive way to do it, but straight recursion won!)

The recursive traversal routine requires another routine, start_traverse, to initialize one register before taking on the tree. The traverse routine itself is a bit cryptic, because it makes very unorthodox use of the stack in relation to the "caller" and "callee" instances of the routine. The trick is that the routine passes its one parameter in a register and exits by reloading that register with its own parent's stacked node pointer *before* returning to the parent (the mov esi, [esp+12] line). This unorthodoxy speeds up traversal by about 10 percent since the parent isn't burdened with a load cycle and an address-generation delay. Some would say this is optimization overkill, but it illustrates the point that there are often creative ways to solve problems by thinking beyond conventional rules, where compilers dare not tread.

### Listing 12-12   Binary Tree Traversal

```
start_traverse proc near C public uses esi, nodeptr:dword
        mov     esi,nodeptr             ;  ;stack first ptr
;       mov     eax,0                   ;  ;optional counter
        call    traverse                ;  ;do the whole tree
        ret                             ;  ;and return

traverse:
        push    esi                     ; 1;save node pointer
        mov     esi,[esi].node.left     ; 0;
        .if esi                         ; 3;
          call  traverse                ; 1;
        .endif                          ;  ;
        mov     esi,[esi].node.right    ; 1;
;       inc     eax                     ; 0;optional node count
        .if esi                         ; 3;
          call  traverse                ; 1;
        .endif                          ;  ;
        mov     esi,[esp+12]            ; 1;restore parent ptr
        pop     edx                     ; 0;discard old pointer
        retn                            ; 2;and return
                                        ;;;;12 cycles typical
start_traverse endp
```

# Conclusion

Linked lists and trees can exhibit some of the best and the worst behaviors of any data structures. Link traversal can be as fast as two cycles per link, and descent through a binary tree can proceed in as little as six cycles per node. But precisely because these speeds are so fast, and because links and nodes may be scattered throughout memory, the delays involved in accessing secondary cache or main memory may sometimes dominate performance. A tree in primary cache can be traversed at about 12 cycles per node, about five times faster than if it were very large and scattered. But even a very large tree, spread out through secondary cache and main memory, can behave very well if it is accessed in very nonrandom patterns which keep just the critical parts in primary cache. An example of a large, fast-running tree is given in Chapter 13.

# Hashing

*Variant of Middle English* hache, *from
Old French, past participle of* hacher, hachier, *to chop up,
from* hache, *ax, of Germanic origin. See* HACHET.
—*Origin of the word* hash, *from the* American Heritage Dictionary

To hash is to chop up or mix up. Hash brown potatoes are chopped up and mixed up. And a *hash value* in computing is just a chopped up, mixed up, pseudorandom number. It's also the key to many fast-data-lookup problems.

This chapter looks at why, when, and how to perform hashed symbol and data object lookups at rates of up to a million per second. A working demonstration program, including all the code shown in this chapter, is capable of "looking up" every word in *War and Peace* in less than a second.

## When to Hash

You need to hash whenever you have to "look up" some multibyte data object from within a large set of such objects quickly, such as looking up a word in a dictionary. More to the point, here's an example from my own experience with assembler construction.

An assembler is a fairly simple machine under the hood. Assemblers and compilers both take in streams of ASCII symbols and produce object or executable code as output, but compilers have to spend a lot of time deciding what assembly language instructions to issue in order to translate the text into an executable code. Conversely, assemblers exercise very little discretion over the code they create.

Each line is an unambiguous directive to generate a specific instruction. So a major limitation on the speed of an assembler can be the speed with which it looks up ASCII symbols, since there is so little logic to execute after the symbol has been found. (For example, once you've located the `clc` symbol, plopping down the 0xF8 opcode takes very little time and logic.) And the fastest symbol lookup is done by hashing.

Assemblers, compilers, interpreters, dictionaries, and phone books all present lookup problems appropriate for hashing.

## How to Hash

The actual hashing operation for which the algorithm is named consists of feeding one's input string through a little number randomizer to produce a handful of random-looking bits. So "checkers" might generate the number 427, while "socks" might generate 83. If "fala" also generates 83 or 427, that's fine, but chances are it will generate an even different number, like 391. Instead of keeping all the known symbols or strings in one long list or big binary tree, you keep them in a few hundred small lists or binary trees, so that when "socks" generates an 83, you would go look to find its match in list or tree number 83. By bypassing all but a tiny fraction of a percent of the symbols using the hash value, you can gain enormous speed on lookup.

If your "hash table," the array of pointers pointing to the start of the lists or trees, contains many more entries than there are strings to be looked up, good hashing almost guarantees direct and immediate access to any string.

## Fast Hashing with `IL_HashFindSymbol()`

With the notion that an ounce of practice usually beats a pound theory, I built what I believe to be just about the fastest general-purpose hashing engine I could imagine for Pentium-class chips, named it `IL_HashFindSymbol()`, and included it in the CHHASH program on the CD-ROM accompanying this book. If you point it at the first character of a symbol and give it a list of valid symbol characters (so that it knows when the symbol terminates), it will climb through a hash table and binary tree structure to find a record of the symbol about as fast as possible.

Written in assembly language, it can "look up" every word in *War and Peace* in less than a second. A C language version of the routine runs at two-thirds the assembly language speed and does the same lookup in just over a second. With minor customization, either version of the routine can be used for a wide variety of hashing applications.

The truly *big* surprise I got when constructing this hash function was that when I reduced the size of the hash table to just one entry, effectively *not* hashing and relying only on a binary tree structure, the *War and Peace* performance was only cut in half! You can actually locate the half-million-plus words in *War and Peace* with binary tree searching in less than two seconds! It turns out that the high frequency of commonly used words in a novel, and the way they are entered into the tree when first encountered, make binary tree searching particularly efficient in this particular case. If the word patterns were more random, you would expect to see a bigger spread between hashing and binary tree performance. Hashing is still the fastest trick in the book, but the binary tree performance is a good reminder that actual performance measurements are still very important when gauging relative algorithm merits.

## `IL_HashFindSymbol()` in C

Listing 13-1 shows a C language version of the `IL_HashFindSymbol()` function. Listing 13-2 shows the three data structures referenced by the function.

### Listing 13-1  `IL_HashFindSymbol_C`

```
IL_HashSymbol **
IL_HashFindSymbol_C(char *symptr, IL_HashTable *table)
{

    unsigned char *p, *xlat, c, *s;
    unsigned long *d, index, len, *l1, *l2, hash;
    long n, lim;
    IL_HashWord hashword;
    IL_HashSymbol *hs, **phs;

    if (!table->strlim) {          // make sure space is available
        if (!table->table) {       // make sure table exists
            if (!(table->table =
                            table->malloc(table->tablesize)))
                return NULL;       // malloc error return
            memset(table->table, 0, table->tablesize); //zero it
        }
        p = table->malloc(table->chunksize); // get symbol space
        if (!p)
            return NULL;           // malloc error return
```

```
        table->string = (long *)(p + sizeof(IL_HashSymbol));
        table->cutoff = (long *)(p + table->chunksize);
        table->strlim = (long *)(((char *)table->string) -
                                                table->negmax);
}
xlat        = table->xlattbl; // set up translation ptr
s           = symptr;         // and character pointer
d           = (unsigned long *)table->string; // and dest
lim         = 0 - table->negmax; // string character limit
hash        = 0;                 // starting hash value
do {
    hashword.hash = 0;           // byte accumulator zeroed
    if (!(hashword.byte[0] = xlat[*s++])) // check char 1
        break;
    if (!(hashword.byte[1] = xlat[*s++])) // check char 2
        break;
    if (!(hashword.byte[2] = xlat[*s++])) // check char 3
        break;
    if (!(hashword.byte[3] = xlat[*s++])) // check char 4
        break;
    *d++ = hashword.hash;                  // save bytes
    hash ^= hashword.hash;                 // xor into hash
    hash = (hash << 1) | (hash >> 31);    // permute hash
} while ((lim -= 4) > 0);                   // until lim hit
if ((lim > 0) && (hashword.hash)) {         // if needed
    *d++ = hashword.hash;                   // save remainder
    hash ^= hashword.hash;                  // and xor hash
}
table->symlen = s - symptr - 1;             // record length
len   = (table->symlen + 3) >> 2;           // alternate len
(((IL_HashSymbol *)(table->string)) - 1)->hash = hash;
(((IL_HashSymbol *)(table->string)) - 1)->len  = len;
index = ((hash ^ ((hash >> 14) | (hash << 18)))
                                & table->msk) >> 2;
phs   = &table->table[index];               // point to table slot
while (hs = *phs) {                          // is it NULL?
    if (hash == hs->hash) {                  // if hash the same
        if (len == hs->len) {                // if len the same
            l1 = (unsigned long *)table->string;
            l2 = (unsigned long *)(hs + 1);
            for (n = 0; n < len; n++)
                if (l1[n] != l2[n]) { // if string different
                    if (l1[n] < l2[n])
                        goto below;   // go below
                    else
                        goto above;   // or above
                }
```

```
            return phs;              // return found!
         } else if (len < hs->len)   // compare len
            goto below;              // go below
         else
            goto above;             // or above
      } else if (hash < hs->hash) {  // compare hash
below:      phs = &hs->below;        // go below
      } else {
above:      phs = &hs->above;        // or above
      }
   }
   return phs;                       // symbol not found
}
```

## Listing 13-2    Hashing Data Structures

```
// IL_HashSymbol - the basic symbol form. Actual translated
//                 string follows the structure body. "Below"
//                 and "above" must be declared next to each
//                 other to accommodate an assembly language
//                 speed feature.
//
typedef struct IL_HashSymbol {
  long                hash;  // hash code
  long                len;   // length in longwords
  struct IL_HashSymbol *below; // must immediately precede above
  struct IL_HashSymbol *above; // must immediately follow below
  long                data;  // arbitrary data
} IL_HashSymbol;

// IL_HashTable - main symbol control table. Maximum symbol
//                 length must be a multiple of 4. "Symlen" is
//                 a return value.
//
typedef struct {
    long    negmax;        // negative of max string byte length
    IL_HashSymbol **table; // pointer to table of hash pointers
    long    tablesize;     // size of table in bytes
    void *(*malloc)(long size); // malloc function
    long    chunksize;     // size for memory symbol chunks
    long    *string;       // ptr to new symbol string storage
    long    *strlim;       // pointer to end of string storage
    long    *cutoff;       // chunk cutoff for strlim value
    long    symlen;        // bytes in latest symbol looked up
    long    msk;           // mask for table lookup
    char    *xlattbl;      // character translation table
} IL_HashTable;
```

```
// IL_HashWord - a longword with byte-addressable components
//              used for translated character accumulation
//
typedef union {
    unsigned char byte[4];
    unsigned long hash;
} IL_HashWord;
```

## The Inner Loop

If you don't know in advance how many characters are going to be in a symbol—such as when you are parsing the symbol straight out of a text file—and you have to detect an end-of-symbol byte, then you have to pick up and inspect each character in sequence to see whether it's part of the symbol and whether it's the end of the symbol. This defines the innermost loop of symbol hashing. (Strings of a standard fixed length can potentially use a version of this loop that runs up to ten times faster.) Listing 13-3 shows the C and assembly language versions of the inner loop.

### Listing 13-3    Symbol Hashing Inner Loop

```
// C language inner loop
//
    do {
        hashword.hash = 0;              // byte accumulator zeroed
        if (!(hashword.byte[0] = xlat[*s++])) // check char 1
            break;
        if (!(hashword.byte[1] = xlat[*s++])) // check char 2
            break;
        if (!(hashword.byte[2] = xlat[*s++])) // check char 3
            break;
        if (!(hashword.byte[3] = xlat[*s++])) // check char 4
            break;
        *d++  = hashword.hash;                 // save bytes
        hash ^= hashword.hash;                 // xor into hash
        hash  = (hash << 1) | (hash >> 31);    // permute hash
    } while ((lim -= 4) > 0);                  // until lim hit

;-----------------------------------------------------------
;
;assembly language inner loop
;
;eax - page-aligned lookup table pointer used with odd chars
;ebx - buffers translated characters for testing, output, hash
;ecx - string I/O index, negative of maximum string length
```

```
;edx - page-aligned lookup table pointer used with even chars
;esi - incoming string pointer
;edi - outgoing translated string pointer
;ebp - holds hash value

        mov     dl,[esi+ecx+0]          ; 1;get first byte
        nop                             ; 0;stop address bus jam
;
;The following instruction, instead of the nop,
;prefetches a cache line, increasing lookup
;speed about 1%.
;       mov     al,[esi+ecx+28]         ; 0;optional prefetch
;
        nop                             ; 0;prevent address jam
        mov     al,[esi+ecx+1]          ; 1;get second byte
        mov     bl,[edx]                ; 0;translate first byte
        test    bl,bl                   ; 1;done?
        je      hash0                   ; 0;yes -> branch
                                        ;;;;13 cycles to here
        .repeat                         ;  ;
          mov   dl,[esi+ecx+2]          ; 1;get byte 4N+2
          mov   bh,[eax]                ; 0;translate 4N+1
          test  bh,bh                   ; 1;done?
          je    hash1                   ; 0;yes -> branch
          rol   ebx,16                  ; 1;lo/hi word swap
          mov   al,[esi+ecx+3]          ; 1;get byte 4N+3
          rol   ebp,1                   ; 1;phase shift hash val
          mov   bl,[edx]                ; 0;translate 4N+2
          test  bl,bl                   ; 1;done?
          je    hash2                   ; 0;yes -> branch
          mov   dl,[esi+ecx+4]          ; 1;get byte 4N+4
          mov   bh,[eax]                ; 0;translate 4N+3
          test  bh,bh                   ; 1;done?
          je    hash3                   ; 0;yes -> branch
          xor   ebp,ebx                 ; 1;add to hash
          mov   [edi+ecx],ebx           ; 0;store 4 bytes of sym
          mov   al,[esi+ecx+5]          ; 1;get byte 4N+5
          mov   bl,[edx]                ; 0;translate 4N+4
          test  bl,bl                   ; 1;done?
          je    hash4                   ; 0;yes -> branch
          add   ecx,4                   ; 1;advance I/O index
        .until !SIGN?                   ; 0;until limit hit
                                        ;;;;;3.3 cyc/char average
```

The C language inner loop is fairly efficient and straightforward. The assembly language version is fast and cryptic, and it takes advantage of pipelining and a page-aligned lookup table to achieve a typical performance of just over *three* cycles per symbol character. (The C version compiles to about *ten* cycles, under Watcom.) The assembly language version of the loop actually produces subtly different hash values than the C language version to save a cycle, but that makes no effective difference in its use. Just don't switch back and forth between the C and assembly language implementations, using the symbol set constructed by one with the other.

The assembly language loop is pipelined in the sense that it is always fetching two bytes ahead of the last byte confirmed to be part of the symbol, not just one. If there is any danger that the second byte fetched ahead could cause a protection error (by crossing into an illegal page just after a symbol), either use the C version or modify the assembly language version to read slower and just one safe byte ahead.

For the optimization extremist, there is a beautiful example in Listing 13-3 of how to outwit the cache to gain speed. Note the disabled instruction `mov al,[esi+ecx+28]`. Since `al` is subsequently overwritten, this instruction appears to do nothing (except chance a protection error by reading a couple of dozen bytes ahead in the stream). But when this instruction replaces the `nop` line, symbol lookup runs about 1 percent faster! By reading ahead in the data stream, you occasionally cause a 6- to 16-cycle delay while data gets read into the cache, but you prevent a subsequent delay of as much as 13 to 28 cycles for rapidly missing the same cache line twice in a row while reading actual symbol characters. It is not at all good style to use a potentially dangerous hardware-specific kludge like this. But if you really need it and you're sure that reading into illegal territory won't be a problem, you can do it.

Here are the steps of the algorithm, in either language:

1. Pick up a byte from the incoming string.
2. Translate it to zero or an assigned "random-looking" bit pattern.
3. If it's zero, meaning that it's not a valid symbol character, exit the loop.
4. You may choose to allow uppercase and lowercase letters to translate to the same value, so that lookup is case-insensitive.
5. Buffer up to four translated characters in a 32-bit register, and then `xor` it into the 32-bit hash value register.
6. Rotate the hash value register one bit so that identical translated characters won't cancel each other on `xor`.
7. Output the four buffered bytes to an output string for subsequent comparisons.
8. After each four-byte output, advance the string index for the next four characters and exit the loop if the string is too long.

And all this happens in an average of just over three cycles per character. In fact, it's so fast that even though it is the primary inner loop for symbol lookup, it typically only accounts for about 20 percent of symbol lookup time in the assembly language version.

## A Few Random Bits

The inner loop just shown generates a 32-bit pseudorandom hash value in the `ebp` register (in assembly) or the variable `hash` (in C). But you rarely need or want much more than a dozen random bits for a hash index. A dozen bits is enough for a 4,096-entry table of pointers taking up 16K of memory, already bigger than the primary cache. In fact, *War and Peace,* with nearly 20,000 unique words, hashes best with 14 bits in the hash value and 16K table entries. As a rule of thumb, if you have about as many hash table array positions as objects or symbols to be looked up, you're probably running at near peak efficiency. The exception to the rule is that when the table gets up toward many tens or hundreds of kilobytes, it starts to defeat the cache and becomes paradoxically, inefficient.

Reducing the 32 bits in the hash value to 14 bits is not a trivial matter. You could just mask off 14 bits, but due to the way the 32-bit hash value is constructed from translated bytes, you would probably get a 14-bit value that is only a function of half of the bytes in the symbol. The solution is to mix together the high and low halves of the 32-bit value and take a 14-bit chunk out of that value. That way labels `loop1` and `loop2`, for instance, won't always automatically generate the same number by systematically ignoring the different last character. The following line shows an example of C code that reduces 32 bits to a smaller number of bits in a slightly arbitrary but effective way.

```
index = ((hash ^ ((hash >> 14) | (hash << 18)))
                                    & table->msk) >> 2;
```

The final shift of two to the right is just there for compatibility with the way the assembly language version of the routine does things. The mask (`msk`) is just a contiguous chunk of bits starting at bit 2. The `index` value produced tends to be a function of every character in the symbol, and so it is fairly random—the point of the exercise.

Just as coming up with a good, fast random-number generator is not trivial, simple, or a matter to be taken lightly, neither is the similar problem of generating hash bits easy to do right. There are an infinite variety of ways to generate bits for hashing, but the best results are only obtained when the regularities of incoming symbols are *not* reflected in any discernible regularities in the hash bits. And it helps to be fast. Some older works on hashing refer to algorithms with division or modulo operations in them. In the present day of RISC architectures, where division times are disproportionately slower than all other common math instructions, that's just asking for performance pain (typically to the tune of 41 cycles or more!). Stick to the one-cycle pairable instructions, and you won't go wrong.

## The Pointer

Once you generate your `index` value, you use it to pick up a pointer to *something* from the hash table:

```
table->table[index]; // the hash table entry
```

Generally speaking, this is either some kind of array index—in effect, an indirect pointer—or a direct memory pointer to something. At this point, the "hashing" is over, and what the pointer points to is entirely up to you; but the two most reasonable "pointees" are linked lists and binary trees. Remember, you've just translated a symbol into a pointer to a small bucket of symbols that lucked into the same hash code. The object of the game now is to find the one you're interested in *without* hashing again.

A linked list of symbols is one option, but if the average length gets very long, list searching time could get very long as well. Putting the same number of symbols in a relatively well balanced binary tree dramatically improves the worst-case performance. As a rule of thumb, if you expect more than about a dozen symbols to be bunched together through the same hash table pointer, you'll likely see improvement with binary trees.

For the `IL_HashFindSymbol()` example, I chose binary trees.

## Comparing Symbols

Remember the 32-bit hash value that was used to generate the smaller hash index into the hash table? Well, don't throw it away. It's a great "fingerprint" for the symbol that can be used to do rapid symbol comparisons. You can detect symbol differences, and hence navigate through a binary tree, based almost entirely on the reliability of these hash value comparisons.

### Listing 13-4    Inner Loops for Binary Tree Descent

```
// main C language binary tree descent loop
//
while (hs = *phs) {                       // is it NULL?
        if (hash == hs->hash) {           // if hash the same
// the body of the symbol confirmation goes here
        } else if (hash < hs->hash) {     // compare hash
```

```
below:      phs = &hs->below;          // go below
        } else {
above:      phs = &hs->above;          // or above
        }
    }


;--------------------------------------------------------------
; main assembly language binary tree descent loop, entered at
; "lpent"
;
hshcar: sbb     edx,edx                         ; 1;edx == 0 or -1
        ;nop                                    ; 0;let address settle
        ;nop                                    ; 1;let address settle
        ;nop                                    ; 0;let address settle
        lea     eax,[ebx+edx*4].IL_HashSymbol.above ; 1;pick
        mov     ebx,[ebx+edx*4].IL_HashSymbol.above ; 0;pick
lpent:  .if ebx                                 ; 1;
        mov     edx,[ebx].IL_HashSymbol.hash ; 1;get hash code
        mov     esi,[ebx].IL_HashSymbol.len  ; 0;and long count
        cmp     ebp,edx                         ; 1;check equality
        jne     hshcar                          ; 0;unequal ->
                                                ;;;;6 cycles
;
; the body of the symbol confirmation goes here
```

Listing 13-4 shows the C and assembly language inner loops for binary tree descent, using the hash value as a fingerprint. Both run rapidly, but the assembly language version descends a level in only six cycles with the help of an unusual cycle-saving technique. When two hash values are compared and found unequal, the carry flag distinguishes between the "below" and "above" tree descent cases. Branching (with `jc` or `jnc`) tends to cost nearly three cycles on average when the branching is fairly random or unpredictable. It's actually faster to generate a 0 or −1 with `sbb edx,edx` and then use that value (times four) to address the next tree descent pointer. The inelegance is that it requires you to remember to always correctly order, and never split up, "below" and "above" pointers in the symbol structure. As programming crimes go, it's no worse than a stiff misdemeanor.

As I mentioned at the beginning of this chapter, I was astonished at the speed with which a binary search for the symbols from *War and Peace* proceeded. It is attributable in large part, I think, to the fast descent loop, which can go ten or twelve levels deep in about the same amount of time as that used by the hash setup overhead.

When two hash values are found to be equal, then it's necessary to check for equality of symbol length, and then for equality of every single byte of the symbol. If anything is found unequal, then use the carry flag or the equivalent to decide which side to descend.

## IL_HashAddSymbol()

There are two ways a search can end. Either you find the pointer to the symbol, or you find a null pointer where the pointer to the symbol should be, meaning it's not in the tree yet. I have structured `IL_HashFindSymbol()` so that it always records its translated string, hash value, and string length (in longwords) in a location suitable to become the next symbol added to the tree. In other words, I tack it onto the end of a buffer of symbols. The value returned by `IL_HashFindSymbol()` is a pointer to the pointer to the symbol. If the latter is null, then the symbol wasn't found. But you can rapidly install it, if you want to, with the `IL_HashAddSymbol()` function, shown in its C version in Listing 13-5.

**Listing 13-5    Adding a Symbol**

```
void
IL_HashAddSymbol_C(IL_HashSymbol **symptr, long val,
                                           IL_HashTable *table)
{
    IL_HashSymbol *hs;
    long           symsize;

    hs = ((IL_HashSymbol *)table->string) - 1; // point to base
    hs->below = NULL;                           // nothing down
    hs->above = NULL;                           // nothing up
    hs->data  = val;                            // set the data
    *symptr   = hs;                             // add to tree
    symsize   = sizeof(IL_HashSymbol) / sizeof(long) + hs->len;
    table->string += symsize;                   // bump up
    if ((table->cutoff - table->strlim) >= symsize)
        table->strlim += symsize;               // bump up
    else
        table->strlim = NULL;                   // or out of room
}
```

There is an assembly language version of this routine as well. It executes in 18 cycles, thanks to the fact that `IL_HashFindSymbol()` does most of the symbol construction work as a side effect of its search.

# The Demo Program: CHHASH.EXE

All the routines mentioned in this chapter, and more, are available on the CD-ROM accompanying this book in the program CHHASH.EXE. CHHASH will count the occurrences of every alphanumeric word in any file you tell it to look at, and you can optionally specify how many bits to use in the hash index and whether it should run in C or assembly language (defaults: 14 bits, assembly). Just invoke it by name without any arguments to see its usage explanation.

By using a hash table to build an index of all the words it encounters, it will tell you how many symbols were found, how many were unique, and how many it processed per second. It will also give you a frequency-sorted list of all the symbols it found. You just have to have enough memory for the input file and the symbol trees at the same time.

# Conclusion

Hashing, often in combination with binary trees, is a tremendously fast way of looking things up. On a Pentium-100, you can hit a million lookups per second. The words in a good stiff novel will run through at the rate of about two-thirds of a million per second. But pure binary tree performance can come surprisingly close to hashing performance in some cases (within a factor of 2).

# 14

# Huffman Compression

*Less is more.*
*—Robert Browning*

In an ordinary text file, the letter *e* and the letter *q* both take up a single 8-bit byte. But unless the text file is a quixotic quiz on queues, quays, and quilting in Quebec, the *e*'s will probably outnumber the *q*'s by about 100 to 1. As it turns out, you can abbreviate *e* in about 3 or 4 bits, at the expense of elongating *q* to 10 or 11 bits; so, likewise, can you encode common text, in general, with about a 40 percent space savings, providing you pick the letter bit codes right.

One David Albert Huffman, in 1952, wrote a paper describing a simple way to select the best bit codes. Even though there are myriad applications using variable-length bit codes for compression, and many of them don't directly use his technique, they pretty much all call themselves "Huffman compression" schemes. And they all compress and decompress pretty much the same way.

This chapter will demonstrate how to quickly calculate true Huffman codes and compress and decompress data using them. The example program on the CD-ROM, CHHUFMN.EXE, can compress or decompress, for instance, *War and Peace* in less than a second.

## A Huffman Example

Suppose you wanted to come up with a set of bit codes to represent the phrase "Huffman examples." An inefficient first choice, straight ASCII text, is shown in Figure 14-1, and an optimal Huffman solution is shown in Figure 14-2. Note that

```
blank = 00100000    "Huffman examples" = 01001000011101010110011
H     = 01001000    0011001100110110101100001011011100010000011
a     = 01100001    0010101111000011000010110110101110000110110
e     = 01100101    00110010101110011
f     = 01100110
l     = 01101100    phrase size: 128 bits
m     = 01101101
n     = 01101110
p     = 01110000
s     = 01110011
u     = 01110101
x     = 01111000
```

**Figure 14-1  "Huffman Examples" Standard ASCII Stream**

```
blank = 1000    "Huffman examples" = 10011110010010011000101
H     = 1001    11000001111100001111001010001110 1
a     = 000
e     = 001
f     = 010
l     = 1010    phrase size: 56 bits
m     = 011
n     = 1011
p     = 1100
s     = 1101
u     = 1110
x     = 1111
```

**Figure 14-2  "Huffman Examples" Huffman Stream**

none of the three-bit codes in Figure 14-2 can be confused with the beginning of any of the four-bit codes in that figure. Keeping short codes from looking like the start of longer codes is a central part of Huffman code generation.

Also note that in Figure 14-2 it doesn't matter whether you swap, for instance, the n 1011 code with the H 1001 code, as far as compression size goes. Huffman coding only necessarily specifies the *length* of codes associated with particular symbols, not their exact bit representations.

# What Huffman Is Good For

If you had "something" to compress, and you had to pick just one compression technique to do the trick, Huffman coding would often be the wrong choice. For instance, the "dictionary-based" compressors, such as the one used by PKZIP, tend to do a better compressing job on plain text. *However*, if you have the opportunity to *combine* multiple compression techniques for the best effect, Huffman coding is almost always a useful component.

Thus JPEG photographic compression is famous for its use of the "discrete cosine transform" and "quantization" phases, but it also relies on a less heralded Huffman compression scheme as well. It's there in MPEG, too. Faxes use hard-wired Huffman codes to compress pages, which explains why white text on black paper transmits much slower than the same text in black on white: The Huffman codes are optimized for transmitting white space and are correspondingly much less efficient at transmitting solid black.

The "dictionary-based" compressors are often implemented with embedded Huffman schemes. Generally speaking, any fixed-bit-length data field that doesn't show a fairly random distribution of values is a good candidate for Huffman encoding, whether the data happens to be part of a compressor, or a database, or a 3D graphics description language. In fact, if it weren't for the overhead of the Huffman descriptor tables themselves, almost any fixed-bit-length data field could be better compressed with Huffman codes.

## Overhead

The "overhead" data of Huffman coding—the description of how many bits to allocate to each symbol—can run from less than 10 bytes (when the order of the associated symbols is trivially simple, as in a sequential run) to about 300 bytes (when encoding by bytes and all byte values are possible), to many thousands of bytes (when thousands of multibyte symbols are involved). The example code on the CD-ROM accompanying this book creates a 312-byte header on compressed output files. Generally speaking, if you're compressing a bunch of small files, it often pays to come up with one fixed Huffman code table that works well on all, and keep one copy of the header separate from the headerless compressed files.

## Adaptive Huffman

There also exist "adaptive Huffman" algorithms that change bit patterns on the fly, based on the history of symbols previously encountered. These algorithms can have zero overhead in terms of not having to carry tables around, and depending on the contents of the data, they can be potentially more efficient than using a fixed Huffman scheme over a large data block. But when it comes time to trade off space for speed, the extra processing time for keeping changeable codes can be prohibitive. Regular Huffman compression and decompression can be largely table-driven and fast, whereas adaptive Huffman requires a fair amount of binary tree traversal and modification and so is generally five to ten times slower at both compression and decompression.

## Beyond Huffman: Arithmetic Coding

In a perfect world, given a text file with 478 characters in it, including 39 *e*'s, it should only take $\log_2(478 / 39)$ bits to encode an *e*. But 478 / 39 is 12.256 . . . , and $\log_2(478 / 39)$ is 3.615. . . Huffman coding will generally pick either a three-bit or a four-bit code to represent the letter *e*, depending on context, but it can't spend fractional bits. Arithmetic coding, a conceptual cousin of Huffman coding, is an alternative to it that can spend almost exactly the required "fractional" bits required for each character for optimal compression. To do this, the bits are scrambled and descrambled with multiplication and division operations. Arithmetic coding usually achieves a relatively few percentage points of improvement over Huffman, at the expense of an order of magnitude of slowdown.

Suppose you have three values, A, B, and C, that are integer numbers in the range 0 to 5, and you want to fit them all into a byte. Chopping them down to three bits each only gets you down to nine bits, which is still too big. But suppose you try this:

```
BYTE = A + (6 * B) + (36 * C)
```

The bits get scrambled, and if you just look at the raw byte, neither A nor B nor C bit patterns are likely to show up. But they can still be extracted by

```
A = BYTE   modulo 6
B = (BYTE / 6) modulo 6
C = BYTE / 36
```

Arithmetic coding works along similar lines. For excellent discussions of both adaptive Huffman and arithmetic coding, *The Data Compression Book* by Mark Nelson is a very good source (see the References). The rest of this chapter will focus on regular Huffman coding.

## Performance

Here are the typical assembly language and C performance figures for typical Huffman compression and decompression. "Typical" means a few hundred distinguishable items (for example, 256 possible byte codes, or, say, 140 different keyword indexes) with an average compressed item size of around half a dozen bits over the whole run.

On a Pentium-100, you can

- Compress 5 million items per second using optimized assembly language routines.
- Compress 3 million items per second using optimized C.
- Decompress 5 million items per second using optimized assembly language routines.
- Decompress 3 million items per second using optimized C.

In this case, good C performs at about 60 percent of the assembly language level. You can compress or decompress *War and Peace* byte by byte, with a compressed size about 60 percent of the decompressed size, in less than a second with assembly language routines. It takes a little more than a second with C.

The demonstration program given on the CD-ROM, CHHUFMN.EXE, will compress and decompress files and report performance statistics. When operating on particularly large files (megabyte range) in particular, the `malloc()` function may cause a 20 percent performance penalty, which might be avoidable in other circumstances with preallocated buffers. So beware that the upper limits of performance may be higher than what is reported by the demo. `Malloc()` timing statistics are displayed and can be factored out.

## Huffman, Step by Step

There are seven discrete steps to compressing data, and compressing it quickly, using a Huffman system:

1. Performing the symbol census
2. Sorting the census data
3. Building the Huffman tree

4. Making the code lengths table

5. Limiting code lengths (optional)

6. Making the encoding table

7. Encoding the data

Of these steps, only the first and last actually scan through the entire data source; these are usually the time-critical routines on large data runs.

Likewise, there are just two main steps to fast decompression:

1. Making the decoding table

2. Decoding the data

The second step is usually the most time-critical. But since Huffman tables can be described, in some circumstances, in as little as ten bytes, situations may arise where it's advantageous to spend the few extra bytes it takes to change tables frequently—and fast—in which case the table-making step can be time-critical too.

The demonstration program, CHHUFMN.EXE, reads in a file and compresses its bytes with Huffman coding before outputting it to another file. It also performs the reverse operation, decompression. The sample code in the following sections is from the demo.

# Huffman Compression

A salesman wants to plan the shortest route through the fifty cities he has to visit in the next three months. At best, a computer can only make a pretty good guess at the solution (because a complete solution would take, effectively, forever to compute). But if the same salesman wants to find the shortest bit codes for compressing the names of the cities, a computer can give him an instant, exact best-case solution using Huffman encoding. Of the following seven steps, step 3 is the heart of Huffman compression.

## Step 1: Performing the Symbol Census

True Huffman encoding makes two passes through the data. The first pass finds the frequencies of the symbols to be compressed so that best-case bit patterns can be found. The second pass performs the compression.

Surprisingly, you can lose a lot of efficiency on a seemingly fast, simple C loop to count byte frequencies, such as that shown in Listing 14-1. Listing 14-2, an optimized assembly language version of the same loop that operates on two bytes in parallel and makes efficient use of the Pentium pipes, runs more than twice as fast. In essence, this routine runs two copies of the same loop in parallel. Done inefficiently, counting the bytes can take over a third of the compression time; done efficiently, it takes less than a quarter of it.

### Listing 14-1    Huffman Census Inner Loop in C

```
do {
    array[*source++].count++;
} while (--loopcount);
```

### Listing 14-2    Huffman Census Inner Loop in Assembly Language

```
                                              ;;;;edi - points to
                                              ;;;;    census counts
                                              ;;;;esi - points to
                                              ;;;;        raw data
                                              ;;;;ebp - counter and
                                              ;;;;   index into data
    .repeat                                   ; ;
      mov ecx,[edi+eax*8].IL_HuffItem.count   ; 1;get item counts
      mov edx,[edi+ebx*8].IL_HuffItem.count   ; 0;
      .if al == bl                            ; 1;if 2 of the same
        add edx,2                             ; 1;bump count by 2
        mov al,[esi+ebp+0]                    ; 0;get byte 1
        mov [edi+ebx*8].IL_HuffItem.count,edx ; 1;update count
        mov bl,[esi+ebp+1]                    ; 0;get byte 2
      .else                                   ; ;
        inc ecx                               ; 1;inc counts
        inc edx                               ; 0;
        mov [edi+eax*8].IL_HuffItem.count,ecx ; 1;update counts
        mov al,[esi+ebp+0]                    ; 0;get byte 1
        mov [edi+ebx*8].IL_HuffItem.count,edx ; 1;
        mov bl,[esi+ebp+1]                    ; 0;get byte 2
      .endif                                  ; ;
      add ebp,2                               ; 1;advance loop cnt
    .until ZERO?                              ; ;
                                              ;;;;6 cycles/loop
                                              ;;;;3 cycles/char
```

The C and assembly language versions of the routine IL_Huffman ByteCensus() on the CD-ROM illustrate this step.

## Step 2: Sorting the Census Data

In anticipation of sorting the census by frequency of character occurrence, each character count should be kept in a little two-item structure along with the character code or value. Here is the form used in this and the previous step:

```
typedef struct {
    long value;
    long count;
} IL_HuffItem
```

Thus the letter *A* would have a value of 65 (its ASCII code) and a count of as many *As* as are found in the data. Sorting the array of 256 such structures, one for each byte code, is the next step.

The routine `IL_HuffItemsSort()` on the CD-ROM does this, sorting the items into an array by ascending count. It uses the C library `qsort()` routine, which is generally fast enough for this step.

Although it's not, in general, necessary to put a special bit code into a Huffman stream to indicate the end of the data, it is sometimes useful to do so in order to not have to run a countdown on the decompression stream. I chose to put a terminator value in (coded with an "impossible" 0x100 byte value in the array) by prepending it to the sorted array as a least frequent 257th value to code. When the decompressor sees this code, it knows to quit.

## Step 3: Building the Huffman Tree

This is the step that made David Huffman famous. Suppose, using the example from the beginning of this chapter, that you have taken a census of the characters in the phrase "Huffman examples" and you've sorted the census. The sorted census should look something like the first line at the top of Figure 14-3. (For simplicity, characters with zero counts and the terminator code are ignored.)

There are two copies of the letters *f*, *m*, *e*, and *a*, and one copy each of the rest. The one-copy letters lead off the list, and the two-copy ones end it.

The rule for building a Huffman tree is simple. Take the two items at the left of the list out of the list; combine them into a "node" with a new count that's the sum of the two counts; and put the new node back in the list in the right sorted order. Repeat until there is only one node in the list; it's the root node of the Huffman tree. The depth of each character within the tree is the number of bits used to represent it.

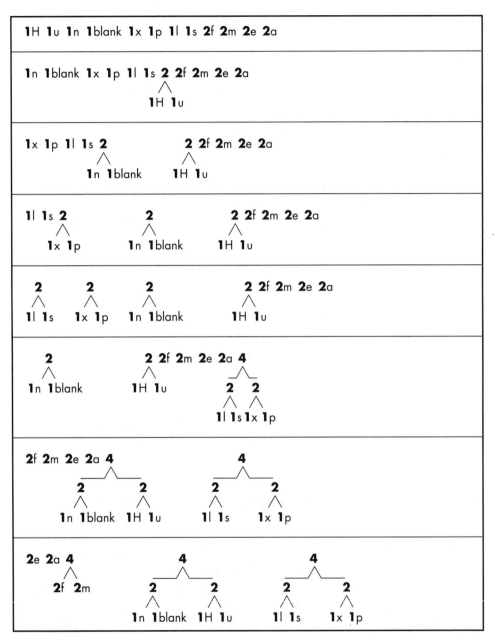

**Figure 14-3** "Huffman Examples" Huffman Tree-Building Steps

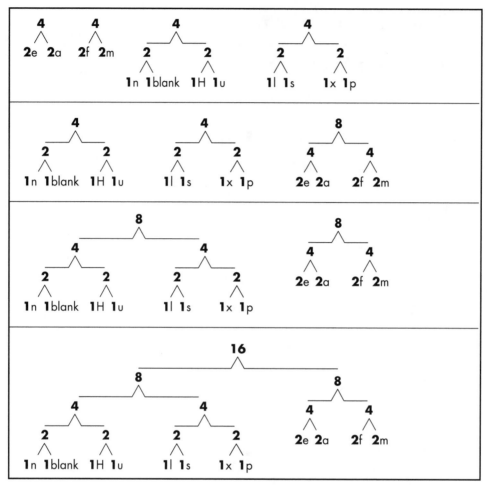

**Figure 14-3 (Continued)** "Huffman Examples" Huffman Tree-Building Steps

In this example, all the two-count characters are buried three levels deep, and the one-count characters are buried four deep. (Depth is code length.) This agrees with the coding example at the beginning of this chapter.

You *could* derive bit codes for the characters from this tree by assigning 0s and 1s to the left and right branches within the tree, but it turns out to be a better idea to just make note of how many codes of each length there are and use a more efficient way to generate the codes. The tree in this example is telling us to use four 3-bit codes and eight 4-bit codes.

**Listing 14-3    Huffman Tree–Building Inner Loop**

```
while (lowerlim != upperlim) {
    index = (lowerlim + upperlim) >> 1;
    if (sum >= array[index].count) {
        lowerlim = index + 1;
    } else {
        upperlim = index;
    }
}
```

Since the sum of the two smallest counts in the sorted list can make a node that gets inserted near the opposite end of the list, I chose to do a kind of binary search of the sorted list to find the right spot to insert the new node. The main alternative, a sequential search, might actually be faster on many reasonably sized sorted symbol sets, since the acts of searching through data and moving it can be combined. (You have to literally bump every item to the left of an inserted node left by one notch on each insertion.)

Listing 14-3 shows the inner loop used to find the node insertion spot. The >= operator on the third line causes new nodes to be inserted in the sorted list as far as possible from the little end of the list. As opposed to the > operator, it biases the tree toward shortest maximum code length, in those cases where there are several best solutions. Usually it is best to bias toward short maximum length for easier decoding. This loop is from the demo routine `IL_MakeHuffTreeFromHuffItems()`. The assembly language version of the routine is also available, but it's not much faster.

When operating on many tens of thousands of symbol counts, the tree-building routine has the potential to bog down badly. Its worst performance speed can be proportional to the square of the number of symbols. But it takes only a millisecond to handle 256 or so.

# Step 4: Making the Code Lengths Table

If you choose to allocate bit codes for symbols that have a count of zero according to the census (not a bad idea if there's a chance the code might ever be applied to different data) the Huffman tree can end up with some ridiculously long codes for symbols that are never used—unless you're sure to bias the tree, as shown in step 3, toward shorter solutions, all else being equal. Even without vacant entries, a census of slightly over a million items can have a natural worst-case code length of 32 bits. The Intel processor family limits hardware shifts to 31 bits, so the fastest compression-decompression algorithms are usually defeated by codes longer than 31 bits. Hence the need to trade a little compression for a fair amount of speed by keeping code lengths shorter than 32 bits.

Another natural (but less rigorous) limit to code bit length is about 11 bits. The reason is that a code of 11 bits or less can be used to look up decoding longwords in the cache. If it is longer than 11 bits, however the decode table is too big for a typical 8K cache. The demonstration on the CD-ROM uses just such bit length–limited tables for rapid decoding. The 11-bit limit is fairly reasonable, in terms of space and speed trade-offs, given about 256 symbols, but it's not great for, say, 1,000 symbols. For 1,000 symbols, it's worth either biting the cache bullet and enlarging the table for more bits *or* keeping binary trees on hand for long codes that the bit-length-limited decoding table flags as undecodable.

All this about limiting code lengths said, it's a simple matter of traversing the binary Huffman tree to get the bit length (alias tree depth) counts, with an optional maximum depth specified. Listing 14-4 shows the inner loop of `IL_MakeCodeLengthsFromHuffTree()`, which just runs through the tree counting nodes at all depths. In a rare paradox of timing, the assembly language version of this routine, written more for clarity than for speed, actually runs slightly *slower* than the C version. Assembly language programmers beware: let your guard down, and a good C optimizing compiler will catch you.

**Listing 14-4    Inner Loop for Counting Huffman Tree Depths**

```
while (1) {
    while (node->left) {
        node = node->left;
        depth++;
    }
    if (depth > maxdepth)
        lengthtable[maxdepth]++;
    else
        lengthtable[depth]++;
    do {
        back   = node;
        source = node->parent;
        if (!depth--)
            return;
    } while (back == node->right);
    node = node->right;
    depth++;
}
```

# Step 5: Limiting Code Lengths (Optional)

If in step 4 you chose not to limit code length, then the list of lengths from step 4 is fine as is and step 5 can be skipped. But if you did choose to limit code lengths, you can be faced with the paradox of having an impossible order to fill. For instance, the tables could request one 1-bit code and three 2-bit codes, an impossibility. You have to modify such requests to fit reality—for instance, substituting four 2-bit codes in the last request.

Devising limited-length code is not a part of true Huffman coding—it's a pragmatic adjustment to pure Huffman, for the sake of improving performance. The demo program uses a brute force approach, breaking up shorter codes into many longer codes, to achieve this end. It's not pretty, and it's not even optimal in terms of compression, but it works fairly well as a quick heuristic.

The demo routine that does this is `IL_HuffDepthsAdjust()`, written only in C. It's fast, it's unlikely to ever become a performance bottleneck, and it has unremarkable inner loops. It's on the CD-ROM for the curious.

## Step 6: Making the Encoding Table

Given a symbol to encode, there are just two things you need to know to put it in the compressed bit stream: how many bits it takes, and what the bits are. And for fast encoding, all you need is a table in which to look up both these values for a given symbol.

If you have a list of all your symbols sorted by frequency, as per step 2, and a list of the appropriate lengths for corresponding Huffman codes, all that remains to be done is to generate the unique Huffman codes, from shortest to longest, and match them to the symbols, from most frequent to least frequent.

Figure 14-4 illustrates the algorithm for assigning unique Huffman codes based on a list of lengths. Huffman codes are assigned from shortest to longest, and in this example there are three 2-bit codes, one 3-bit code, and two 4-bit codes to be assigned. Starting with an all-zero bit pattern, you first assign the two highest bits (00) to the first 2-bit code. Then you add binary 01 to the two highest bits of the pattern and repeat the process. The next code, therefore, is 01, followed by 10. The next code extracted, three bits, is 110, followed by the addition of 001 to the three highest bits of the pattern. The first 4-bit code, then, is 1110, and after adding 0001, the last 4-bit code is 1111. And this is how a table of code lengths is transformed into the actual working Huffman codes.

The only thing particularly tricky about assigning Huffman codes is that on Intel's architecture the natural order for bits in a continuous stream is from low bit to high bit within bytes, and then from low byte addresses to high. In other words, the way we like to write Huffman codes on paper is the reverse of the way we like to stuff them into bytes. Thus the codes 1011 and 0001, in that order, would look like 10001101 in a byte looked at in a debugger.

Huffman code generation for the following length table:

| length | how many |
|--------|----------|
| 1 | 0 |
| 2 | 3 |
| 3 | 1 |
| 4 | 2 |
| 5 and up | 0 |

00000000000    —>    extract left 2 bits    —>    code 00

          +

01_____                  add 2-bit spacer

01000000000    —>    extract left 2 bits    —>    code 01

          +

01_____                  add 2-bit spacer

10000000000    —>    extract left 2 bits    —>    code 10

          +

01_____                  add 2-bit spacer

11000000000    —>    extract left 3 bits    —>    code 110

          +

001_____                  add 3-bit spacer

11100000000    —>    extract left 4 bits    —>    code 1110

          +

0001_____                  add 4-bit spacer

11110000000    —>    extract left 4 bits    —>    code 1111

          +

0001_____                  add 4-bit spacer

00000000000                  0 means code space full

**Figure 14-4    Assigning Huffman Codes, Given Lengths**

The routine `IL_MakeHuffmanEncodeTable()`, written only in C, is not likely to be a performance bottleneck. The only remarkable thing about its innards is that it performs additions in bit-reversed order (with carrys propagating toward lower bits, not higher bits) to get the Huffman codes in proper bit order. It's there in full on the demo CD-ROM.

# Step 7: Encoding the Data

Just as it usually takes longer to pack the trunk of a car well for vacation than it does to unpack it, it's common for compression algorithms to take longer to compress than to decompress. Huffman coding is an exception. Since code lengths are easily known at compression time but have to be figured out from the contents of the compressed bit stream at decompression time, Huffman compression can run slightly to significantly faster than decompression, depending on how heavily table-driven the decompression is.

Listing 14-5 shows both the C and the assembly language versions of the first two inner loops of `IL_HuffEncodeBytes()`. It's not very big, and as is common, the assembly language version runs 50 percent faster than the C version.

These loops gain speed by starting off with at least 32 symbols available for encoding from the input stream. Since each symbol takes at least one bit to encode, the loops can be built around the assumption that they can stuff a 32-bit longword full of data and send it to the output stream without running out of data. Not having to check internally for the end of input speeds things up.

C loses a little ground by not having a good option to use the assembly language `shrd` instruction, which does the work of two shifts and an `or` operation.

The innermost assembly loop is pretty heavily wrapped around itself, with instructions from three different phases processing three successive symbols on each pass through the loop. It is shown in its more readable, unwrapped form as a comment in the assembly listing. When fully wrapped up on itself, though, it runs in about seven cycles per symbol. Slowed by the occasional cache miss and a 14-cycle first outer loop after every half dozen or so symbols, its effective symbol-crunching rate is one every dozen or so cycles, for a 7-million-symbol-per-second rate on a Pentium-100. Taken together with the other compression steps, a sustained 5-million-symbol-per-second rate is possible.

**Listing 14-5   Huffman Encoding Inner Loops in C and Assembly Language**

```
do {
    goto lpstart;
    do {
```

```
                accum   = (accum >> wid) | (bits << (32 - wid));
lpstart:        val     = *source++;
                wid     = table[val].wid;
                bits    = table[val].bits;
            } while ((available -= wid) >= 0);
        wid       += available;
        if (wid)
            accum   = (accum >> wid) | (bits << (32 - wid));
        *dest++   = accum;
        wid       -= available;
        accum     = bits << (32 - wid);
        available += 32;
    } while (source < sourcelim);
```

```
            .repeat                     ;   ;
;
;The natural order of execution of the inner loop of this
;routine is shown here for clarity.
;
;               mov al,[esi]                ; 1;1-get encode val
;               inc esi                     ; 0;2-advance byte ptr
;               mov ecx,[ebx+eax*8].IL_HuffEncode.wid
;                                           ; 1;3-get bit width
;               mov edx,[ebx+eax*8].IL_HuffEncode.bits
;                                           ; 0;4-get code bits
;               sub edi,ecx                 ; 1;5-enough room?
;               jc  out_of_loop             ; 0;6-no -> exit
;               shrd ebp,edx,cl             ; 4;7-shift bits in
;
;


            .repeat                     ;   ;
              shrd ebp,edx,cl             ; 4;7-shift bits in
              mov ecx,[ebx+eax*8].IL_HuffEncode.wid
                                          ; 1;3-get bit width
              mov edx,[ebx+eax*8].IL_HuffEncode.bits
                                          ; 0;4-get code bits
              mov al,[esi]                ; 1;1-get encode val
              inc esi                     ; 0;2-advance byte ptr
              sub edi,ecx                 ; 1;5-enough room?
            .until CARRY?                 ; 0;6-yes -> branch
                                          ;;;;7 cycles
                                          ; 4;
            add ecx,edi                 ; 1;cl gets max shift
            mov ebx,outptr              ; 0;ready to output
            shrd ebp,edx,cl             ; 4;fill ebp
            mov [ebx],ebp               ; 1;store output
```

```
        sub ecx,edi            ; 0;ecx now original
        add edi,32             ; 1;new remaining
        add ebx,4              ; 0;advance output ptr
        mov outptr,ebx         ; 1;store output ptr
        mov ebx,esilim         ; 0;get lim to check
        cmp esi,ebx            ; 1;past lim?
        mov ebx,encodetbl      ; 0;restore ebx
    .until CARRY?              ; 1;and
                               ;;;;14-cycle refill
```

# Huffman Decompression

Usually, the fastest way to decompress Huffman codes is to take about 11 bits out of the compressed data stream and use it as an index into a decode table. When the decoded symbols are bytes, the decode entries can be as small as two bytes—a byte holding the number of bits used to encode the symbol and a byte for the symbol itself.

There are just two major steps to the decompression.

## Step 1: Making the Decoding Table

Step 6 of the encoding process is quite similar to this decoding step. But instead of using symbols to index code bits and lengths, you use code bits to look up symbols and lengths. IL_MakeHuffmanDecodeTable() is the routine, implemented in both C and assembly language, that does this.

I once implemented a 15-frame-per-second video playback system that required three different decoding tables for each frame. That's 45 per second. If making the decoding tables had taken even a hundredth of a second each, I'd have lost half my CPU to building the tables. Fortunately, it only *needs* to take a sixth of a millisecond, using *less* than 1 percent of the CPU during full-motion video.

The same caveats that came with encoding in step 6 apply here. The code to create this table looks a little odd, with its need to do bit-reversed arithmetic. It's available on the CD-ROM. But the innermost loop that keeps things fast is shown in Listing 14-6. Using an 11-bit index to decode Huffman values requires that, for instance, all three-bit codes have 256 duplicate entries in the table ($2^8 = 256$, $8 + 3 = 11$) to account for the effect of the random eight bits following the first three bits of the code. So, rapidly planting duplicate copies of the decoding information for a particular code throughout the table is the key to speed. The two-cycle loop to do this in assembly language is shown. The C version takes about 70 percent longer.

**Listing 14-6    Inner Loop to Make Decoding Table, C and Assembly Language**

```
do {
    *outp  = temp;
    outp  += repspace;
} while (--count);


.repeat              ;  ;
  mov [edi+edx],eax  ; 1;store a copy of decode
  add edi,ebx        ; 0;advance via spacer
  dec ecx            ; 1;done?
.until ZERO?         ; 0;no -> loop
                     ;;;;2-cycle loop
```

# Step 2: Decoding the Data

There are 64,000 pixels on the lowest-resolution 256-color screen commonly used on PCs, known as VGA mode 13 (hexadecimal). To achieve true full-motion video, you have to update them all 15 times per second. That's nearly a million individual pixel updates per second. Assuming a CD-ROM drive is hogging 60 percent of the CPU and you can only afford to spend half of the remaining 40 percent on a Huffman decompression scheme to feed the video update pixel by pixel, is Huffman fast enough to decompress the 1 million values per second on a mere 20 percent of the CPU? The answer is yes—just barely.

Huffman-compressed text decompresses at 5 million characters per second, and well-thought-out pixel information should do as well or better. On 20 percent of a Pentium-100's CPU, you can produce 1 million decompressed values per second. Per-pixel Huffman is possible!

Listing 14-7 shows the assembly language inner loop responsible for the speed of the decompression routine `IL_DecompressHuffman()`. The equivalent C routine is much slower (by about a factor of 2), less photogenic (it's mixed with outer loop code), but available on the CD-ROM, for the curious.

**Listing 14-7    Huffman Decoding Inner Loop in Assembly Language**

```
;eax - holds negative bits remaining in ebp
;ebx - holds backup bitstream bits
;ecx - holds current byte decode and its bit length
;edx - holds decode table pointer
;esi - input pointer
```

```
;edi - output pointer
;ebp - holds next bitstream bits
;
;EDXMASK is 0fffff001H
;
;In-order loop instructions:
;
;           mov    ebx,ebp             ; 1;1-start to put bits in
;           and    ebx,not EDXMASK     ; 1;2-mask region
;           mov    ecx,[edx+ebx*2]     ; 2;3-pick up cl,ch decode
;           add    al,cl               ; 1;4-check code length
;           .until CARRY?              ; 0;5-loop if OK
;           shr    ebp,cl              ; 4;6-adjust ebp
;           mov    [edi],ch            ; 1;7-save the byte
;           inc    edi                 ; 0;8-advance the pointer
;                                      ;  ;
           .repeat                     ;  ;
             shr ebp,cl                ; 4;6-adjust ebp
             mov [edi],ch              ; 1;7-save the byte
start:       mov ebx,ebp               ; 0;1-start to put bits in
             and ebx,not EDXMASK       ; 1;2-mask region
             inc edi                   ; 0;8-advance the pointer
             mov ecx,[edx+ebx*2]       ; 2;3-pick up cl,ch decode
             add al,cl                 ; 1;4-check code length
           .until CARRY?               ; 0;5-loop if OK
                                       ;;;;9-cycle loop
```

Nearly half the inner loop processing time goes to the dreadfully slow—but necessary—shr instruction. A heavy-duty outer loop that refills the inner loop's registers with fresh compressed bits takes a lot of cycles and approximately doubles the average time per decompressed value, from 9 to between 15 and 20 cycles. But even at 20 cycles, you've still got 5 million decompressions per second!

# Conclusion

Huffman coding is among the most common and useful forms of compression available to any programmer. The encoding process is nontrivial in its several complexities, but it can be very fast. Decoding can also run quite quickly when all or most of the codes in a compressed stream are no longer than about 11 bits. Encoding and decoding can both run at up to 5 million symbols per second on the Pentium-100.

There are opportunities to customize Huffman algorithms in many directions for various purposes. It is possible, for instance, to allow codes up to 31 bits in length into a stream with only a small loss of speed, as long as the vast majority of codes encountered obey the 11-bit rule of thumb. Symbols larger than a byte can be encoded. Control codes in addition to the terminator code can be added. There is a lot of room for experimentation, optimization, and growth within this trusty old workhorse system.

# References

Nelson, M. 1992. *The Data Compression Book*. San Mateo, Calif.: M&T Books.

# 15

## A Fast Sort

*And of every living thing of all flesh,*
*two of every sort shalt thou bring into the ark.*
—God, in Genesis 6:19, ordering the first binary sort

There are many ways to sort, and the fastest way to sort something often depends on the number of items to be sorted and the anticipated distribution of data. What works well on a dozen items may fail miserably on ten thousand, and vice versa. In fact, there's a niche of optimal performance for just about every sorting scheme ever devised. This chapter takes a look at one of the most powerful algorithms for sorting very large numbers of items, anywhere from a few hundred up to millions of items arrayed in memory. It's a form known as a "distribution" sort, and as computer memories, and hence in-memory data record capacities, have grown, it has in many cases become the fastest sorting option available.

## Order N Sorting

Most of the well-known sorting algorithms, including quicksort, heap sort, and merge sort, bog down somewhat the more items they are given to sort. For instance, if they sort 100 records at a rate of one microsecond per record, they tend to "bog down" to about two microseconds per record at 10,000 records and three microseconds (or, in practice, often more) at 1 million. In terms of time, most of these algorithms are said to execute on the order of $N\log_2(N)$, where N is the number of items being sorted. If the data being sorted is fairly nonrandomly arranged, performance may be considerably better or worse, but given random data, $N\log_2(N)$ is typical. And since $\log_2(100 \times 100)$ has twice the value of $\log_2(100)$, for instance, 10,000 items ($100 \times 100$) tend to sort at half the speed per item as 100 items. But there is a sorting algorithm that operates at the rate of order N—the distribution sort—and given a big enough sort job, it can beat the $N\log_2(N)$ algorithms.

## The Distribution Sort

Here's how it works. Suppose you have one thousand 10-byte records and you want to sort them into ascending order according to the value of their first byte. One way to do it is to first take a census of the values found in the first byte of every record. Suppose you find out that twelve have value 0, seventeen have value 1, nine have value 2, and so forth. Once you know all this, you can prepare an area of memory into which you can copy the records, reserving the first 12 positions for records with a first byte of 0, the next 17 positions for records with a first byte of 1, and so forth. Then you build a 256-entry table of pointers (one for each possible byte value) to the first positions to be occupied in the new table area by the records corresponding to each initial byte value. The first pointer points to the start of the copy area; the second points 12 records later; the third points 17 records still later, and so on. Finally, you go through the original records one by one, use their first byte as an index into the pointer table, copy the record to the area pointed to, and increment the table pointer so that it points to the next successive record position. The result is a new array of records sorted in order according to the value of their first byte.

The amazing thing about this kind of sorting is that when you feed the results of the sort on the first byte position into a similar sort on the next position, the result is the same as if you had done a sort on an Intel-format two-byte unsigned integer in the first two positions. Sorting on the first four bytes in succession is like sorting a 32-bit unsigned integer. In fact, if you can define the sort order of records in terms of most significant byte down through successively less significant bytes to a least significant byte for the sort, then by executing just this kind of byte-oriented sort from least significant to most significant, you accomplish the intended multifield sort. And it runs in time proportional to the number of records sorted.

To be sure, there are limitations to this kind of sorting. It has a significant amount of fixed overhead in terms of setting up census and pointer tables, so it's not particularly efficient on fewer than, say, about 100 items or records to be sorted. Since this kind of sorting relies heavily on having the data in fixed record positions, it doesn't work well when null-terminated strings of variable length need to be used for string comparisons as part of the sort. And the more passes it has to make through the data on low-priority bytes, the less competitive it becomes. (Most other sorts operate at similar speeds whether they are sorting 1 or 20 fields, because most ordering decisions can be made without considering the low-order bytes of the comparison. The distribution sort has to go through all of them.) Another drawback is that it is not an "in place" sort, meaning that it takes a significant amount of extra free memory to perform it. And it doesn't operate well on floating-point values. Nevertheless, the distribution sort is very competitive at large volumes (100+ records) and with fewer than about a dozen byte fields to sort.

## The CHSORT.EXE Program

On the CD-ROM accompanying this book is the full source and executable code of the test program CHSORT.EXE. It can read in a file and a command line description of fixed-length records and fields to be sorted and then execute a fast distribution sort and write the sorted output to a file. All fields can be described as integers of various byte widths, either Intel or Motorola format, signed or unsigned, and ascending or descending in order. The signed-unsigned, ascending-descending, Intel-Motorola aspects of the sort are implemented as simple variations on pointer table construction and byte sort order. The program puts out comparative timing data showing how well it performs with its inner loops implemented in assembly language, in C, or replaced with the C library's quicksort routine. Just run it with no arguments for further information on how it operates. The source code shown subsequently in this chapter is drawn from this program.

## The First Inner Loop of the Distribution Sort

When a sort routine has to move large records around repeatedly, it may spend most of its time just moving memory around. So for speed's sake, it is usually faster to sort, for instance, one thousand pointers to one thousand 32-byte records than to sort the one thousand 32-byte records directly. Once the pointers have been sorted, they can be used to copy the actual records into sorted order. As a rule of thumb, unless the record being sorted is four bytes or less in size, it's probably faster to structure a sort around pointers to the records, whatever sort one may choose.

The distribution sort implemented here is built with the expectation of sorting an array of pointers to records. It carries an overhead memory requirement of nine bytes per record sorted, which includes the four bytes per record used by the array of pointers, four bytes per record for yet another such array used temporarily during sorting, and one byte per record for a temporary array of bytes drawn from the records.

## Listing 15-1 The Census Phase of the Distribution Sort in C

```
void
IL_DistributionSortPart1_C(unsigned long *countarray,
                           long offset, unsigned char **sourceptr,
                           unsigned char *bytelist, long count)
{
    int n;
    for (n = 0; n < 0x100; n++)
        countarray[n] = 0;
    for (n = 0; n < count; n++)
        countarray[bytelist[n] = sourceptr[n][offset]]++;
}
```

Listing 15-1 shows the C version of the census phase of the distribution sort algorithm. The inner loop of this routine is, simply

```
for (n = 0; n < count; n++)
    countarray[bytelist[n] = sourceptr[n][offset]]++;
```

Yet for all its simplicity, a fast Pentium version of this same simple loop takes up the better part of a page, as shown in Listing 15-2.

These two versions of the same routine both operate on an array of pointers to the records to be sorted. This first inner loop performs an unusual optimization by not only picking up bytes and recording them in the census count but also writing them to an array of bytes. For very large sorts, one of the slowest parts of the code is the part that reads a byte out of a record. Such reads tend to appear like very random memory references to the processor, and they can often take about 50 cycles. In the usual way one sees a distribution sort implemented, the first and second inner loops both perform the same sequence of reads from records, potentially racking up about 100 cycles in delays. But by storing the bytes read by the first inner loop in a linear array of bytes in memory, the second inner loop can access them from the array instead, at a cost of about 1 cycle per byte instead of the potential 50.

The most obvious general optimization visible in Listing 15-2 is the parallel census operations being performed in the U pipe and the V pipe. C compilers are unlikely to think of running two fetch-index-increment-store cycles in parallel, but it's a natural way to solve the problem fast. Note also that the U and V pipes operate on pointers that are four positions apart in the pointer array, so that when storing bytes to the output byte array, they're stored four bytes apart and don't contend for the same bus into the cache (preventing a possible one-cycle loss—an example of rather extreme optimization).

By way of further optimizations, the `ecx` register serves not only as the count-up loop counter but also as the index register for addressing both byte and pointer arrays. And the presumably more frequently executed code is given the preferred `else` position in the `.if-.else-.endif` sequence. The census count is kept on the stack due to the lack of a free register to point to an array elsewhere in memory.

The Achilles' heel of this tandem loop strategy is the potential for a double cache miss when reading bytes from the records:

```
mov    al,[edi+ebp]            ; 1;cache miss likely
mov    bl,[edx+ebp]            ; 0;2nd miss likely
```

A single primary cache, secondary cache, and page table miss costs about 48 cycles. Two such misses occurring simultaneously cost about 102 cycles (48 + 6 + 48), since there are approximately 6 cycles of unfinished business being tended to after the first miss completes before the second miss can get started (residual cache line transfer).

As shown in Listing 15-2, the doubled loop runs an average of about nine cycles (4.3 × 2, approximately) between double cache misses. So it processes two sort items in about 111 cycles (102 + 9). But if a tight single loop could run in, say, 6 cycles (which, indeed, it can), then it could complete two loops in 108 cycles (48 + 6 + 48 + 6). The penalty of a double cache miss can actually allow a seemingly less efficient single loop to run faster than a seemingly faster doubled loop sometimes. It's not a big performance loss, but it is a reminder that paradoxical behavior is not uncommon in computer performance.

## Listing 15-2  Census Phase of Distribution Sort in Assembly Language

```
RADBYT0     textequ                  <esp+4*(100H+0)>
RADBYT4     textequ                  <esp+4*(100H+1)>
RADOFST     textequ        <dword ptr [esp+4*(100H+2)]>
RADBPTR     textequ        <dword ptr [esp+4*(100H+3)]>
RADCNTARY   textequ        <dword ptr [esp+4*(100H+4)]>


radmac      macro num                        ;  ;
            mov    edi,[esi+ecx*4+(0+num)*4] ; 1;pick up next pair
            mov    edx,[esi+ecx*4+(4+num)*4] ; 0;of record pointers
            if num ne 0                      ;  ;
              mov [RADBYT0+num-1],al         ; 1;record previous
              mov [RADBYT4+num-1],bl         ; 0;sort bytes
            endif                            ;  ;
```

```
        mov    al,[edi+ebp]         ; 1;get new sort bytes
        mov    bl,[edx+ebp]         ; 0;
        .if eax == ebx              ; 1;if sort bytes are
          mov edi,[esp+eax*4]       ; 1;the same
          if num eq 3               ;  ;
            mov ebp,RADBPTR         ; 0;load and advance
          endif                     ;  ;byte pointer
          add edi,2                 ; 1;add 2 to the count
          mov [esp+eax*4],edi       ; 1;
        .else                       ; 0;
          mov edi,[esp+eax*4]       ; 1;
          mov edx,[esp+ebx*4]       ; 0;
          inc edi                   ; 1;increment 1st count
          inc edx                   ; 0;increment 2nd count
          mov [esp+eax*4],edi       ; 1;
          mov [esp+ebx*4],edx       ; 0;
          if num eq 3               ;  ;on last of a set of 4
            mov ebp,RADBPTR         ; 1;load and advance
          endif                     ;  ;byte pointer
        .endif                      ;  ;
        if num eq 3                 ;  ;on last of a set of 4
          mov [RADBYT0+3],al        ; 0;save sort bytes
          mov [RADBYT4+3],bl        ; 1;
          mov edi,[RADBYT0]         ; 0;pick up 8 sort bytes
          mov edx,[RADBYT4]         ; 1;
          mov [ecx+ebp],edi         ; 0;and deposit them
          mov [ecx+ebp+4],edx       ; 1;
          mov ebp,RADOFST           ; 0;and restore ebp
        endif                       ;  ;to ofst
        endm                        ;;;;7  cycles typical
                                    ;;;;12 cycles if num==3
                                    ;  ;

        xor    eax,eax              ; 1;
        xor    ebx,ebx              ; 0;
        .repeat                     ;  ;
          radmac 0                  ; 7;do 2
          radmac 1                  ; 7;do 2
          radmac 2                  ; 7;do 2
          radmac 3                  ;12;do 2 and save results
          add    ecx,8              ; 1;increment counter
        .until ZERO?                ; 0;and loop
                                    ;;;;34 cycles per 8 recs
                                    ;;;;4.3 cycles per record
```

Nominally executing in less than 5 cycles per record, when running in the primary cache, the loop in Listing 15-2 can be brought to its knees, exceeding 50 cycles per record, on sorts involving many megabytes of very random data, in which most record byte fetches can cause a page table miss.

# The Second Inner Loop of the Distribution Sort

The second inner loop of the distribution sort, in which a new sorted pointer array is built, is shown in Listings 15-3 and 15-4, in C and assembly language, respectively. Again, the C loop looks deceptively simple, while the assembly language version runs parallel operations in the U and V pipes and so takes considerably more lines of code.

There is one odd timing note wherein a line of code is listed as costing 0.5 cycles. In that particular case, two adjacent bytes are being fetched by two instructions trying to share the same cycle. I arranged the execution of this loop so that the first fetch is always to an odd address and the next fetch to an address one higher. Half the time, the two fetches collide on the way to the cache and cause a one-cycle delay; but the other half of the time, they address different doublewords and are not delayed. This is a rare instance of taking advantage of oddly aligned data references to pick up a little speed, (again, optimization in the extreme).

As usual, all seven general-purpose registers are in use, as they were in the first inner loop. The `ebp` register is tremendously useful in a majority of optimized algorithms.

### Listing 15-3　The Second Phase of the Distribution Sort in C

```
void
IL_DistributionSortPart2_C(unsigned char ***destptr,
                unsigned char **srcptr,
                unsigned char *bytelist, long count)
{
    int n;

    for (n = 0; n < count; n++)
        *++destptr[bytelist[n]] = srcptr[n];
}
```

### Listing 15-4　The Second Phase of the Distribution Sort in Assembly Language

```
                                ;;;;esi - sort byte ptr
                                ;;;;edi - record
                                ;;;;        pointer-list
                                ;;;;        pointer
                                ;;;;ebp - counter
            .repeat             ;  ;
              xor eax,eax       ; 1;clear out regs for
```

```
        xor ebx,ebx              ; 0;indexing
        mov al,[esi+ebp]         ; 1;pick up sort bytes
        mov bl,[esi+ebp+1]       ;.5;bus bank contention half
                                 ;   ;the time
        .if eax == ebx           ; 1;check for same byte value
          mov edx,[esp+eax*4]    ; 1;get pointer for next spot
          add edx,2*4            ; 1;advance it 2 positions
          mov ebx,[edi+ebp*4+4]  ; 0;pick up record pointer 2
          mov [esp+eax*4],edx    ; 1;store advanced spot ptr
          mov eax,[edi+ebp*4+0]  ; 0;pick up record pointer 1
          mov [edx-4],eax        ; 1;store sorted record ptr 1
          mov [edx],ebx          ; 0;store sorted record ptr 2
        .else                    ; 1;
          mov ecx,[esp+eax*4]    ; 1;get pointer for spot 1
          mov edx,[esp+ebx*4]    ; 0;get pointer for spot 2
          add ecx,4              ; 1;advance it 1 position
          add edx,4              ; 0;advance it 1 position
          mov [esp+eax*4],ecx    ; 1;store spot pointer 1
          mov [esp+ebx*4],edx    ; 0;store spot pointer 2
          mov eax,[edi+ebp*4+0]  ; 1;pick up record pointer 1
          mov ebx,[edi+ebp*4+4]  ; 0;pick up record pointer 2
          mov [ecx],eax          ; 1;store sorted record ptr 1
          mov [edx],ebx          ; 0;store sorted record ptr 2
        .endif                   ;  ;
        add ebp,2                ; 1;advance by 2 sort bytes
.until ZERO?                     ; 0;and loop
                                 ;;;;9.5 cycles + branch
                                 ;;;;misprediction
                                 ;;;;5 cycles per rec approx.
```

## Performance

Generally speaking, the distribution sort implemented here beats C quicksort above about 100 records being sorted on a 32-bit key field. The distribution sort performs best relative to other sort algorithms when it is sorting a single byte field. To sort on a 32-bit integer, it has to do four byte sorts. To sort three such integers in declining precedence, it has to make a dozen passes.

For the purpose of comparison, and in the interest of leveling the playing field, I chose a single 32-bit integer field in varying record sizes to test the relative performance of the assembly language distribution sort against the C version and two implementations using the C library's quicksort, one sorting pointers to records and the other sorting (and moving) the records directly. All tests were conducted on files of random numbers.

## Quicksort on Records

The only situation in which quicksorting records was faster than quicksorting pointers to records was when the records themselves were about the same size as the pointers, four bytes. Generally speaking, it's faster to sort pointers to records than it is to sort records themselves when the pointer is smaller than the record.

## Quicksort on Pointers

Quicksorting the array of pointers to the records was consistently the fastest solution at 100 records and fewer, but it beat the distribution sort by only a nose at the 100-record mark. Just above the 100-record mark, the distribution sort consistently won.

## Distribution Sort in Assembly Language

The distribution sort in assembly language reached peak efficiency, about 100 cycles per record (or 25 cycles per sorted byte per record), when operating on about two thousand 4-byte records, enough to just fill the primary cache. Since it takes fewer records of larger sizes to fill the cache and it takes quite a few records to amortize the general algorithm overhead (about 25,000 cycles), it turns out that for larger record sizes, peak efficiency of about 150 cycles per record occurred closer to a total record volume of 64K. Heavy primary cache, secondary cache, and page table misses caused things to slow down significantly at very large volumes, approaching a limit of just under 300 cycles per record (75 cycles per sorted byte per record) at an arbitrarily large sorting volume.

## Distribution Sort in C

At its relative worst, when the distribution sort in assembly language was running at its best (100 cycles per record), the distribution sort in C ran at two-thirds that speed. On the other hand, it usually ran as well as or sometimes even slightly better than the assembly language routine in situations where heavy cache misses occured, generally above 8,000 records. The paradox of the double cache miss, mentioned previously, seems to be the source of this occassional C victory over assembly language. In response to this paradox, I wrote up an optimal single (as opposed to double) assembly language first inner loop for the distribution sort, as shown in Listing 15-5. It is a very tightly coiled single loop, as evidenced by the out-of-order instruction sequence numbers in the comment field. It runs faster than the C equivalent, and it not infrequently beats the double loop's performance at very high record counts.

Table 15-1 shows performance statistics for the various sort routines on sorts of one hundred thousand 40-byte records and of 1 million 4-byte records. Note that at these large volumes, the distribution sort runs about four times faster than quicksort.

### Listing 15-5  Coiled First Inner Loop of Distribution Sort

```
                                    ;  ;eax - count value
                                    ;  ;ebx - byte referenced
                                    ;  ;ecx - negative count
                                    ;  ;edx - byte list ptr-1
                                    ;  ;esi - pts to src ptrs
                                    ;  ;edi - record ptr
                                    ;  ;ebp - offset in rec
.if ecx                             ; 1;
  mov   edi,[esi+ecx*4]             ; 1;1
  mov   bl,[edi+ebp]                ; 0;2
  inc   ecx                         ; 1;3
  .if !ZERO?                        ;  ;4
    .repeat                         ;  ;
      mov     edi,[esi+ecx*4]       ; 1;1 - fetch record ptr
      mov     eax,[esp+ebx*4]       ; 0;5 - pick up count val
      mov     [edx+ecx],bl          ; 1;6 - store rec byte
      inc     eax                   ; 0;7 - increment count
      mov     [esp+ebx*4],eax       ; 1;8 - store the count
      mov     bl,[edi+ebp]          ; 0;2 - fetch rec byte
      inc     ecx                   ; 1;3 - inc loop counter
    .until ZERO?                    ; 0;4 - and loop if OK
                                    ;;;;4-cycle inner loop
  .endif                            ;  ;
  mov   eax,[esp+ebx*4]             ; 0;5
  mov   [edx+ecx],bl                ; 1;6
  inc   eax                         ; 0;7
  mov   [esp+ebx*4],eax             ; 1;8
.endif                              ;  ;
```

| Table 15-1    Sort Performance Statistics on Large Data Sets | |
| --- | --- |
| *Sort of 1 million 4-byte records* | |
| Radix sort, assembly language, double loop: | 311.7 cycles per rec |
| Radix sort, assembly language, single loop: | 285.8 cycles per rec |
| Radix sort, C: | 339.4 cycles per rec |
| C library pointer quicksort: | 1226.2 cycles per rec |
| C library record quicksort: | 802.0 cycles per rec |

| Table 15-1 (Continued) Sort Performance Statistics on Large Data Sets | |
|---|---|
| *Sort of 100,000 40-byte records* | |
| Radix sort, assembly language, double loop: | 284.0 cycles per rec |
| Radix sort, assembly language, single loop: | 284.8 cycles per rec |
| Radix sort, C: | 328.2 cycles per rec |
| C library pointer quicksort: | 1021.2 cycles per rec |
| C library record quicksort: | 2203.3 cycles per rec |

# The Implications of Nlog$_2$(N)

The reason that many of the most common sort algorithms follow Nlog$_2$(N) performance is that each of the N elements being sorted has to be compared to another element, on average, log$_2$(N) times. If you were sorting 30 things, log$_2$(N) is about 5 (since $2^5$ is 32, which is close to 30). That means that each element would be compared to another element about five times. For a million items, log$_2$(N) is closer to 20. And since this number is generally a multiplier applied to an item-comparison speed, it says something about how fast those comparisons need to be to stay competitive.

At a million records (and above), the distribution sort performs at a rate of about 300 Pentium cycles per record sorted on a 32-bit key. For quicksort or any other Nlog$_2$(N) sort to beat it, that sort would have to perform its basic comparison operation in less than 15 cycles (300/log$_2$(1,000,000)) including the time taken waiting for cache misses. Any pointer-based sort, where the pointers to records are sorted instead of the records themselves, will probably experience heavy memory reference delays, most likely as bad as or worse than those experienced by the distribution sort. After all, the distribution sort only pseudorandomly accesses a record 4 times (for a 32-bit integer sort), but the Nlog$_2$(N) sorts touch the record 20 times (although possibly in less random patterns).

At a million records, the distribution sort spends about 80 percent of its time waiting for memory, so if an Nlog$_2$(N) sort merely did no worse waiting for memory, it would have to do its comparisons in 3 cycles (20 percent of the 15 cycles per comparison previously derived). Actual measurement shows that the C library quicksort routine runs at about one-quarter the speed of the distribution sort in this record range, apparently losing a lot of speed to the 20-reference problem.

## Recommendations

For very large sorting tasks involving just a few sortable bytes per record, the distribution sort is the clear winner over quicksort. On very large sorting tasks, it spends most of its time waiting for main memory to deliver data. As a result, there is relatively little difference (only about 10 percent) in the performance of the C implementation of the sort and the assembly language versions. The two assembly language versions generally perform within a few percent of each other's speed, but the double loop (also called a tandem loop) version seems to win the race more often. Because the C version has a smaller startup overhead than the assembly language versions (since it doesn't need to copy the census table data), the C version can actually run faster than the assembly language versions below about a thousand records.

When sorting on a four-byte field, I would recommend

- Quicksort up to about 100 records
- The distribution sort as implemented in C up to about 1,000 records
- The distribution sort as implemented with the double loop in assembly language above 1,000 records
- The distribution sort as implemented with the single loop in assembly language above 1,000 records if empirical testing shows that it runs faster on test data

The execution speed of the distribution sort is proportional to the number of bytes in the record being used as part of the sorting key. The quicksort–distribution sort trade-off point is affected accordingly.

# The Loop Not Taken

Sometimes, after writing support code around a fast inner loop for a day or two, I wonder about the loop not taken—that other good-contender loop, the dark horse option I passed over at an early design stage. In the case of the code for this chapter, I had second thoughts after noticing how having two simultaneous cache misses could slow the code. And, in fact, I found an even more efficient single coiled loop as a result. But what about the virtues of the original double loop? Can't double loops be run without making their cache misses coincide? I rewrote the basic macro that defines the first inner loop of the distribution sort, as shown in Listing 15-6. Instead of pairing nearly identical instructions in the U and V pipes, I chose to shift the U and V pipe loops three instructions out of phase with each other, so that their cache misses would alternate instead of coincide.

A first distribution sort inner loop, built around this macro, stands a chance of marginally besting the other assembly language versions in some circumstances. I leave it as a stone unturned for the ambitious reader's experimentation.

### Listing 15-6    An Alternate First Distribution Sort Loop

```
radmac   macro    num

         mov edi,[esi+ecx*4+(0+num*2)*4]  ; 1;loop 1 - get pointer
         mov edx,[esp+ebx*4]              ; 1;loop 2 - fetch counter

         mov [RADBYT+num*2-2],al          ; 1;loop 1 - store prev byte
         inc edx                          ; 0;loop 2 - increment count

         mov al,[edi+ebp]                 ; 1;loop 1 - fetch byte
         mov [esp+eax*4],edx              ; 0;loop 2 - store counter

         mov edi,[esp+eax*4]              ; 2;loop 1 - fetch counter
         mov edx,[esi+ecx*4+(1+num*2)*4]  ; 0;loop 2 - get pointer

         inc edi                          ; 1;loop 1 - increment count
         mov [RADBYT+num*2-1],al          ; 0;loop 2 - store prev byte

         mov [esp+eax*4],edi              ; 1;loop 1 - store counter
         mov bl,[edx+ebp]                 ; 0;loop 2 - fetch byte

         endm
```

# Conclusion

With all but very small record sizes (on the order of four bytes), it is usually faster to sort pointers to data records than to move the data records around themselves. Accordingly, you can sort a million random 32-bit values in just over two seconds using the distribution sort. The C library's quicksort (in this particular case, Watcom's, but it could be just about anybody's) takes up to four times as long. Many of the common sort routines are burdened by having to reference a record about

20 times to sort it if there are a million or so records in the set. The distribution sort, for a 32-bit value, references the record only four times, regardless of the total number of records, and so it can usually maintain a speed advantage with large record counts.

Providing that the sort can be accomplished via byte-wise comparisons at fixed record positions, the distribution sort becomes relatively efficient above 100 records. It excels at 10,000 and shines at a million.

# Matrix Multiplication

*Middle English* matrice, *from Old French, from Late Latin* matrix,
matric-, *from Latin, breeding-animal, from* mater, matr-, *mother.*
— *Origin of the word* matrix, *the* American Heritage Dictionary

A matrix, in mathematics, is usually thought of as a two-dimensional array of numbers often used to "multiply" other one- or two-dimensional arrays of numbers. This is not, of course, a rigorous or complete definition of what a matrix is, but it covers a large percentage of real-world matrix applications. This chapter specifically examines the speed limits for floating-point matrix math, both on very large matrices and on the small matrices used to rotate objects in three-dimensional space.

## Matrix Review

Suppose you had a set of points in three-dimensional space that described the corners of an object you wanted to visualize on a screen. Each point has an X, Y, and Z coordinate, and a simple way to visualize the object is to ignore the Z coordinate and plot the points on a screen at their given X and Y coordinates. If you wish to add perspective, there is a simple adjustment calculation involving the Z coordinate as well, but it still boils down to plotting the X and Y pairs.

Now, suppose you want to rotate the object about the origin, the location where X, Y, and Z are all zero. You need to "multiply" each point by a rotation matrix to do that job. A simple numeric example of this kind of multiplication is given in Figure 16-1. The matrix is the three-by-three grid of numbers at the left side. The X, Y, and Z values are the vertical triplet with values 2.1, 1.8, and 9.0, respectively. The next

| 2.7 | 3.5 | 8.2 | | 2.1 | | 2.1*2.7 + 1.8*3.5 + 9.0*8.2 | | 85.77 |
|---|---|---|---|---|---|---|---|---|
| 0.7 | –1.0 | 12.2 | X | 1.8 | = | 2.1*0.7 – 1.8*1.0 + 9.0*12.2 | = | 109.47 |
| 6.4 | 0.3 | –4.2 | | 9.0 | | 2.1*6.4 + 1.8*0.3 – 9.0*4.2 | | –23.82 |

**Figure 16-1    A Numeric Example of Multiplication by a Matrix**

array to the right shows the mathematical expressions for the transformed triplet, and the rightmost triplet of numbers is the final result. The numbers that would be involved in an actual rotation matrix would typically be small numbers, with absolute values no greater than 1 and many many digits after the decimal point, but the mechanics of multiplication are the same as those shown here.

The rotation of an aircraft is often referred to by the aeronautical terms *pitch*, *yaw*, and *roll*. We can use these same terms to describe the rotation of any object in space, where there are three degrees of rotational freedom. When a plane pitches, its nose moves in the up-and-down direction. When it yaws, the nose is moving left and right. And when it rolls, the nose may be pointed straight ahead, but the pilots are tilted to one side or even upside down. *Pitch*, *yaw*, and *roll* are analogous to rotations about the X, Y, and Z axes, and you can model rotation matrices on these angular parameters.

Figure 16-2 shows how each of the nine values in a pitch-yaw-roll matrix is calculated. The matrix only has to be calculated once for any given rotational state, but you can use it to rotate as many XYZ points as you like.

|  | R11 R12 R13 |
|---|---|
|  | R21 R22 R23 |
|  | R31 R32 R33 |

R11 = cos(yaw ) * cos(roll)
R12 = sin(pitch) * sin(yaw ) * cos(roll ) – cos(pitch) * sin(roll)
R13 = cos(pitch) * sin(yaw ) * cos(roll ) + sin(pitch) * sin(roll)

R21 = cos(yaw ) * sin(roll)
R22 = cos(pitch) * cos(roll) + sin(pitch) * sin(yaw ) * sin(roll)
R23 = cos(pitch) * sin(yaw ) * sin(roll ) – sin(pitch) * cos(roll)

R31 = –sin(yaw )
R32 = sin(pitch) * cos(yaw )
R33 = cos(pitch) * cos(yaw )

**Figure 16-2    Value Expansions for a Pitch-Yaw-Roll Matrix**

In the depths of engineering and scientific mathematics, there are uses for matrices with thousands of elements and vertical and horizontal dimensions in the hundreds. But the principles of multiplication are the same—lots of multiplications and additions.

# Fast Multiplication with a Three-by-Three Matrix

So, how fast can you shovel data points through a rotation matrix on a Pentium-100? As it turns out, you can process up to 2 million points per second, or up to 64K points every thirtieth of a second, a common unit of animation time.

Listing 16-1 shows the C implementation of a function that reads in an array of points and puts out an array of transformed points. In addition to performing the $3 \times 3$ multiplication, this function also adds a constant offset to each output value. It is very common to want to do a rotation on an object relative to its own internal point of origin and then move the entire object to some other part of space using X, Y, and Z offsets. That is what this routine is built to do.

### Listing 16-1    A C Function to Rotate a Point Array

```
void
IL_3DRotateAndDisplace_C(float *dest, float *source,
                                 float *matrix, long count)
{
    long n;

    for (n = 0; n < count; n++) {
        dest[0] = source[0] * matrix[0+0*4] +
                  source[1] * matrix[1+0*4] +
                  source[2] * matrix[2+0*4] +
                            matrix[3+0*4];
        dest[1] = source[0] * matrix[0+1*4] +
                  source[1] * matrix[1+1*4] +
                  source[2] * matrix[2+1*4] +
                            matrix[3+1*4];
        dest[2] = source[0] * matrix[0+2*4] +
                  source[1] * matrix[1+2*4] +
                  source[2] * matrix[2+2*4] +
                            matrix[3+2*4];
```

```
        source += 3;
        dest   += 3;
    }
}
```

Listing 16-2 shows the same function implemented in assembly language, where it runs about 60 percent faster than the C in Listing 16-1. When running in the primary cache, the inner loop, predicted by cycle counting to be 34 cycles, actually measures in at about 39 cycles, fairly close to the prediction.

The code itself is a major exercise in floating-point unit stack-oriented processing. Writing optimized code for the floating-point unit requires meticulous care in terms of knowing what's where on the stack. In fact, all the comments in the main loop are devoted to a shorthand notation to describe the stack. The comment to the right of each instruction indicates the state of the stack after executing that instruction. By way of example, $i2$ refers to the second of the three values in a particular point coordinate set, $m31$ refers to the matrix element in the third row and first column of the matrix, and values starting with the letter $s$ represent intermediate or final sums of multiplied elements. Because the matrix array includes a constant offset element, it is actually a $4 \times 3$ array, where the fourth element is simply added in without a multiplication step; hence the positioning of matrix rows four floating-point positions apart in memory.

The main trick to writing efficient floating-point code, besides keeping track of the mind-numbing details of the stack, is to allow three cycles to pass from the time an addition or multiplication is initiated to the time the value is used for anything else except an `fxch` exchange instruction. Fortunately, in matrix math there are enough operations that can potentially be performed in parallel that it is rarely necessary to waste a cycle waiting for any one operation to complete.

## Listing 16-2   An Assembly Language Function to Rotate a Point Array

```
FPTR    textequ <dword ptr>             ;   ;pointer for floats
FSIZE   textequ <4>                     ;   ;size of floats

IL_3DRotateAndDisplace_A proc near C public uses esi edi ebx,
        dest:dword, source:dword, matrix:dword, count:dword
        mov     ecx,count               ;   ;get item count
        mov     esi,source              ;   ;get source array ptr
        mov     ebx,dest                ;   ;get dest array ptr
        mov     edi,matrix              ;   ;point to matrix
        imul    ecx,ecx,3*FSIZE         ;   ;ecx is size of array
        add     esi,ecx                 ;   ;esi points to
                                        ;   ;source end
```

```
add     ebx,ecx                         ;  ;edi points to
                                        ;  ;dest end
neg     ecx                             ;  ;ecx ready for
                                        ;  ;count-up
.if !ecx                                ;  ;catch zero case
  ret                                   ;  ;
.endif                                  ;  ;
.repeat                                 ;  ;
  fld   FPTR [esi+ecx+0*FSIZE]          ; 1;i1
  fmul  FPTR [edi+(0+0*4)*FSIZE]        ; 1;m11
  fld   FPTR [esi+ecx+1*FSIZE]          ; 1;m11 i2
  fmul  FPTR [edi+(1+0*4)*FSIZE]        ; 1;m11 m12
  fld   FPTR [esi+ecx+2*FSIZE]          ; 1;m11 m12 i3
  fmul  FPTR [edi+(2+0*4)*FSIZE]        ; 1;m11 m12 m13
  fxch  st(1)                           ; 0;m11 m13 m12
  faddp st(2),st                        ; 1;s1a m13
  fld   FPTR [esi+ecx+0*FSIZE]          ; 1;s1a m13 i1
  fmul  FPTR [edi+(0+1*4)*FSIZE]        ; 1;s1a m13 m21
  fxch  st(1)                           ; 0;s1a m21 m13
  faddp st(2),st                        ; 1;s1b m21
  fld   FPTR [esi+ecx+1*FSIZE]          ; 1;s1b m21 i2
  fmul  FPTR [edi+(1+1*4)*FSIZE]        ; 1;s1b m21 m22
  fld   FPTR [esi+ecx+2*FSIZE]          ; 1;s1b m21 m22 i3
  fmul  FPTR [edi+(2+1*4)*FSIZE]        ; 1;s1b m21 m22 m23
  fxch  st(1)                           ; 0;s1b m21 m23 m22
  faddp st(2),st                        ; 1;s1b s2a m23
  fld   FPTR [esi+ecx+0*FSIZE]          ; 1;s1b s2a m23 i1
  fmul  FPTR [edi+(0+2*4)*FSIZE]        ; 1;s1b s2a m23 m31
  fxch  st(1)                           ; 0;s1b s2a m31 m23
  faddp st(2),st                        ; 1;s1b s2b m31
  fld   FPTR [esi+ecx+1*FSIZE]          ; 1;s1b s2b m31 i2
  fmul  FPTR [edi+(1+2*4)*FSIZE]        ; 1;s1b s2b m31 m32
  fld   FPTR [esi+ecx+2*FSIZE]          ; 1;s1b s2b m31 m32 i3
  fmul  FPTR [edi+(2+2*4)*FSIZE]        ; 1;s1b s2b m31 m32 m33
  fxch  st(1)                           ; 0;s1b s2b m31 m33 m32
  faddp st(2),st                        ; 1;s1b s2b s3a m33
  fxch  st(3)                           ; 0;m33 s2b s3a s1b
  fadd  FPTR [edi+(3+0*4)*FSIZE]        ; 1;m33 s2b s3a s1c
  fxch  st(1)                           ; 0;m33 s2b s1c s3a
  faddp st(3),st                        ; 1;s3b s2b s1c
  fxch  st(1)                           ; 0;s3b s1c s2b
  fadd  FPTR [edi+(3+1*4)*FSIZE]        ; 1;s3b s1c s2c
  fxch  st(2)                           ; 0;s2c s1c s3b
  fadd  FPTR [edi+(3+2*4)*FSIZE]        ; 1;s2c s1c s3c
  fxch  st(1)                           ; 0;s2c s3c s1c
  fstp  FPTR [ebx+ecx+0*FSIZE]          ; 2;s2c s3c
  fxch  st(1)                           ; 0;s3c s2c
```

```
        fstp  FPTR [ebx+ecx+1*FSIZE]    ; 2;s3c
        fstp  FPTR [ebx+ecx+2*FSIZE]    ; 2;
        add   ecx,3*FSIZE               ; 1;
    .until ZERO?                        ; 0;
                                        ;;;;34 cycles predicted
                                        ;;;;39 cycles measured
        ret                             ; ;

IL_3DRotateAndDisplace_A endp
```

It may seem odd that the code reloads each element of the point coordinate three times instead of loading all three elements of the XYZ point onto the stack and performing all subsequent accesses through the stack. This would, indeed, reduce memory traffic to the primary cache, but it would not reduce the cycle count. Unless you're willing to let the stack values be destroyed in the process, it takes two instructions to load a matrix element and multiply it by a point coordinate element, regardless of whether that element is on the floating-point stack or out in memory.

# The CHMATRX.EXE Demonstration Program

On the CD-ROM accompanying this book are the source and executable versions of the demonstration program CHMATRX.EXE. This program uses the fast point rotation code to let you interactively rotate and move an object made of a potentially very large set of points in real time. The program performs a perspective calculation on the points generated by the rotation and displacement routine, so the objects look more "real" as they move. You may define and test your own objects using a simple text file of point coordinates and colors.

# Large Matrices

When matrices become very large, the main multiplication inner loop reduces to approximately the following:

```
for (n = 0, sum = 0.0; n < Xdimension; n++)
    sum += inputptr[n] * matrixptr[n];
```

This is often referred to as a MAC loop, referring to the "multiply and accumulate" operation. Many digital signal processing applications perform extensive MAC loops when processing serial data points from signals, and large matrices do it too.

There is a very simple four-instruction floating-point building block that executes a MAC unit, as follows:

```
MAC     macro   num                         ;   ;MAC with doubles
        fld     qword ptr [esi+8*num]       ; 1;load a double
        fmul    qword ptr [edi+8*num]       ; 1;times a double
        fxch    st(1)                       ; 0;swap for old result
        faddp   st(2),st                    ; 1;add old val into sum
        endm                                ;;;;3 cycles
```

Using successive integer arguments for num, you can chain these together to do a MAC chain of arbitrary length:

```
        fldz                                ; 2;sum starts as zero
        fld     qword ptr [esi+8*0]         ; 1;
        fmul    qword ptr [edi+8*0]         ; 1;do the first multiply
        MAC     1                           ; 3;then chain MACs
        MAC     2                           ; 3;
        MAC     3                           ; 3;
        ;...                                ;   ;more MACs here
        faddp   st(1),st                    ; 2;do final add
        fstp    qword ptr [ebx+ecx]         ; 5;final store
```

The MAC macro works efficiently by constantly swapping the multiplication in progress with the previous, completed multiplication on the stack. This way its addition operation is not delayed waiting for the most recent multiplication to complete.

On another note, there is a serious memory access problem that is frequently encountered in large-matrix math. Sometimes, instead of reading items one after another from a matrix row, where they are stored consecutively in memory, you want to access elements one after another from a column, where they are generally not stored in consecutive memory locations. When this happens, performance can be dominated by memory delays. One solution is to keep a copy of the matrix "turned on its side," so that columns are consecutive in memory and rows are non-consecutive. If a large matrix can be oriented so that every row starts on a cache line boundary, then turning a matrix on its side can be done with minimized pain by identifying and operating on cache line zones of the matrix that, with some permutation of their contents, can be swapped.

# Conclusion

Efficient matrix math implementation is dominated by the multiply-and-accumulate operation. When pipelined, this is inherently a three-cycle operation on the Pentium. If you have a large matrix multiplication operation to perform, chances are good that, unless memory access delays bog things down, it can be executed in a little over three cycles per multiplication.

Given an appropriate matrix to perform it, calculation of the location of a rotated and displaced point somewhere in three-dimensional space costs about 39 cycles before accounting for any memory delays. (Adding a true perspective calculation, involving a division operation, takes a minimum of about 25 cycles more.) It is possible to calculate tens of thousands of such points in the time used by a typical frame of animation.

# JPEG

*A picture is worth a thousand words.*
*—A common saying descriptive of*
*JPEG compression at a coarse quality setting*

JPEG, which stands for Joint Photographic Experts Group, is the acronym associated with one of the most popular and powerful image compression techniques in use today. As generally used, it is a "lossy" technique (meaning that a decompressed image will be slightly different than the original) that attempts to keep only the most visually important part of an image while discarding bits of information that are less likely to be missed.

The JPEG algorithm has a fascinating pair of inner loops. In fact, as inner loops go, they're quite large. When compressing, the main inner loop is referred to as a discrete cosine transform (DCT). When the main inner loop is decompressing, a sort of mirror-image reversal called the inverse discrete cosine transformation (IDCT) is performed. After a brief sketch of the way JPEG compression and decompression work, this chapter takes a close look at the IDCT inner loop used to quickly decompress graphic images and then demonstrates parallel implementations in C and assembly language.

The code given in this chapter is *not* a full implementation of JPEG image decompression but rather a fast implementation of the IDCT inner loop (as opposed to a slower but slightly more visually accurate IDCT implementation). Spanning a number of pages, it illustrates what I believe to be an effective way to write interleaved C and assembly language implementations of the same routine, juxtaposing a few lines of C at a time with their assembly language correlates. It also demonstrates a variety of strategies to cut down the cycle count, ultimately running about 30 percent faster in assembly language than in the C equivalent.

**323**

The code in this chapter was derived from the Independent JPEG Group's fast IDCT routine, a part of their very large and freely distributed JPEG source code package. A copy of their entire distribution is provided on the CD-ROM for the JPEG-curious.

# How JPEG Works

There are extraordinarily complex ways to explain JPEG, and there are much simpler ways to explain the gist of it. This explanation shoots for the simple gist.

## The Eight-by-Eight Unit of Compression

Suppose you had a $320 \times 240$ gray-scale computer image to compress. Each pixel would most likely be represented by a single byte, with 0 representing black, 255 representing white, and values like 23 and 194 representing shades of gray in between.

The first thing JPEG would do with such a picture would be to divide it into 1,200 little $8 \times 8$ squares of pixels: 320/8 = 40 columns of squares, 240/8 = 30 rows of squares, and $30 \times 40 = 1,200$. JPEG would then compress each one separately, appending the compressed results together in the output stream. Thus, no matter what size the image, JPEG always performs its compression magic on individual $8 \times 8$ squares. Dividing a picture into such squares and later reconstructing it from them is very straightforward.

Figure 17-1 shows a simple $8 \times 8$ piece of a picture, in this case apparently dark at the bottom and lighter at the top. This is exactly the kind of fundamental unit JPEG compresses.

```
182 194 201 169 168 187 175 169
176 146 161 182 157 141 156 174
150 147 141 150 150 140 135 146
106 106 126 116 116 129 129 140
 93  94  78  87  85 112 116  94
 73 121 106  95  88  71  87  77
 22  22  29  22  21  20  20  26
  2   3   3   2   3   3   3   3
```

**Figure 17-1    An 8 × 8 Piece of an Image**

# The Magical DCT Algorithm

Usually referred to as the DCT or the forward DCT, this next step is a bit magical. Conceptually, what happens is that the 8 × 8 piece of the image gets multiplied by two other 8 × 8 matrices to produce a derivative 8 × 8 matrix. In other words, the original 8 × 8 matrix gets transformed into a new 8 × 8 matrix via some seemingly very heavy number crunching.

Ordinarily, two 8 × 8 matrix multiplications would require 1,024 (64 × 8 × 2) multiplication steps. Part of the magic of the DCT is that the very special matrices chosen for this step have a lot of internal symmetries, so there is a way to execute the math with only 80 multiplication steps. It is this symmetry that saves the day for JPEG and keeps the algorithm fairly fast.

Figure 17-2 shows the results of performing a DCT using integer math (subject to slight rounding error) on the image from Figure 17-1. Odd as it may seem, this matrix contains essentially the same information as the original and can be converted back into the original with two more matrix multiplications. The image information hasn't been lost; it's just been changed in form.

| | | | | | | | |
|---|---|---|---|---|---|---|---|
| -206 | 3 | 4 | -15 | -7 | 2 | 1 | -2 |
| 461 | 6 | 4 | -1 | 10 | 7 | 12 | -1 |
| -70 | 25 | -2 | -5 | 4 | 0 | 8 | 5 |
| 74 | 17 | -1 | -5 | -30 | -5 | -10 | 0 |
| -20 | -23 | 7 | 17 | -24 | 1 | 12 | -2 |
| -7 | -1 | -4 | -6 | -14 | -12 | 14 | 6 |
| 48 | 23 | -10 | -3 | -18 | -18 | -12 | 1 |
| -31 | -1 | 6 | 26 | -3 | 1 | 1 | -6 |

**Figure 17-2   Raw Results of the Forward DCT**

Now, instead of having 64 pixel values, we have 64 wave pattern coefficients that describe the same image. Just as you can construct an image from 64 separate pixels, you can take sixty-four 8 × 8 patterns of pixels that look like various combinations of vertical and horizontal waves, scale them by these coefficients, and add them together to produce the same image. The main thing to understand is that the numbers at the upper left describe big, slow waves, those at the lower right describe frantic little waves, and those in between describe waves of intermediate frequencies.

The human visual system pays much more attention to the big slow waves than to the rapidly oscillating waves. For instance, the value 461, near the upper left-hand corner of the matrix, no doubt represents the top-to-bottom, light-to-dark trend so easily noticed in the original image data by simple inspection. That's a big (light to dark), slow (peak to trough, it takes all eight pixels from top to bottom) wave. The −6 at the lower right-hand corner represents small back-and-forth, up-and-down variations from one pixel to the next across the entire image. Chances are good that its visual effect is indistinguishable from noise.

The way JPEG achieves its lossy compression is to systematically toss out information from such a wave matrix. The farther away a coefficient is from the upper left-hand corner, the more of its information content gets thrown out. This is done in the next step.

## Applying the Quantization Matrix

JPEG relies on one of the simplest tricks in the book to toss out information: integer division. Figure 17-3 shows an $8 \times 8$ matrix of values used to "quantize" the result of the DCT. It is called "quantization" because when you divide a value by, say, 7 and then try to reconstruct the original value by multiplying by 7, you're guaranteed to get a multiple of 7 (such as 0, 7, 14, 21, and so on) as a result. There is a quantum distance of seven between the possible reconstructed values.

To quantize the matrix in Figure 17-2 using the quantization matrix in Figure 17-3, you just divide every value in Figure 17-2 by the number in the corresponding matrix position in Figure 17-3. The result is shown in Figure 17-4. Actual quantization matrices in general use are less regular than the matrix in Figure 17-3, but they share the general trend of small numbers turning into large numbers as you go from upper left to lower right.

Quality-level index numbers are assigned various quantization tables, with low quality levels usually associated with low index numbers (and large values in the quantization matrix) and high quality levels associated with high index numbers (and small values in the quantization matrix). The larger the values in the quantization matrix, the more 0s in the quantized matrix, the greater the compression, and the more visible the visual artifacts.

| | | | | | | | |
|---|---|---|---|---|---|---|---|
| 3 | 5 | 7 | 9 | 11 | 13 | 15 | 17 |
| 5 | 7 | 9 | 11 | 13 | 15 | 17 | 19 |
| 7 | 9 | 11 | 13 | 15 | 17 | 19 | 21 |
| 9 | 11 | 13 | 15 | 17 | 19 | 21 | 23 |
| 11 | 13 | 15 | 17 | 19 | 21 | 23 | 25 |
| 13 | 15 | 17 | 19 | 21 | 23 | 25 | 27 |
| 15 | 17 | 19 | 21 | 23 | 25 | 27 | 29 |
| 17 | 19 | 21 | 23 | 25 | 27 | 29 | 31 |

**Figure 17-3  A Quantization Matrix**

```
-68    0    0   -1    0    0    0    0
 92    0    0    0    0    0    0    0
-10    2    0    0    0    0    0    0
  8    1    0    0   -1    0    0    0
 -1   -1    0    1   -1    0    0    0
  0    0    0    0    0    0    0    0
  3    1    0    0    0    0    0    0
 -1    0    0    1    0    0    0    0
```

**Figure 17-4   Quantized 8 × 8 Image Data**

## Compressing the Quantized Data

At this point, a giant light bulb should go off in the mind of anyone thinking about compression. The resultant matrix is mostly 0s with mostly very small integers making up the rest of the positions. It's a great candidate for some form of Huffman encoding. In fact, it's usually compressed using a predefined fixed Huffman table to encode adjacent elements of the matrix, starting from the upper left-hand corner and progressing to the lower right-hand corner, going back and forth diagonally through the data in a zigzag pattern. Runs of 0s have special codes, and when there is nothing left but 0s to encode, an end token terminates the data stream. The lower the quality (and the larger the entries) of the quantization matrix, the more 0s and very small integers that are generated in the quantized image data. This is where JPEG gets its compression power.

Figure 17-5, read from top to bottom and left to right, shows the sequence in which the matrix values are finally processed into Huffmanized values from the data in Figure 17-4. This storage order tends to collect most of the 0s at the end of the sequence, where they can be replaced by a single end code.

At this point, compression is complete.

```
                -68
                0  92
           -10   0   0
           -1   0   2   8
        -1   1   0   0   0
        0   0   0   0  -1   0
     3   0   0   0   0   0   0
  0   0   0  -1   1   0   1  -1
     0   0   0  -1   0   0   0
        0   0   0   0   0   0
              1    END
```

**Figure 17-5   Zigzag Sequence of Final Compression**

## Decompressing the Quantized Data

The matrix in Figure 17-4 is straightforwardly reconstructed from the compressed Huffman stream at decompression time.

## Reapplying the Quantization Matrix

At compression time, the quantization matrix elements are used for division. On decompression, each element of the quantization matrix shown in Figure 17-3 is multiplied by the corresponding element in the matrix shown in Figure 17-4 to produce the matrix shown in Figure 17-6. Note that the result is similar to the matrix in Figure 17-2, differing in the precision with which the original values are reconstructed. This matrix is now ready for the inverse DCT.

```
-204    0    0   -9    0    0    0    0
 460    0    0    0    0    0    0    0
 -70   18    0    0    0    0    0    0
  72   11    0    0  -17    0    0    0
 -11  -13    0   17  -19    0    0    0
   0    0    0    0    0    0    0    0
  45   17    0    0    0    0    0    0
 -17    0    0   23    0    0    0    0
```

**Figure 17-6   Matrix Ready for the Inverse DCT**

## The Inverse DCT

The inverse DCT is computationally very similar to the forward DCT. It takes a shortcut requiring only 80 multiplications to execute the equivalent of two large $8 \times 8$ matrix multiplications. The result, shown in Figure 17-7, is similar to the original shown in Figure 17-1. This same cellular process repeated hundreds or thousands of times per image reproduces the original picture.

```
185  192  188  177  178  187  183  170
155  157  163  166  157  148  154  168
153  142  142  152  151  140  139  150
108  115  121  121  120  123  129  133
 93   95   91   89   99  112  109   94
 84   94  100   92   79   73   79   86
 26   24   25   28   26   21   22   27
  5    4    3    3    3    2    2    2
```

**Figure 17-7   The Reconstructed 8 × 8 Pixel Image**

## Color Pictures

Compression of color pictures is just a variant of grayscale compression. There are three types of color receptor cells in our eyes, one each (more or less) for red, green, and blue. There are also many, many receptors for different shades of gray; these respond to some degree to each of the primary colors as well. You could encode color pictures as separate red, green, and blue component images and combine them to make a color picture, but it turns out there is a more efficient way of doing it.

Instead of encoding red, green, and blue images, it makes sense to encode one very detailed grayscale image and two other less detailed images that describe how to "colorize" the grayscale image. The colorization images don't need to be nearly as precise as the main, grayscale one, because we can't see a transition from, say, red to green as easily as we see a transition from light to dark. It is not unusual for beautiful color images to have 80 percent or more of their compressed information devoted to grayscale.

# Taking on the Inverse DCT

The inverse DCT is certainly the main time-critical inner loop for grayscale image decompression, and it is usually the most critical for color images, too, unless extravagant measures are taken to adapt the image to a 256-color display. It is generally implemented as a series of applications of one-dimensional inverse DCTs that operate on a single row or column of eight numbers at a time, producing eight numbers as output. Using 16 one-dimensional inverse DCTs, you get the effect of the two $8 \times 8$ matrix multiplications.

The DCT and inverse DCT are also integral to much of MPEG compression and decompression.

## The Flowgraph

The one-dimensional inverse DCT is elegantly described by a flowgraph such as that shown in Figure 17-8. The flowgraph is read from left to right. On the left-hand side are the eight starting points of the eight matrix row or column values that are to undergo transformation, one on each line. On the right-hand side the eight transformed results emerge. In between, there is a lot of addition, subtraction, and some multiplication.

In the flowgraph, values move from left to right. Where a line splits, a copy of the value follows both paths. Where two lines merge, an addition takes place. Where

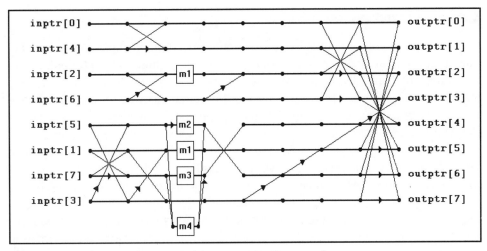

**Figure 17-8    A One-Dimensional Inverse DCT Flowgraph**

a value passes an arrow, it is negated. And where it passes through a box, it is multiplied by a constant. Where thin lines happen to cross each other, no interaction is implied. The values of the constants *m1* through *m4* are 1.414, 2.613, 1.082, and 1.847, respectively.

These rules and this flowgraph are a concise description of one of the most interesting and important inner loops in image compression. The reverse process, the forward DCT, has a very similar look to the IDCT flowgraph run in reverse. That is, if you reverse the arrows and run the values through the flowgraph from right to left, you come fairly close to getting the forward DCT specification, which has similar numbers of additions, negations, and multiplications. It was this elegant mirrorlike reversibility that led to the description of the DCT as a "symmetrical" algorithm. The notion of symmetry has since been replaced in popular perception by the idea of compressing and decompressing at similar rates.

## The Code

Although optimizing the complete JPEG codec is beyond the scope of this book, I chose to take a simplified version of the fast inverse DCT algorithm in C, as put out by the Independent JPEG Group, and see how much it could be improved with assembly language. The answer: it's about 30 percent faster. Listing 17-1 shows the interleaved C and assembly language listing of the routine. The Independent JPEG Group code was an extremely efficient starting point, and the simplifications I applied were mainly cosmetic, such as replacing macros with specific expansions. For clarity in the context of this chapter, I also removed some code that checked for special cases in the input data (a lot of zero coefficients in a row) where certain computations could be skipped. This routine actually combines the dequantization step with the IDCT, but the dequantization just consists of eight multiplications as the quantized input parameters are first read. The code was derived from the `jpeg_idct_ifast()` function in the source file JIDCTFST.C in the included IJG code.

This particular routine is designed to run fast with integer arithmetic and fixed-point math at the expense of losing a little precision in the result. There are other possible implementations of the IDCT algorithm, and theses have been written on the topic, but this is among the quickest of approaches in software. (Hardware implementations are a whole other matter.) The code is optimized for the Pentium processor.

## Listing 17-1   Parallel Inverse DCT Code in C and Assembly Language

```
;/*`.................. assembly language ....................
        .586
        .model flat


_IL_DATA segment page use32 public 'DATA'
_IL_DATA ends
_IL_TEXT segment page use32 public 'CODE'
_IL_TEXT ends


  comment `..................... C language ..................*/
#include <stdio.h>
#pragma aux MS_C "_*"                                    \
        parm caller []                                  \
        value struct float struct routine [eax] \
        modify [eax ecx edx es];
#pragma aux (MS_C) IL_idct_A;
void              IL_idct_A(unsigned char  *range_limit,
                           int *quantptr, int *inptr,
                           unsigned char **output_buf,
                           unsigned int output_col);
;/*`.................. assembly language ....................
  comment `..................... C language ..................*/

#define C277  277           // 1.082...
#define C362  362           // 1.414...
#define C473  473           // 1.847...
#define C669  669           // 2.613...


;/*`.................. assembly language ....................

_IL_TEXT segment
```

```
mul277   macro   reg, t1, t2      ;   ;multiply by binary 100010101
         lea     t1,[reg*4]       ; 1;
         mov     t2,reg           ; 0;
         shl     t2,4             ; 1;
         add     reg,t1           ; 0;0...101
         shl     t1,6             ; 1;
         add     reg,t2           ; 0;0...10101
         add     reg,t1           ; 1;0...100010101
         endm                     ;;;;4 cycles


mul362   macro   reg, t1, t2      ;   ;multiply by binary 101101010
         mov     t1,reg           ; 1;
         mov     t2,reg           ; 0;
         shl     t1,3             ; 1;
         add     reg,reg          ; 0;0...10
         shl     t2,5             ; 1;
         add     reg,t1           ; 0;0...1010
         shl     t1,3             ; 1;
         add     reg,t2           ; 0;0...101010
         shl     t2,3             ; 1;
         add     reg,t1           ; 0;0...1101010
         add     reg,t2           ; 1;0...101101010
         endm                     ;;;;6 cycles


mul473   macro   reg, t1, t2      ;   ;multiply by binary 111011001
         mov     t1,reg           ; 1;
         mov     t2,reg           ; 0;
         shl     t2,4             ; 1;
         lea     reg,[reg+reg*8]  ; 0;0...1001
         shl     t1,6             ; 1;
         add     reg,t2           ; 0;0...11001
         shl     t2,5             ; 1;
         sub     reg,t1           ; 0;1...111111011001
         add     reg,t2           ; 1;0...000111011001
         endm                     ;;;;5 cycles


mul669n  macro   reg, t1, t2      ;   ;multiply by binary-1010011101
         mov     t1,reg           ; 1;alias ...111110101100011
         lea     t2,[reg*2]       ; 0;
         shl     t1,5             ; 1;
         add     reg,t2           ; 0;0...11
         shl     t2,5             ; 1;
         add     reg,t1           ; 0;0...100011
         shl     t1,3             ; 1;
         add     reg,t2           ; 0;0...1100011
         shl     t2,4             ; 1;
         add     reg,t1           ; 0;0...101100011
```

```
        sub     reg,t2           ; 1;1...111110101100011
        endm                     ;;;;6 cycles
```

```
    comment `..................... C language .................*/
```

```
// IL_idct_A is based on jpeg_idct_ifast

void
IL_idct_C(unsigned char  *range_limit,
        int             *quantptr,      // dct table ptr
        int             *inptr,         // coefficient block ptr
        unsigned char **output_buf,
        unsigned int    output_col)
{
```

```
;/*`................... assembly language .....................
```

```
IL_idct_A proc near C public uses esi edi ebx ebp,
                                range_limit_:dword,
                                quantptr_   :dword,
                                inptr_      :dword,
                                output_buf_ :dword,
                                output_col_ :dword
```

```
    comment `..................... C language .................*/
```

```
    int             tmp0, tmp1, tmp2, tmp3, tmp4, tmp5, tmp6;
    int             tmp7, tmp10, tmp11, tmp12, tmp13;
    int             z5, z10, z11, z12, z13;
    int             *wsptr;
    unsigned char *outptr;
    int             ctr;
    int             workspace[64]; /*buffers data between passes*/
```

```
;/*`................... assembly language .....................
```

```
stackspace      textequ         <400>

range_limit     textequ         <dword ptr [esp+00*4]>
quantptr        textequ         <dword ptr [esp+01*4]>
inptr           textequ         <dword ptr [esp+02*4]>
output_buf      textequ         <dword ptr [esp+03*4]>
output_col      textequ         <dword ptr [esp+04*4]>
tmp0            textequ         <dword ptr [esp+05*4]>
tmp1            textequ         <dword ptr [esp+06*4]>
tmp2            textequ         <dword ptr [esp+07*4]>
tmp3            textequ         <dword ptr [esp+08*4]>
```

```
push1          textequ              <dword ptr [esp+09*4]>
push2          textequ              <dword ptr [esp+10*4]>
push3          textequ              <dword ptr [esp+11*4]>
wsptr          textequ              <dword ptr [esp+12*4]>
ctr            textequ              <dword ptr [esp+13*4]>
workspace      textequ              <dword ptr [esp+14*4]>

                                    ; 2;entry overhead
        sub    esp,stackspace       ; 1;clear enough stack
                                    ;   ;variable space
        mov    eax,range_limit_     ; 2;transfer passed
                                    ;   ;parameters
        mov    range_limit,eax      ; 1;for [esp+xx] stack
                                    ;   ;addressing
        mov    eax,quantptr_        ; 0;
        mov    quantptr,eax         ; 1;
        mov    eax,inptr_           ; 0;
        mov    inptr,eax            ; 1;
        mov    eax,output_buf_      ; 0;
        mov    output_buf,eax       ; 1;
        mov    eax,output_col_      ; 0;
        mov    output_col,eax       ; 1;
                                    ;;;;10 cycles in this seg


 comment `.................... C language ..................*/


    wsptr = workspace;
    ctr   = 8;


;/*`.................. assembly language ....................

        lea    eax,workspace        ; 0;
        mov    wsptr,eax            ; 1; wsptr = workspace
        mov    eax,8                ; 0;
        mov    ctr,eax             ; 1; ctr   = 8
                                    ;;;;2 cycles in this seg


 comment `.................... C language ..................*/

    do {
        tmp0 = inptr[8*0] * quantptr[8*0];
        tmp1 = inptr[8*2] * quantptr[8*2];
        tmp2 = inptr[8*4] * quantptr[8*4];
        tmp3 = inptr[8*6] * quantptr[8*6];
```

```
;/*`.................... assembly language ....................

        mov       esi,inptr                   ; 1;
        mov       edi,quantptr                ; 0;
                                              ;;;;1 cycle in this piece
                                              ;;;;13 cycles to start of
                                              ; ;first loop
      .repeat                                  ; ;
        mov       eax,[esi+0*8*4]             ; 1;
        mov       ebx,[esi+2*8*4]             ; 0;
        mov       ecx,[esi+4*8*4]             ; 1;
        mov       edx,[esi+6*8*4]             ; 0;
        imul      eax,[edi+0*8*4]             ; 9; eax - tmp0
        imul      ebx,[edi+2*8*4]             ;10; ebx - tmp1
        imul      ecx,[edi+4*8*4]             ;10; ecx - tmp2
        imul      edx,[edi+6*8*4]             ;10; edx - tmp3
                                              ;;;;41 cycles, this piece

comment `..................... C language ..................*/

        tmp10 = tmp0 + tmp2;
        tmp11 = tmp0 - tmp2;
        tmp13 = tmp1 + tmp3;
        tmp12 = (((tmp1 - tmp3) * C362) >> 8) - tmp13;
        tmp0  = tmp10 + tmp13;

;/*`.................... assembly language ....................

        lea       ebp,[eax+ecx]               ; 1; tmp10 = tmp0 + tmp2
        sub       eax,ecx                     ; 0; tmp11 = tmp0 - tmp2
        lea       ecx,[ebx+edx]               ; 1; tmp13 = tmp1 + tmp3
        sub       ebx,edx                     ; 0;         tmp1 - tmp3
        mul362    ebx,esi,edi                 ; 6; * C362
        sar       ebx,8                       ; 1; >> 8
        sub       ebx,ecx                     ; 0; tmp12 = ... - tmp13
        lea       edx,[ebp+ecx]               ; 1; tmp0  = tmp10+tmp13
                                              ;;;;10 cycles, this piece
                                              ; ;ebp -   tmp10
                                              ; ;eax -   tmp11
                                              ; ;ecx -   tmp13
                                              ; ;ebx -   tmp12
                                              ; ;edx -   tmp0

comment `..................... C language ..................*/

        tmp3 = tmp10 - tmp13;
        tmp1 = tmp11 + tmp12;
        tmp2 = tmp11 - tmp12;
```

```
;/*`.................. assembly language .....................

        sub     ebp,ecx                 ; 0; tmp3 = tmp10 - tmp13
        lea     ecx,[eax+ebx]           ; 1; tmp1 = tmp11 + tmp12
        sub     eax,ebx                 ; 0; tmp2 = tmp11 - tmp12
        mov     tmp0,edx                ; 1; edx -    tmp0
        mov     tmp1,ecx                ; 0; ecx -    tmp1
        mov     tmp2,eax                ; 1; eax -    tmp2
        mov     tmp3,ebp                ; 0; ebp -    tmp3
                                        ;;;;3 cycles, this piece

comment `..................... C language ..................*/

        tmp4 = inptr[8*1] * quantptr[8*1];
        tmp5 = inptr[8*3] * quantptr[8*3];
        tmp6 = inptr[8*5] * quantptr[8*5];
        tmp7 = inptr[8*7] * quantptr[8*7];

;/*`.................. assembly language .....................

        mov     esi,inptr               ; 1;
        mov     edi,quantptr            ; 0;
        mov     eax,[esi+1*8*4]         ; 2;
        mov     ebx,[esi+3*8*4]         ; 0;
        mov     ecx,[esi+5*8*4]         ; 1;
        mov     edx,[esi+7*8*4]         ; 0;
        imul    eax,[edi+1*8*4]         ; 9; eax -    temp4
        imul    ebx,[edi+3*8*4]         ;10; ebx -    temp5
        imul    ecx,[edi+5*8*4]         ;10; ecx -    temp6
        imul    edx,[edi+7*8*4]         ;10; edx -    temp7
                                        ;;;;43 cycles, this piece

comment `..................... C language ..................*/

        z13     = tmp6 + tmp5;
        z10     = tmp6 - tmp5;
        z11     = tmp4 + tmp7;
        z12     = tmp4 - tmp7;

;/*`.................. assembly language .....................

        lea     ebp,[ebx+ecx]           ; 1;ebp - z13 = tmp6+tmp5
        sub     ecx,ebx                 ; 0;ecx - z10 = tmp6-tmp5
        lea     ebx,[eax+edx]           ; 1;ebx - z11 = tmp4+tmp7
        sub     eax,edx                 ; 0;eax - z12 = tmp4-tmp7
                                        ;;;;2 cycles, this piece
```

```
comment `..................... C language .................*/

        tmp7  =    z11 + z13                    ;
        tmp11 = ((z11 - z13) *  C362) >> 8      ;
        z5    = ((z10 + z12) *  C473) >> 8      ;
        tmp10 = ((z12        *  C277) >> 8) - z5;
        tmp12 = ((z10        * -C669) >> 8) + z5;

;/*`.................. assembly language ....................

        lea     edx,[ebx+ebp]        ; 1; tmp7 = z11 + z13
        sub     ebx,ebp              ; 0;        z11 - z13
        mul362  ebx,esi,edi          ; 6; * C362
        sar     ebx,8                ; 1; >> 8          (tmp11)
        lea     ebp,[ecx+eax]        ; 0; z10 + z12
        mul473  ebp,esi,edi          ; 5; * C473
        sar     ebp,8                ; 1; >> 8             (z5)
        mul277  eax,esi,edi          ; 4; z12 *  C277
        sar     eax,8                ; 1; >> 8
        mul669n ecx,esi,edi          ; 6; z10 * -C669
        sar     ecx,8                ; 1; >> 8
        sub     eax,ebp              ; 0; tmp10 = ... - z5
        add     ecx,ebp              ; 1; tmp12 = ... + z5
                                     ;;;;27 cycles, this piece
                                     ;  ;edx -   tmp7
                                     ;  ;eax -   tmp10
                                     ;  ;ebx -   tmp11
                                     ;  ;ecx -   tmp12

comment `..................... C language .................*/

        tmp6 = tmp12 - tmp7;
        tmp5 = tmp11 - tmp6;
        tmp4 = tmp10 + tmp5;

;/*`.................. assembly language ....................

        sub     ecx,edx              ; 1; tmp6 = tmp12 - tmp7
        sub     ebx,ecx              ; 1; tmp5 = tmp11 - tmp6
        add     eax,ebx              ; 1; tmp4 = tmp10 - tmp5
                                     ;;;;3 cycles, this piece
                                     ;  ; eax - tmp4
                                     ;  ; ebx - tmp5
                                     ;  ; ecx - tmp6
                                     ;  ; edx - tmp7
```

```
comment `..................... C language ...................*/

        wsptr[8*0] = tmp0 + tmp7;
        wsptr[8*7] = tmp0 - tmp7;
        wsptr[8*1] = tmp1 + tmp6;
        wsptr[8*6] = tmp1 - tmp6;
        wsptr[8*2] = tmp2 + tmp5;
        wsptr[8*5] = tmp2 - tmp5;
        wsptr[8*4] = tmp3 + tmp4;
        wsptr[8*3] = tmp3 - tmp4;

;/*`.................. assembly language .....................

        mov     esi,wsptr               ; 1;
        mov     ebp,tmp0                ; 0;
        lea     edi,[ebp+edx]           ; 2; tmp0 + tmp7
        sub     ebp,edx                 ; 0; tmp0 - tmp7
        mov     [esi+4*8*0],edi         ; 1; wsptr[8*0]=tmp0+tmp7
        mov     edx,tmp1                ; 0;
        mov     [esi+4*8*7],ebp         ; 1; wsptr[8*7]=tmp0-tmp7
        nop                             ; 0;
        lea     ebp,[edx+ecx]           ; 1; tmp1 + tmp6
        sub     edx,ecx                 ; 0; tmp1 - tmp6
        mov     [esi+4*8*1],ebp         ; 1; wsptr[8*1]=tmp1+tmp6
        mov     ecx,tmp2                ; 0;
        mov     [esi+4*8*6],edx         ; 1; wsptr[8*6]=tmp1-tmp6
        nop                             ; 0;
        lea     ebp,[ebx+ecx]           ; 1; tmp2 + tmp5
        sub     ecx,ebx                 ; 0; tmp2 - tmp5
        mov     [esi+4*8*2],ebp         ; 1; wsptr[8*2]=tmp2+tmp5
        mov     edx,tmp3                ; 0;
        mov     [esi+4*8*5],ecx         ; 1; wsptr[8*5]=tmp2-tmp5
        nop                             ; 0;
        lea     ebp,[eax+edx]           ; 1; tmp3 + tmp4
        sub     edx,eax                 ; 0; tmp3 - tmp4
        mov     [esi+4*8*4],ebp         ; 1; wsptr[8*4]=tmp3+tmp4
        mov     [esi+4*8*3],edx         ; 0; wsptr[8*3]=tmp3-tmp4
                                        ;;;;13 cycles, this piece

comment `..................... C language ...................*/

        inptr++;
        quantptr++;
        wsptr++;
    } while (--ctr);
```

```
;/*`.................. assembly language ..................

        lea     eax,[esi+4]             ; 1;wsptr++
        mov     esi,inptr               ; 0;
        mov     edi,quantptr            ; 1;
        mov     wsptr,eax               ; 0;
        add     esi,4                   ; 1;inptr++
        add     edi,4                   ; 0;quantptr++
        mov     inptr,esi               ; 1;
        mov     ecx,ctr                 ; 0;
        mov     quantptr,edi            ; 1;
        dec     ecx                     ; 0;
        mov     ctr,ecx                 ; 1;
    .until ZERO?                        ; 0;
                                        ;;;;6 cycles, this piece
                                        ;;;;148 cycles in loop
                                        ;;;;8 iterations
                                        ;;;;    = 8 * 148 = 1184
                                        ;;;; + 1 branch
                                        ;;;;misprediction (4 cyc)
                                        ;;;;1188 cycles spent
                                        ;;;;in this loop

  comment `.................... C language .................*/

    wsptr = workspace;
    ctr   = 0;

;/*`.................. assembly language ..................

        lea     eax,workspace           ; 0;
        mov     wsptr,eax               ; 1; wsptr = workspace
        xor     eax,eax                 ; 0; eax   = 0
        mov     ctr,eax                 ; 1; ctr   = 0
                                        ;;;;2 cycles, this piece

  comment `.................... C language .................*/

    do {
        tmp10 = wsptr[0] + wsptr[4];
        tmp11 = wsptr[0] - wsptr[4];
        tmp13 = wsptr[2] + wsptr[6];
        tmp12 = (((wsptr[2] - wsptr[6]) * C362) >> 8) - tmp13;

;/*`.................. assembly language ..................

    mov       esi,wsptr                 ; 0;
                                        ;;;;0 cycles, this piece
```

```
        .repeat                        ;  ;
          mov      ebx,[esi+0*4]       ; 1;
          mov      ecx,[esi+4*4]       ; 0;
          mov      edx,[esi+2*4]       ; 1;
          mov      ebp,[esi+6*4]       ; 0;
          lea      eax,[ebx+ecx]       ; 1; tmp10 =
                                       ;  ;     wsptr[0]+wsptr[4]
          sub      ebx,ecx             ; 0; tmp11 =
                                       ;  ;     wsptr[0]-wsptr[4]
          lea      ecx,[edx+ebp]       ; 1; tmp13 =
                                       ;  ;     wsptr[2]+wsptr[6]
          sub      edx,ebp             ; 0;     wsptr[2]-wsptr[6]
          mul362   edx,ebp,edi         ; 6; * C362
          sar      edx,8               ; 1; >> 8
          sub      edx,ecx             ; 1; tmp12 = ... - tmp13
                                       ;;;;12 cycles, this piece
                                       ;  ; eax -   tmp10
                                       ;  ; ebx -   tmp11
                                       ;  ; ecx -   tmp13
                                       ;  ; edx -   tmp12

    comment `.................... C language .................*/

          tmp0 = tmp10 + tmp13;
          tmp3 = tmp10 - tmp13;
          tmp1 = tmp11 + tmp12;
          tmp2 = tmp11 - tmp12;

;/*`.................. assembly language ....................

          lea      ebp,[eax+ecx]       ; 1; tmp0 = tmp10 + tmp13
          sub      eax,ecx             ; 0; tmp3 = tmp10 - tmp13
          lea      ecx,[ebx+edx]       ; 1; tmp1 = tmp11 + tmp12
          sub      ebx,edx             ; 0; tmp2 = tmp11 - tmp12
          mov      tmp0,ebp            ; 1;
          mov      tmp3,eax            ; 0;
          mov      tmp1,ecx            ; 1;
          mov      tmp2,ebx            ; 0;
                                       ;;;;4 cycles, this piece

    comment `.................... C language .................*/

          z13   = wsptr[5] + wsptr[3];
          z10   = wsptr[5] - wsptr[3];
          z11   = wsptr[1] + wsptr[7];
          z12   = wsptr[1] - wsptr[7];
```

```
;/*`.................. assembly language ..................

        mov     ebx,[esi+5*4]           ; 1;
        mov     ecx,[esi+3*4]           ; 0;
        mov     edx,[esi+1*4]           ; 1;
        mov     ebp,[esi+7*4]           ; 0;
        lea     eax,[ebx+ecx]           ; 1; z13 =
                                        ; ;     wsptr[5]+wsptr[3]
        sub     ebx,ecx                 ; 0; z10 =
                                        ; ;     wsptr[5]-wsptr[3]
        lea     ecx,[edx+ebp]           ; 1; z11 =
                                        ; ;     wsptr[1]+wsptr[7]
        sub     edx,ebp                 ; 0; z12 =
                                        ; ;     wsptr[1]-wsptr[7]
                                        ;;;;4 cycles, this piece
                                        ; ;z10 -    ebx
                                        ; ;z11 -    ecx
                                        ; ;z12 -    edx
                                        ; ;z13 -    eax

    comment `.................... C language ................*/

        tmp7    =     z11 + z13;
        tmp11   = (((z11 - z13) * C362) >> 8)      ;
        z5      = (((z10 + z12) * C473) >> 8)      ;
        tmp10   = (( z12        * C277) >> 8) - z5;
        tmp12   = (( z10        * -C669) >> 8) + z5;

;/*`.................. assembly language ..................

        lea     ebp,[ecx+eax]           ; 1; tmp7 = z11 + z13
        sub     ecx,eax                 ; 0;          z11 - z13
        mul362  ecx,esi,edi             ; 6; * C362
        sar     ecx,8                   ; 1; >> 8           (tmp11)
        lea     eax,[ebx+edx]           ; 0;          z10 + z12
        mul473  eax,esi,edi             ; 5; * C473
        sar     eax,8                   ; 1; >> 8            (z5)
        mul277  edx,esi,edi             ; 4; * C277
        sar     edx,8                   ; 1; >> 8
        mul669n ebx,esi,edi             ; 6; * -C669
        sar     ebx,8                   ; 1; >> 8
        sub     edx,eax                 ; 0; tmp10 = ... - z5
        add     ebx,eax                 ; 1; tmp12 = ... + z5
                                        ;;;;27 cycles, this piece
                                        ; ; ebp -    tmp7
                                        ; ; ecx -    tmp11
                                        ; ; edx -    tmp10
                                        ; ; ebx -    tmp12
```

```
comment `..................... C language ...................*/

        tmp6  = tmp12 - tmp7;
        tmp5  = tmp11 - tmp6;
        tmp4  = tmp10 + tmp5;
        outptr = output_buf[ctr] + output_col;

;/*`.................... assembly language ....................

        mov     edi,output_buf          ; 1;
        mov     esi,ctr                 ; 0;
        sub     ebx,ebp                 ; 1; tmp6  = tmp12 - tmp7
        mov     eax,output_col          ; 0;
        sub     ecx,ebx                 ; 1; tmp5  = tmp11 - tmp6
        mov     edi,[edi+4*esi]         ; 0;
        add     edx,ecx                 ; 1; tmp4  = tmp10 + tmp5
        add     edi,eax                 ; 0; outptr = ...
                                        ;;;;4 cycles, this piece
                                        ;  ; edx -     tmp4
                                        ;  ; ecx -     tmp5
                                        ;  ; ebx -     tmp6
                                        ;  ; ebp -     tmp7

comment `..................... C language ...................*/

        outptr[0] = range_limit[((tmp0 + tmp7) >> 5) & 0x3ff];
        outptr[7] = range_limit[((tmp0 - tmp7) >> 5) & 0x3ff];
        outptr[1] = range_limit[((tmp1 + tmp6) >> 5) & 0x3ff];
        outptr[6] = range_limit[((tmp1 - tmp6) >> 5) & 0x3ff];
        outptr[2] = range_limit[((tmp2 + tmp5) >> 5) & 0x3ff];
        outptr[5] = range_limit[((tmp2 - tmp5) >> 5) & 0x3ff];
        outptr[4] = range_limit[((tmp3 + tmp4) >> 5) & 0x3ff];
        outptr[3] = range_limit[((tmp3 - tmp4) >> 5) & 0x3ff];

;/*`.................... assembly language ....................

        mov     eax,tmp0                ; 1;
        mov     esi,tmp1                ; 0;
        sub     eax,ebp                 ; 1;tmp0 - tmp7
        add     ebp,ebp                 ; 0;
        add     ebp,eax                 ; 1;tmp0 + tmp7
        sar     eax,5                   ; 1;
        sar     ebp,5                   ; 1;
        and     eax,3ffH                ; 0;
        mov     push1,eax               ; 1;push pointer
        and     ebp,3ffH                ; 0;for outptr[7]
        mov     push2,ebp               ; 1;push pointer
```

```
lea     ebp,[ebx+esi]        ; 0;for outptr[0]
sar     ebp,5                ; 1;
sub     esi,ebx              ; 0;tmp1 - tmp6
sar     esi,5                ; 1;
and     ebp,3ffH             ; 0;
mov     push3,ebp            ; 1;push pointer
                             ;   ;for outptr[1]
and     esi,3ffH             ; 0;esi has pointer
                             ;   ;for outptr[6]
mov     eax,tmp2             ; 1;
mov     ebp,tmp3             ; 0;
sub     eax,ecx              ; 1;tmp2 - tmp5
add     ecx,ecx              ; 0;
sub     ebp,edx              ; 1;tmp3 - tmp4
add     edx,edx              ; 0;
add     ecx,eax              ; 1;tmp2 + tmp5
add     edx,ebp              ; 0;tmp3 + tmp4
sar     ecx,5                ; 1;
mov     ebx,range_limit      ; 0;
sar     edx,5                ; 1;
and     ecx,3ffH             ; 0;
sar     eax,5                ; 1;
and     edx,3ffH             ; 0;
sar     ebp,5                ; 1;
and     eax,3ffH             ; 0;
and     ebp,3ffH             ; 1;
mov     cl,[ebx+ecx]         ; 0;
mov     [edi+2],cl           ; 1;outptr[2]
mov     cl,[ebx+edx]         ; 0;
mov     [edi+4],cl           ; 1;outptr[4]
mov     cl,[ebx+eax]         ; 0;
mov     eax,push3            ; 1;
mov     edx,push2            ; 0;
mov     [edi+5],cl           ; 1;outptr[5]
mov     cl,[ebx+ebp]         ; 0;
mov     [edi+3],cl           ; 1;outptr[3]
mov     cl,[ebx+eax]         ; 0;
mov     [edi+1],cl           ; 1;outptr[1]
mov     cl,[ebx+edx]         ; 0;
mov     ebp,push1            ; 1;
mov     [edi+0],cl           ; 0;outptr[0]
mov     cl,[ebx+esi]         ; 1;
mov     [edi+6],cl           ; 0;outptr[6]
mov     cl,[ebx+ebp]         ; 1;
mov     [edi+7],cl           ; 0;outptr[7]
                             ;;;;28 cycles, this piece
```

```
    comment `..................... C language ..................*/

        wsptr += 8;
    } while (++ctr < 8);
}

;/*`.................... assembly language .....................

        mov     esi,wsptr               ; 1;
        mov     ebx,ctr                 ; 0;
        add     esi,8*4                 ; 1;
        inc     ebx                     ; 0;
        mov     wsptr,esi               ; 1;wsptr += 8
        mov     ctr,ebx                 ; 0;++ctr
      .until ebx == 8                   ; 1;
                                        ;;;;4 cycles, this piece
                                        ;;;;83 cycles in loop
                                        ;;;;8 iterations =
                                        ;;;;        8 * 83 = 664
                                        ;;;; + 1 branch
                                        ;;;;misprediction (1 cyc)
                                        ;;;;668 cycles spent
                                        ;;;;in this loop
        add     esp,stackspace          ; 1;
        ret                             ; 5;includes AGI and
                                        ;   ;stack pops
                                        ;;;;6 cycles, this piece

;Cycle Count Breakdown:     21 cycles entry/exit overhead
;                         1188 cycles in first loop
;                          668 cycles in second loop
;                         --------------------------------
;                         1877 cycles predicted (if running
;                                          entirely on cache)
;
;Note: On a 100 MHz Pentium, the predicted running time for
;      1,000,000 iterations of this routine, if all memory
;      references were cache hits, is 19 seconds. Actual measured
;      time was 21 seconds. The C equivalent took 28 seconds.
;

IL_idct_A  endp

_IL_TEXT ends
         end
```

```
      comment `.................... C language ................*/
unsigned char range_lim[0x400];
int         quant_table[64] = {              // for quality
              3, 5, 7, 9,11,13,15,17,        // factor
              5, 7, 9,11,13,15,17,19,
              7, 9,11,13,15,17,19,21,
              9,11,13,15,17,19,21,23,
             11,13,15,17,19,21,23,25,
             13,15,17,19,21,23,25,27,
             15,17,19,21,23,25,27,29,
             17,19,21,23,25,27,29,31
};
int         in_block[64] = {                 // a piece of
            -68, 0, 0,-1, 0, 0, 0, 0,        // a picture
             92, 0, 0, 0, 0, 0, 0, 0,
            -10, 2, 0, 0, 0, 0, 0, 0,
              8, 1, 0, 0,-1, 0, 0, 0,
             -1,-1, 0, 1,-1, 0, 0, 0,
              0, 0, 0, 0, 0, 0, 0, 0,
              3, 1, 0, 0, 0, 0, 0, 0,
             -1, 0, 0, 1, 0, 0, 0, 0
};
unsigned char  out_buf[64];
unsigned char *buf_ptr[8] = {
              out_buf+0*8,
              out_buf+1*8,
              out_buf+2*8,
              out_buf+3*8,
              out_buf+4*8,
              out_buf+5*8,
              out_buf+6*8,
              out_buf+7*8
};

void (*IL_idct)(unsigned char *range_limit, int *quantptr,
                int *inptr, unsigned char **output_buf,
                unsigned int output_col)
                = IL_idct_C;

main()
{
    int n, m, ar[64], *p;

    printf("\n");
    printf(
```

```
            "This program demonstrates at source code level the parallel  \n"
            "design of C and assembly language IDCT routines.              \n"
            "                                                              \n"
            "Press enter to see matrices produced by the two routines and \n"
            "visually confirm that they produce identical results.         \n"
            );
        getchar();
        printf("\n");

        for (n = 0; n < 0x400; n++) {
            if (n & 0x200) {
                m = (n - 0x400) * 5;
            } else {
                m = n * 5;
            }
            m += 128;
            range_lim[n] = (m < 0) ? 0 : ((m > 255) ? 255 : m);
        }
        IL_idct = IL_idct_C;
        IL_idct(range_lim, quant_table, in_block, buf_ptr, 0);

        printf("C results:\n");
        for (n = 0; n < 8; n++) {
            for (m = 0; m < 8; m++) {
                printf("%3d ", buf_ptr[n][m]);
            }
            printf("\n");
        }
        printf("\n");

        IL_idct = IL_idct_A;
        IL_idct(range_lim, quant_table, in_block, buf_ptr, 0);

        printf("assembly language results:\n");
        for (n = 0; n < 8; n++) {
            for (m = 0; m < 8; m++) {
                printf("%3d ", buf_ptr[n][m]);
            }
            printf("\n");
        }
        printf("\n");
    }
```

# The Optimizations

The optimizations of note in this code are as follows.

## Sum and Difference Calculations in a Single Cycle

There are a lot of places in the algorithm where two values are converted into their sum and their difference. This can be done in a single cycle as per the following:

```
lea     ecx,[ebx+eax]       ; 1;
sub     ebx,eax             ; 0;
                            ;;;;1 cycle
```

The resultant values don't occupy exactly the same registers as the originals, but as long as there is just one register free, this is the fastest way to accomplish both calculations at once.

## Fast Fixed-Value Multiplication Using Three Registers

At the beginning of the assembly code are four macros for multiplying registers by fixed values. The general strategy is to make two copies of the value to be multiplied and perform shift-and-add arithmetic, shifting one register while adding the results of the previous shift of the other. With most fixed values up to about 16 bits in length, this actually beats using hardware multiplication. Of course, it requires two spare registers, and it can take two more cycles to save and restore them if they weren't initially free.

## "Pushing" to Fixed Stack Locations

Toward the end of the routine, a classic urge to push registers occurs. Because the code is implemented with stack-pointer-relative addressing of stack variables, it's not desirable to move the stack pointer. So for each item that would otherwise have been pushed, a dedicated position in the local variables is reserved. It takes no longer to store and fetch a stack variable than to push and pop the same. Pushing is averted, and the `ebp` register remains free for general use.

## Pipelining Final Output Value Address Calculations

The C code that outputs the final matrix values involves eight evaluations of moderately complex expressions. It turns out that if you calculate one expression and then calculate its output address, you usually waste a cycle on an AGI. But if you do all the expression evaluation at once and then do all the address calculation and output at once, you can avoid the processor stalls.

## Optimizations Yet to Be Tried

Because the assembly code was written to closely parallel the highly efficient C original, there were a few opportunities for shaving a cycle here and there that I skipped in the interest of readability. It should also be noted that at the very beginning of the IDCT routine there are eight multiplications representing multiplication by the quantization matrix values, the step just prior to the IDCT. It may save a few cycles to combine this step with the IDCT, but there are some faster possible ways to multiply by quantization values, and checking for a matrix value of 0 before multiplying can save cycles when the matrix is heavily populated with 0s. If all but the first of the eight coefficients input to a one-dimensional IDCT calculation are 0, all eight outputs are a constant value derived from the first coefficient, and the arduous calculation step can be skipped. (This was the optimization that I actually removed from the original C source for the sake of didactic simplicity.)

The range limit table used in the C code and the assembly language copy is really just intended to force calculated integers into the range 0 to 255. Due to quantization and integer-rounding effects, it is possible that reconstructed pixels will fall slightly outside this range and have to be forced back in before they are output. An alternative way to do the same thing and possibly save a few cycles would be

```
.if  edx > 255     ; 1;check edx for unsigned range
   sar   edx,31    ; 1;copy down the sign bit
   not   edx       ; 1;invert it
.endif             ; 0;
                   ;;;;1 cycle in most cases
```

## Speed

The measured speed of the assembly language optimized IDCT plus quantization matrix multiplication was 33 cycles per pixel (versus the 30 ideally predicted). Depending upon data patterns, the number could be substantially lower if the seven-0-coefficient bypass were also implemented. Based on the analysis in Chapter 14, the Huffman decompression time may run as high as 20 cycles per pixel, although matrices heavily populated with 0s and early end points should bring the average down considerably. So a grayscale image could reasonably be expected to JPEG-decompress at no more than about 60 cycles per pixel, or about 4 million cycles per $320 \times 200$ screen. That's 25 screens per second on a Pentium-100—*if* the Pentium has nothing else to do. If it's streaming in frames from CD-ROM, 10 or 12 might be a more reasonable limit. Color adds more complexity to pixel construction and display and can slow things down anywhere from a little to a lot, depending upon how faithful a reproduction is to be produced. This is why, as of yet, full-motion, full-screen JPEG video is still slightly beyond the reach of the processing power of a bare Pentium CPU.

# Conclusion

JPEG has one of the most interesting inner loops to be found anywhere. It's big, and it looks terribly impressive in flowgraph form. Given the complex matrix math that underlies it, it operates remarkably quickly, thanks to symmetry shortcuts. Boiled down to its essentials, its most important decompression inner loop weighs in at about 33 cycles per pixel on a Pentium. And thanks again to symmetry, that must be approximately the speed of the equivalent compression step.

# References

Nelson, M. 1992. *The Data Compression Book*. San Mateo, Calif.: M&T Books. This book includes an actual, if simplified, working example of some JPEG compression and decompression code. Although it does not present the algorithm tuned for speed, it fills in many of the details alluded to here.

Pennebaker, W. B., and Mitchell, J. L. 1993. *JPEG Still Image Compression Standard*. New York: Van Nostrand Reinhold. This book is a large and thorough treatment of the JPEG standard, appropriate for those with professional interests in JPEG implementation. And, for the curious, it has more flowgraphs, including a one-dimensional forward DCT symmetrically similar to the IDCT shown in this chapter.

The Independent JPEG Group's code is a great place to find working real-world JPEG code. It is available in DOS format, as of this writing, at ftp.coast.net: /SimTel/msdos/graphics or on Compuserve at "GO GRAPHSUP" in Library 12. The official residence, though, of the latest version is at ftp.uu.net in the graphics/jpeg directory, where it is found compressed in Unix tar form. Further information about related resources is available in the IJG README file on the CD-ROM accompanying this book.

# Epilogue

There is an endlessly fascinating inner loop at the heart of a ten-billion-dollar industry today. In fact, if it weren't endlessly fascinating, the industry wouldn't exist. It's the roughly 100-millisecond loop between on-screen events in a video game and a player's reactions to them, which in turn affects the events, which in turn affects the reactions and keeps the player dropping tokens or buying game cartridges and CDs.

Within the 100-millisecond loop is a 20-millisecond nested loop, which is the time it takes the eye to distinguish motion. It is this inner loop of retinal perception that drives the inner loops of MPEG. And if completing the manufacture of a dot of color in a tenth of a microsecond seems like a lot to ask of a pixel-producing process, well . . . those rod cells hanging off the optic nerve are at least that hungry for photons.

Anatomically, the retina is part of the brain. It's a web of cells on which light falls, about a conductive inch from the seat of consciousness, and five inches from the gray matter bitmap that detects object motions and shapes. From there, an organic choir of lobes and cortical folds analyzes and reports. Text objects, processed in parallel at about ten milliseconds per letter, run through pattern-matching and linguistic centers and take on meaning. Background motion compensation takes place. And at the end of 100 milliseconds, the thumb moves!

The brain has an endless appetite for information and interaction. And it seems to enjoy running fast, trying to keep pace with a 100-millisecond feedback cycle. The inner loops of computers are often just mirrors of the inner loops of the brain. And we have only just begun to explore what thirsts of thought the inner loops of computers can quench in the restive mind. Where will computer-generated 3D worlds of arbitrary complexity lead? I don't know. But I'm sure that the race between mind and machine will go on and on. The inner loops of machines will be pressed ever faster, in pursuit of the inner loops of man.

It was a pleasure and a great learning experience to research and write this book, and with e-mail and the Internet, I hope to continue the saga in cyberspace. For *Inner Loops* updates, errata, clarifications, and hopefully some online expansions, my World Wide Web address is

http://ourworld.compuserve.com/homepages/rbooth/

I can also be reached by e-mail at

73642.1707@compuserve.com

or    rbooth@compuserve.com

(The latter more memorable address becomes effective when Compuserve completes its mail address system overhaul, scheduled for late 1996.)

Good luck, reader, with your own inner loops, wherever you may find them.

# Index

Numbers followed by the letter f indicate figures; numbers followed by the letter t indicate tables.

! operator, 61
!= operator, 61
< operator, 61
<= operator, 61
== operator, 61
> operator, 61
>= operator, 61
& operator, 61
&& operator, 61
|| operator, 61

**A**

aaa instruction, 39
aad instruction, 39
aam instruction, 39
aas instruction, 39
Abrash, Michael, 88
Adaptive Huffman compression, 283–284
adc instruction, 44, 164–165
   speed on Pentium Pro, 133
add instruction, 44
Address displacement, 95
Addressing of memory, 24, 27–28

AGI (address generation interlock), 87–88, 118–119, 138
   defeating, 165–167, 347
AH register, 29
AL register, 29
Algorithms
   DCT, 325–326
   for random numbers, 227–245
   RC4, 226, 247–248
   rethinking, 143–146
Alias checking, 182
align statement, 85, 116
and instruction, 44
*Application Note AP–526*, 124
Arithmetic coding, 284
Arithmetic instructions, 34
arpl instruction, 38
Arrays, 174–175
Assembly language
   advantages of, 7, 21
   advantages of optimization of, 146
   built into C compilers, 49
   C's relationship to, 52–55, 172–180
   coiled, 165–166
   improving speed of, xiii–xv
   prefix byte for 16-bit instruction, 25, 97
   processor structure used by, 26–27
   sample program in, 50–52

Assembly language *(continued)*
    structured. *See* Structured assembly
        language
    syntax of, 30
Audio, 20
AX register, 29

**B**

BH register, 29
Bidirectional node, 254–255
Binary coded decimal instructions, 38–39
Binary tree, 178
    bidirectional, 255
    searching of, 261–264
    simple, 255
    traversal of, 264–265
Bit-testing instructions, 39
Bitmaps, 200
Bitwise operators, 31
BL register, 29
Block memory moves
    alignment in, 208–210
    on Pentium Pro, 134
bound instruction, 37
BP register, 29
Brain, function of, 349
Branch prediction, 97–98
    on Pentium Pro, 137–138
break C statement, 175
break instruction, 64
break if instruction, 64
bsf instruction, 39
bsr instruction, 39
bswap instruction, 42
    and MMX, 186
    speed on 486, 74
bt instruction, 39
btc instruction, 38
btr instruction, 38
bts instruction, 38
Buses, 15
BX register, 29
Byte registers, 88

**C**

C flag bit, 31
C language
    assemblers built into compilers of, 49
    data structures of, 172–175
    functions in, 180
    keywords of, 175–178
    operators in, 178–179
    optimizing, 180–183
    relationship to assembly language,
        52–55, 172–180
Cache, 13
    code vs. data in, 83–84
    delays from misses, 82–83
    on 486, 80–82
    four-way, 81
    on MMX machines, 188–189
    on Pentium, 109–115
    prefetching into, 160–161, 166
    primary, 13, 80–82
    secondary, 13, 82, 135
    two-way, 110–112
Cache-to-cache memory moves, on
    Pentium Pro, 134
Calculated shift operations, on Pentium
    Pro, 132
call instruction, 44
Calling and returning, 55
    conventions regarding, 56
Carry flag, 30f, 31
Carry flag instructions, 41
CARRY? flag status bit, 61
case C statement, 175
cbw instruction, 39
    replacement for, 39
CD-ROM, 16–17
    data transfer rates of, 17t
cdq instruction, 39
    replacement for, 39
CH register, 29
CH486.EXE timing program, 68
char data type, 172
CHHASH.EXE demo program, 279

Chi-square test, 220, 222
    code for, 241–243
Child nodes, 261
CHMATRX.EXE demo program, 320
CHMEM.EXE timing program, 208
CHPENT.BAT timing program, 92
CHPPRO.EXE timing program, 124
CHRANDM.EXE demo, 221–222, 243,
    250
CHSORT.EXE demo program, 303
CISC (complex instruction set computer)
    processors, 26
CL register, 29
clc instruction, 40, 41
cld instruction, 41
cli instruction, 41
clts instruction, 38
cmc instruction, 40, 41
cmov Pentium Pro instruction, 129
cmp instruction, 44, 60
cmps instruction, 25
cmpxchg instruction, 38
cmpxchg8b instruction, 38
Code
    alignment of, 86–87, 117–118
    reordering of, 153, 181
Code lengths table, for Huffman encoding,
    291–293
Coiled loops, 157–158, 165–167
Color pictures, compression of, 329
Comments, delimiters of, xi
Comparisons, 32
Compiled code, alignment of, 86, 117
Compression
    arithmetic coding, 284
    dictionary-based, 283
    Huffman, 281–300, 327
    JPEG, 323–329, 347–348
    MPEG, 283, 329
Conditional branches, prediction of, 97–98
continue C statement, 175
continue instruction, 64
continue if instruction, 64
Copy loop paradox, 211–212

cpuid instruction, 42, 102, 185
Cryptography, random numbers and, 226,
    247–248
cwd instruction, 39
cwde instruction, 39
    replacement for, 40
CX register, 29
Cycle counting, 45–46

**D**

daa instruction, 39
das instruction, 39
Data and code alignment, 147–148, 172
    in block memory transfers, 208–210
    on 486, 85–87
    on Pentium, 116–118
    on Pentium Pro, 136
Data structures, 57–58
    in C, 172–175
DCT algorithm, 325–326
dec instruction, 44
Decoding, Huffman, 297–299
default C statement, 175
Destination pointer, 29
DH register, 29
DI register, 29
Direction flag, 41, 57
Distribution sort, 302–303, 309–310
    efficiency of, 308, 311
    first inner loop of, 303–306
    recommendations for, 312
    second inner loop of, 307–308
div instruction, 42
Division
    via inverse multiplication, 181
    speed of, 275
DL register, 29
do C statement, 175
do ... while statement, 59
DOS4GW.EXE, xii
double data type, 172
Double loops, 312–313
    example of, 303–308

Double precision format, 33
    random numbers in, 224–225
Double slash (//) convention, xi
DX register, 29
Dynamic execution, 124–126

**E**

EAX register, 29
EBP register, 28
    dangers of using, 150
    freeing, 148–150
    preservation of, 56
EBX register, 29
    preservation of, 56
ECX register, 29
EDI register, 29
    preservation of, 56
EDX register, 29
Efficiency analysis, 7
Eight-by-eight compression, 324
EISA (Extended Industry Standard
        Architecture) bus, 15
else C statement, 175
else statement, 63
elseif statement, 63
emms MMX instruction, 195
Encoding table, for Huffman encoding,
        293, 294f, 295–297
Enlarge register instructions, 39
enter instruction, replacement for, 36
ESI register, 29
    preservation of, 56
ESP register, 28, 149
    and AGI, 87–88, 118–119
Exchange register instructions, 39
Expressions, evaluating, 60–61

**F**

fadd instruction, 34
    speed on 486, 78

speed on Pentium, 108
speed on Pentium Pro, 134
fcmov Pentium Pro instruction, 129
fcomi Pentium Pro instruction, 129
fdiv instruction, 34
    speed on 486, 79
    speed on Pentium, 108
    speed on Pentium Pro, 134
FIFO, 84, 115, 212
fild instruction, 78t, 107t
fist instruction, 78t, 107t
Flags, 30–33, 41
    setting, 161–162
Flat programming model, 24
fld instruction, 34, 78t, 107t
fldcw instruction, 79, 108
float data type, 172
Floating-point alignment
    on 486, 85–86
    on Pentium, 117
Floating-point instructions, 34, 77–80,
        106–107
    arithmetic, 78–79, 108
    flags, 79–80, 108
    loading and storing, 78, 107
    precision control, 79, 108
Floating-point random numbers, 224
Floating-point unit, 12, 33–34
    on 486, 85–86
    moving noncached memory via,
        214–216
    on Pentium, 106–109
    on Pentium Pro, 134
Floppy disk, 16
fmul instruction, 34
    speed on 486, 79
    speed on Pentium, 108
    speed on Pentium Pro, 134
for C statement, 177
486
    cache of, 80–84
    data and code alignment on, 85–87

floating-point unit on, 85–86
    instruction set of, 69–80
    optimizing, 87–89
    output queue of, 84
486 instruction set, 69–70
    floating point, 77–80
    timings of, 70t–72t, 73–77
Four-way cache, 81
fst instruction, 34, 78t, 107t
fsub instruction, 34
    speed on 486, 78
    speed on Pentium, 108
    speed on Pentium Pro, 134
fxch instruction, 109

**G**

goto C statement, 175
Graphics
    compressing, 283, 324–329, 347–348
    overlaying, 200–202

**H**

Hard disk, 16
Hash table, 268
Hashing
    for comparing symbols, 276–278
    fast, 268–272
    indications for, 267–268
    pointers in, 276
    procedures for, 268
    random values in, 268, 275–276
    using inner loop, 272–275
hlt instruction, 38
Huffman, David Albert, 281, 288
Huffman compression
    adaptive, 283–284
    example of, 281–282
    JPEG use of, 283, 327–328
    overhead of, 283
    performance of, 285

procedure for, 285–297
    uses of, 283
Huffman decompression, 297–299, 328

**I**

I flag bit, 31
IDE controller, 16
idiv instruction, 42
    speed on Pentium Pro, 133
if C statement, 176
if statement, 58–59
    structured, 62–63
IL_Combined Random, 220t, 239–240,
    245f
IL_FindPrimes, 220
IL_HashAddSymbol, 278
IL_HashFindSymbol, 268–272
IL_HashRandom, 220t, 237–239, 245f
IL_MemCopyAlignedRepMovsd, 207,
    210, 210t
IL_MemCopyLoadStoreLoop, 207
IL_MemCopyToMainMemory, 208, 216t
IL_MemCopyToSecondaryCache, 207,
    212–214, 216
IL_MixRandom, 220t, 231–234, 244f
IL_PiByMonteCarlo, 220, 243, 246–247
IL_PickRandomSeed, 220t, 240–241,
    245f
IL_R250Random, 220t, 235–236, 244f
IL_RandomChiSquareTest, 220, 241–243
IL_Shift32Random, 220t, 230–231, 245f
IL_SimpleRandom, 220t, 229–230, 244f
IL_StandardRandom, 220t, 227–229, 244f
Image compression, 283
    of color pictures, 329
    JPEG, 323–349
    MPEG, 283, 329
imul instruction, 42
    speed on 486, 74
    speed on Pentium, 104
    speed on Pentium Pro, 133

in instruction, 41
   speed on 486, 75
   speed on Pentium, 105
inc instruction, 44
Index value, in hashing, 275
Indexing, through binary tree, 262–264
Inner loops, 258–259
   importance of, 6
   on Pentium Pro, 138
ins instruction, 41
Instruction pairing, 93–94
   exceptions to, 94–95
   multicycle, 95–96
Instruction set, 34–45
   of 486, 69–80
   MMX, 190–195
   of Pentium, 98–109
   of Pentium Pro, 130–134
int data type, 172
int instruction, 42
Integer alignment
   on 486, 85
   on Pentium, 116
Integer math instructions, 42–43
Integration, 225–226
*Intel486 Microprocessor Family
   Programmer's Reference Manual,*
   73
Interleaved file, 54
Interrupt enable, 41
Interrupt entry and exit, 41–42
Interrupt flag, 30f, 31
Interrupts, 31
into instruction, 42
invd instruction, 38
Inverse DCT (inverse discrete cosine transformation), 323, 328
   code of, 330–346
   flowgraph of, 329–330, 330f
   speed of, 348
invlpg instruction, 38
iretd instruction, 42

ISA (Industry Standard Architecture) bus,
   15

**J**

ja instruction, 32
jae instruction, 32
jb instruction, 32
jbe instruction, 32
jc instruction, 32
jCC instruction, 44
jcxz instruction, 25
je instruction, 32
jecxz instruction, replacement for, 37
jg instruction, 32
jge instruction, 32
jl instruction, 32
jle instruction, 32
jmp instruction, 44, 60
jna instruction, 32
jnae instruction, 32
jnb instruction, 32
jnbe instruction, 32
jnc instruction, 32
jne instruction, 32
jng instruction, 32
jnge instruction, 32
jnl instruction, 32
jnle instruction, 32
jno instruction, 32
jnp instruction, 32
jns instruction, 32
jnz instruction, 32
jo instruction, 32
jp instruction, 32
jpe instruction, 32
JPEG compression, 283
   inner loops in, 323
   mechanism of, 324–329
   optimization of, 347–348
jpo instruction, 32
js instruction, 32

Jump tables, 156, 177
jz instruction, 32

**K**

Kelvin, William Lord, 1

**L**

Labels, 60
lahf instruction, 32, 41
lar instruction, 38
lds instruction, 38
lea instruction, 44, 163
leave instruction, replacement for, 36
les instruction, 38
lfs instruction, 38
lgdt instruction, 38
lgs instruction, 38
lidt instruction, 38
Linked list, 253–257
    searching of, 259–261
    speed issues related to, 257–258
lldt instruction, 38
lmsw instruction, 38
Local variables, 56
lock instruction, 38
    speed on 486, 76
    speed on Pentium, 105
lods instruction, 25, 130
    replacement for, 35
Logical operators, 44
    64-bit, 193
long data type, 172
Long double precision format, 33
Long integer format, 33
Loop
    coiled, 157–158, 165–167
    inner, 6, 138, 258–259
    tandem, 158–160
    unrolled, 151–153, 181
Loop counter, 29
    efficiency of, 154

loop instruction, 25
    replacement for, 35
    speed on 486, 73
loopnz instruction, replacement for, 36
loopz instruction, replacement for, 36
lsl instruction, 38
lss instruction, 38
ltr instruction, 38

**M**

Machine-independent code, 1–2
Main memory, 14
malloc() C function, 258
MASM 6, xi, 6
    compatibility of, 49–50
Matrix multiplication, 315–317, 316f
    of large matrices, 320–321
    pitch-yaw-roll, 316–320, 316f
MCA (Microchannel Architecture) bus, 15
memcpy() C function, 207, 208, 209t
Memory
    cache, 13. *See also* Cache
    main, 14
    moving, 207–217
    nondestructive tests on, 60
    PC addressing of, 24
    on Pentium Pro vs. Pentium, 132
    32-bit addressing of, 27–28
Micro-ops, 126, 127–129, 138
    execution units of, 127f, 128
MMX
    enhancements of, 186–189
    instruction set of, 190–196
    registers of, 189–190
    software emulation of, 196–202
Modem, 18
Motorola assembler, 30
mov instruction, 44
Move alignment, 86, 117
movq MMX instruction, 191
movsx instruction, 39
    and MMX, 186

movsx instruction *(continued)*
  on Pentium Pro, 132
  replacement for, 40
movzx instruction, 39
  and MMX, 186
  on Pentium Pro, 132
  replacement for, 40
MPEG compression, 283, 329
mul instruction, 42
  speed on 486, 74
  speed on Pentium, 104
Multiplication
  matrix, 315–321
  MMX, 195, 198–200
  optimizing, 162–163, 347

**N**

neg instruction, 43
Network connections, 18
Nodes, 253–257
nop instruction, 44, 119–120
not instruction, 43
Null pointer, 256

**O**

O flag bit, 31
Octree node, 255–256
Operating systems, 21–22
Optimization, xiii–xv
  and algorithm rearrangement, 143–146
  goals of, 11
  precautions in, 6, 142–143
  reasons for, 142–143
  for 32-bit PC, 1–2
or instruction, 45
out instruction, 41
  speed on 486, 75
  speed on Pentium, 105
Outer loops, importance of, 7
Output queue, 84, 115–116, 212
  MMX and, 187
outs instruction, 41

Overflow flag, 30f, 31
OVERFLOW? flag status bit, 61
Overlaying, 200–202

**P**

P flag bit, 31
Packing
  with signed saturation, 191, 196–197
  with unsigned saturation, 191, 197–198
packssdw MMX instruction, 191
packsswb MMX instruction, 191
packuswb MMX instruction, 191
paddb MMX instruction, 192
paddd MMX instruction, 192
paddsb MMX instruction, 192
paddsw MMX instruction, 192
paddusb MMX instruction, 192
paddusw MMX instruction, 192
paddw MMX instruction, 192
Page tables, 14
pand MMX instruction, 193
Parallel processing, 12
Parity flag, 30f, 31
PARITY? flag status bit, 61
Partial register stall, 136–137, 138
Partial registers, 88, 119
Passed parameters, 56
PCI bus, 15
pcmpeqb MMX instruction, 194
pcmpeqd MMX instruction, 194
pcmpeqw MMX instruction, 194
pcmpgtb MMX instruction, 194
pcmpgtd MMX instruction, 194
pcmpgtw MMX instruction, 194
Pentium
  branch prediction on, 97–98
  cache of, 82, 109–115
  cycle clock of, 29, 92
  data and code alignment on, 116–118
  floating-point unit of, 106–109
  instruction pairing on, 93–96
  instruction stream timing oddities on,
    119–121

optimizing, 118–121
output queue of, 115–116, 212
overview of, 12, 92–93
pipes of, 97, 115, 158
read-before-write function on, 212–214
top speed of, 134
Pentium cache
architecture of, 109–110
buses into, 112–113
code, 109
data, 109
delays from misses, 113–115
Pentium instruction set, 98–99
floating point, 106–109
new elements of, 102
timings of, 99, 99t–101t, 101–102,
103–106
Pentium Pro
branch prediction on, 137–138
cache on, 135
copy loop paradox on, 211–212
data and code alignment on, 136
dynamic execution on, 124–126
floating-point unit of, 134
memory speedups for, 132
micro-ops on, 126, 127–129
partial register stall on, 136–137
pipes of, 128
slowdowns on, 133–134
speedups on, 131–133
top speed of, 134
Pentium Pro instruction set, timing of,
130–134, 130t–131t
Pentium systems
data transfer rates of, 22t
memory of, 13–14
overview of, 12
speed of, 13–16
Pi, calculating, 243, 246–247
Pipes, 97, 115, 128, 158
Pitch-yaw-roll matrix, 316, 316f
multiplication of, 317–320
PKZIP, 283
pmaddwd MMX instruction, 195

pmulhw MMX instruction, 195
pmullw MMX instruction, 195
pnand MMX instruction, 193
Pointers, 28
contained in nodes, 254
for hash table, 276
minimizing increments to, 154–155
speed issues regarding, 257–258
pop instruction, 45
speed on 486, 73
popad instruction, 39, 40
popf instruction, 32
popfd instruction, 32, 41
por MMX instruction, 193
Port I/O group, 41
Portability
loss of, 6
speed hit from, 1–2
pragma statement, 51
Precision control, 79, 108
Prefetching, cache, 160–161, 166
Prefixed opcodes, 25, 97
and MMX, 186
and Pentium Pro, 133
Primary cache, 13
on 486, 80–82
on MMX, 186
on Pentium, 82
Process synchronization, 38
Processor stall condition, 46
Processor structure, 26–27
pslld MMX instruction, 194
psllw MMX instruction, 194
psrad MMX instruction, 194
psraw MMX instruction, 194
psrld MMX instruction, 194
psrlq MMX instruction, 194
psrlw MMX instruction, 194
psslq MMX instruction, 194
punpckhbw MMX instruction, 192
punpckhdq MMX instruction, 192
punpckhwd MMX instruction, 192
punpcklbw MMX instruction, 192
punpckldq MMX instruction, 192

punpcklwd MMX instruction, 192
push instruction, 45
    to fixed stack locations, 347
pusha instruction, 116
    speed on 486, 76, 84
    speed on Pentium, 105
pushad instruction, 39, 40, 116
    speed on 486, 76, 84
    speed on Pentium, 105
pushf instruction, 32
pushfd instruction, 32, 41
pxor MMX instruction, 193

**Q**

Quadtree node, 255
Quantization matrix, 326–327, 328
Quicksort C routine, 308–309
    efficiency of, 311
    recommendations for, 312

**R**

Random numbers
    algorithms for generating, 220–222,
        227–245
    combining, 223
    double-precision, 224–225
    extreme, 227
    floating-point, 224
    ranges of, 223–224
    theory of, 222–225
    uses of, 219, 226–227, 246–250
    Website for, 227
RC4 algorithm, 226, 247–248
rcl instruction, 45
rcr instruction, 45
rdmsr instruction, 38
rdtsc instruction, xi, 102
Read-after-write pairing exception, 94
Read-before-write, 212–214
Registers, 24, 28–29
    conventions regarding, 56–57

need for, 149
nesting of, 27f
MMX, 189–190
nondestructive tests on, 60
on Pentium Pro, 125–126
reg,mem instructions, 132, 138
Reordering code, 153, 181
rep instructions, 25
    speed on 486, 76–77
    speed on Pentium, 106
rep lods instruction, 76t, 77, 106t
rep movs instruction, 29, 57, 76t, 106t
rep movsd instruction, 86, 117, 207
    on Pentium Pro, 211
rep stos instruction, 37, 76t, 106t
repe cmps instruction, 37, 76t, 106t
repe scas instruction, 37, 76t, 106t
repne scas instruction, 37, 177
ret instruction, 55, 56, 188
retf instruction, 38
Retina, 349
retn instruction, 43
return C statement, 175
Return stack buffer
    on MMX Pentium, 187–188
    on Pentium Pro, 138
RISC (reduced instruction set computer)
    processors, 26
rol instruction, 45, 146
    speed on 486, 74–75
    speed on Pentium, 103
ror instruction, 45, 146
    speed on Pentium, 103
Rotate operators, speed on Pentium,
    103–104
rsm instruction, 38

**S**

S flag bit, 31
sahf instruction, 32, 41
Sampling rate, 20
sar instruction, 45

sbb instruction, 45
  speed on Pentium Pro, 133
scas instruction,
  replacement for, 35
Secondary cache, 13, 82
  on Pentium Pro, 135
Seeds, random, 225
Segment instructions, 38
Segment registers, 24, 28–29, 38
Semicolon character, 52
setCC instruction, 43
  and MMX, 186
  speed on 486, 75
  speed on Pentium, 104
sgdt instruction, 38
Shift operators, 31
  64-bit, 194–195
  speed on Pentium, 103–104
shl instruction, 45
shld instruction, 43
  and MMX, 186
  speed on 486, 74
  speed on Pentium, 104
short data type, 172
shr instruction, 45
shrd instruction, 43
  and MMX, 186
  speed on 486, 74
  speed on Pentium, 104
Shuffling, 223
SI register, 29
sidt instruction, 38
Sieve of Eratosthenes, 248–250
Sign flag, 30f, 31
SIGN? flag status bit, 61
Signed comparisons, 32
Signed saturation, packing with, 191,
  196–197
Simple node, 254
Single precision format, 33
16-bit assembler, 24–26
64-bit instructions, 190–195
Slash-star (/*...*/) convention, xi, 52

sldt instruction, 38
smsw instruction, 38
Sorting
  distribution, 302–311
  order N, 301–302, 311–312
  recommendations for, 312–313
  speed of, 310t–311t
Source data pointer, 29
SP register, 29
Spare registers, 25–26
Sphere, volume of, 246
Stack alignment, 147–148
Stack frame pointer, 28, 56, 148
Stack pointer, 28
Staggered tandem loops, 159–160
stc instruction, 40, 41
std instruction, 41
sti instruction, 41
Still images, size of, 19
stos instruction, 25
  replacement for, 35
str instruction, 38
String instructions, 37
struct C statement, 173
Structured assembly language, 6, 7, 58–61
  debugging of, 65
  efficiency of, 61–63
sub instruction, 45
Subroutine return, 43
switch C statement, 177
Symbol census, for Huffman encoding,
  286–288
Symbols
  adding, 278
  comparing, 276–277
Systems programming instructions, 37–38

**T**

Table lookup, 144–145, 150–151
Tandem loops, 158–159, 312
  staggered, 159–160
Termination strategies, 256–257

Ternary tree, 255
test instruction, 45, 60
   speed on Pentium, 103
Text
   compression of, 28
   transfer of, 20
32-bit assembler. *See* Assembler
Transparency, overlaying with, 201–202
traverse C function, 264
Tree
   binary, 178, 255, 261–265
   Huffman, 288, 289f–290f, 290–291
   structure of, 253
Two-register shifts, 43
Two-way cache, 110–111
   disadvantages of, 111–112

**U**

U pipe, 97, 115
   and MMX, 187
   on Pentium Pro, 128
Unions, 174
Unrolling loops, 151–153, 181
Unsigned comparisons, 32
Unsigned saturation, packing with, 191,
   197–198

**V**

V pipe, 97, 115
   and MMX, 186–187
   on Pentium Pro, 128
Variables, reversing, 153
verr instruction, 38
verw instruction, 38
VESA local bus, 15

Video, standards of, 19–20
Virtual memory, mapping of, 14
VL bus, 15

**W**

Watcom C compiler, 51–52
wbinvd instruction, 38
while C statement, 176, 177
while statement, 59
Word counting, optimization example,
   144–146, 163–167
Write queue, 84, 115–116, 212
   MMX and, 187
Write-after-write pairing exception, 95
Write-back cache, 109, 112
Write-through cache, 82
wrmsr instruction, 38

**X**

xadd instruction, 38
xchg instruction, 39
   speed on 486, 76
   speed on Pentium, 105
xlat instruction, 25
   replacement for, 36
xor instruction, 45

**Z**

Z flag bit, 31
*Zen of Code Optimization*, 88
zero flag, 30f, 31
ZERO? flag status bit, 61

## TEST PROGRAM ALERT

One of the test programs on the CD-ROM, **CHPENT,** the Pentium chip timing program, may give the following error message when first run:

```
Stub exec failed:
dos4gw.exe
No such file or directory
```

If this happens, either copy the CD-ROM file \DOS4GW.EXE to any directory named in your DOS environment PATH list or execute the following DOS commands (assuming, in this example, that the hard disk is C: and the CD-ROM is D:) to execute from a hard disk directory:

```
C:\>md chpent
C:\>cd chpent
C:\CHPENT>copy d:\chpent\*.*
C:\CHPENT>copy d:\dos4gw.exe
C:\CHPENT>chpent
```

The **CHHUFMN** program tends to report a bogus decompression time when run in DOS underneath Windows. It generally reports a correct value undertrue (booted) DOS.

The **CHHASH** program works correctly with null-terminated text files as input but may sometimes count a few words past the end of the file on text files that are not null-terminated. Timing statistics reported in either case are valid.